D1789798

Do It!
Play Strings

A World of Musical Enjoyment At Your Fingertips

James O. Froseth
Bret P. Smith

Instrument	Book 1 & CD	Book 2 & CD
Violin	M526	M531
Viola	M527	M532
Cello	M528	M533
Bass	M529	M534
Teacher's Resource Edition with Full Score & CDs	M530	M535
Recorder	M440	
Teacher's Resource Edition For Recorder with 2 CDs	M441	

Contents

CD Indexes: **To the Teacher's Resource Edition:** . . . . ii – vii

                              To the Student's Texts: 48

Student's Violin Text (With Chord Symbols Added to the Music) . . . . 6 – 48

                         Fingering Charts: Violin . . . . I-A

                                             Viola . . . . I-B

                                             Cello . . . . I-C

                                             Bass . . . . I-D

                    Performance Pedagogy: Violin 2-A, 3-A

                                              Viola 2-B, 3-B

                                              Cello 2-C, 3-C

                                              Bass 2-D, 3-D

                              Dictionaries: Music Signs and Symbols Dictionary 4, 5

                                           Music Terms Dictionary 42, 43, 44, 45

                                           Rhythmic Pattern Dictionary 46, 47

Teacher's Resource Edition . . . . 6-A – 41-N

Resource Indexes to the Teacher's Edition:

Resource Index #1 *A World of Musical Styles at Your Fingertips* . . . . viii, ix

Resource Index #2 *"You Can Look It Up" - Resources for Musical Independence* x

Resource Index #3 *Easy Listen-Play Exercises for Media Generated Group Instruction* xi

Resource Index #4 *Ensembles and Opportunities for Individualizing Group Instruction* xii

Resource Index #5 *Musical Rounds for Independent Study and Ensemble Performance* xiii

Resource Index #6 *Music Literacy - Optional Rhythmic Reading Flashcards* . . . . xiv, xv

Resource Index #7 *Music Literacy - Rhythmic Rounds and Rhythmic Reading Exercises* xvi

Resource Index #8 *One Octave Major and Minor Scales and Arpeggios* xvii

Resource Index #9 *Foundation Studies for Creative Musicianship* . . . . xviii, xix

Resource Index #10 *Creative Musicianship - Improvisation and Composition* . . . . xx, xxi

Resource Index #11 *Resources for Teaching to the National Content Standards for Music* . . . . xxii, xxiii

Performing Artists, Credits, and Acknowledgements 47-A

ORDER OF PRESENTATION
Teacher's Resource Edition - COMPACT DISC NO. I

CD I Track #s	pg #	Title
I	**5-A**	*Listen and Play* - Getting Started on Open D: Pizzicato
I-2	**5-A**	*Listen and Play* - Getting Started on Open A: Pizzicato
I-3	**5-A**	*Listen and Play* - Getting Started on Open D and Open A: Pizzicato
2	**5-B**	*Listen and Play* - Getting Started on Open D: Arco
2-2	**5-B**	*Listen and Play* - Getting Started on Open A: Arco
2-3	**5-B**	*Listen and Play* - Getting Started on Open D and Open A: Arco
3	**5-C**	*Listen* - Articulation - Separated and Connected
4	**5-C**	*Listen and Play* - Separated Style of Articulation on Open D
4-2	**5-C**	*Listen and Play* - Connected Style of Articulation on Open D
4-3	**5-C**	*Listen and Play* - Separated Style of Articulation on Open A
4-4	**5-C**	*Listen and Play* - Connected Style of Articulation on Open A
4-5	**5-C**	*Listen and Play* - Articulation - Open D
4-6	**5-C**	*Listen and Play* - Articulation - Open A
5	**5-D**	Blues in D - Accompaniment for *Teacher Call - Student Response*
6	**5-E**	*Listen and Play* - Getting Started on F♯
7	**5-E**	*Listen and Play* - Getting Started on E
8	**5-E**	*Listen and Play* - Getting Started on D
9	**5-B**	D Major Triad - Accompaniment for *Teacher Call - Student Response* and Rhythmic Reading in 2s
10	**6-A**	*Listen and Play* - Hot Cross Buns - Melodic Ear-to-Hand Training and Assessment
II	**6-I**	Hot Cross Buns - Violin Model
12	**6-I**	Hot Cross Buns - Viola Model
13	**6-I**	Hot Cross Buns - Cello Model
14	**6-I**	Hot Cross Buns - Bass Model
15	**6-I**	Hot Cross Buns - Accompaniment
16	**6-2**	Hot Cross Buns (Honky Tonk Style) - Violin Model
17	**6-2**	Hot Cross Buns (Honky Tonk Style) - Cello Model
18	**6-2**	Hot Cross Buns (Honky Tonk Style) - Accompaniment
19	**6-3**	Hot Cross Buns (Rock and Roll Style) - Violin Model
20	**6-3**	Hot Cross Buns (Rock and Roll Style) - Cello Model
21	**6-3**	Hot Cross Buns (Rock and Roll Style) - Accompaniment
22	**6-B**	*Listen and Play* - Notes - Melodic Ear-to-Hand Assessment
23	**6-4**	Notes (D) - Viola Model
24	**6-4**	Notes (D) - Bass Model
25	**6-4**	Notes (D) - Accompaniment
26	**6-D**	*Listen and Play* - Mary Had a Little Lamb - Melodic Ear-to-Hand Assessment
27	**6-5**	Mary Had a Little Lamb (Bluegrass Style) - Violin Model
28	**6-5**	Mary Had a Little Lamb (Bluegrass Style) - Viola Model
29	**6-5**	Mary Had a Little Lamb (Bluegrass Style) - Cello Model
30	**6-5**	Mary Had a Little Lamb (Bluegrass Style) - Bass Model
31	**6-5**	Mary Had a Little Lamb (Bluegrass Style) - Accompaniment
32	**6-6**	Mary Had a Little Lamb (Reggae Style) - Viola Model
33	**6-6**	Mary Had a Little Lamb (Reggae Style) - Bass Model
34	**6-6**	Mary Had a Little Lamb (Reggae Style) - Accompaniment
35	**6-E**	Hot Cross Buns in A (Honky Tonk Style) - Accompaniment
36	**6-E**	Hot Cross Buns in G (Polka Style) - Accompaniment
37	**6-E**	Notes in A - Accompaniment
38	**6-F**	Notes in G - Accompaniment
39	**6-F**	Mary Had a Little Lamb in A (Bluegrass Style) - Accompaniment
40	**6-F**	Mary Had a Little Lamb in G (Reggae Style) - Accompaniment
41	**7-I**	Stepping and Skipping - Viola Model
42	**7-I**	Stepping and Skipping - Bass Model
43	**7-I**	Stepping and Skipping - Accompaniment
44	**7-B**	*Listen and Play* - Au Claire de la Lune - Melodic Ear-to-Hand Training and Assessment
45	**7-4**	Au Claire de la Lune (D) - Violin Model

CD 1 Track #s	pg #	Title
46	7-4	Au Claire de la Lune (D) - Cello Model
47	7-4	Au Claire de la Lune (D) - Accompaniment
48	8-2	Rocket Cruiser - Violin Model
49	8-2	Rocket Cruiser - Cello Model
50	8-2	Rocket Cruiser - Accompaniment
51	8-5	Down By the Station - Violin Model
52	8-5	Down By the Station - Bass Model
53	8-5	Down By the Station - Accompaniment
54	8-6	Down By the Station (Jazz Style) - Viola Model
55	8-6	Down By the Station (Jazz Style) - Cello Model
56	8-6	Down By the Station (Jazz Style) - Accompaniment
57	8-6	Down By the Station (Jazz Style) - Extended Accompaniment
58	9-A	*Listen and Play* - Old King Cole - Melodic Ear-to-Hand Training and Assessment
59	9-1	Old King Cole (G) - Violin Model
60	9-1	Old King Cole (G) - Bass Model
61	9-1	Old King Cole (G) - Accompaniment
62	9-B	*Listen and Play* - Jacob Drink - Rhythmic, Bowing, and Articulation Ear-to-Hand Training and Assessment
63	9-2	Jacob Drink (G) - Violin Model
64	9-2	Jacob Drink (G) - Cello Model
65	9-2	Jacob Drink (G) - Accompaniment
66	10-1	Bile 'em Cabbage Down - Violin Model
67	10-1	Bile 'em Cabbage Down - Cello Model
68	10-1	Bile 'em Cabbage Down - Accompaniment
69	10-2	Juba (D) - Violin Model
70	10-2	Juba (D) - Cello Model
71	10-2	Juba (D) - Accompaniment
72	10-2	Juba (D) - Extended Accompaniment for Rhythmic Improvisation
73	10-4	Cobbler, Cobbler (Em) - Violin Model
74	10-4	Cobbler, Cobbler (Em) - Bass Model
75	10-4	Cobbler, Cobbler (Em) - Accompaniment
76	10-4	Cobbler, Cobbler (Em) - Extended Accompaniment for Rhythmic Improvisation
77	11-1	Fais do do (D) - Violin Model
78	11-1	Fais do do (D) - Cello Model
79	11-1	Fais do do (D) - Accompaniment
80	11-2	Waltz (G) - Violin Model
81	11-2	Waltz (G) - Bass Model
82	11-2	Waltz (G) - Accompaniment
83	11-6	Champaigne Branle - Violin Model
84	11-6	Champaigne Branle - Cello Model
85	11-6	Champaigne Branle - Accompaniment
86	12-1	Au Claire de la Lune (Em) - Violin Model
87	12-1	Au Claire de la Lune (Em) - Cello Model
88	12-1	Au Claire de la Lune (Em) - Accompaniment
89	12-2	Fais do do (Em) - Violin Model
90	12-2	Fais do do (Em) - Cello Model
91	12-2	Fais do do (Em) - Accompaniment
92	12-A	Au Claire de la Lune (Gm) - Accompaniment
93	12-B	Fais do do (Gm) - Accompaniment
94	12-B	Au Claire de la Lune (Am) - Accompaniment
95	12-B	Fais do do (Am) - Accompaniment
96	12-C	Au Claire de la Lune (Dm) - Accompaniment
97	12-C	Fais do do (Dm) - Accompaniment
98	——	Funky Blues in D - Accompaniment for *Teacher Call- Student Response* and Rhythmic Reading in 2s
99	——	D Dorian - Accompaniment for *Teacher Call- Student Response* and Rhythmic Reading in 3s

ORDER OF PRESENTATION
Teacher's Resource Edition - COMPACT DISC NO. 2

CD 2 Track #s	pg #	Title
1	12-3	Polka - Violin Model
2	12-3	Polka - Bass Model
3	12-3	Polka - Accompaniment
4	13-A	*Listen and Play* - Notes Leap, Hush My Baby, Cowboy Ballad, and Practice Every Day March - Melodic Ear-to-Hand Training and Assessment
5	13-1	Notes Leap - Violin Model
6	13-1	Notes Leap - Cello Model
7	13-1	Notes Leap - Accompaniment
8	13-2	Hush My Baby - Violin Model
9	13-2	Hush My Baby - Bass Model
10	13-2	Hush My Baby - Accompaniment
11	13-3	Cowboy Ballad - Violin Model
12	13-3	Cowboy Ballad - Cello Model
13	13-3	Cowboy Ballad - Accompaniment
14	13-4	Practice Every Day March - Violin Model
15	13-4	Practice Every Day March - Bass Model
16	13-4	Practice Every Day March - Accompaniment
17	13-5	Vesper Hymn - Viola Model
18	13-5	Vesper Hymn - Cello Model
19	13-5	Vesper Hymn - Accompaniment
20	14-1	Lightly Row - Violin Model
21	14-1	Lightly Row - Bass Model
22	14-1	Lightly Row - Accompaniment
23	14-2	Lightly Row (Honky Tonk Style) - Violin Model
24	14-2	Lightly Row (Honky Tonk Style) - Cello Model
25	14-2	Lightly Row (Honky Tonk Style) - Accompaniment
26	14-3	Lightly Row (Quick Time) - Viola Model
27	14-3	Lightly Row (Quick Time) - Cello Model
28	14-3	Lightly Row (Quick Time) - Accompaniment
29	14-4	Oh When the Saints Go Marching In ("By Ear" Starting on D) - Violin Model
30	14-4	Oh When the Saints Go Marching In ("By Ear" Starting on D) - Cello Model
31	14-4	Oh When the Saints Go Marching In ("By Ear" Starting on D) - Accompaniment
32	14-5	Rain, Rain - Call and Response - Violin Model
32-2	14-5	Rain, Rain - Call and Response - Viola Model
32-3	14-5	Rain, Rain - Call and Response - Viola Model
33	14-5	Rain, Rain - Call and Response - Cello Model
33-2	14-5	Rain, Rain - Call and Response - Bass Model
33-3	14-5	Rain, Rain - Call and Response - Cello Model
34	15-1	Twinkle, Twinkle, Little Star - Violin Model
35	15-1	Twinkle, Twinkle, Little Star - Viola Model
36	15-1	Twinkle, Twinkle, Little Star - Cello Model
37	15-1	Twinkle, Twinkle, Little Star - Bass Model
38	15-1	Twinkle, Twinkle, Little Star - Accompaniment
39	15-4	Twinkle, Twinkle, Little Star (Swing Style) - Violin Model
40	15-4	Twinkle, Twinkle, Little Star (Swing Style) - Cello Model
41	15-4	Twinkle, Twinkle, Little Star (Swing Style) - Accompaniment
42	16-1	Shepherd's Hey - Viola Model
43	16-1	Shepherd's Hey - Bass Model
44	16-1	Shepherd's Hey - Accompaniment
45	16-4	Shepherd's Hey (Quick Time) - Violin Model
46	16-4	Shepherd's Hey (Quick Time) - Cello Model
47	16-4	Shepherd's Hey (Quick Time) - Accompaniment

CD 2 Track #s	pg #	Title
48	16-6	Jolly Old Saint Nicholas - Violin Model
49	16-6	Jolly Old Saint Nicholas - Cello Model
50	16-6	Jolly Old Saint Nicholas - Accompaniment
51	16-7	Jolly Old Saint Nicholas (Jazz Ballad Style) - Violin Model
52	16-7	Jolly Old Saint Nicholas (Jazz Ballad Style) - Cello Model
53	16-7	Jolly Old Saint Nicholas (Jazz Ballad Style) - Accompaniment
54	17-1	By the Fireside - Violin Model
55	17-1	By the Fireside - Cello Model
56	17-1	By the Fireside - Accompaniment
57	17-5	The Birch Tree - Viola Model
58	17-5	The Birch Tree - Bass Model
59	17-5	The Birch Tree - Accompaniment
60	18-A	*Listen and Play* - Scotland's Burning and Old King Cole - Melodic Ear to Hand Training and Assessment
61	18-B	*Listen and Play* - Scotland's Burning and Old King Cole - Rhythmic, Bowing, and Articulation Ear-to-Hand Training and Assessment
62	18-3	Old King Cole (D) - Violin Model
63	18-3	Old King Cole (D) - Cello Model
64	18-3	Old King Cole (D) - Accompaniment
65	19-1	Dance in the Circle - Viola Model
66	19-1	Dance in the Circle - Bass Model
67	19-1	Dance in the Circle - Accompaniment
68	19-2	French Folk Song - Violin Model
69	19-2	French Folk Song - Cello Model
70	19-2	French Folk Song - Accompaniment
71	19-3	On Top of Old Smokey - Violin Model
72	19-3	On Top of Old Smokey - Cello Model
73	19-3	On Top of Old Smokey - Accompaniment
74	20-A	*Listen and Play* - Notes, Stepping and Skipping, Hot Cross Buns, and Mary Had a Little Lamb (With Slurs) - Melodic and Bowing Ear-to-Hand Training and Assessment
75	20-A	*Listen and Play* - Cowboy Ballad (With Slurs) - Melodic and Bowing Ear-to-Hand Training and Assessment
76	20-1	Notes (A- With Slurs) - Violin Model
77	20-1	Notes (A- With Slurs) - Bass Model
78	20-1	Notes (A- With Slurs) - Accompaniment
79	20-2	Stepping and Skipping (A - With Slurs) - Violin Model
80	20-2	Stepping and Skipping (A - With Slurs) - Cello Model
81	20-2	Stepping and Skipping (A - With Slurs) - Accompaniment
82	21-2	Cuckoo Song - Violin Model
83	21-2	Cuckoo Song - Cello Model
84	21-2	Cuckoo Song - Accompaniment
85	21-3	Cuckoo Song (Jazz Waltz Style) - Violin Model
86	21-3	Cuckoo Song (Jazz Waltz Style) - Cello Model
87	21-3	Cuckoo Song (Jazz Waltz Style) - Accompaniment
88	21-4	Nonsense Song - Viola Model
89	21-4	Nonsense Song - Cello Model
90	21-4	Nonsense Song - Accompaniment
91	22-1	Juba (G) - Violin Model
92	22-1	Juba (G) - Cello Model
93	22-1	Juba (G) - Accompaniment
94	22-3	A Paris - Violin Model
95	22-3	A Paris - Cello Model
96	22-3	A Paris - Accompaniment
97	——	Triple Reggae in D - Accompaniment for *Teacher Call - Student Response* and Rhythmic Reading in 3s
98	——	Cool Jazz - Accompaniment for *Teacher Call - Student Response*

ORDER OF PRESENTATION
COMPACT DISC NO. 3
Teacher's Resource Edition

CD 3 Track #s	pg #	Title
1	22-4	Cobbler, Cobbler (Am) - Violin Model
2	22-4	Cobbler, Cobbler (Am) - Cello Model
3	22-4	Cobbler, Cobbler (Am) - Accompaniment
4	22-4	Cobbler, Cobbler (Am) - Extended Accompaniment for Melodic Improvisation
5	23-1	Jacob Drink (C) - Viola Model
6	23-1	Jacob Drink (C) - Bass Model
7	23-1	Jacob Drink (C) - Accompaniment
8	23-3	Waltz (C) - Viola Model
9	23-3	Waltz (C) - Cello Model
10	23-3	Waltz (C) - Accompaniment
11	23-5	Golya, Golya, Gilice (The Storks) - Viola Model
12	23-5	Golya, Golya, Gilice (The Storks) - Cello Model
13	23-5	Golya, Golya, Gilice (The Storks) - Accompaniment
14	24-1	Up on the Housetop - Viola Model
15	24-1	Up on the Housetop - Cello Model
16	24-1	Up on the Housetop - Accompaniment
17	24-2	Up on the Housetop (Swing Style) - Violin Model
18	24-2	Up on the Housetop (Swing Style) - Cello Model
19	24-2	Up on the Housetop (Swing Style) - Accompaniment
20	24-4	Die Abendglocke (Evening Bells) - Violin Model
21	24-4	Die Abendglocke (Evening Bells) - Cello Model
22	24-4	Die Abendglocke (Evening Bells) - Accompaniment
23	25-1	Lightly Bounce the Bow to Lightly Row - Accompaniment
24	25-4	Norwegian Dance - Violin Model
25	25-4	Norwegian Dance - Bass Model
26	25-4	Norwegian Dance - Accompaniment
27	25-5	Bouffons - Violin Model
28	25-5	Bouffons - Cello Model
29	25-5	Bouffons - Accompaniment
30	26-3	Blues in D - Viola Model
31	26-3	Blues in D - Cello Model
32	26-4	*Listen and Play* - Blues In D (Imitative Call and Response) - Violin Model
33	26-6	Blues in D - Extended Accompaniment for *Teacher Call - Student Response*
34	27-1	Shoheen Sho - Violin Model
35	27-1	Shoheen Sho - Cello Model
36	27-1	Shoheen Sho - Accompaniment
37	27-2	Intry Mintry - Viola Model (C String)
38	27-2	Intry Mintry - Bass Model
39	27-1	Intry Mintry - Extended Accompaniment for *Teacher Call - Student Response*
40	27-6	Yangtze Boatman Chanty - Viola Model
41	27-6	Yangtze Boatman Chanty - Cello Model
42	27-6	Yangtze Boatman Chanty - Accompaniment
43	28-1	Some Folks Do - Violin Model
44	28-1	Some Folks Do - Cello Model
45	28-1	Some Folks Do - Accompaniment
46	28-2	Silent, Silent - Violin Model
47	28-2	Silent, Silent - Cello Model
48	28-2	Silent, Silent - Accompaniment
49	29-1	Baa, Baa, Black Sheep - Violin Model

CD 3 Track #s	pg #	Title
50	29-1	Baa, Baa, Black Sheep - Cello Model
51	29-1	Baa, Baa, Black Sheep - Accompaniment
52	29-2	Bingo - Violin Model
53	29-2	Bingo - Cello Model
54	29-2	Bingo - Accompaniment
55	30-1	Raindrops - Violin Model
56	30-1	Raindrops - Cello Model
57	30-1	Raindrops - Accompaniment
58	30-3	Aura Lee - Viola Model
59	30-3	Aura Lee - Cello Model
60	30-3	Aura Lee - Accompaniment
61	30-4	Sleep, Baby, Sleep - Violin Model
62	30-4	Sleep, Baby, Sleep - Cello Model
63	30-4	Sleep, Baby, Sleep - Accompaniment
64	31-1	Sur la Pont D'Avignon (On the Bridge of Avignon) - Violin Model
65	31-1	Sur la Pont D'Avignon (On the Bridge of Avignon) - Cello Model
66	31-1	Sur la Pont D'Avignon (On the Bridge of Avignon) - Accompaniment
67	31-3	Amazing Grace - Violin Model
68	31-3	Amazing Grace - Cello Model
69	31-3	Amazing Grace - Accompaniment
70	31-4	Amazing Grace (Gospel Style) - Violin Model
71	31-4	Amazing Grace (Gospel Style) - Cello Model
72	31-4	Amazing Grace (Gospel Style) - Accompaniment
73	32-3	Little Tom Tinker - Violin Model
74	32-3	Little Tom Tinker - Cello Model
75	32-3	Little Tom Tinker - Accompaniment
76	33-1	Patsy, Ory, Ory, Aye - Violin Model
77	33-1	Patsy, Ory, Ory, Aye - Bass Model
78	33-1	Patsy, Ory, Ory, Aye - Accompaniment
79	33-4	Oats, Peas, Beans - Violin Model
80	33-4	Oats, Peas, Beans - Cello Model
81	33-4	Oats, Peas, Beans - Accompaniment
82	34-1	The Shining Young Moon - Violin Model
83	34-1	The Shining Young Moon - Cello Model
84	34-1	The Shining Young Moon - Accompaniment
85	36-3	Can Can Theme - Violin Model
86	36-3	Can Can Theme - Cello Model
87	36-3	Can Can - Accompaniment
88	37-1	Starlight - Viola Model
89	37-1	Starlight - Cello Model
90	37-1	Starlight - Accompaniment
91	37-2	Jacob Drink (B♭) - Violin Model
92	37-2	Jacob Drink (B♭) - Cello Model
93	37-2	Jacob Drink (B♭) - Accompaniment
94	38-1	Mary Had a Little Lamb (E♭) - Violin Model
95	38-1	Mary Had a Little Lamb (E♭) - Bass Model
96	38-1	Mary Had a Little Lamb (E♭) - Accompaniment
97	38-3	Scarborough Fair - Viola Model
98	38-3	Scarborough Fair - Cello Model
99	38-3	Scarborough Fair - Accompaniment

I. MUSIC OF THE AMERICAS

A. The United States

1. Folk Music

Down By the Station - p. 8
Shave and a Haircut - p. 9
Bile 'em Cabbage Down - p. 10
**Oh, When the Saints Go
   Marching In "By Ear"** - p. 14
By the Fireside - p. 17
Dance In the Circle - p. 19
On Top of Old Smokey - p. 19
Intry Mintry - p. 27
Some Folks Do - p. 28
Bingo - p. 29
Aura Lee - p. 30
Row, Row, Row Your Boat - p. 33
Time and Tide - p. 37

2. Blues

Blues In D - p. 26

3. March

Practice Every Day March - p. 13

4. Jazz

Down By the Station - *Swinging
   Jazz Style* - p. 8
Twinkle, Twinkle, Little Star - *Swinging
   Jazz Style* - p. 15
Jolly Old St. Nicholas - *Jazz
   Ballad Style* - p. 16
Cuckoo Song - *Jazz Waltz Style* - p. 21
Up on the Housetop - *Swing Style* - p. 24

5. Dixieland Jazz

**Oh, When the Saints Go
   Marching In "By Ear"** - p. 14

6. Country Style

Some Folks Do - p. 28

7. Country Swing

Lightly Row - p. 14

8. African-American

Juba - p. 10, p. 22

9. Bluegrass

Mary Had a Little Lamb - p. 7

10. Honky Tonk

Hot Cross Buns - p. 6

11. Spiritual

Amazing Grace - p. 31

12. Gospel

Amazing Grace - *Gospel Style* - p. 31

13. Rock and Roll

Hot Cross Buns - p. 6
Up On the Housetop - p. 24
Intry Mintry - p. 27

B. The Caribbean

1. Reggae

Mary Had a Little Lamb - p. 5
Cobbler, Cobbler - p. 10, p. 22

II. MUSIC OF THE WORLD

A. England

Hot Cross Buns - p. 6
Old King Cole - p. 9, p.18
Shepherd's Hey - p. 16
**London Bridge is Falling
   Down "By Ear"** - p. 17
Lady My - p. 20, p. 28
Tallis Canon - p. 29

Santy Maloney - p. 33
Oats, Peas, Beans - p. 33
My Dame's Lame, Tame Crane - p. 33
Singing Goose - p. 36
The Hart, He Loves the High - p. 37
Scarborough Fair - p. 38

B. Ireland

Patsy Ory, Ory, Aye - p. 33

C. Wales

Shoheen Sho - p. 27

D. France

Au Claire de la Lune - p. 7, p. 12
Chamaigne Branle - p. 11
Fais do do - p. 11, p. 12
Twinkle, Twinkle, Little Star - p. 15
French Folk Song - p. 19
A Paris - p. 22
Bouffons - p. 25
Baa, Baa, Black Sheep - p. 29
French Cathedrals - p. 29
Sur la pont d'Avignon - p. 31
Can Can - p. 36

E. Germany

Lightly Row - p. 14
Lightly Row - *Quick Time* - p. 14
Cuckoo Song - p. 21
**Die Abendglocke (Oh How Lovely Is
    the Evening)** - p. 24
Silent, Silent - p. 28
Sleep, Baby, Sleep - p. 30

F. Hungary

Nonsense Song - p. 21
Golya, Golye, Gilice (The Storks) - p. 23

G. Israel

S'evinon Round (Spin My Top) - p. 21

H. Norway

Norwegian Dance - p. 25

I. Poland

Jacob Drink - p. 9, p. 23, p. 37

J. Russia

Vesper Hymn - p. 13
Birch Tree, The - p. 17
Shining Young Moon, The - p. 34-35

K. China

Yangtze Boatman Chanty - p. 27

L. Japan

Sakura - p. 40-41

III. SPECIAL STYLES AND FORMS

A. Ballad

Cowboy Ballad - p.13
Aura Lee - p. 30
Scarborough Fair - p. 38

B. Lullaby

Fais do do - p. 11, p. 12
Silent, Silent - p. 28
French Cathedrals - p. 29
Sleep, Baby Sleep - p. 30

C. Polka

Polka - p. 12

D. Waltz

Waltz - p. 11, p. 23

E. Theme and Variations

Stepping and Skipping - p. 7
Waltz - p. 11
Polka - p. 12
Shepherd's Hey - p. 16
**Lightly Bounce the Bow to
    Lightly Row** - p. 25
Shining Young Moon, The - p. 34-35

F. Celebration Themes

**Oh, When the Saints Go
    Marching In** - *Dixieland Jazz Style* - p. 14
Jolly Old St. Nicholas - p. 16
Up On the Housetop - *Rock and
    Roll Style* - p. 24

ix

RESOURCE INDEX #2

"You Can Look It Up"

Resources For Musical Independence

INSTRUMENTAL TECHNIQUE

- **PLAYING POSTURE - STUDENT'S TEXT PAGE 2**
- **RIGHT AND LEFT HAND POSITION • STUDENT'S TEXT PAGE 3**

INFORMATION RESOURCES

- **MUSIC SIGNS AND SYMBOLS DICTIONARY • STUDENT'S TEXT PAGES 4 and 5**

- **MUSIC TERMS DICTIONARY • STUDENT'S TEXT PAGES 42, 43, 44, and 45**

- **RHYTHMIC PATTERN DICTIONARY • STUDENT'S TEXT PAGES 46 and 47**

- **FINGERING CHART • STUDENT'S TEXT INSIDE FRONT COVER**

- **CD MUSIC INDEX • STUDENT'S TEXT PAGE 48**

RESOURCE INDEX #3

MEDIA GENERATED GROUP INSTRUCTION
- EASY "LISTEN-PLAY" EXERCISES -

CD 1 Track #s	pg #	Title
1	5-A	*Listen and Play* - Getting Started on Open D: Pizzicato
1-2	5-A	*Listen and Play* - Getting Started on Open A: Pizzicato
1-3	5-A	*Listen and Play* - Getting Started on Open D and Open A: Pizzicato
2	5-B	*Listen and Play* - Getting Started on Open D: Arco
2-2	5-B	*Listen and Play* - Getting Started on Open A: Arco
2-3	5-B	*Listen and Play* - Getting Started on Open D and Open A: Arco
3	5-C	*Listen* - Articulation - Separated and Connected
4	5-C	*Listen and Play* - Separated Style of Articulation on Open D
4-2	5-C	*Listen and Play* - Connected Style of Articulation on Open D
4-3	5-C	*Listen and Play* - Separated Style of Articulation on Open A
4-4	5-C	*Listen and Play* - Connected Style of Articulation on Open A
4-5	5-C	*Listen and Play* - Articulation - Open D
4-6	5-C	*Listen and Play* - Articulation - Open A
5	5-D	Blues in D - Accompaniment for *Teacher Call - Student Response*
6	5-E	*Listen and Play* - Getting Started on F♯
7	5-E	*Listen and Play* - Getting Started on E
8	5-E	*Listen and Play* - Getting Started on D
9	5-B	D Major Triad - Accompaniment for *Teacher Call - Student Response* and Rhythmic Reading in 2s
10	6-A	*Listen and Play* - Hot Cross Buns - Melodic Ear-to-Hand Training and Assessment
22	6-B	*Listen and Play* - Notes - Melodic Ear-to-Hand Assessment
26	6-D	*Listen and Play* - Mary Had a Little Lamb - Melodic Ear-to-Hand Assessment
44	7-B	*Listen and Play* - Au Claire de la Lune - Melodic Ear-to-Hand Training and Assessment
58	9-A	*Listen and Play* - Old King Cole - Melodic Ear-to-Hand Training and Assessment
62	9-B	*Listen and Play* - Jacob Drink- Rhythmic, Bowing, and Articulation Ear-to-Hand Training and Assessment
98	——	Funky Blues in D- Accompaniment for *Teacher Call- Student Response* and Rhythmic Reading in 2s
99	——	D Dorian - Accompaniment for *Teacher Call - Student Response* and Rhythmic Reading in 3s

CD 2 Track #s	pg #	Title
4	13-A	*Listen and Play* - Notes Leap, Hush My Baby, Cowboy Ballad, and Practice Every Day March - Melodic Ear-to-Hand Training and Assessment
60	18-A	*Listen and Play* - Scotland's Burning and Old King Cole - Melodic Ear to Hand Training and Assessment
61	18-B	*Listen and Play* - Scotland's Burning and Old King Cole - Rhythmic, Bowing, and Articulation Ear-to-Hand Training and Assessment
74	20-A	*Listen and Play* - Notes, Stepping and Skipping, Hot Cross Buns, and Mary Had a Little Lamb (With Slurs) - Melodic and Bowing Ear-to-Hand Training and Assessment
75	20-A	*Listen and Play* - Cowboy Ballad (With Slurs) - Melodic and Bowing Ear-to-Hand Training and Assessment
97	——	Triple Reggae in D - Accompaniment for *Teacher Call - Student Response* and Rhythmic Reading in 3s
99	——	Cool Jazz - Accompaniment for *Teacher Call - Student Response*

CD 3 Track #s	pg #	Title
32	26-4	*Listen and Play* - Blues In D (Imitative Call and Response) - Violin Model
33	26-6	Blues in D - Extended Accompaniment for *Teacher Call - Student Response*
39	27-1	Intry Mintry - Extended Accompaniment for *Teacher Call - Student Response*

RESOURCE INDEX #4

Ensembles with Opportunities for Individualizing Group Instruction

Student's Text Page #	Teacher's CD-1 Track #	Title
8	25	Eighth Notes Duet (Duet)
9	65	Jacob Drink (4 Parts)

Student's Text Page #	Teacher's CD-2 Track #	Title
15	38	Twinkle, Twinkle Little Star (3 Parts)
17	56	By the Fireside (4 Parts)

Student's Text Page #	Teacher's CD-3 Track #	Title
28	45	Some Folks Do (Duet)
28	48	Silent, Silent (Duet)
31	66	Sur la Pont d'Avignon (Duet with 4 Melodic Ostinatos)
36	—	Woodchuck (4 Parts)
38	—	St. Paul's Steeple (Duet)

String Orchestra Arrangement for Concert Performance

Student's Text Page #	Track #	Title
39	—	Theme from "Spring"

Solo (with piano accompaniment) for Concert Performance

Student's Text Page #	Track #	Title
40	—	Sakura

RESOURCE INDEX #5
Musical Rounds for Independent Study and Ensemble Performance

Student's Text and Tch's Resource Ed Page #	Title
15	We are Met (Unaccompanied)
18	Scotland's Burning (Individualized and Unaccompanied)
20	Lady My (D Major - With Slurs - Unaccompanied)
21	S'evivon Round (Spin, My Top) (Individualized and Unaccompanied)
24	Die Abendglocke (Evening Bells) (With CD Accompaniment - CD 3 Track 22) Oh, How Lovely is the Evening
24	Day is Done (Unaccompanied)
26	Round Evening (Individualized and Unaccompanied)
27	Lady My (G Major - Unaccompanied)
29	Tallis Canon (Unaccompanied)
29	French Cathedrals (Unaccompanied)
32	Scotland's A-Burning (Individualized and Unaccompanied)
32	Little Tom Tinker (Individualized with CD Accompaniment - CD 3 Track 75)
32	Santy Maloney (Unaccompanied)
33	Row, Row, Row Your Boat (Individualized and Unaccompanied)
33	My Dame's Lame, Tame Crane (Unaccompanied)
36	Singing Goose (Unaccompanied)
37	Tide and Time (Unaccompanied)
37	The Hart, He Loves the High Wood (Unaccompanied)

RESOURCE INDEX #6

Music Literacy - Optional Rhythmic Reading Flashcards*

Student's Text Page #	Tch's Resource Ed Page #	Rhythmic flashcards	Title
7	7-A	R-3, R-5, R-6	Au Claire de la Lune
30	30-A	R-3, R-4, R-5, R-6, R-43, R-44	Aura Lee
29	29-A	R-1 R-2, R-11, R-15, R-26, R-27	Baa, Baa, Black Sheep (In Minor Tonality)
10	10-A	R-10, R-14	Bile 'em Cabbage Down
29	29-A	R-10, R-12, R-14, R-20	Bingo
17	17-A	R-2, R-10, R-13, R-14, R-19, R-20	By the Fireside, Accompaniments, and Obbligato
10	10-A	R-8, R-13	Cobbler, Cobbler and Variation on Cobbler, Cobbler
8	8-A	R-11, R-14, R-15	Down By the Station
23	23-A	R-2, R-13, R-14	Gólya, Gólya, Gilice
6	6-A	R-1, R-2	Hot Cross Buns
8	8-A	R-1, R-10	Hot Cross Buns (With Subdivisions)
9	9-B	R-10, R-13, R-14, R-17, R-25	Jacob Drink, Accompaniments, and Obbligato
16	16-A	R-11, R-13	Jolly Old Saint Nicholas
10	10-A	R-2, R-13	Juba and Variation on Juba
20, 28	28-A	R-1, R-2	Lady My
14	14-A	R-3, R-4, R-5, R-11, R-13, R-17	Lightly Row and Lightly Row (Quick Time)
32	32-A	R-28, R-29, R-30, R-31, R-32	Little Tom Tinker
6	6-C	R-3, R-4, R-5	Mary Had a Little Lamb
8	8-A	R-1, R-11, R-12	More Notes
25	25-A	R-10, R-14	Norwegian Dance

*Rhythmic Reading Flashcards - Set A MLR 421

Music Literacy – Optional Rhythmic Reading Flashcards*
(continued)

Student's Text Page #	Tch's Resource Ed Page #	Rhythmic flashcards	Title
6	6-B	R-1, R-2	Notes
13	13-A	R-1, R-2 , R-19	Notes Leap, Hush My Baby, Cowboy Ballad, and Practice Every Day March
33	33-A	R-33, R-34	Oats, Peas, Beans
9, 18	9-A, 18-A	R-1, R-2, R-19	Old King Cole
33	33-A	R-33, R-34	Patsy-Ory-Ory-Aye
12	12-A	R-1, R-2, R-10, R-11, R-13, R-14	Polka, Variation One on Polka, Variation Two on Polka
14	14-A	R-13, R-20	Rain, Rain
30	30-A	R-2, R-10, R-11, R-13, R-14	Raindrops and Raindrops Variation
8	8-A	R-1, R-10, R-11, R-12	Rocket Cruiser
33	33-A	R-28, R-30, R-31, R-37	Row, Row, Row Your Boat and Variation
18	18-A	R-2, R-10	Scotland's Burning
9	9-B	R-15, R-16	Shave and a Haircut
16	16-A	R-1, R-2, R-10, R-14, R-18, R-19	Shepherd's Hey, Variation One, and Variation Two
28	28-A	R-2, R-11, R-17	Silent, Silent
28	28-A	R-1, R-2, R-11, R-17	Some Folks Do
7	7-A	R-1, R-2	Stepping and Skipping
7	7-A	R-8, R-9	Stepping and Skipping Variations One and Two
31	31-A	R-1, R-2, R-10, R-13, R-17, R-19	Sur la Pont d'Avignon and Melodic Ostinatos
15	15-A	R-1, R-2	Twinkle, Twinkle, Little Star
24	24-A	R-1, R-2, R-15, R-25, R-26, R-38	Up On the Housetop
13	13-A	R-3, R-4	Vesper Hymn

*Rhythmic Reading Flashcards - Set A MLR 421

RESOURCE INDEX #7

MUSIC LITERACY - RHYTHMIC ROUNDS AND RHYTHMIC READING EXERCISES
- For Overhead Projection or Supplementary Rhythmic Reading Handouts -

Tch's Resource Ed Page #	Description
8-A	4-Line Rhythmic Reading Exercise in 2/4
8-E	Rhythmic Patterns for Technical Development
11-A	5-Line Rhythmic Reading Exercise in 3/4
11-A	4-Part Rhythmic Round in 3/4
11-A	4-Part Rhythmic Round in 3/4
11-A	COMPOSE A RHYTHMIC ROUND IN 3/4
16-A	4-Part Rhythmic Round in 2/4
16-A	4-Line Rhythmic Reading Exercise in 2/4
19-A	4-Part Rhythmic Round in 3/4
19-A	4-Line Rhythmic Reading Exercise in 3/4
23-A	4-Part Rhythmic Round in 2/4
23-A	4-Line Rhythmic Reading Exercise in 2/4
23-A	COMPOSE A RHYTHMIC ROUND IN 2/4
24-A	4-Line Rhythmic Reading Exercise in 2/4
24-A	4-Part Rhythmic Round in 2/4
29-A	4-Part Rhythmic Round in 2/4
29-A	4-Line Rhythmic Reading Exercise in 2/4
30-A	5-Line Rhythmic Reading Exercise in 4/4
30-A	4-Part Rhythmic Round in 4/4
31-A	4-Line Rhythmic Reading Exercise in 2/4
31-A	4-Part Rhythmic Round in 2/4
32-A	Rhythmic Bowing Patterns for Technical Development in 6/8
33-A	4-Line Rhythmic Reading Exercise in 6/8
33-A	4-Part Rhythmic Round in 6/8

RESOURCE INDEX #8

One Octave Scales and Arpeggios for Warm-Up and Technical Development

xvii

D major, G major, C major, F major, B♭ major, E natural minor, A natural minor, D natural minor

Tch's Resource Ed Page #	Title
41-J	Scales and Arpeggios for Violin
41-K	Scales and Arpeggios for Viola
41-L	Scales and Arpeggios for Cello
41-M	Scales and Arpeggios for Bass

RESOURCE INDEX #9
Foundation Studies for Creative Musicianship

AURAL TRANSCRIPTION
- FAMILIAR SONGS LEARNED "BY EAR" WITHOUT THE AID OF MUSIC NOTATION -

Student's Text and Tch's Resource Ed Page #	Title	Description
6	*Hot Cross Buns*	Honky Tonk Style
6	*Hot Cross Buns*	Rock and Roll Style
6	*Mary Had a Little Lamb*	Reggae Style
8	*Down By the Station*	Jazz Style
14	*Oh, When the Saints Go Marching In*	Dixieland Jazz
15	*Twinkle, Twinkle Little Star*	Jazz Style
16	*Shepherd's Hey (Quick Time)*	Country Dance
16	*Jolly Old Saint Nicholas*	Jazz Ballad Style
17	*London Bridge is Falling Down*	Bluegrass or Reggae Style
21	*Cuckoo Song*	Jazz Waltz Style
24	*Up on the Housetop*	Swing Style
31	*Amazing Grace*	Gospel Style

AURAL TRANSPOSITION
- FAMILIAR SONGS PLAYED ON A DIFFERENT STARTING NOTE -

Tch's Resource Ed Page #	Title	Description
6-E	*Hot Cross Buns*	English folk song starting on C#
6-E	*Hot Cross Buns*	English folk song starting on B
6-E	*Notes*	Traditional song starting on C#
6-F	*Notes*	Traditional song starting on B
6-F	*Mary Had a Little Lamb*	Traditional song starting on C#
6-F	*Mary Had a Little Lamb*	Traditional song starting on B
12-A	*Au Claire de la Lune (in Minor Tonality)*	French folk song starting on G
12-B	*Fais do do (in Minor Tonality)*	French folk song starting on B♭
12-B	*Au Claire de la Lune (in Minor Tonality)*	French folk song starting on A
12-B	*Fais do do (in Minor Tonality)*	French folk song starting on C
12-C	*Au Claire de la Lune (in Minor Tonality)*	French folk song starting on D
12-B	*Fais do do (in Minor Tonality)*	French folk song starting on F

Foundation Studies for Creative Musicianship
(continued)

CD RECORDED "CALL AND RESPONSE"
- LISTEN & PLAY -

Student's Text Page #	Tch's Resource Ed Page #	Title	Description
14	14-E	*Rain, Rain*	"Call and Response" in a Fantasy Style
26	26-A	*Blues in D*	"Call and Response" in a Swinging Style

TEACHER "CALL" - STUDENT "RESPONSE"
- LISTEN & PLAY -

Tch's Resource Ed Page #	Title	Description
5-C	*Blues in D*	"Teacher Call (Open Strings) - Student Response"
8-C	*Blues in D*	"Teacher Call - Student Response"
16-B	*Blues in D*	"Teacher Call - Student Response"
17-B	*Cobbler, Cobbler*	"Teacher Call - Student Paraphrase"
18-B	*Cool Jazz*	"Teacher Call (Vocal) - Student Response"
22-B	*Cool Jazz*	"Teacher Call (Instr) - Student Response"
24-B	*Cobbler, Cobbler*	"Teacher Call - Student Paraphrase"
26-B	*Blues in D*	"Teacher Call (Vocal) - Student Response"
27-A	*Intry Mintry*	"Teacher Call (Vocal) - Student Response"
27-D	*Cool Jazz*	"Teacher Call - Student Response"
28-F	*Cobbler, Cobbler*	"Teacher Call - Student Dialogue"
28-G	*Cool Jazz*	"Teacher Call - Student Response"
29-B	*Blues in D*	"Teacher Call - Student Response"
30-D	*Down By the Station*	"Teacher Call - Student Dialogue"
31-D	*Cool Jazz*	"Teacher Call - Student Response"
37-A	*Blues in D*	"Teacher Call - Student Response"

RESOURCE INDEX #10
Creative Musicianship - Improvisation and Composition

- CREATING A SAFE ENVIRONMENT FOR SPONTANEOUS MUSIC-MAKING -

Student's Text Page #	Tch's Resource Ed Page #	Title	Description	Number of Notes Required
8	8-B	*Down By the Station*	Jazz	3
10	10-B	*Cobbler, Cobbler*	Reggae	3

- GETTING STARTED WITH RHYTHMIC IMPROVISATION -

8	8-B	*Down By the Station*	Jazz	3
10	10-B	*Cobbler, Cobbler*	Reggae	3
10	10-A	*Juba*	Bluegrass	4
16	16-A	*Jolly Old Saint Nicholas*	Jazz Ballad Style	6

- EXPANDING THE OPTIONS FOR IMPROVISATION IN A SAFE ENVIRONMENT -

—	8-C	*Blues In D*	Swinging Style	3
—	9-C	*Down By the Station*	Jazz	3
—	11-B	*Down By the Station*	Jazz	3
—	13-B	*Down By the Station*	Jazz	5
—	14-A, B	*Rain, Rain*	Fantasy Style	5
—	16-B	*Blues in D*	Swinging Style	5
—	17-B	*Cobbler, Cobbler*	Reggae	3 or 5
—	18-B	*Cool Jazz*	Swinging Style	1
—	22-A	*Cobbler, Cobbler*	Reggae	4-6
—	22-B	*Cool Jazz*	Swinging Style	4
—	24-B	*Cobbler, Cobbler*	Reggae	3-9
26	26-B, C	*Blues in D*	Swinging Style	4
27	27-A, B	*Intry Mintry*	Rock and Roll	4-10
—	27-D, H	*Cool Jazz*	Swinging Style	3
—	28-D, E	*Down By the Station*	Jazz	3-6
—	28-F	*Cobbler, Cobbler*	Reggae	3-6
—	28-G	*Cool Jazz*	Swinging Style	4
—	29-B, C	*Blues in D*	Swinging Style	7
—	29-D	*Cool Jazz*	Swinging Style	4
—	30-D	*Down By the Station*	Jazz	3-6
—	31-C, D	*Cool Jazz*	Swinging Style	4-6
—	37-A	*Blues in D*	Swinging Style	9

- CD RECORDED CALL AND RESPONSE - REPLICATED OR IMPROVISED RESPONSE -

14	14, 14-A, 14-B	*Rain, Rain*	Fantasy Style	4
26	26, 26-A	*Blues in D*	Swinging Style	4

Creative Musicianship - Improvisation and Composition
(Continued)

- OPTIONS FOR MUSIC COMPOSITION -

—	11-A	*Compose a Rhythmic Round in 3/4*
—	14-B, 21-A	*Compose a Melody Based on a Single Musical Idea (Rain, Rain)*
—	23-A	*Compose a Rhythmic Round in 2/4*
—	26-D, E	*Compose a Riffs and Melodies to the Blues in D*
—	30-C, D	*Compose a Melody Based on an Original Musical Motif*
—	37-C	*Compose a Melody Based on an Original Musical Motif*
—	41-D	*Composition Worksheet for "Cobbler, Cobbler (Am)"*
—	41-E	*Composition Worksheet for "Cobbler, Cobbler (Em)*
—	41-F	*Composition Worksheet for "Cool Jazz"*
—	41-G	*Composition Worksheet for "Blues in D"*
—	41-H	*Composition Worksheet for "Intry Mintry"*
—	41-I	PRINCIPLES OF MUSIC NOTATION

- APPLYING EXPRESSIVE AND STRUCTURAL ELEMENTS TO IMPROVISATION -

Tch's Resource Ed Page #   **Description and Title**

SOUND AND SILENCE AS AN EXPRESSIVE ELEMENT

9-C   *Down By the Station (Jazz Style)*

MUSICAL DYNAMICS AS AN EXPRESSIVE ELEMENT

11-B   *Down by the Station (Jazz Style)*

RHYTHMIC SUBDIVISION AS AN EXPRESSIVE ELEMENT

13-B   *Down By the Station (Jazz Style)*

REPETITION AND VARIATION AS STRUCTURAL ELEMENTS

14-B   *Rain, Rain (Fantasy Style)*

THE MUSICAL PARAPHRASE AS AN EXPRESSIVE ELEMENT

17-B, 24-B   *Cobbler, Cobbler (Reggae)*

THE MUSICAL DIALOGUE AS AN EXPRESSIVE ELEMENT

21-C, 28-F   *Cobbler, Cobbler (Reggae)*

RETURN TO THE MUSICAL DIALOGUE AS AN EXPRESSIVE ELEMENT

30-D   *Down By the Station (Jazz Style)*

REVIEW OF STRATEGIES FOR CREATING MUSIC IMPROVISATIONS

36-A, B, C   *Down By the Station (Jazz Style)*

- ENTRY-LEVEL OPPORTUNITIES FOR MUSIC IMPROVISATION -
THE TEACHER "CALL" AND THE STUDENT "RESPONSE"

See **RESOURCE INDEX #9**, page xix

TEACHING TO THE NATIONAL CONTENT STANDARDS FOR MUSIC

Students should know and be able to do these things in music:

#1   **Sing, alone and with others (in small and large ensembles), a varied repertoire of music (representing diverse genres and cultures)**

All *Do It! Play Strings* song repertoire includes text to encourage singing alone and with others.

Refer to **Resource Index #1** *A World of Musical Styles at Your Fingertips*
(Note that song repertoire represents a wide variety of musical genres and cultures.)

#2   **Perform on instruments, alone and with others (in small and large ensembles), a varied repertoire of music (representing diverse genres and cultures)**

Do It! Play Strings provides extensive opportunities to develop solo and ensemble performance skills through repertoire that represents a wide variety of musical genres and cultures.

Refer to **Resource Index #1** *A World of Musical Styles at Your Fingertips*

Refer to **Resource Index #4** *Ensembles and Opportunities for Individualizing Group Instruction*

Refer to **Resource Index #5** *Musical Rounds for Independent Study and Ensemble Performance*

#3   **Improvise melodies, variations, and accompaniments**

Do It! Play Strings integrates creative musicianship skills with traditional instrumental performance skills from the start.

Refer to **Resource Index #9** *Foundation Studies for Creative Musicianship* for a listing of preparatory exercises that provide an aural and technical foundation for creative musicianship.

Refer to **Resource Index #10** *Creative Musicianship - Improvisation* for a listing of opportunities specifically designed to develop improvisation skills.

#4   **Compose and arrange music (for voices and various acoustic and electronic instruments) within specified guidelines**

The **Teacher's Resource Edition** of *Do It! Play Strings* provides extensive options and opportunities to encourage students to engage in music learning that leads to music composition and arranging.

Refer to **Resource Index #10** *Creative Musicianship - Composition* for a listing of opportunities and strategies designed to develop composition and arranging skills.

#5   **Read and notate music**

The **Teacher's Resource Edition** of *Do It! Play Strings* provides extensive options and opportunities to develop music reading and music notation skills.

Refer to **Resource Index #6** *Music Literacy Options - Rhythmic Reading Flashcards* for music reading options.

Refer to **Resource Index #7 Music** *Literacy - Rhythmic Rounds and Rhythmic Reading Exercises*

Refer to **Resource Index #10** *Creative Musicianship - Improvisation and Composition* for notation options associated with music composition.

#6   **Listen to, analyze, and describe music (representing diverse genres and cultures)**

The *Do It! Play Strings* **CD** provides boundless opportunities for listening, analyzing, and describing recorded music representing diverse genres and cultures.

Refer to **Resource Index #1** *A World of Musical Styles at Your Fingertips*

#7   **Evaluate music and music performances**

The *Do It! Play Strings* **CD** provides extensive opportunities for evaluating music, recorded music performances, and student music performances.

Refer to **Resource Index #1** *A World of Musical Styles at Your Fingertips*

#8   **Understand relationships between music, the other arts, and disciplines outside the arts (in different historical periods and cultures)**

The multi-musical styles, historical periods, and cultures represented by the printed and recorded music of *Do It! Play Strings* provide extensive opportunities for an expanded study of the relationship between music, the other arts, and disciplines outside the arts.

Refer to **Resource Index #1** *A World of Musical Styles at Your Fingertips*

#9   **Understand music in relation to history and culture**

Do It! Play Strings provides extensive opportunities for an expanded study of music in relation to history and culture.

Refer to **Resource Index #1** *A World of Musical Styles at Your Fingertips*

Source: National Standards for Arts Education (Reston, VA: MENC, 1994)

PRACTICE RECORD

Student   School

Day

Wk	MON	TUES	WED	THURS	FRI	SAT	SUN	Wk Total	Parent's Signature
1									
2									
3									
4									
5									
6									
7									
8									
9									
10									
11									
12									
13									
14									
15									
16									
17									
18									
19									
20									
21									
22									
23									
24									
25									
26									
27									
28									
29									
30									
31									
32									
33									
34									
35									
36									

BLANK PAGE

PARTS OF THE VIOLIN AND BOW

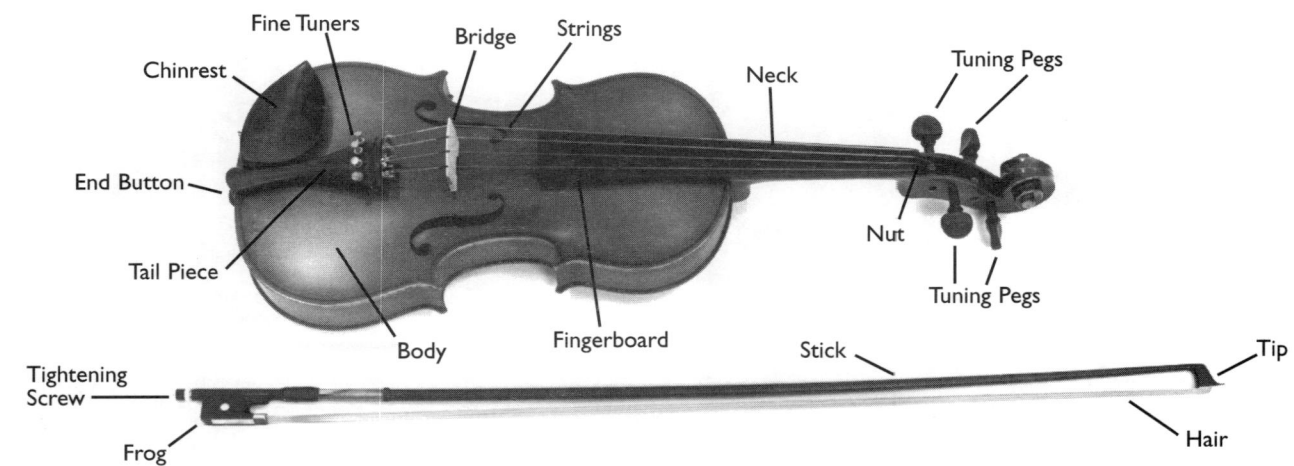

OPEN CASE AND ACCESSORIES

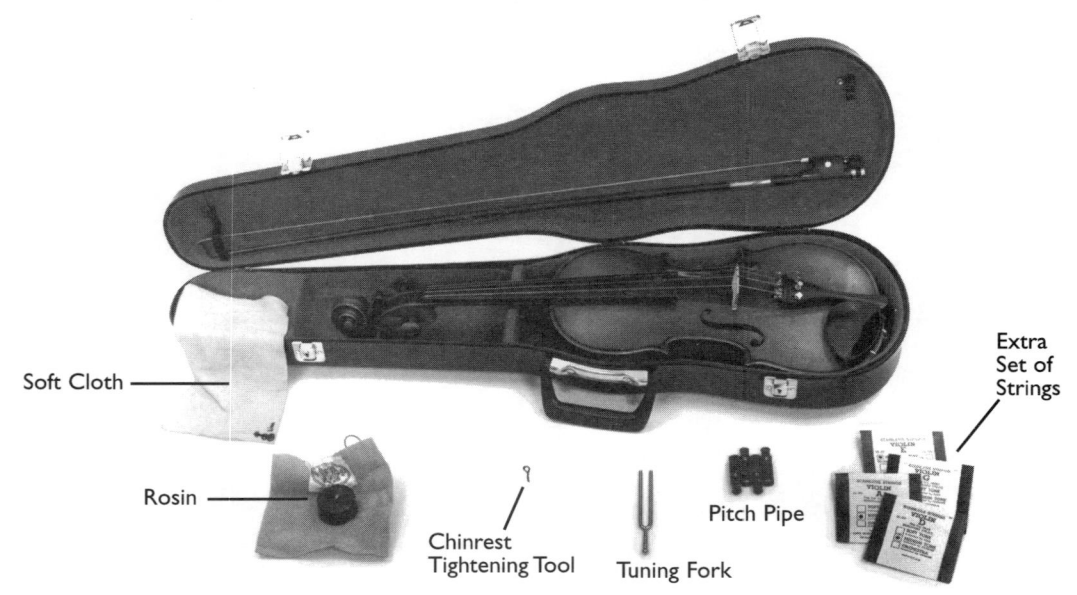

VIOLIN FINGERING CHART

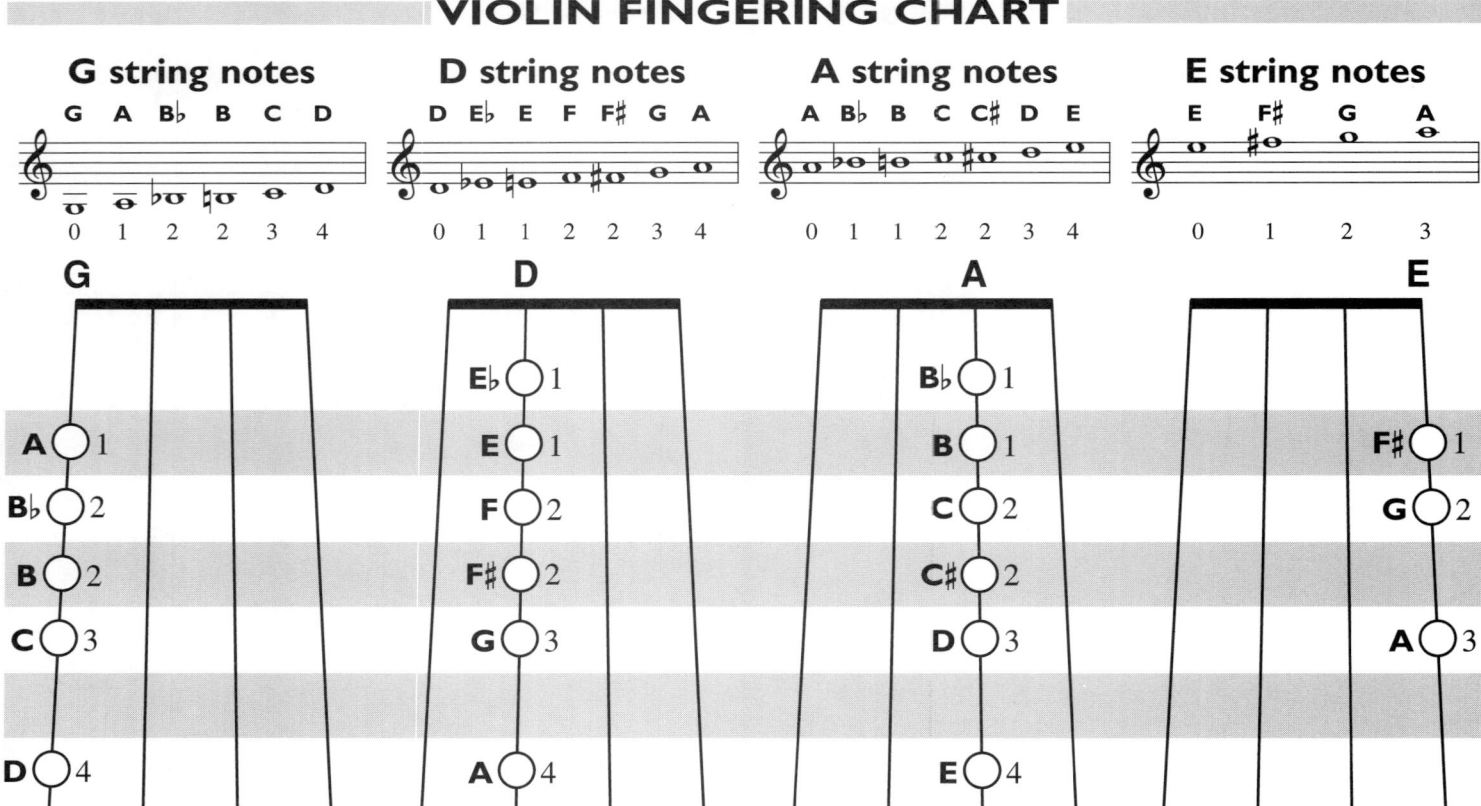

PARTS OF THE VIOLA AND BOW

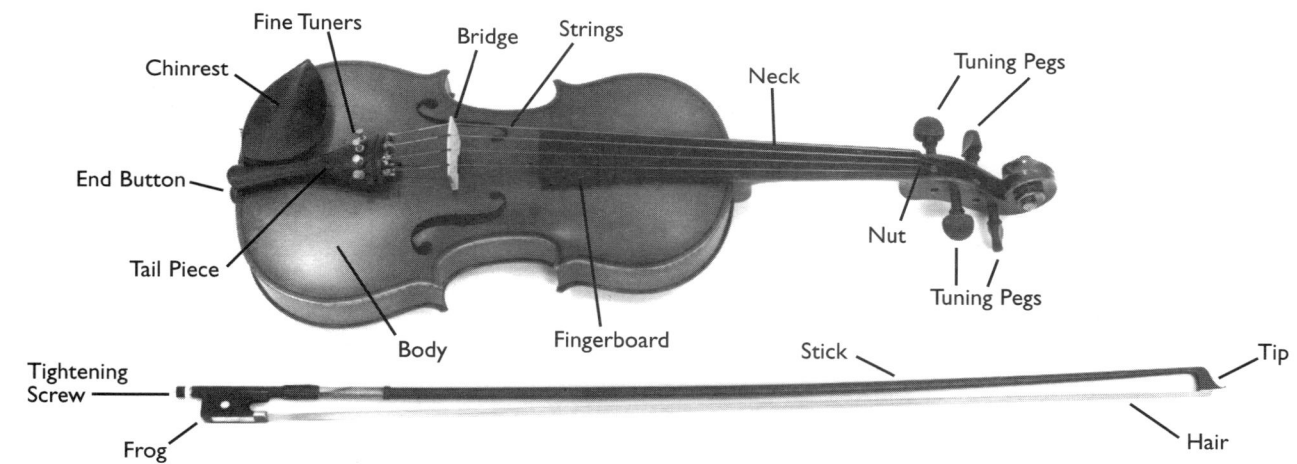

OPEN CASE AND ACCESSORIES

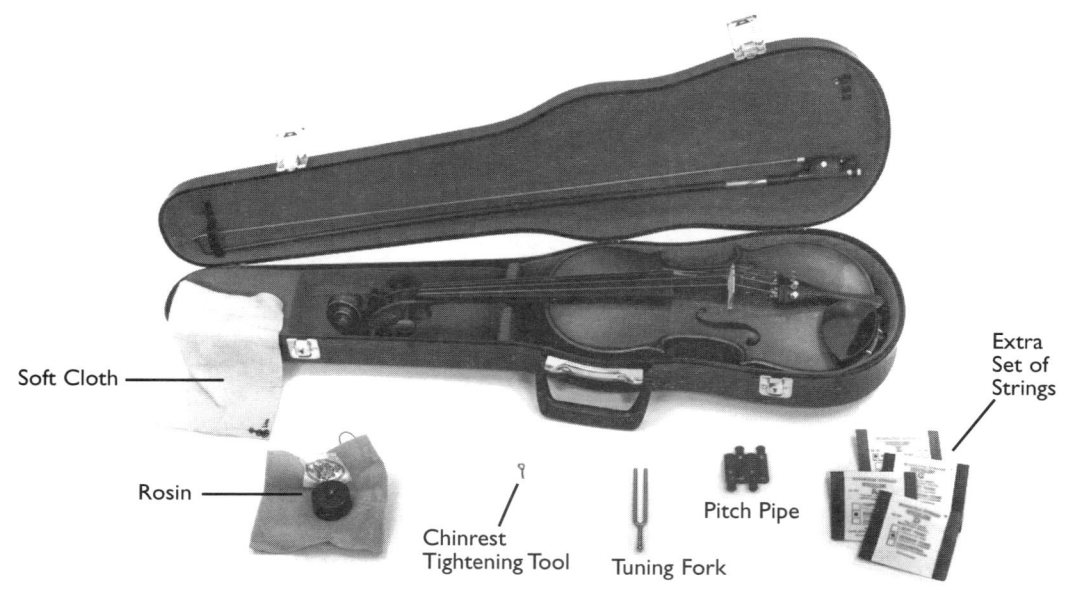

VIOLA FINGERING CHART

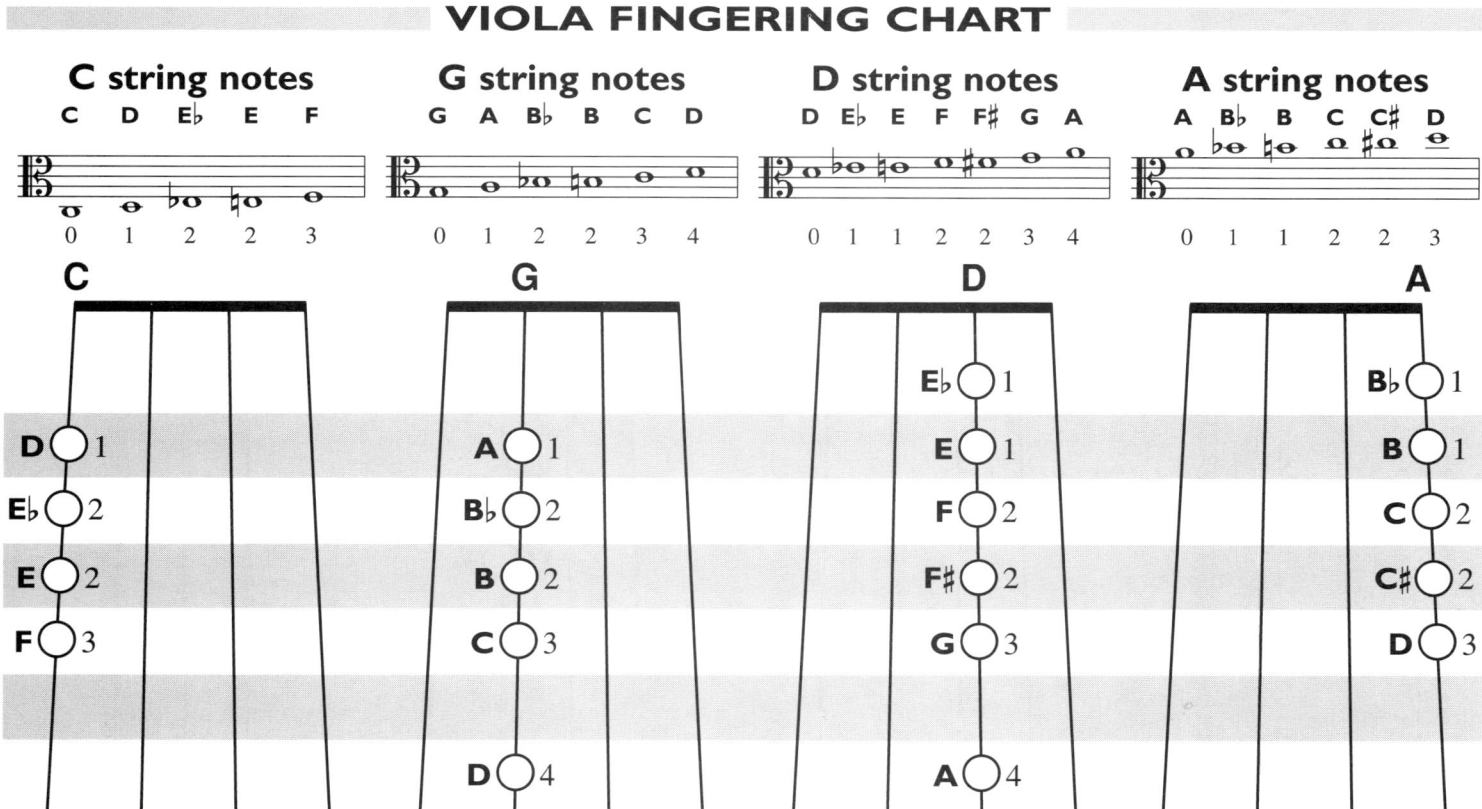

PARTS OF THE CELLO AND BOW

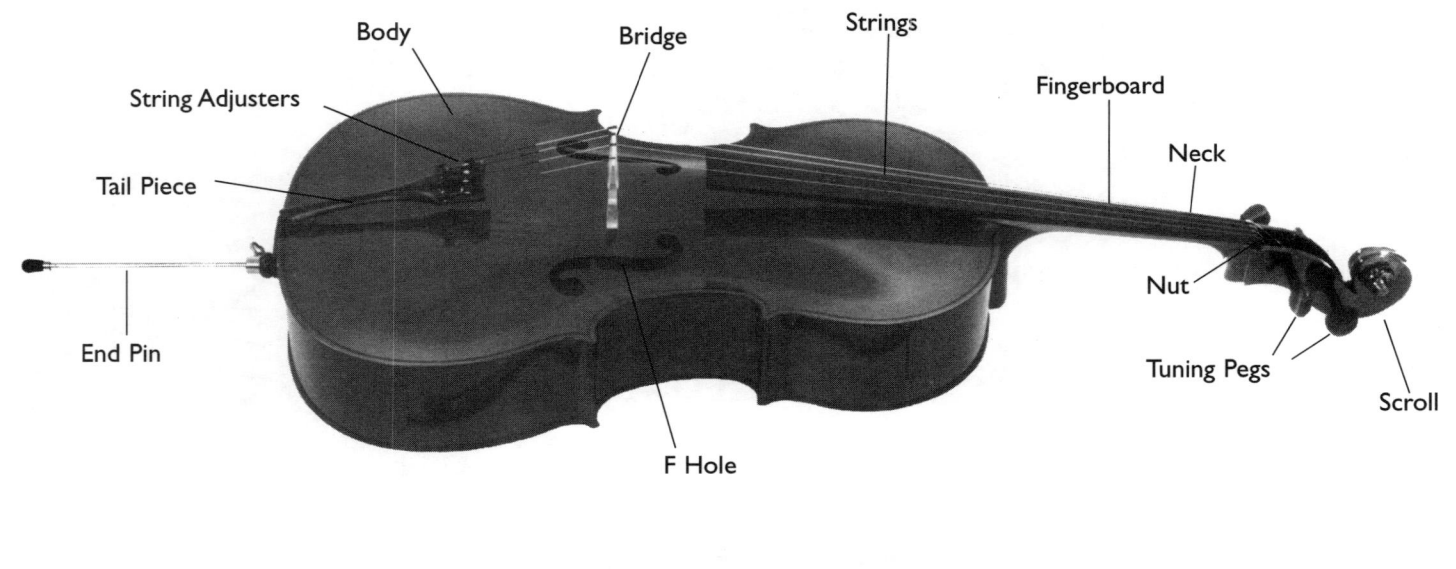

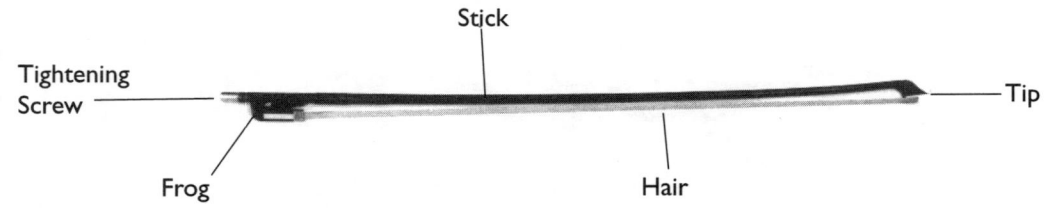

CELLO FINGERING CHART

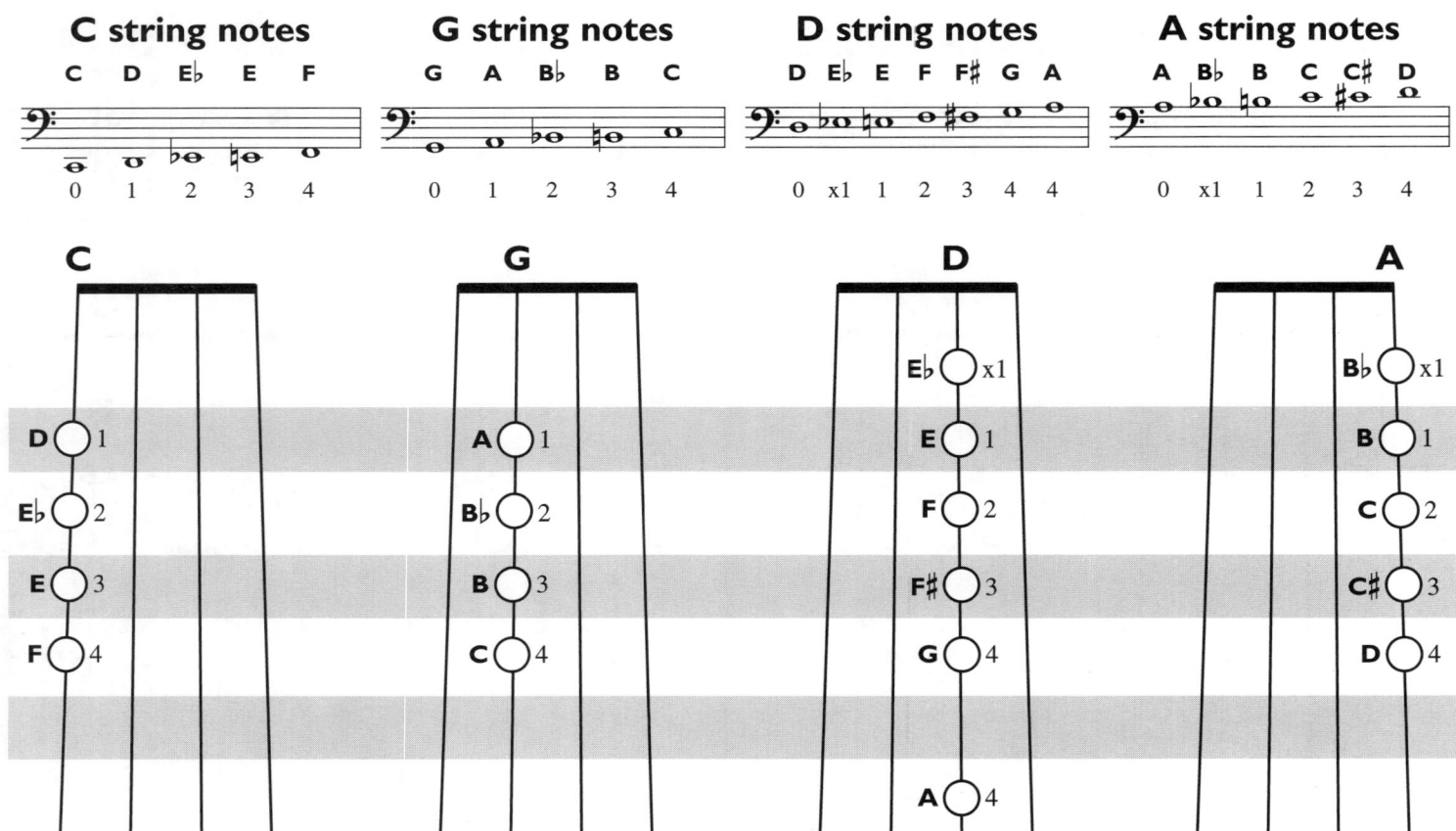

PARTS OF THE BASS AND BOW

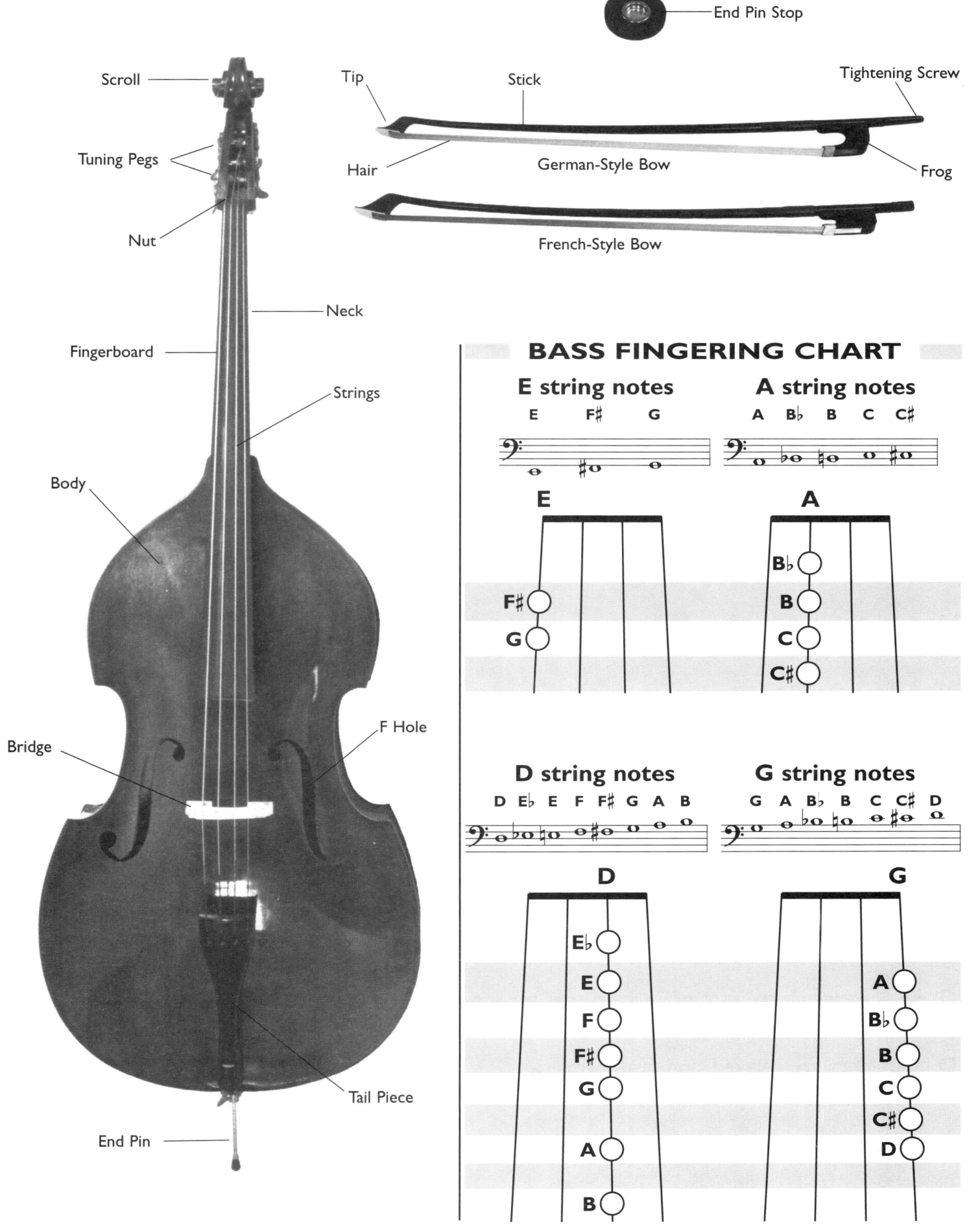

End Pin Stop

Scroll

Tuning Pegs

Nut

Neck

Fingerboard

Strings

Body

Bridge

F Hole

Tail Piece

End Pin

Tip

Stick

Hair

German-Style Bow

French-Style Bow

Tightening Screw

Frog

BASS FINGERING CHART

E string notes
E   F♯   G

A string notes
A B♭ B C C♯

E

F♯

G

A

B♭

B

C

C♯

D string notes
D E♭ E F F♯ G A B

G string notes
G A B♭ B C C♯ D

D

E♭

E

F

F♯

G

A

B

G

A

B♭

B

C

C♯

D

VIOLIN PLAYING POSTURE

SEATED POSITION

A. Body is lengthened.

B. Body weight is balanced on the front of chair and on both feet.

C. Body weight is free to move from side to side.

D. Shoulders are relaxed, and both arms can move freely.

STANDING POSITION

A. Body is lengthened.

B. Body weight is balanced on both feet, left foot slightly forward.

C. Body weight is free to move from side to side.

D. Shoulders are relaxed, and both arms can move freely.

[Mirror image]

RIGHT HAND POSITION

A. Fingers are relaxed, curved, and flexible.

B. Thumb is curved and flexible, tip touching stick and edge of frog.

C. Instrument supports the bow.

D. Hand gently guides the bow, without gripping tightly.

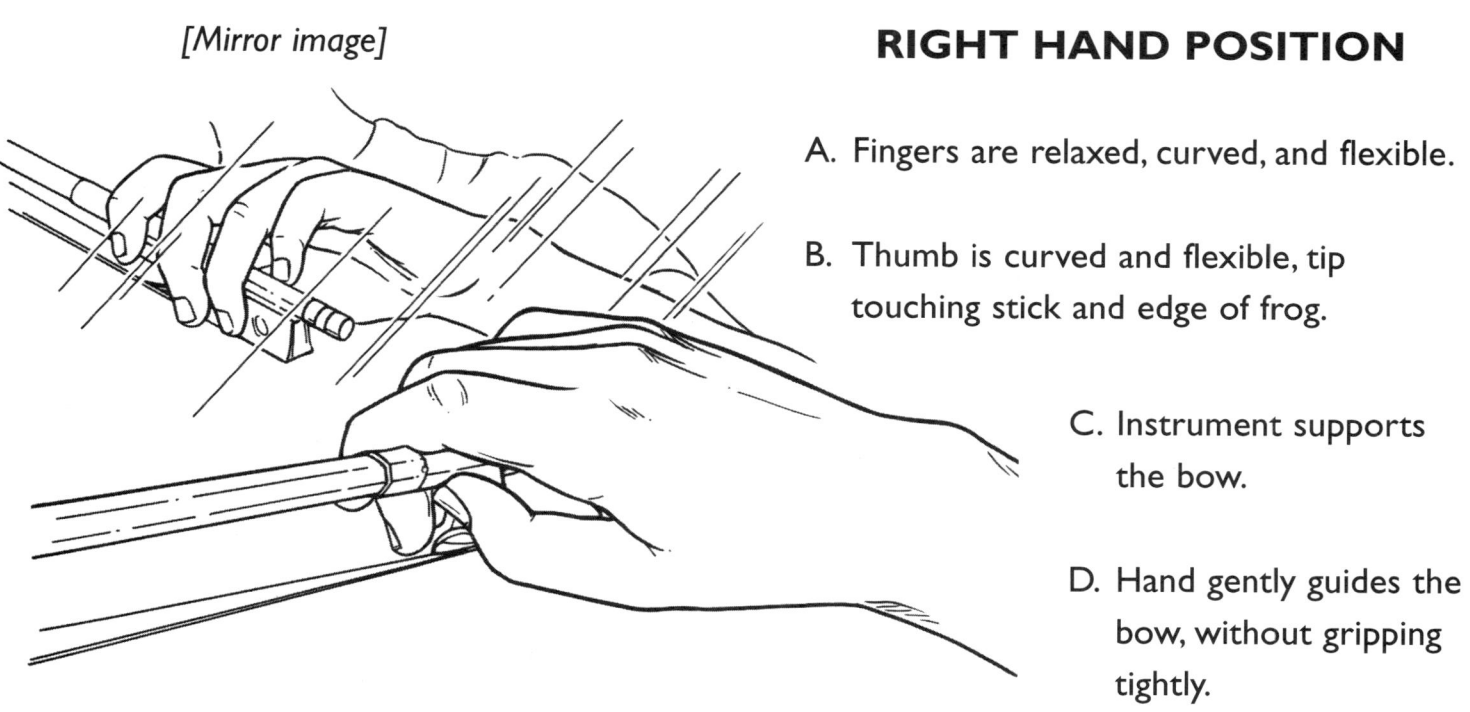

Check your position in a mirror

LEFT HAND POSITION

A. Fingers are curved, tips touching the string.

B. Instrument is held lightly by thumb and base knuckle of index finger.

C. Wrist is flexible and not bent.

D. Elbow hangs below instrument.

[Mirror image]

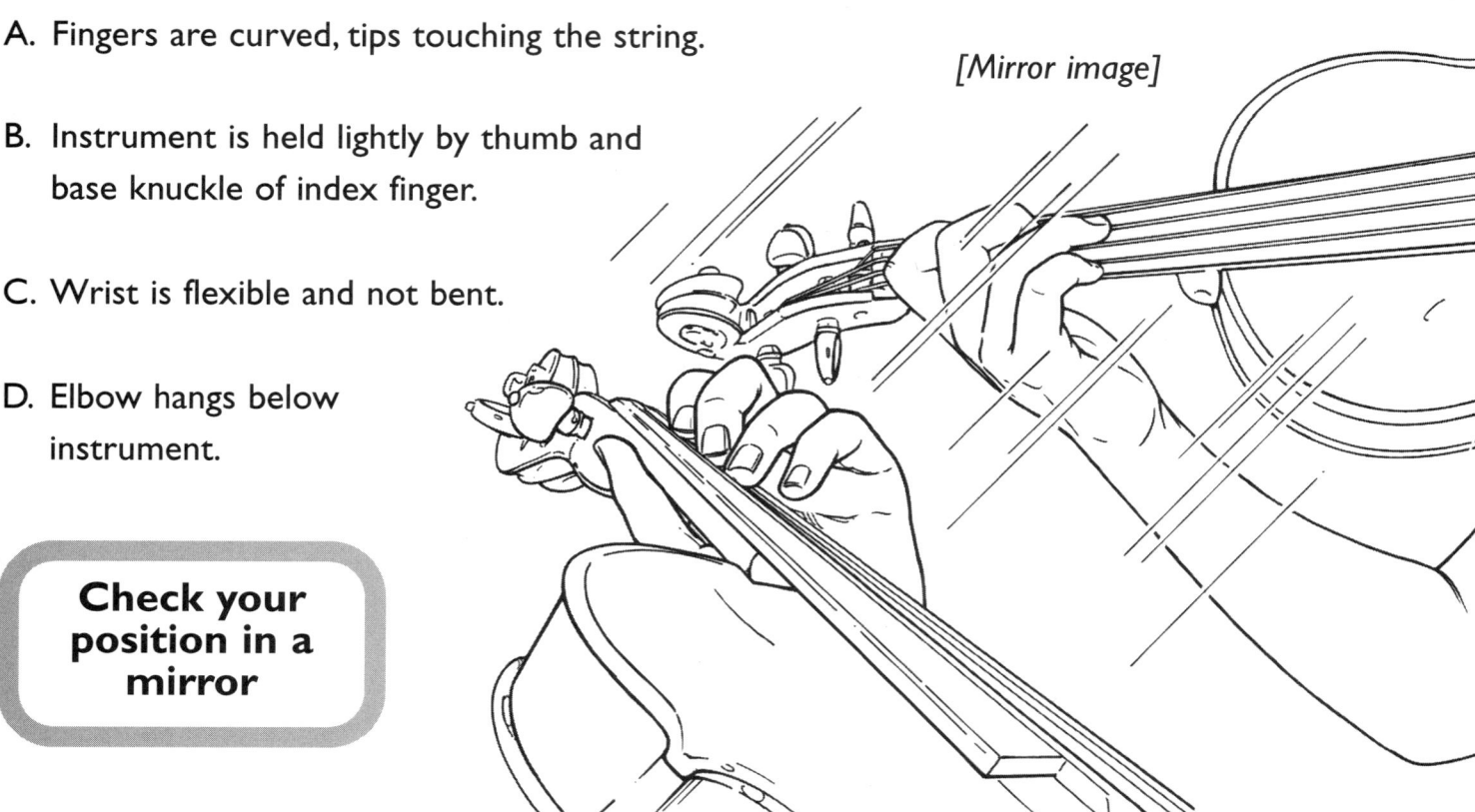

Check your position in a mirror

VIOLA PLAYING POSTURE

SEATED POSITION

A. Body is lengthened.

B. Body weight is balanced on the front of chair and on both feet.

C. Body weight is free to move from side to side.

D. Shoulders are relaxed, and both arms can move freely.

STANDING POSITION

A. Body is lengthened.

B. Body weight is balanced on both feet, left foot slightly forward.

C. Body weight is free to move from side to side.

D. Shoulders are relaxed, and both arms can move freely.

[Mirror image]

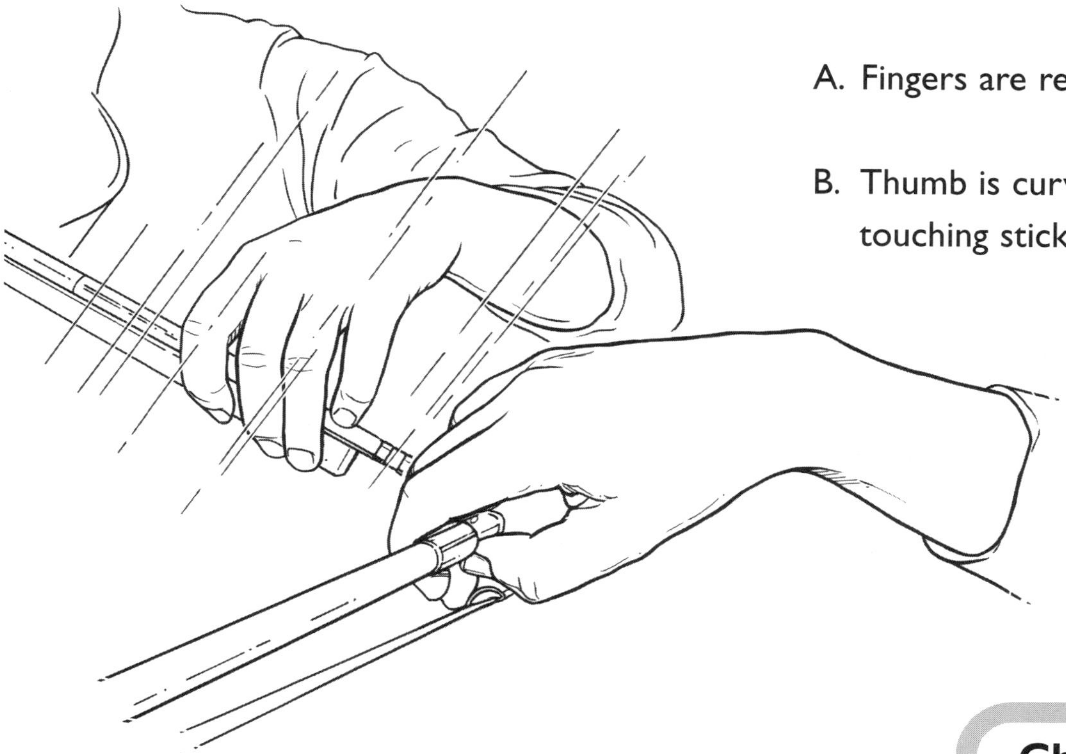

RIGHT HAND POSITION

A. Fingers are relaxed, curved, and flexible.

B. Thumb is curved and flexible, tip touching stick and edge of frog.

C. Instrument supports the bow.

D. Hand gently guides the bow, without gripping tightly.

Check your position in a mirror

LEFT HAND POSITION

A. Fingers are curved, tips touching the string.

B. Instrument is held lightly by thumb and base knuckle of index finger.

C. Wrist is flexible and not bent.

D. Elbow hangs below instrument.

[Mirror image]

Check your position in a mirror

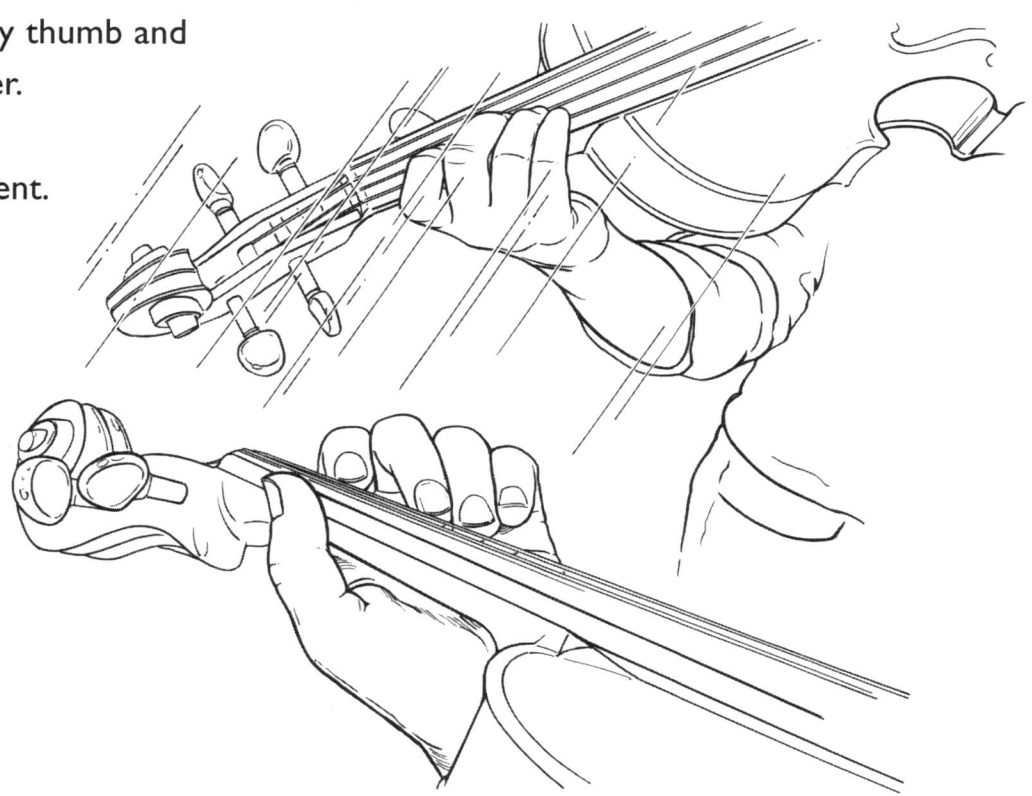

CELLO PLAYING POSTURE

A. Body is lengthened.

B. Body weight is balanced on the front of chair and on both feet.

C. Body weight is free to move from side to side.

D. Shoulders are relaxed, and both arms can move freely.

E. Instrument is supported by floor, front of torso, and left knee.

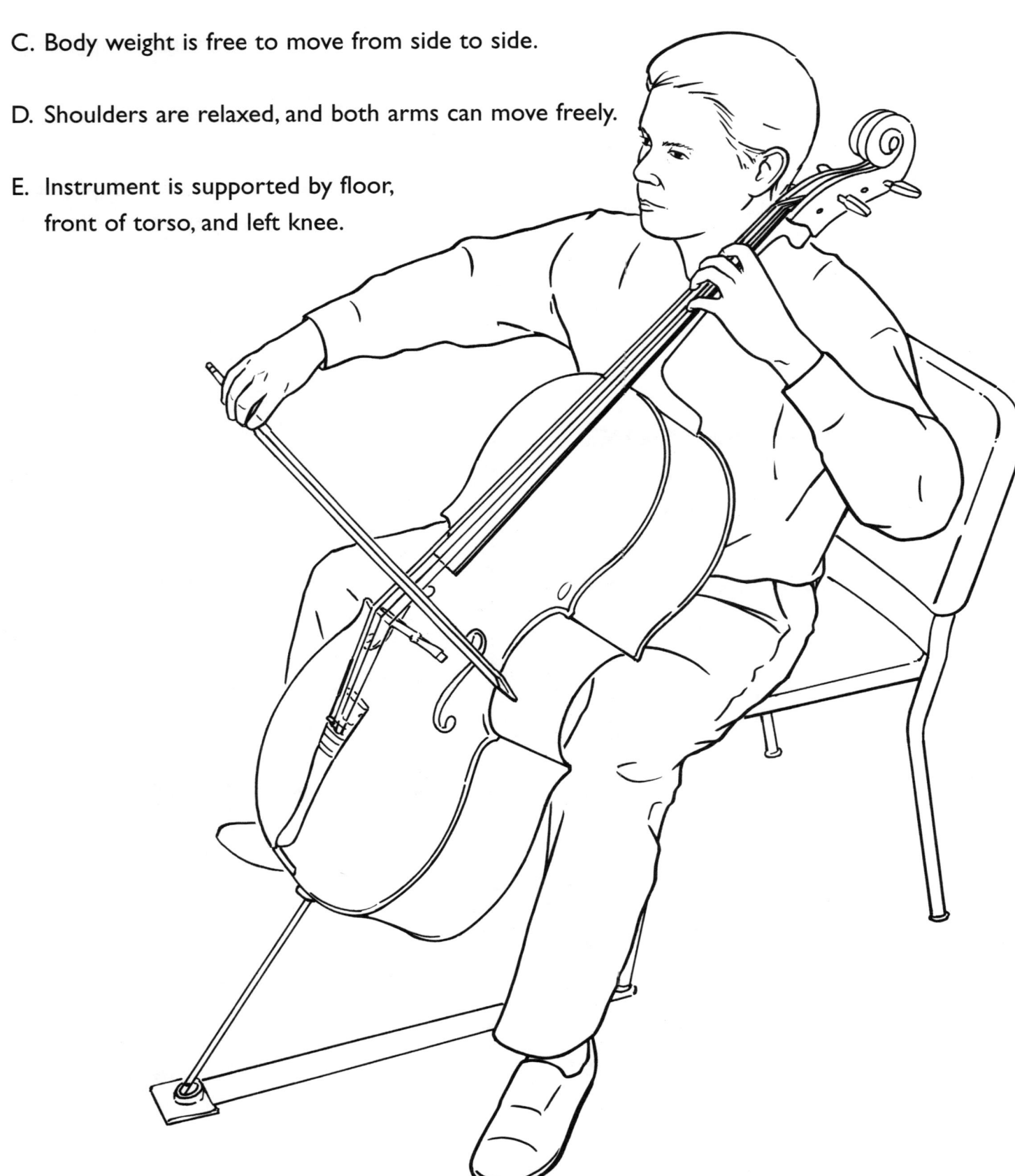

[Mirror image]

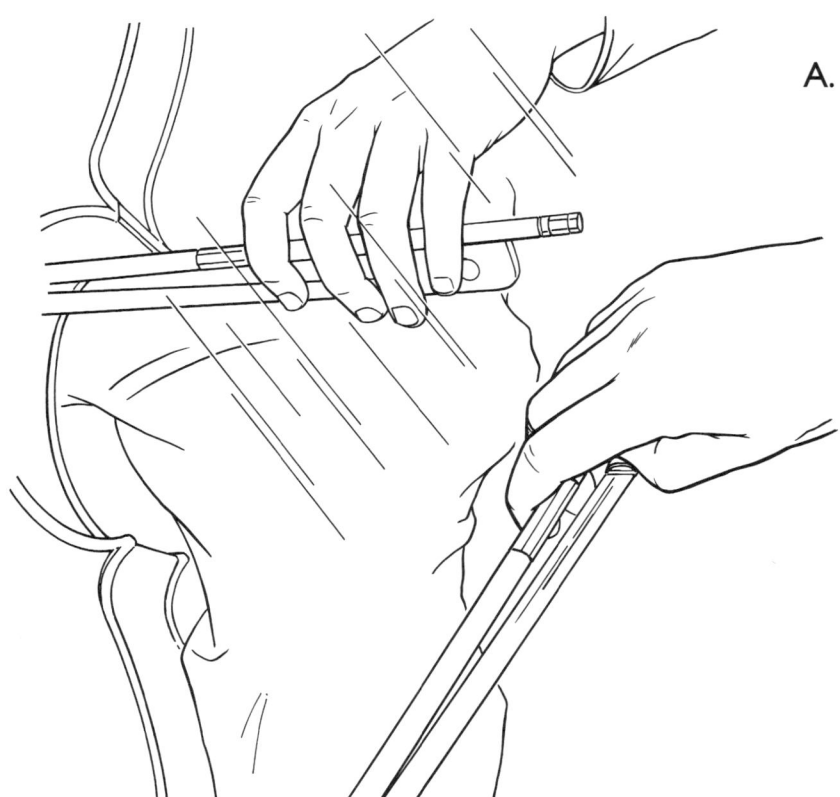

RIGHT HAND POSITION

A. Fingers are relaxed, curved and flexible.

B. Thumb is curved and flexible, tip touching stick and edge of frog.

C. Instrument supports the bow.

D. Hand gently guides the bow, without gripping tightly.

Check your position in a mirror

LEFT HAND POSITION

A. Fingers are slightly curved, hand is open.

B. Thumb is relaxed and free to move, lightly touching neck opposite index finger.

C. Wrist is not bent, arm weight holds down string.

D. Elbow is free to move, held away from the body.

BASS PLAYING POSTURE

SEATED POSITION

A. Body is lengthened.

B. Body weight is balanced on front of stool and on both feet.

C. Body weight is free to move from side to side.

D. Shoulders are relaxed, and both arms can move freely.

E. Top edge of instrument is balanced by left leg.

STANDING POSITION

A. Body is lengthened.

B. Body weight is balanced on both feet, left foot slightly forward.

C. Body weight is free to move from side to side.

D. Shoulders are relaxed, and both arms can move freely.

E. Top edge of instrument is balanced inside left hip.

RIGHT HAND POSITION

FRENCH BOW

A. Fingers are relaxed, curved, and flexible.

B. Thumb is curved and flexible, tip touching stick and edge of frog.

C. Instrument supports the bow.

D. Hand gently guides the bow, without gripping tightly.

[Mirror image]

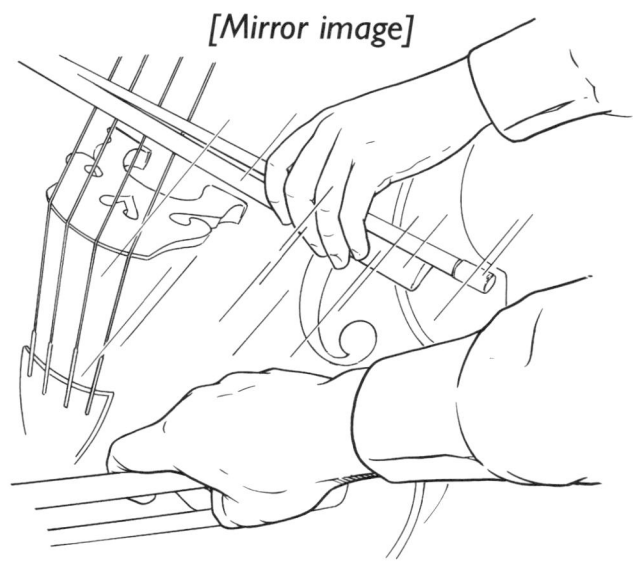

Check your position in a mirror

GERMAN BOW

[Mirror image]

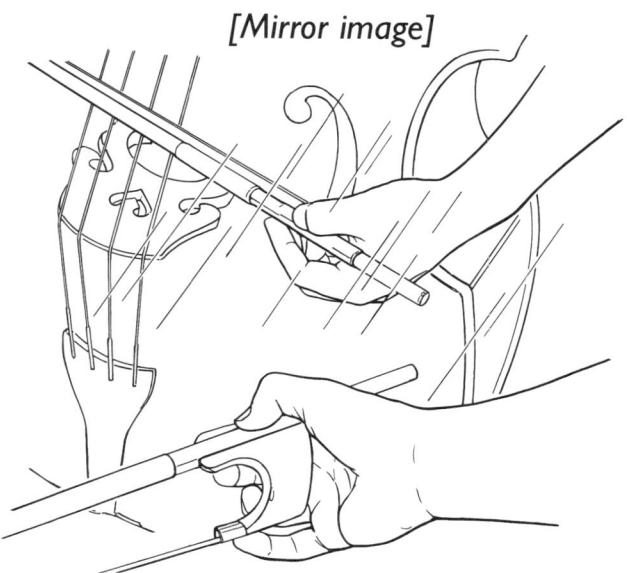

Check your position in a mirror

A. Fingers are relaxed, curved, and flexible.

B. Thumb is flexible, tip touching side of stick and frog.

C. Instrument and index finger support the bow.

D. Hand gently guides the bow, without gripping tightly.

LEFT HAND POSITION

A. Fingers are curved, hand is open.

B. Thumb is relaxed and free to move, lightly touching neck opposite index finger.

C. Wrist is relaxed, arm weight holds down string.

D. Elbow is free to move, held away from body.

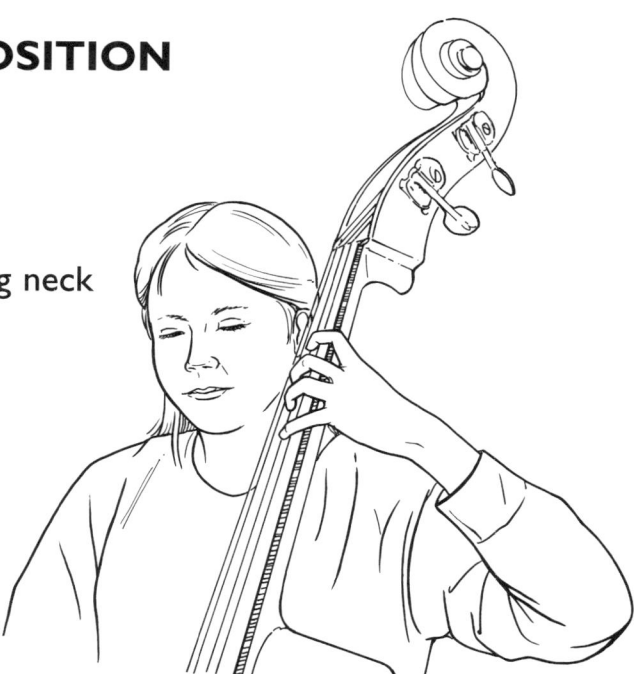

"YOU CAN LOOK IT UP"
MUSIC SIGNS AND SYMBOLS DICTIONARY
VOCABULARY NEEDED TO NAME, IDENTIFY, AND DESCRIBE

SIGN/SYMBOL and NAME   **DESCRIPTION/INTERPRETATION**

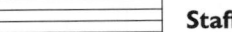 **Staff**   The **Staff** is composed of five lines and four spaces.

— **Ledger Line**   The **Ledger Line** is a short line used to extend the staff.

Bar Line
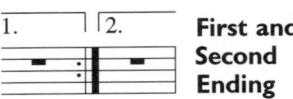 **Double Bar Line**   The **Bar Line** is a vertical line used to divide a staff into measures.

The **Double Bar Line** is two lines used to indicate the end of the music or the end of a section of music.

Measure   Measure   The space between two bar lines is called a **Measure**

 **Repeat Sign**   **Repeat Sign**: "Repeat from the beginning or repeat a section between two repeat signs."

First and Second Ending   **First and Second Ending:** "Play from the beginning and to the repeat sign in the first ending. Then, return to the beginning. On the repeat, skip the first ending and continue through the second ending."

Treble Clef (G Clef)   The **Treble Clef** is a sign used to fix the pitch of the second line of the staff to G.

LINES   SPACES

Letter Names are letters of the alphabet used to name and to identify the lines and spaces of the Treble Clef.

E G B D F   C G B E

Alto Clef (C Clef)   The **Alto Clef** is a sign used to fix the pitch of the third line of the staff to middle C.

LINES   SPACES

Letter Names are letters of the alphabet used to name and to identify the lines and spaces of the Alto Clef.

Bass Clef (F Clef)   The **Bass Clef** is a sign used to fix the pitch of the fourth line of the staff to F.

LINES   SPACES

Letter Names are letters of the alphabet used to name and to identify the lines and spaces of the Bass Clef.

G B D F   A A C E G

♯ **Sharp**   A **Sharp** is a sign used to raise the pitch of a note one half-step (one semi-tone).

♭ **Flat**   A **Flat** is a sign to lower the pitch of a note one half-step (one semi-tone).

♮ **Natural**   A **Natural** is a sign used to cancel a sharp or flat in a measure or in the key signature.

Key Signatures

A **Key Signature** is the particular arrangement of flats or sharps that appears at the beginning of each staff to indicate the key of a piece or composition.

| C Major | G Major | D Major | F Major | Bb Major | Eb Major |
| A Minor | E Minor | B Minor | D Minor | D Minor | C Minor |

Accent   An **Accent** is a symbol to indicate special stress or emphasis on a certain note.

Staccato   A **Staccato** sign is used to indicate a shortened or separated style of articulation.

Tenuto   A **Tenuto** sign over or below a note is used to indicate a sustained (connected) style of articulation.

	Tie	The **Tie** is a curved line used to connect two notes of the same pitch resulting in one longer tone.
	Slur	The **Slur** is a curved line above or below two or more notes of different pitch to indicate no change of bow direction, resulting in a continous, smooth style of articulation.
,	**Bow Lift**	Lift the bow from the string and replace it nearer the frog.
⊓	**Down Bow**	Draw the bow toward the tip.
V	**Up Bow**	Draw the bow toward the frog.

NOTES   RESTS

NOTES	RESTS	
o		**Whole (United Kingdom - Semi Breve)**
♩	▬	**Half (UK - Minim)**
♩.	▬·	**Dotted Half (UK - Dotted Minim)**
♩	𝄽	**Quarter (UK - Crotchet)**
♩.	𝄽 ♪	**Dotted Quarter (UK - Dotted Crotchet)**
♪	♪	**Eighth (UK - Quaver)**
♫		**Barred Eighths (UK - Barred Quavers)**
♬	𝄾	**Sixteenth (UK - Semi Quaver)**
♬♬		**Barred Sixteenths (UK - Barred Semi Quavers)**

INTERPRETATION
The Rhythmic Values of Notes and Rests Are Determined By the Measure Signature. (See Measure Signatures below.)

MEASURE (TIME) SIGNATURES

2/4	**Two-Quarter Measure Signature**	Two Beats In Each Measure The Quarter Note Is The Primary Beat (Crotchet)	
2/2 or ¢	**Two-Half (Cut-Time) Measure Signature**	Two Beats In Each Measure The Half Note Is The Primary Beat (Minim)	
4/4 or C	**Four-Quarter (Common) Measure Signature**	Four Beats In Each Measure The Quarter Note Is The Primary Beat (Crotchet)	
3/4	**Three-Quarter Measure Signature**	1. One Beat In Each Measure The Dotted Half Note Is The Primary Beat (Dotted Minim)	
		2. Three Beats In Each Measure The Quarter Note Is The Primary Beat (Crotchet)	
6/8	**Six-Eighth Measure Signature**	1. Two Beats In Each Measure The Dotted Quarter Note Is The Primary Beat (Dotted Crotchet)	
		2. Six Beats In Each Measure The Eighth Note Is The Primary Beat (Quaver)	

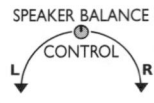

SPEAKER BALANCE
CONTROL
L   R

This symbol indicates that the Left speaker to Right speaker balance of the music can be controlled by the Speaker Balance Control Knob on your stereo. For accompaniment only, turn the Speaker Balance Control Knob to the extreme right.

Getting Started on Open D and Open A: Pizzicato

TEXT: "Listen and Play. Pizzicato. The tone is D."

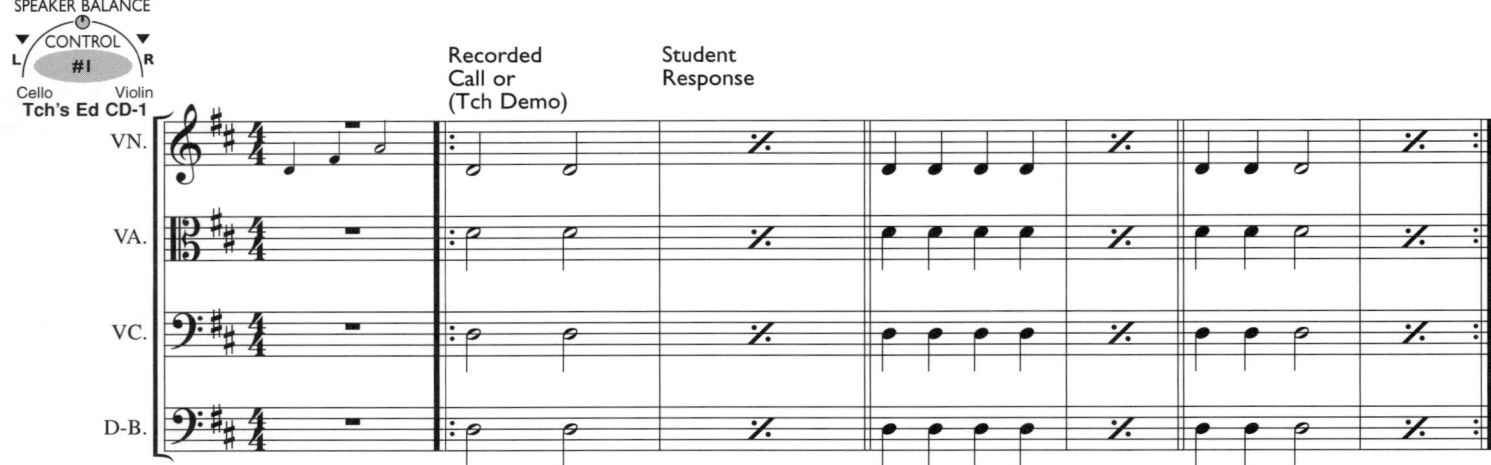

TEXT: "Listen and Play. Pizzicato. The tone is A."

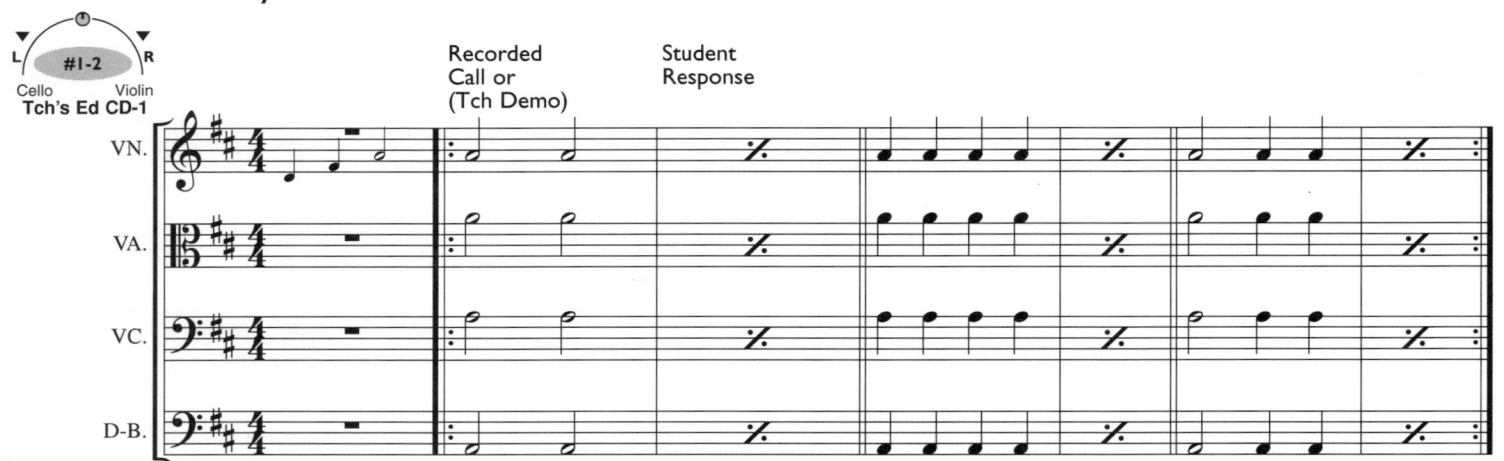

TEXT: "Listen and Play. Pizzicato. The starting tone is D."

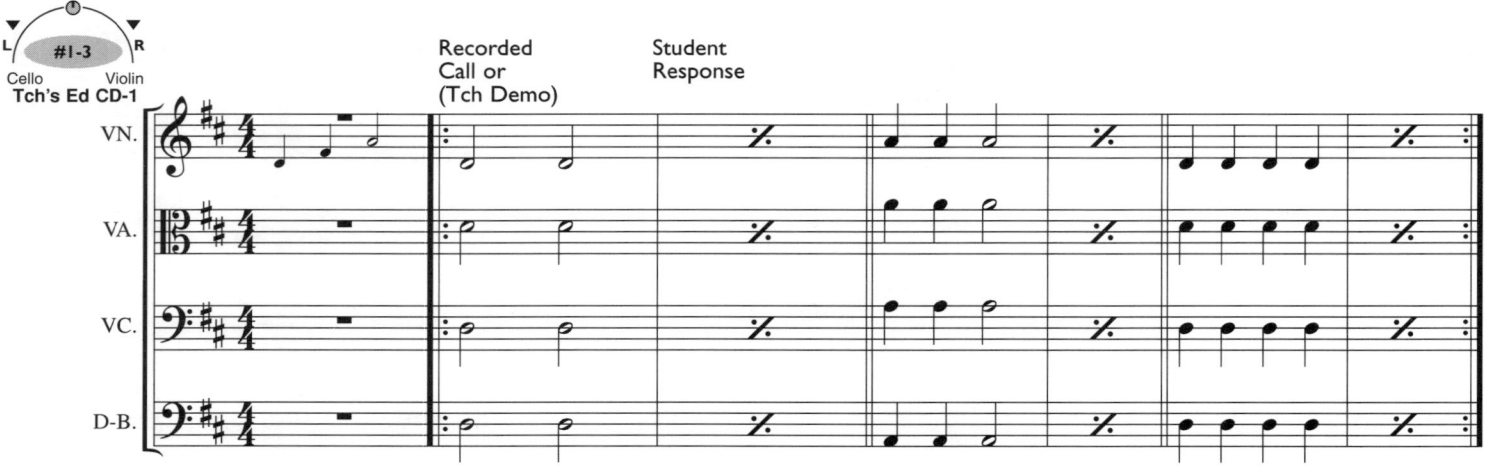

SPECIAL OPTION: **For teacher-initiated Call and Response, use Teacher's Resource Edition CD-1 Track 9 or 98 (duple meter in D).**

Getting Started on Open D and Open A: Arco

TEXT: "Listen and Play. Arco. The tone is D."

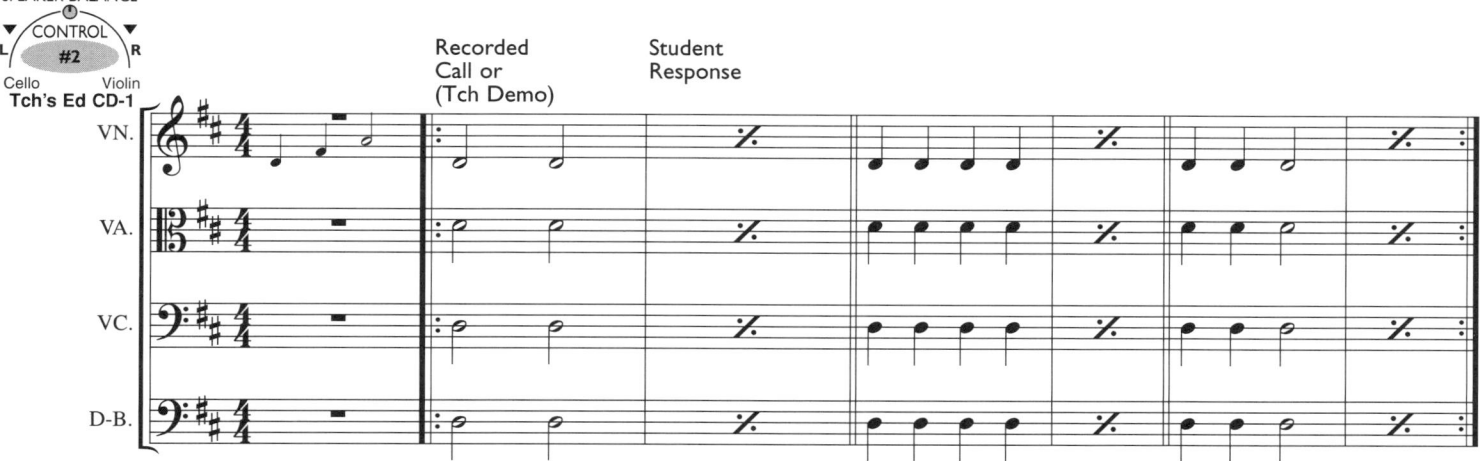

TEXT: "Listen and Play. Arco. The tone is A."

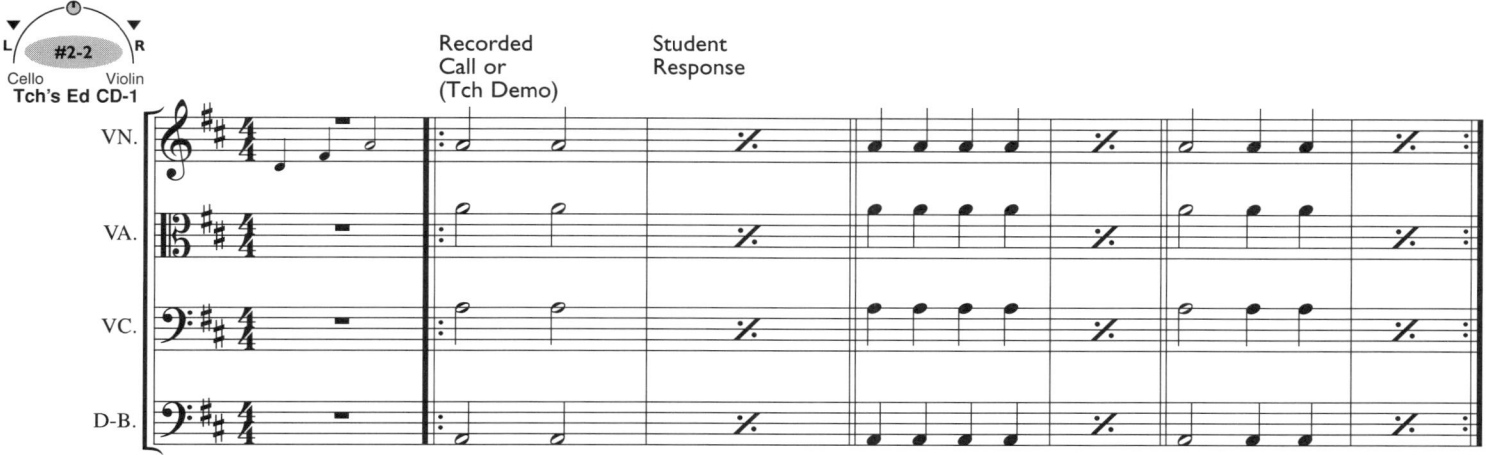

TEXT: "Listen and Play. Pizzicato. The starting tone is D."

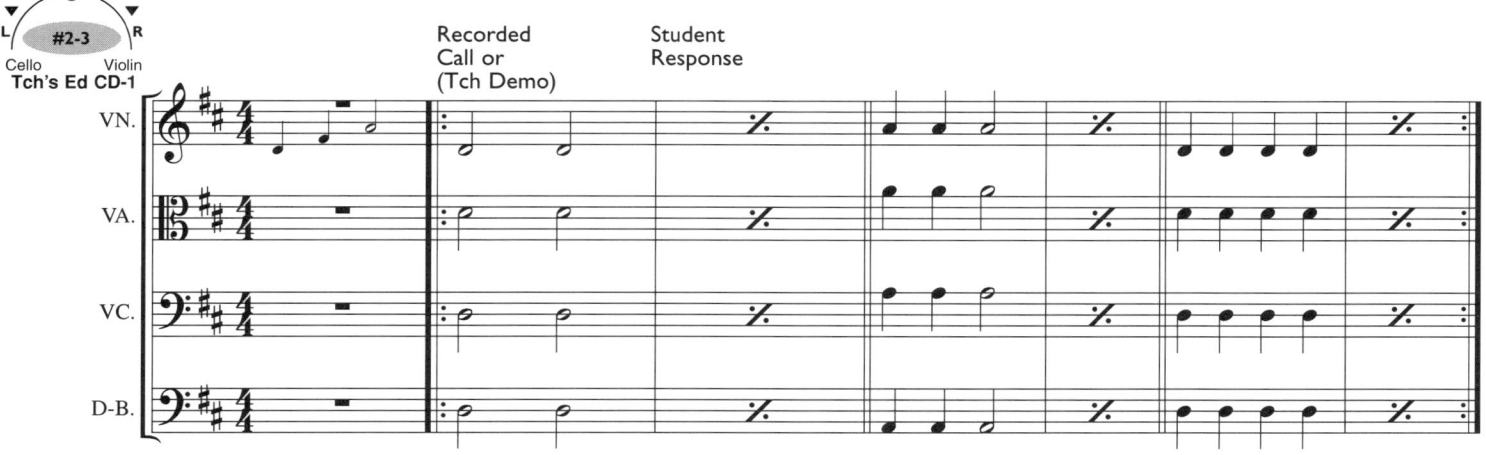

SPECIAL OPTION: **For teacher-initiated Call and Response, use Teacher's Resource Edition CD-1 Track 9 or 98 (duple meter in D).**

Separated and Connected Styles of Articulation

TEXT: "Articulation - Separated and Connected. Just Listen."

TEXT: "Separated style of articulation. Listen and Play. The tone is D."

TEXT: "Connected style of articulation. Listen and Play. The tone is D."

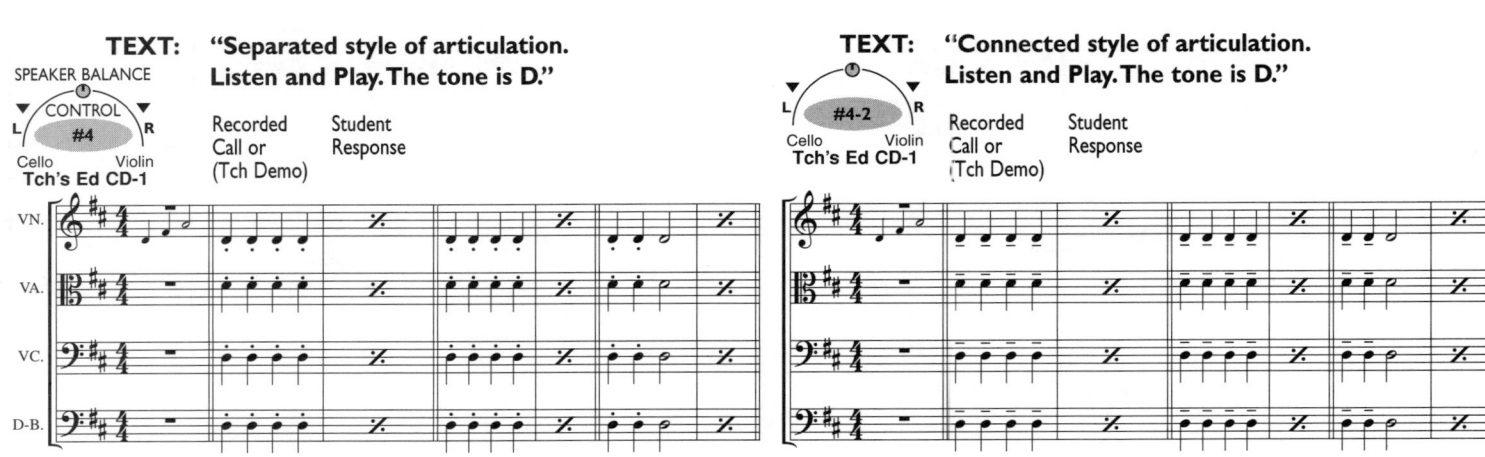

TEXT: "Separated style of articulation. Listen and Play. The tone is A."

TEXT: "Connected style of articulation. Listen and Play. The tone is A."

TEXT: "Listen and play what you hear. Pay close attention to the style of articulation. The tone is D."

TEXT: "Connected style of articulation. Pay close attention to the style of articulation. The tone is A."

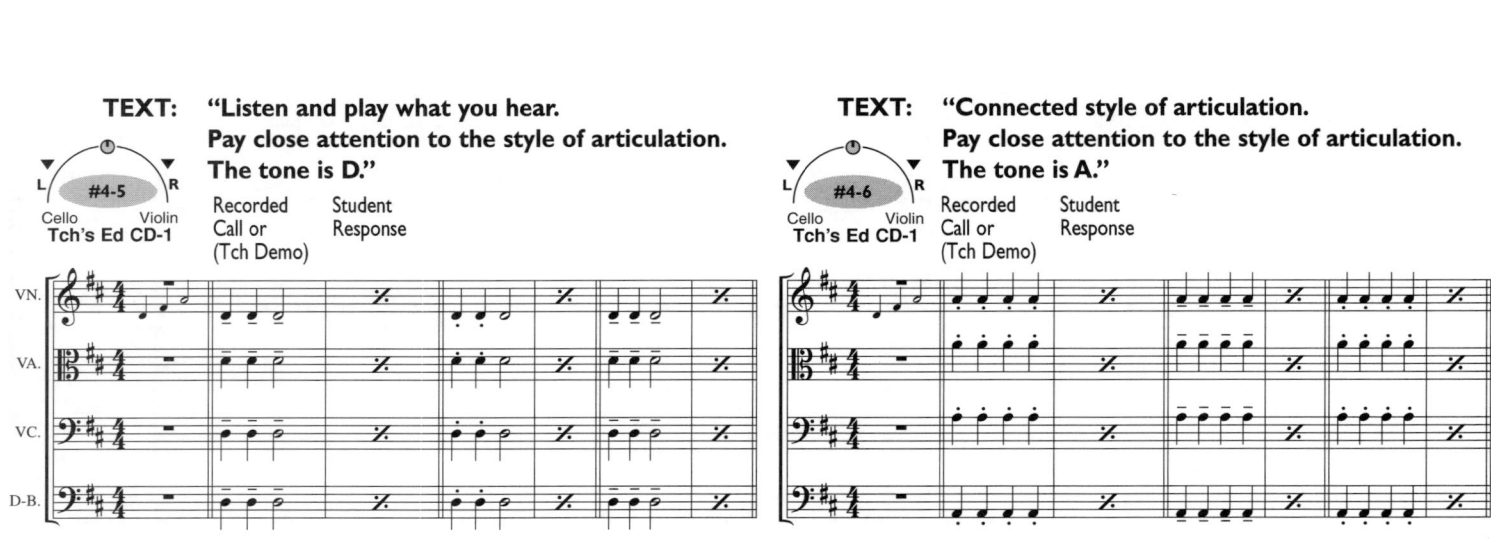

SPECIAL OPTION FOR GETTING STARTED WITH OPEN STRINGS

Tracking the "Open String Blues" in D

Call and Response
(As Performed by the Teacher)

ADDITIONAL OPTIONS FOR TECHNICAL AND RHYTHMIC DEVELOPMENT

- Vary style of articulation (separated/connected), use pizzicato
- Use a variety of quarter note, half note, or whole note rhythm patterns
- Sing pitches and note names

Getting Started on F♯, E, and D.

TEXT: "Listen and Play. The tone is F♯."

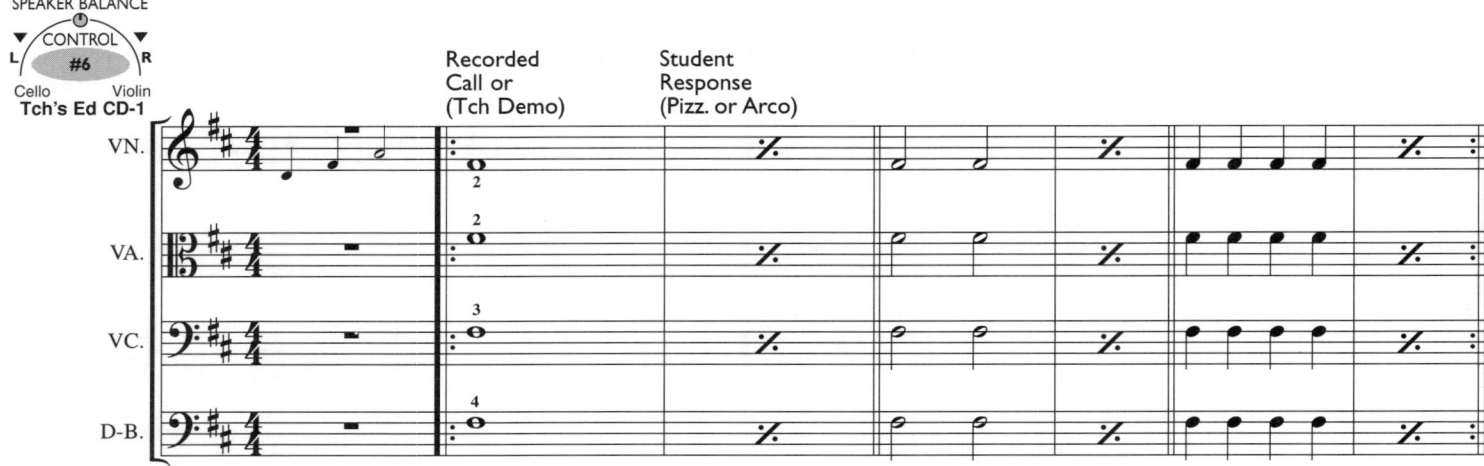

TEXT: "Listen and Play. The tone is E."

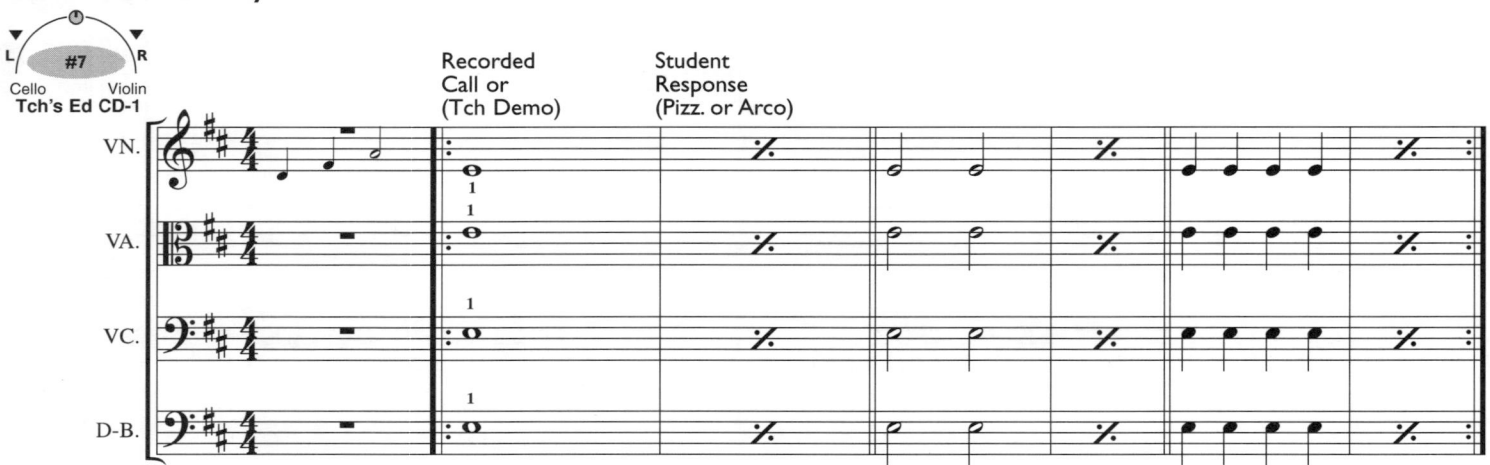

TEXT: "Listen and Play. The tone is D."

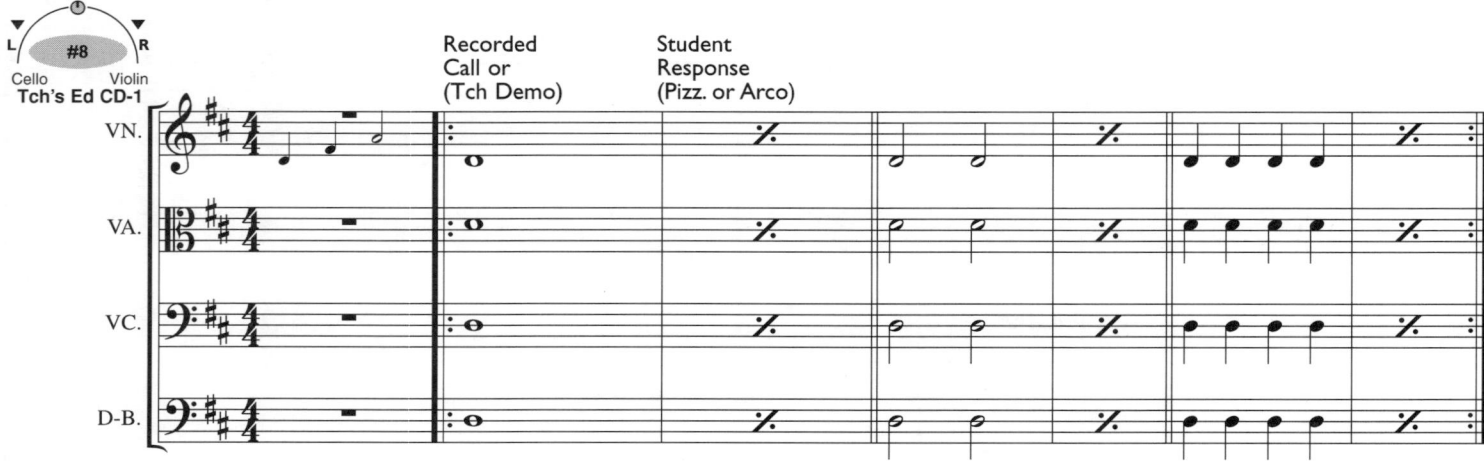

SPECIAL OPTION: **For teacher-initiated Call and Response, use Teacher's Resource Edition CD-1 Track 9 or 98 (duple meter in D).**

SET YOUR MUSICAL STANDARDS IN SOUND
"STUDY IN SCHOOL AND AT HOME WITH AN ARTIST"

- THE ACHIEVEMENT LOOP -

I   **A "SOUND" MUSIC LEARNING OBJECTIVE**

Music repertoire contained on Compact Disc, performed by an artist, and set in an authentic music context that defines the elements of:

A. Rhythm (Tempo, Meter, Melodic Rhythm)

B. Melody (Tonality)

C. Harmony

D. Tone Quality (Timbre)

E. Intonation

F. Phrasing

G. Style of Articulation

H. Expressive Nuance, and

I. Ethnicity (Music Culture)

A sound concept of the music learning objective motivates students for:

II   **PREPARATION AND FACILITATION**

Something the teacher does to get students ready for:

III   **PRACTICE**

Something the student does that leads to:

IV   **ACHIEVEMENT**

A result that pleases everyone and motivates the student to take on:

V   **A NEW MUSIC LEARNING OBJECTIVE "SET IN SOUND" (STEP I)**

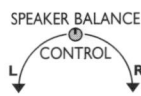

SPEAKER BALANCE CONTROL
L   R

This symbol indicates that the Left speaker to Right speaker balance of the music can be controlled by the Speaker Balance Control Knob on your stereo. For accompaniment only, turn the Speaker Balance Control Knob to the extreme right.

FIRST TONES: F♯, E, D

FOLK SONG — *A song reflecting the traditions of the people of a country or region and forming part of their characteristic culture.*

SOLO — *One player, alone, with or without accompaniment.*

STUDENT CD

SPEAKER BALANCE CONTROL
CD Trk 1
L   R
Violin   Accom.
Cello

CD Trk 2
L   R
Viola   Accom.
Bass

1 Hot Cross Buns   **FULL SCORE ON P. 6-H**

English Folk Song

Hot cross buns,   Hot cross buns,   One cent,   Two cents,   Hot cross buns.

HONKY TONK — *A rowdy musical style characterized by a lively piano accompaniment.*

CD Trk 3
L   R
Violin   Accom.
Cello

2   ★ SOLO — **Hot Cross Buns** (HONKY TONK STYLE STARTING ON F♯)

ROCK AND ROLL — *A mid-1950s style of popular music featuring guitar and driving rhythms with accents on the off-beats:* 1 **2** | 1 **2**

CD Trk 4
L   R
Violin   Accom.
Cello

3   ★★ SOLO — **Hot Cross Buns** (ROCK AND ROLL STYLE STARTING ON F♯)

CD Trk 5
L   R
Viola   Accom.
Bass

4 Notes   **FULL SCORE ON P. 6-I**

U.S.

Notes step down,   Notes step up,   Notes re - peat and notes can skip.

BLUEGRASS — *A type of Anglo-American folk music originating around the mid-1940s in rural Appalachia.*

CD Trk 6
L   R
Violin   Accom.
Cello

CD Trk 7
L   R
Viola   Accom.
Bass

5 Mary Had a Little Lamb   **FULL SCORE ON P. 6-I**

Traditional Folk Song

Mar - y had a lit - tle lamb,   lit - tle lamb,   little lamb.

Mar - y had a lit - tle lamb whose fleece was white as snow.

REGGAE — *A musical style mixing African and Caribbean rhythms often attributed to Jamaican sources.*

CD Trk 8
L   R
Viola   Accom.
Bass

6   ★ SOLO — **Mary Had a Little Lamb** (REGGAE STYLE STARTING ON F♯)

? *Forget the meaning of something?* **You Can Look It Up** *in the* **Music Terms Dictionary** *on pages 42, 43, 44, and 45.*

Rhythmic Flashcard Reading Option for *Hot Cross Buns*

R-1 *NEW*   **R-2** *NEW*

Melodic Ear-to-Hand Training and Assessment for *Hot Cross Buns*.

TEXT: "Listen and Play What You Hear. The Starting Tone is F♯."

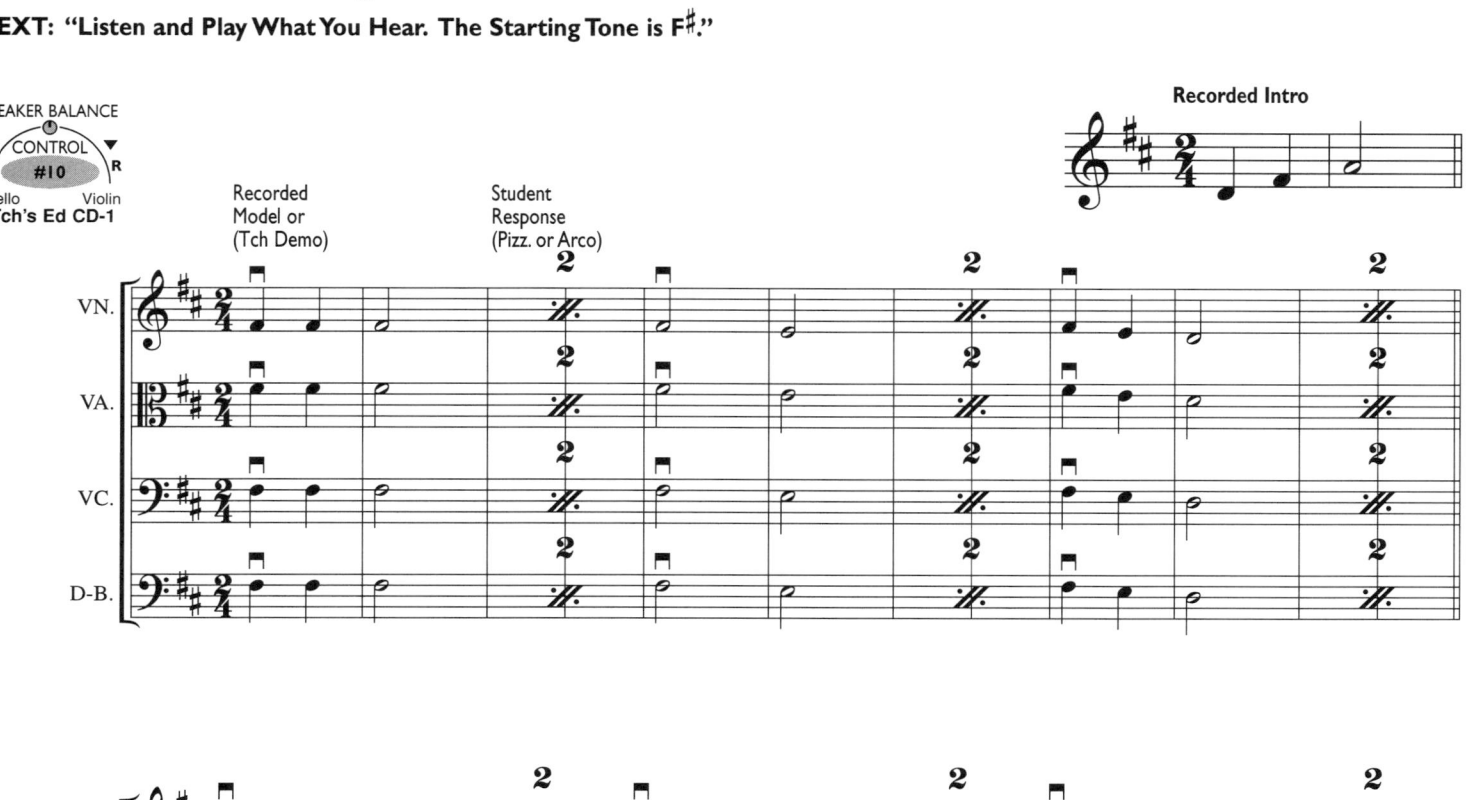

Rhythmic Flashcard Reading Option for *Notes*

R-1   **R-2**

Melodic Ear-to-Hand Preparation for *Notes*. Instruct Students to "Listen and Play What You Hear. The Starting Tone is F#."

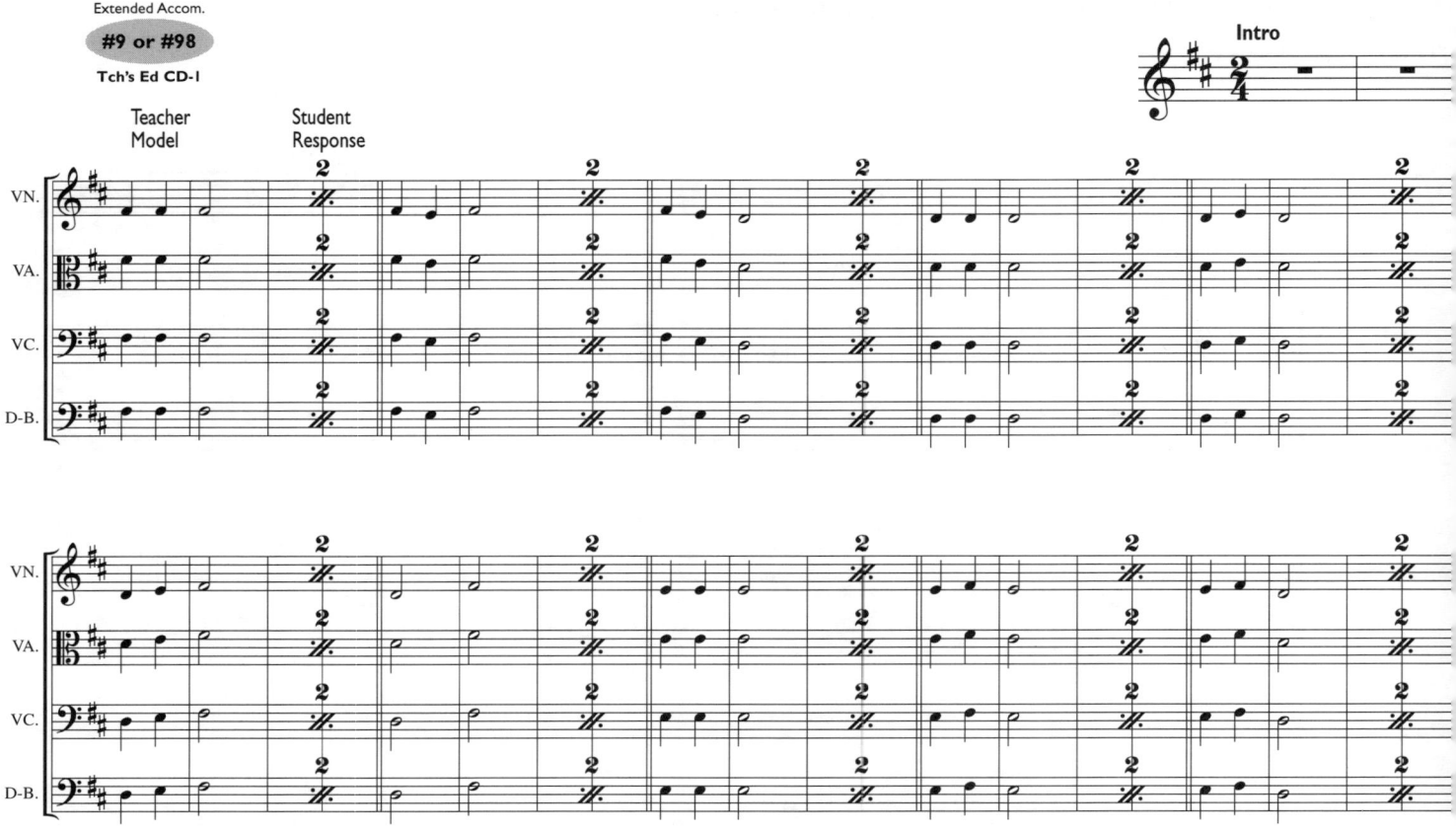

Melodic Ear-to-Hand Assessment for *Notes*. TEXT: "Listen and Play What You Hear. The Starting Tone is F#."

Rhythmic Flashcard Reading Option for *Mary Had a Little Lamb*

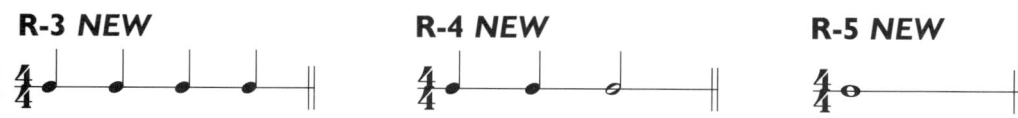

R-3 *NEW*

R-4 *NEW*

R-5 *NEW*

Melodic Ear-to-Hand Preparation for *Mary Had a Little Lamb.*

Instruct Students to "Listen and Play What You Hear. The Starting Tone is F♯."

Extended Accom.

#9 or #98

Tch's Ed CD-1

Intro

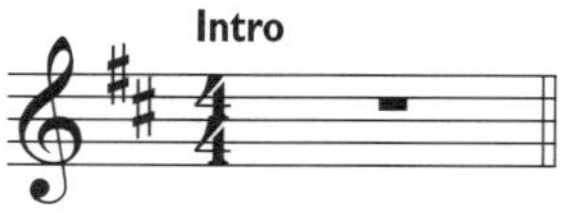

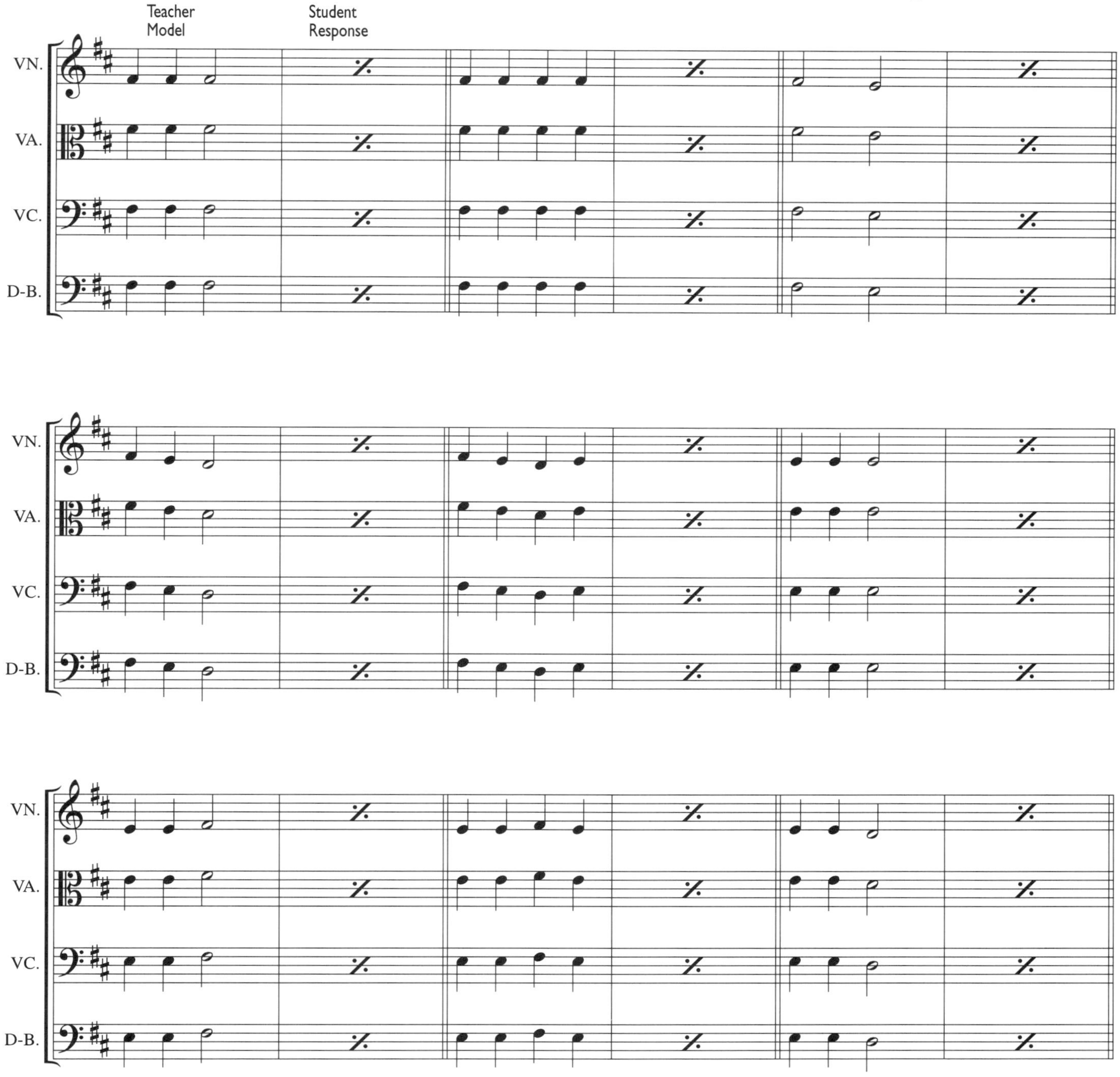

Melodic Ear-to-Hand Assessment for *Mary Had a Little Lamb*. TEXT: "Listen and Play What You Hear. The Starting Tone is F♯."

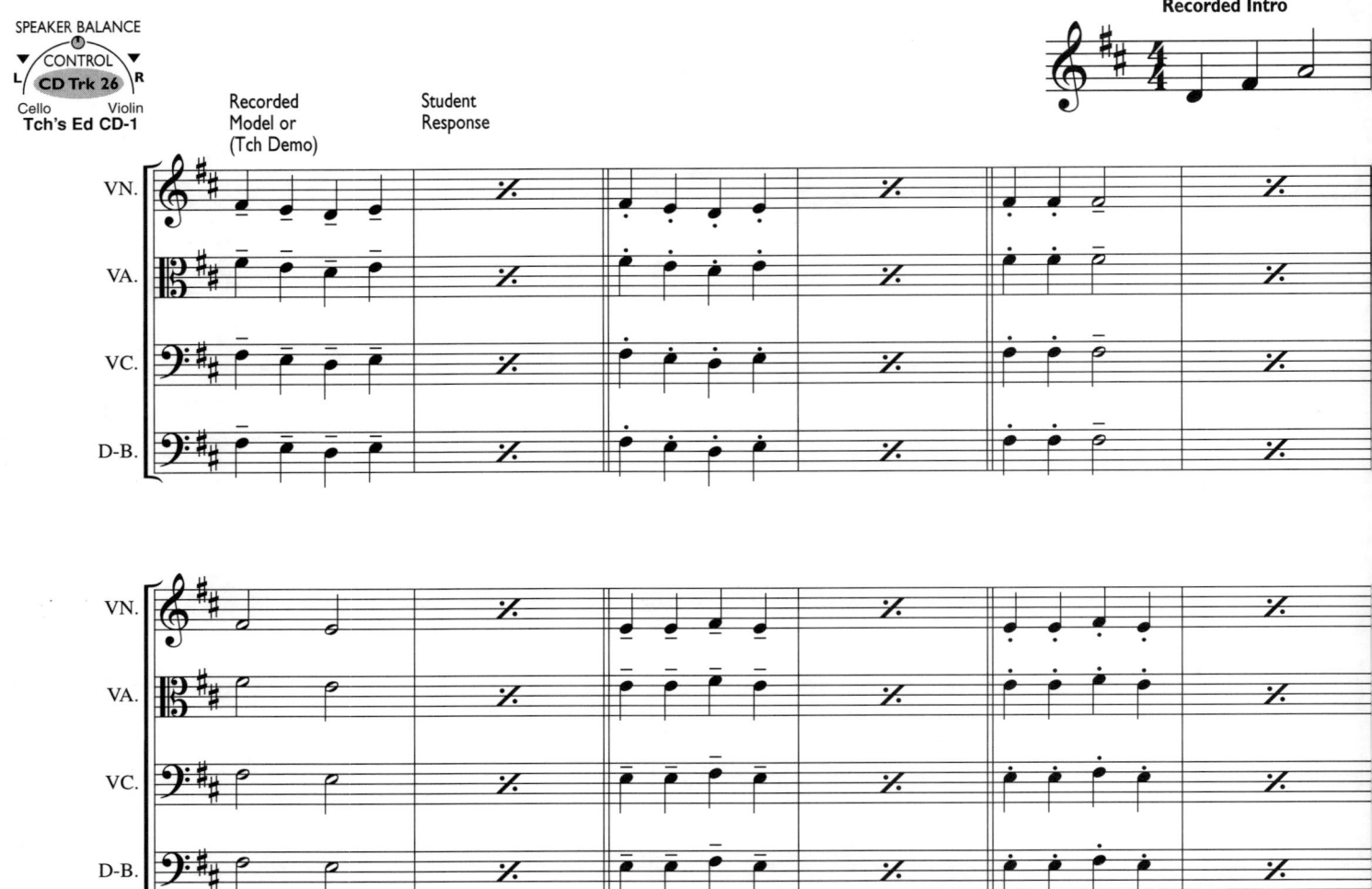

SPECIAL OPTIONS FOR TECHNICAL AND AURAL DEVELOPMENT
HOT CROSS BUNS, NOTES, AND MARY HAD A LITTLE LAMB

TRANSPOSE FAMILIAR SONGS "BY EAR"

Procedure: Direct students to "Use the same bow rhythms and left hand finger patterns on a new string."

Hot Cross Buns (IN A - HONKY TONK STYLE, STARTING ON C♯ ON THE A STRING "BY EAR")

Hot Cross Buns (IN G - POLKA, STARTING ON B ON THE G STRING "BY EAR")

Notes (IN A - STARTING ON C♯ ON THE A STRING "BY EAR")

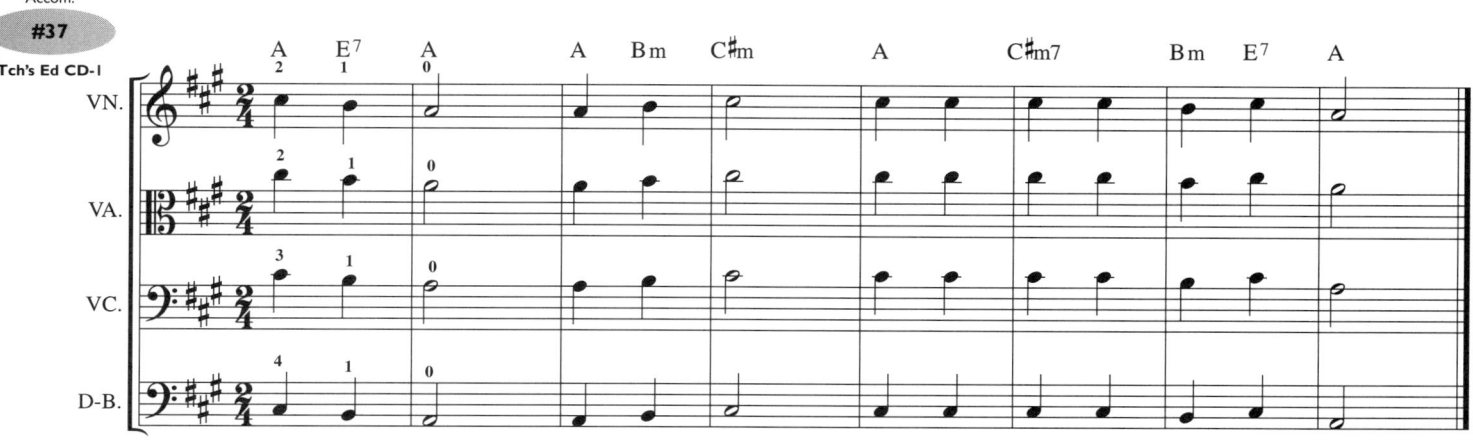

Notes (IN G - STARTING ON B ON THE G STRING "BY EAR")

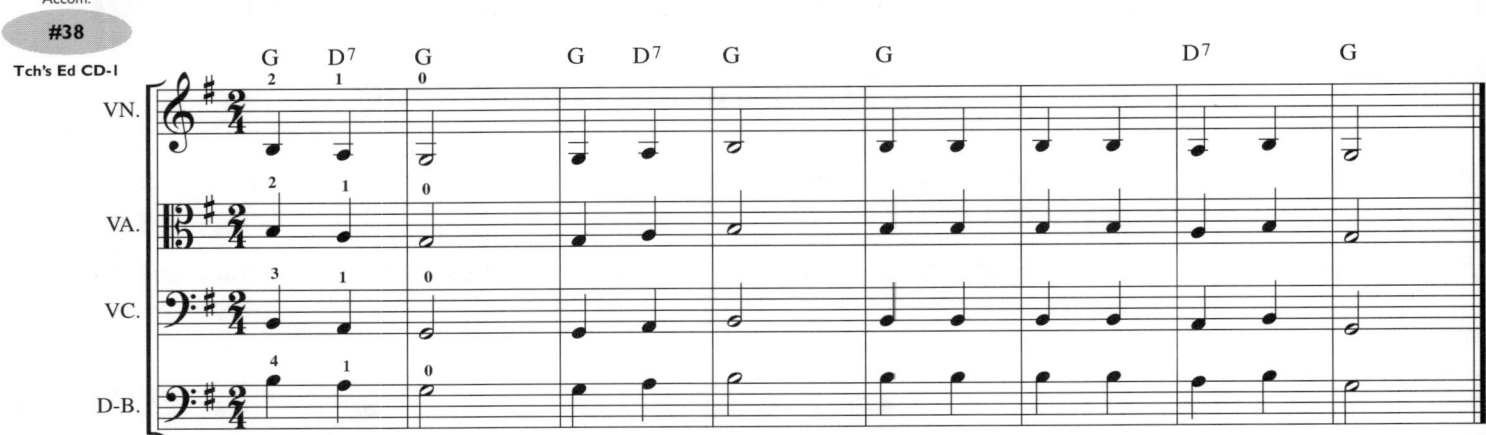

Mary Had a Little Lamb (IN A - BLUEGRASS STYLE, STARTING ON C# ON THE A STRING "BY EAR")

Mary Had a Little Lamb (IN G - REGGAE STYLE, STARTING ON B ON THE G STRING "BY EAR")

OPTIONS FOR INDIVIDUALIZING INSTRUCTION IN A GROUP SETTING

- Half the group plays pizzicato, half the group plays arco
- Half the group plays (pizz. or arco), half the group sings
- Half the group plays (pizz. or arco), half finger alone
- Half the group plays (pizz. or arco), half "air" or "shadow" bow

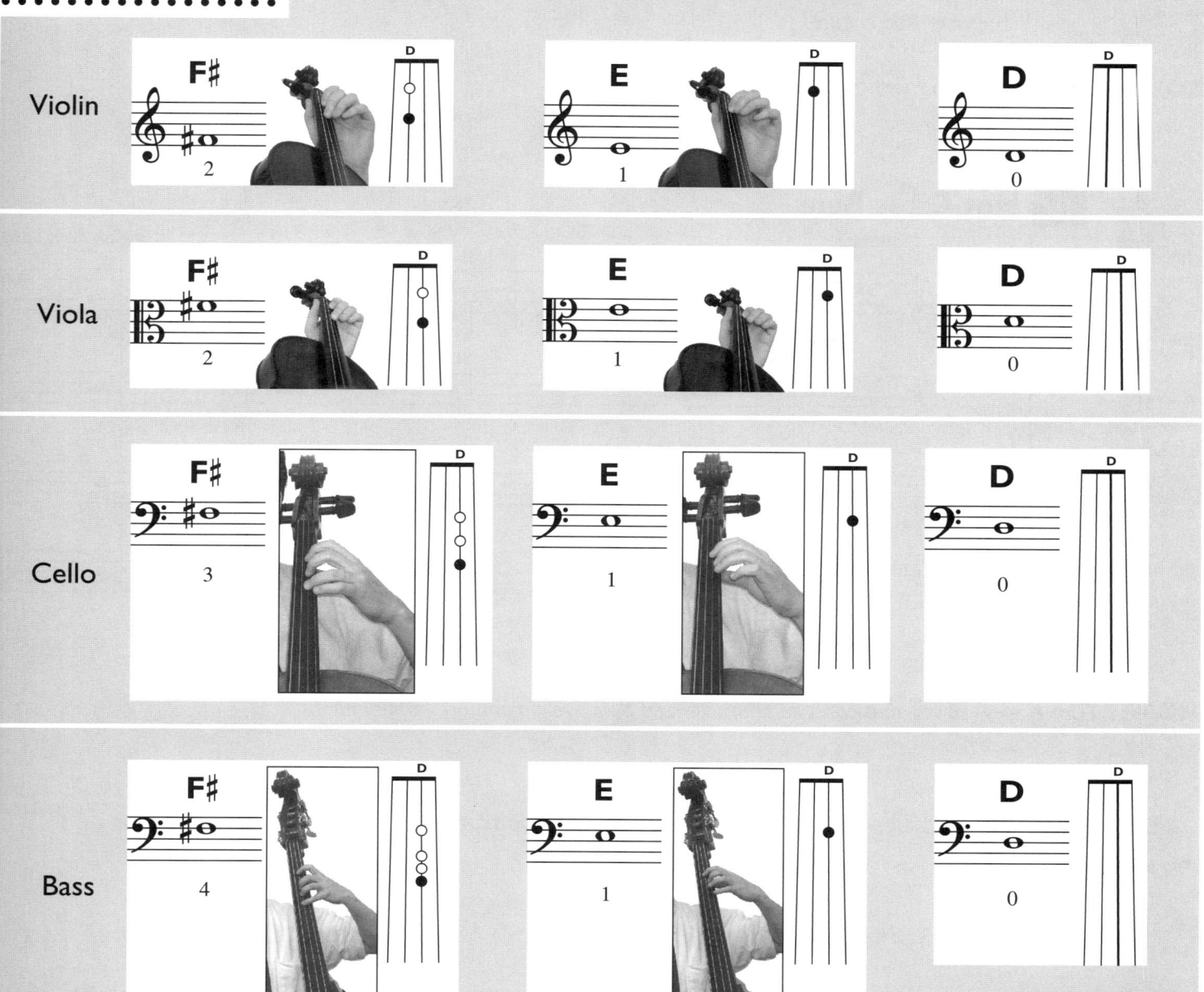

FIRST TONES

Violin

Viola

Cello

Bass

FOLK SONG — *A song reflecting the traditions of the people of a country or region and forming part of their characteristic culture.*

SOLO — *One player, alone, with or without accompaniment.*

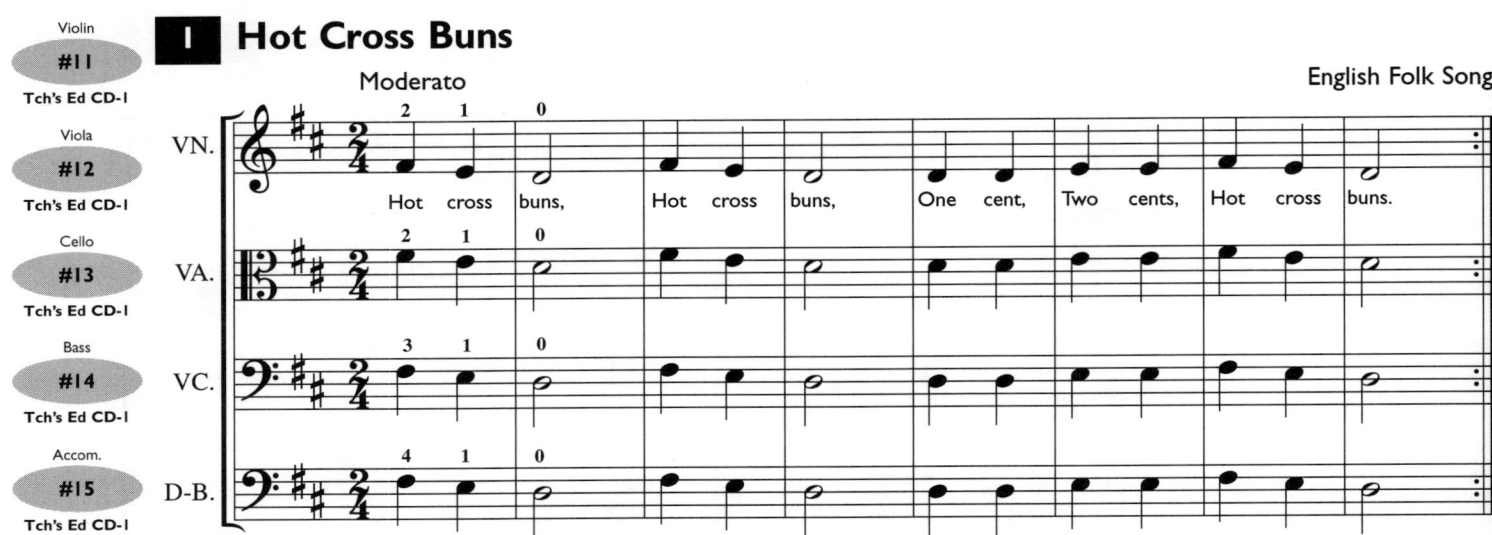

HONKY TONK — *A rowdy musical style characterized by a lively piano accompaniment.*

ROCK AND ROLL — *A mid-1950s style of popular music featuring guitar and driving rhythms with accents on the off-beats: I **2** I **2***

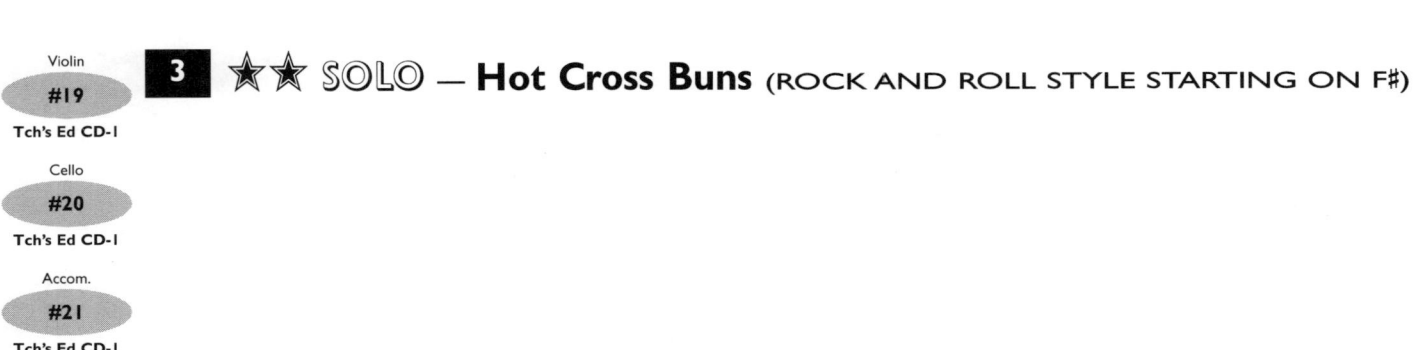

Viola #23 Tch's Ed CD-1
Bass #24 Tch's Ed CD-1
Accom. #25 Tch's Ed CD-1

4 Notes

Moderato — U.S.

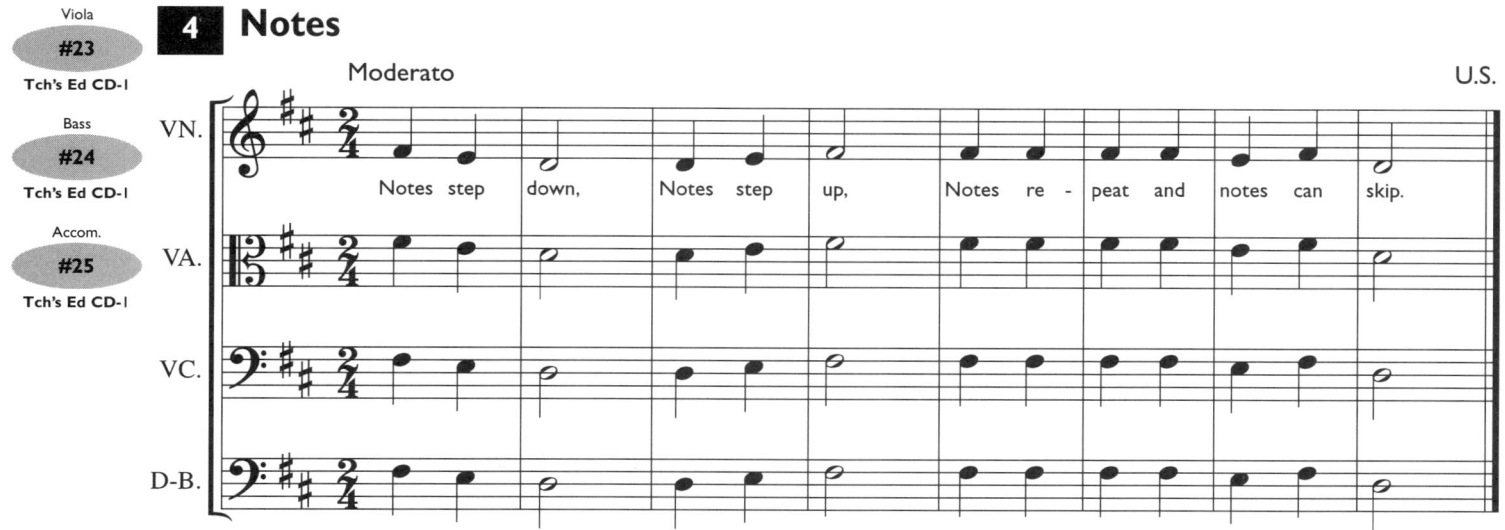

BLUEGRASS *— A type of Anglo-American folk music originating around the mid-1940s in rural Appalachia.*

Violin #27 Tch's Ed CD-1
Viola #28 Tch's Ed CD-1
Cello #29 Tch's Ed CD-1
Bass #30 Tch's Ed CD-1
Accom. #31 Tch's Ed CD-1

5 Mary Had a Little lamb

Lively — Traditional Folk Song

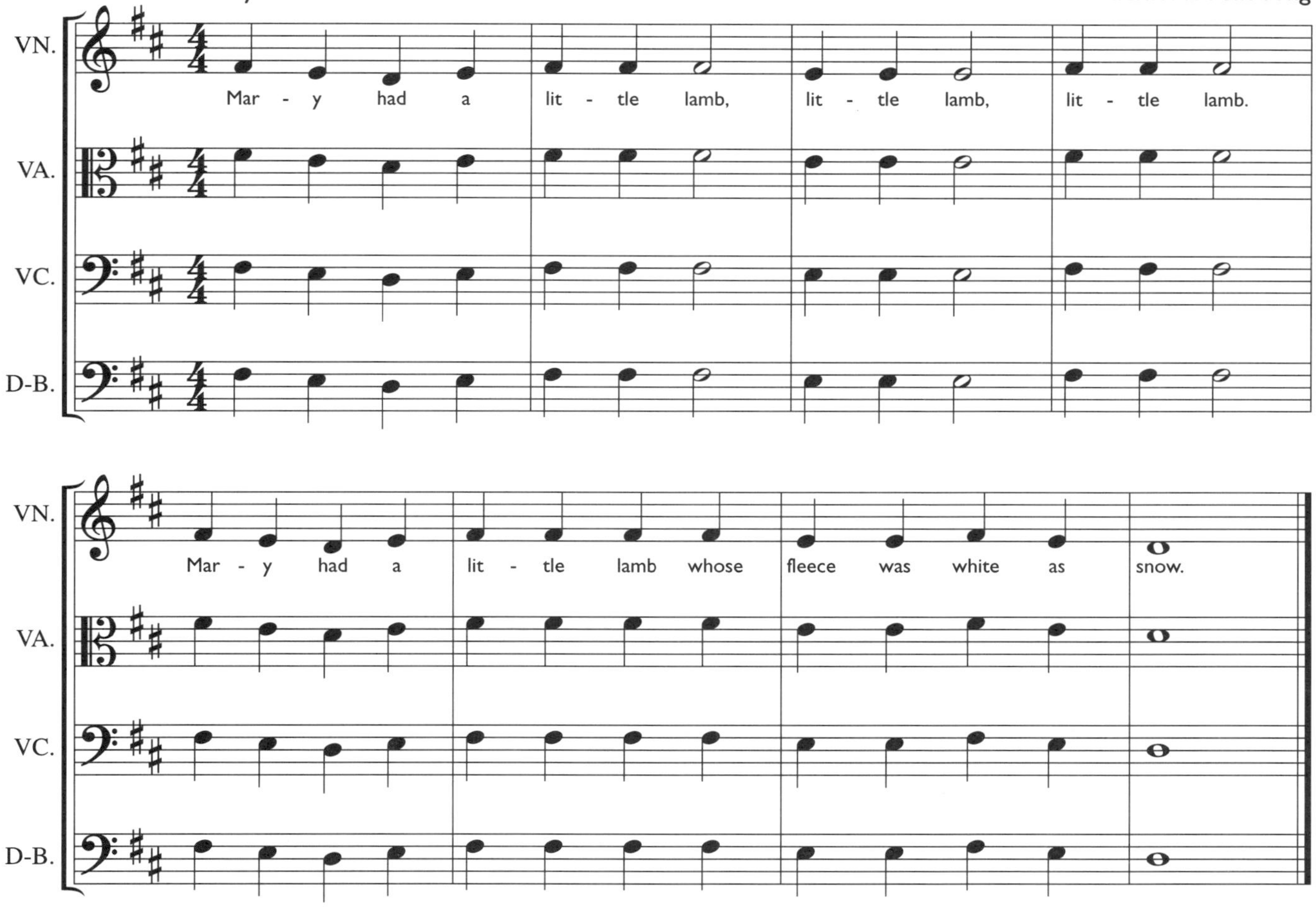

REGGAE *— A musical style mixing African and Caribbean rhythms often attributed to Jamaican sources.*

Viola #32 Tch's Ed CD-1
Bass #33 Tch's Ed CD-1
Accom. #34 Tch's Ed CD-1

6 ★ SOLO — Mary Had a Little Lamb (REGGAE STYLE STARTING ON F♯)

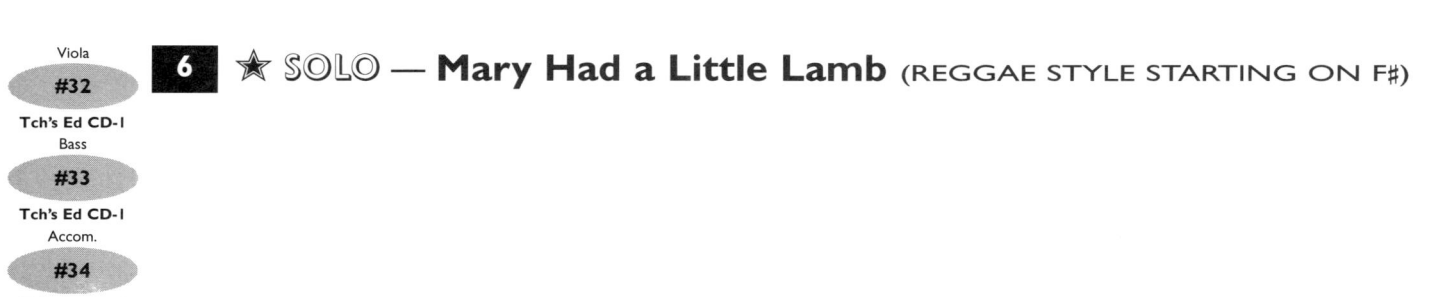

SPECIAL PROJECT — ★★★ **Practice Variations "By Ear"**
- *Practice melody pizzicato (plucking) and arco (with bow)*
- *Play melody on each of the four strings*
- *Practice rhythm patterns without left hand on an open string*

THEME AND VARIATIONS — *A musical form based upon a melody followed by a succession of composed rhythmic/melodic variations.*

STUDENT CD

SPEAKER BALANCE
CONTROL
CD Trk 9
L   R
Viola   Accom.
Bass

1 **Stepping and Skipping** (THEME)   **FULL SCORE ON P. 7-C**   U.S.

DOWN BOW (⊓) — *Draw the bow toward the tip.*

UP BOW (∨) — *Draw the bow toward the frog.*

BOW LIFT (,) — *Lift the bow from the string and replace it nearer the frog.*

CD Trk 9 R
Accom.

2 **Variation One on** *Stepping and Skipping*   **FULL SCORE ON P. 7-C**

CD Trk 9 R
Accom.

3 **Variation Two on** *Stepping and Skipping*   **FULL SCORE ON P. 7-C**

LEGATO — *With a smooth and connected style of articulation.*

DÉTACHÉ — *The bow stroke used to produce a legato style.*

CD Trk 10 R
L   R
Violin   Accom.
Cello

4 **Au Claire de la Lune**   **FULL SCORE ON P. 7-D**   French Folk Song

SPECIAL PROJECT — ★★★ **Use Practice Variations with** *Stepping and Skipping* **and** *Au Claire de la Lune*

Rhythmic Flashcard Reading Option for *Stepping and Skipping*

Rhythmic Flashcard Reading Option for *Stepping and Skipping Variations One and Two*

Rhythm and Bowing Preparation for *Stepping and Skipping Variations One and Two.*
Instruct Students to "Look and Listen. The Starting Tone is D."

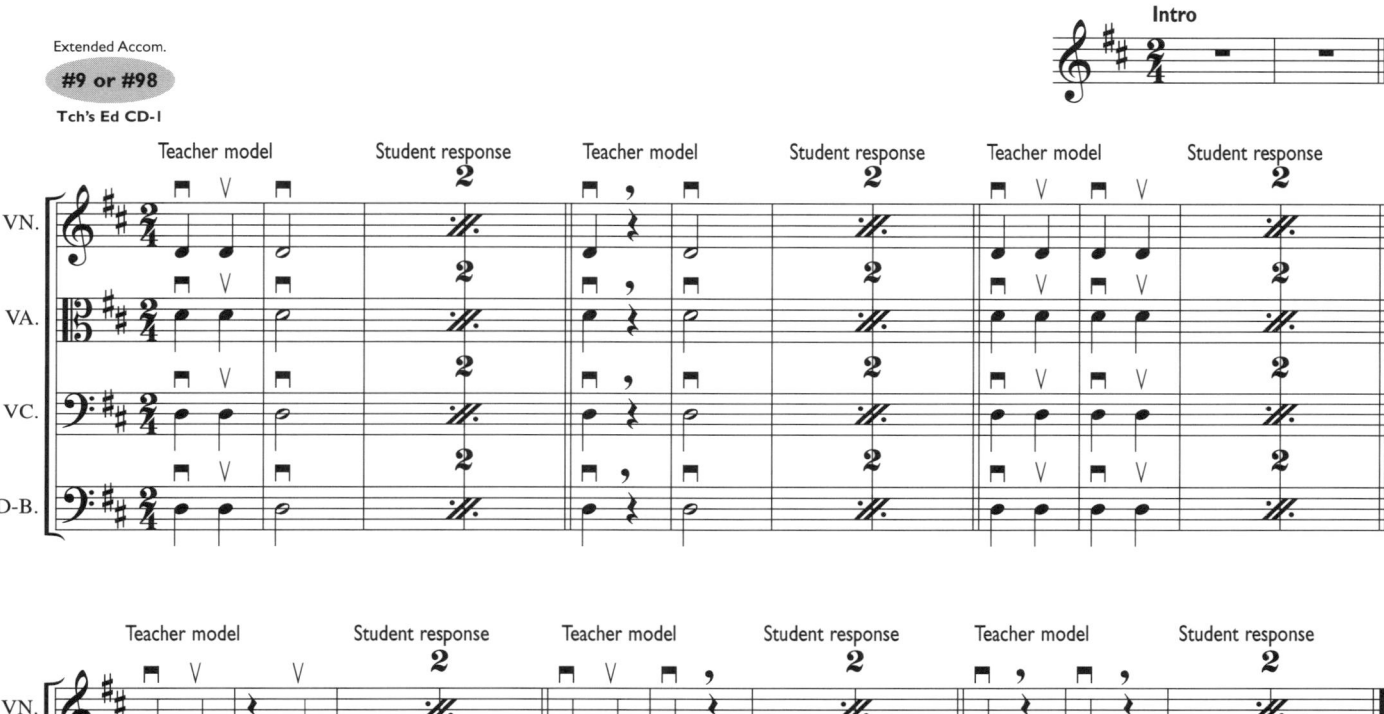

Rhythmic Flashcard Reading Option for *Au Claire de la Lune*

Melodic Ear-to-Hand Training and Assessment for *Au Claire de la Lune*
TEXT: "Listen and Play What You Hear. The Starting Tone is D."

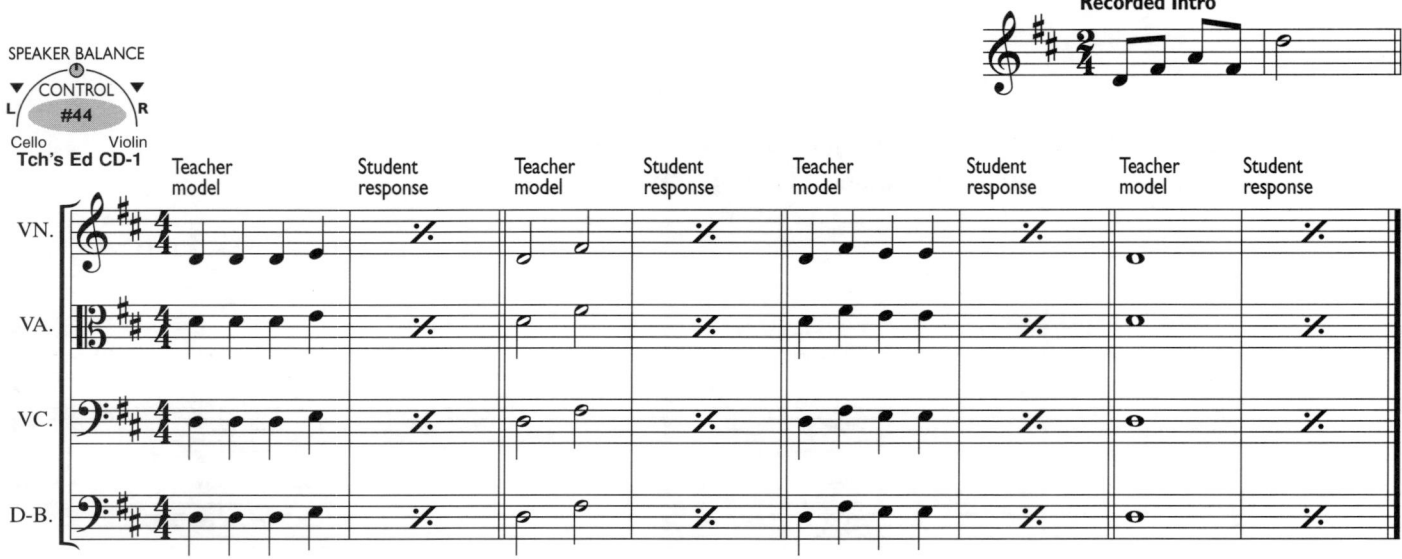

Bowing Variation Option - *Au Claire de la Lune:* add bow lift before second phrase

Articulation and Dynamic Variation Option - *Au Claire de la Lune*

- **Use separated and connected articulation**
- **Model loud and soft dynamic levels**

SPECIAL PROJECT — ★★★ Practice Variations "By Ear"

- *Practice melody pizzicato (plucking) and arco (with bow)*
- *Play melody on each of the four strings*
- *Practice rhythm patterns without left hand on an open string*

THEME AND VARIATIONS — *A musical form based upon a melody followed by a succession of composed rhythmic/melodic variations.*

1 Stepping and Skipping (THEME)

Viola #41 Tch's Ed CD-1
Bass #42 Tch's Ed CD-1
Accom. #43 Tch's Ed CD-1

U.S.

DOWN BOW (⊓) — *Draw the bow toward the tip.*
UP BOW (∨) — *Draw the bow toward the frog.*
BOW LIFT (') — *Lift the bow from the string and replace it nearer the frog.*

Accom. #43 Tch's Ed CD-1

2 Variation One on *Stepping and Skipping*

Accom. #43 Tch's Ed CD-1

3 Variation Two on *Stepping and Skipping*

LEGATO — *With a smooth and connected style of articulation.*

DÉTACHÉ — *The bow stroke used to produce a legato style.*

Violin
#45
Tch's Ed CD-1

Cello
#46
Tch's Ed CD-1

Accom.
#47
Tch's Ed CD-1

4 **Au Claire de la Lune**

French Folk Song

Legato

Au claire de la lu - ne, Mon a - mi Pier - rot,
In the moon's pale shim - mer, My dear friend Pier - rot,

Prét - e - moi ta plu - me, Pour é - crite un mot.
I would like to write you, Just a word or so.

SPECIAL PROJECT — ★★★ **Use Practice Variations with *Stepping and Skipping* and *Au Claire de la Lune***

BLANK PAGE

SUBDIVISION — *The process of dividing a steady beat into even twos or threes.*

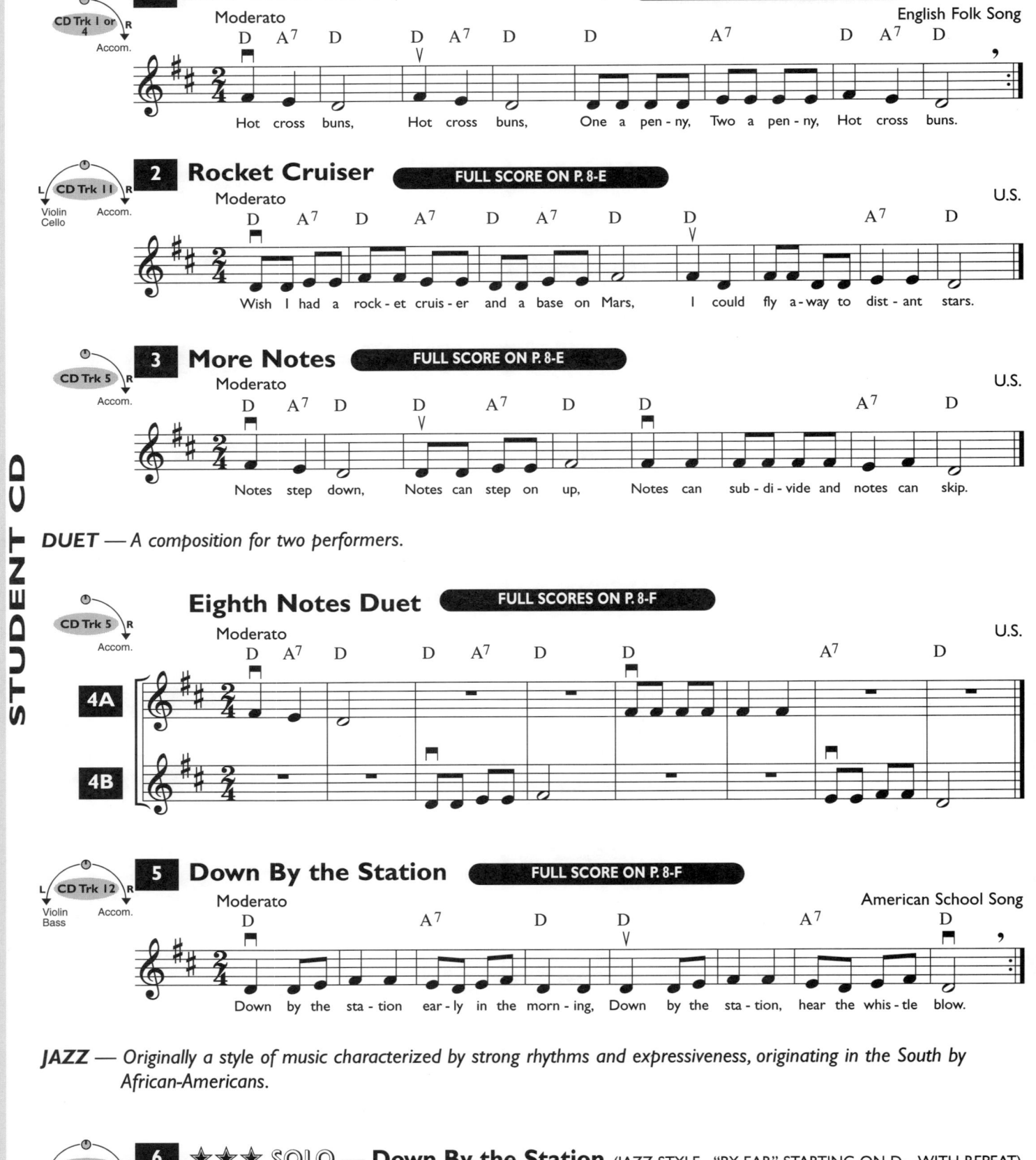

STUDENT CD

SPEAKER BALANCE

CD Trk 1 or 4
Accom.

1 **Hot Cross Buns** (WITH SUBDIVISIONS)   FULL SCORE ON P. 8-E

Moderato

English Folk Song

D A⁷ D   D A⁷ D   D   A⁷   D A⁷ D

Hot cross buns,   Hot cross buns,   One a pen-ny, Two a pen-ny, Hot cross buns.

CD Trk 11
Violin   Accom.
Cello

2 **Rocket Cruiser**   FULL SCORE ON P. 8-E

Moderato

U.S.

D A⁷ D A⁷ D A⁷ D   D   A⁷   D

Wish I had a rock-et cruis-er and a base on Mars,   I could fly a-way to dist-ant stars.

CD Trk 5
Accom.

3 **More Notes**   FULL SCORE ON P. 8-E

Moderato

U.S.

D A⁷ D   D A⁷ D   D   A⁷   D

Notes step down,   Notes can step on up,   Notes can sub-di-vide and notes can skip.

DUET — *A composition for two performers.*

CD Trk 5
Accom.

Eighth Notes Duet   FULL SCORES ON P. 8-F

Moderato

U.S.

D A⁷ D   D A⁷ D   D   A⁷   D

4A

4B

CD Trk 12
Violin   Accom.
Bass

5 **Down By the Station**   FULL SCORE ON P. 8-F

Moderato

American School Song

D   A⁷   D   D   A⁷   D

Down by the sta-tion ear-ly in the morn-ing, Down by the sta-tion, hear the whis-tle blow.

JAZZ — *Originally a style of music characterized by strong rhythms and expressiveness, originating in the South by African-Americans.*

CD Trk 13
Viola   Accom.
Cello

6 ★★★ SOLO — **Down By the Station** (JAZZ STYLE - "BY EAR" STARTING ON D – WITH REPEAT)

Rhythmic Flashcard Reading Option for *Hot Cross Buns (WITH SUBDIVISIONS)*

R-I   **R-10** *NEW*

Rhythmic Flashcard Reading Option for *Rocket Cruiser*

R-10   **R-11** *NEW*   **R-12** *NEW*   **R-1**

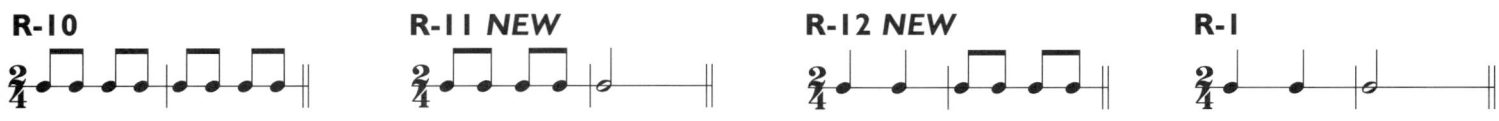

Rhythmic Flashcard Reading Option for *More Notes*

R-1   **R-11**   **R-12**

Rhythmic Flashcard Reading Option for *Down By the Station*

R-15 *NEW*   **R-14** *NEW*   **R-11**

Down By the Station (FOR EXTENDED JAZZ ACCOMPANIMENT - USE TCHS ED. CD-1 TRACK 57)

RHYTHMIC READING EXERCISE – The rhythmic reading exercise is designed to develop pattern reading skills and musical independence. It can also be employed to individualize group instruction. Following are suggestions for the use of the Rhythmic Reading Exercise.

1. Assign lines A, B, C, and D to students based upon their rhythmic reading achievement.

2. Read (Sing, Say, or Play) through the exercise by line (A, B, C, D) with or without accompaniment.

3. Snake through the exercise one measure at a time to encourage pattern reading. (Follow the arrows - 1st measure of Line A, down to 1st measure of Line B, down to 1st measure of Line C, down to 1st measure of Line D, over, up, up, up, over, down, down, down, over, up, and so on ending at the last measure of Line A.)

Rhythmic Reading Exercise

G.I.A. Publications, Inc. grants permission to the purchaser to duplicate this worksheet as an overhead transparency or student handout.

CREATING A SAFE ENVIRONMENT FOR SPONTANEOUS MUSIC MAKING

DOWN BY THE STATION - Jazz Style

Extended Accom.

#57

Tch's Ed CD-1

PRINCIPLE #1: *Keep it Simple (Too many options can inhibit creativity).*

Procedure 1. Direct students to "Use only the tones F♯, E, and D."

PRINCIPLE #2: *Keep Everyone Involved (Peer observation can be intimidating).*

Procedure 2a. Direct students to simultaneously improvise rhythmic variations on *Down By the Station*.

Procedure 2b. Teach everyone an 8-beat riff (melodic ostinato).
(**Note:** Riffs may be improvised and taught to the class by the teacher or by the students.)

Example (As notated)

Example (As performed in a swinging style ♫ = ♪♪ **)**

Procedure 3. Direct students to "Repeat the riff until the music ends."

PRINCIPLE #3: *Allow for Self-Selection of Tasks (Absence of options can stifle creativity).*

Procedure 4. When individual students are chosen or volunteer, suggest that they:

A. "Play the riff."

B. "Improvise a rhythmic variation on the riff, or"

C. "Improvise a rhythmic/melodic variation on the riff."

PRINCIPLE #4: *Avoid Common Creativity Killers Including Expressions of Approval or Disapproval, Surveillance, Evaluation, Reward Systems, and Competition.*

TRACKING THE BLUES IN D

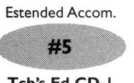

Estended Accom.
#5
Tch's Ed CD-I

Blues in D "Call and Response" (AS PERFORMED BY THE TEACHER)

Intro

TEACHER CALL   D^7 | **STUDENT RESPONSE** Imitated or Improvised | **TEACHER CALL**   D^7 | **STUDENT RESPONSE** Imitated or Improvised

CALL   G^7 | **RESPONSE** | **CALL**   D^7 | **RESPONSE**

CALL   A^7 | **RESPONSE** | **CALL**   D^7 | **RESPONSE**

CALL   D^7 | **RESPONSE** | **CALL**   D^7 | **RESPONSE**

CALL   G^7 | **RESPONSE** | **CALL**   D^7 | **RESPONSE**

CALL   A^7 | **RESPONSE** | **CALL**   D^7 | **RESPONSE**

Blues in D "Call and Response" (AS PERFORMED BY THE TEACHER)

RHYTHMIC PATTERNS FOR TECHNICAL DEVELOPMENT

Use extended D major accompaniment

#9 or #98

Tch's Ed CD-1

Procedure 1: Listen and Play. Direct students to "Listen and play what you hear."

> **Procedure 1a:** Using vocal or instrumental model, perform rhythmic patterns before student response.

Procedure 2: Listen and Associate. Direct students to "Listen and look at the rhythmic pattern, then play what you hear and see."

> **Procedure 2a:** Using vocal model, sing and display rhythmic flashcard before student response.

Procedure 3: Recognize and Reproduce Notated Rhythmic Patterns. Direct students to "Look at the rhythm pattern, then play what you see."

> **Procedure 3a:** Prompted Flash. Prompt students with "Ready, Now, Look and Play." Remove flashcard during student response.

> **Procedure 3b:** Rapid Flash. Display next flashcard while students play previous pattern.

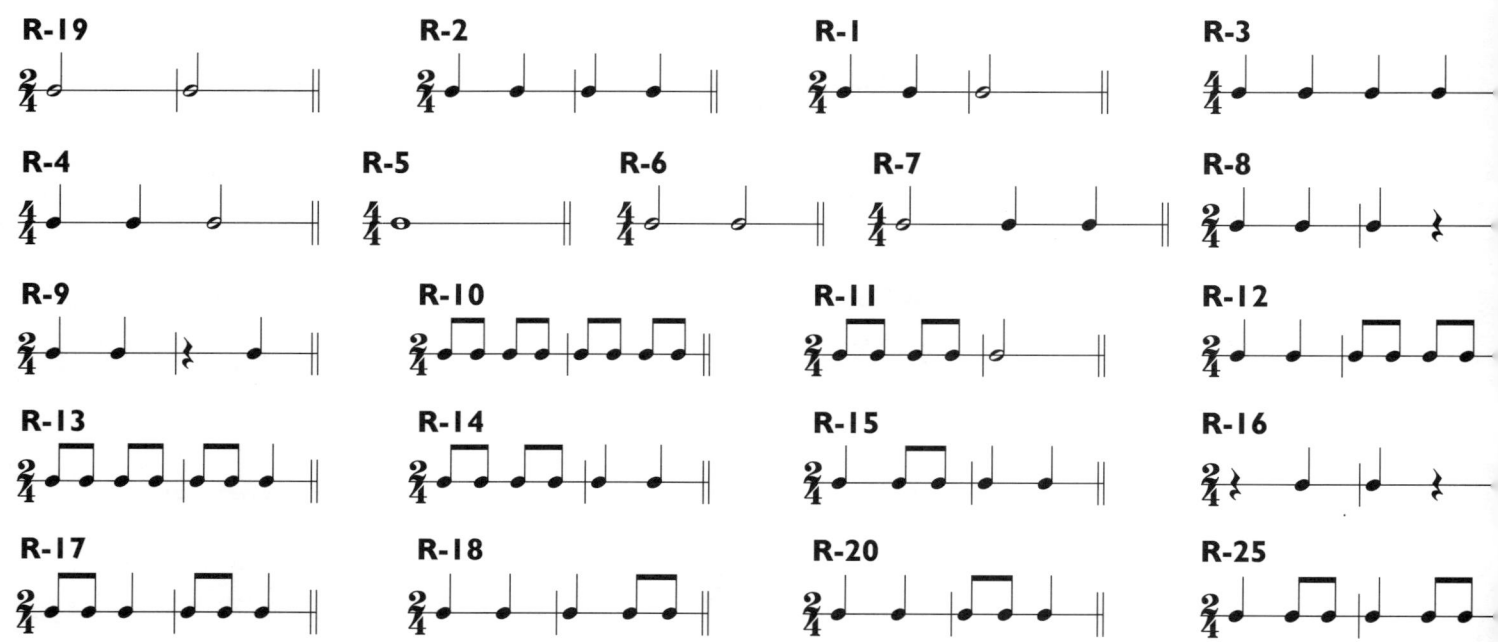

*Numbers refer to Rhythmic Flashcard set MLR-421.

ADDITIONAL OPTIONS FOR TECHNICAL AND RHYTHMIC DEVELOPMENT

- **Vary style of articulation (separated/connected), use pizzicato**
- **Use different pitches**
- **Introduce harmonics**
- **Use rhythmic patterns of student names**
- **Associate rhythmic patterns with rhythmic syllables**
- **Allow student leaders to model rhythmic patterns**
- **Practice "shadow bowing" with cardboard tissue tubes or plastic plumbing pipe**
- **Have student partners monitor bow holds, contact point, and straight bows**

SUBDIVISION — *The process of dividing a steady beat into even twos or threes.*

1 Hot Cross Buns (WITH SUBDIVISIONS)

English Folk Song

2 Rocket Cruiser

U.S.

3 More Notes

U.S.

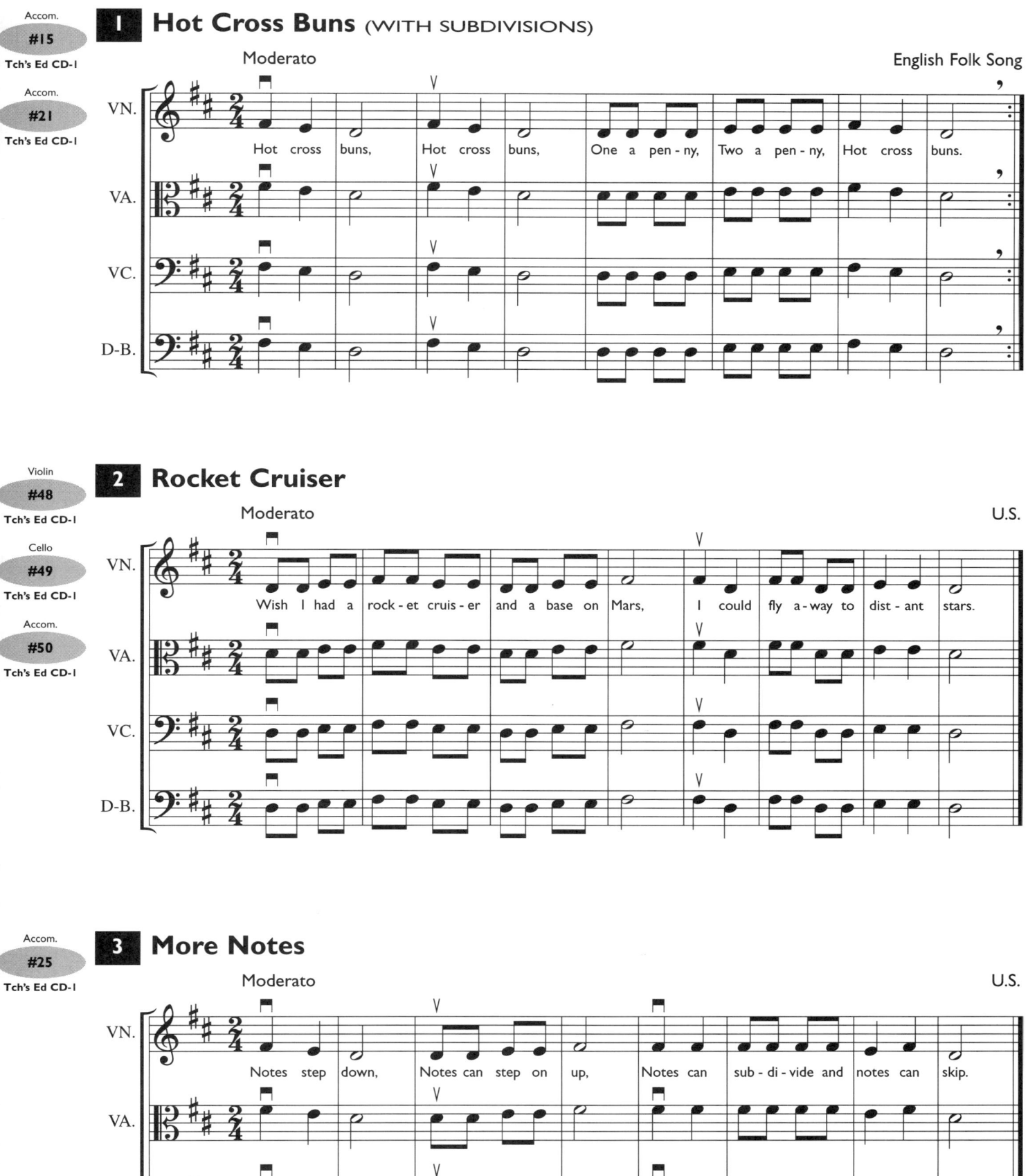

DUET — *A composition for two performers.*

4A **Eighth Notes Duet** (PART A)

Accom.
#25

Tch's Ed CD-1

Moderato

U.S.

VN.

VA.

VC.

D-B.

Part B

4B **Eighth Notes Duet** (PART B)

Moderato

U.S.

VN.

VA.

VC.

D-B.

Part A

5 **Down By the Station**

Violin
#51

Tch's Ed CD-1

Bass
#52

Tch's Ed CD-1

Accom.
#53

Tch's Ed CD-1

Moderato

American School Song

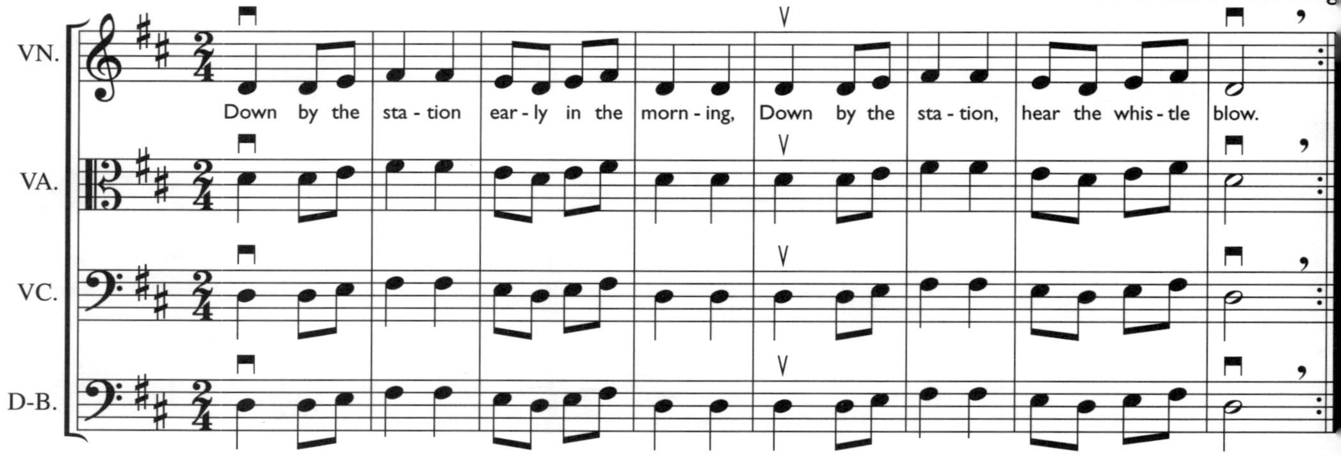

VN.

Down by the sta - tion ear - ly in the morn - ing, Down by the sta - tion, hear the whis - tle blow.

VA.

VC.

D-B.

JAZZ — *Originally a style of music characterized by strong rhythms and expressiveness, originating in the South by African-Americans.*

Violin
#54

Tch's Ed CD-1

6 ★★★ SOLO — **Down By the Station** (JAZZ STYLE - "BY EAR" STARTING ON D – WITH REPEAT)

Cello
#55

Tch's Ed CD-1

Accom.
#56

Tch's Ed CD-1

Extended Accom.
#57

Tch's Ed CD-1

BLANK PAGE

BLANK PAGE

9

See Bass Alternative Fingerings F♯, G: p. 9-D

NEW NOTE: G

STUDENT CD

SPEAKER BALANCE
CONTROL
CD Trk 14
L Violin Bass   R Accom.

1 Old King Cole   FULL SCORE ON P. 9-E

Moderato

Adaptation of an Old Folk Tune

Old King Cole's a mer-ry soul, mer-ry soul is he, is he.
Has his pipe and has his bowl, has his fid-'lers three, all three.

Dance with fid-'lers, dance with fid-'lers, dance with fid-'lers three, three.

Violin Cello
Solo Trk 15
Accom. Trk 15-2

2 Jacob Drink (SOLO, ENSEMBLE 2-5 PARTS)   FULL SCORE ON P. 9-E

With enthusiasm

Polish Folk Song

3 Variation on *Jacob Drink*   FULL SCORE ON P. 9-F

4 Accompaniment Number One to *Jacob Drink*   FULL SCORE ON P. 9-F

5 Accompaniment Number Two to *Jacob Drink*   FULL SCORE ON P. 9-F

6 ★ Obbligato to *Jacob Drink*   FULL SCORE ON P. 9-G

7 Shave and a Haircut   FULL SCORE ON P. 9-G

As quickly as possible

Early American

Shave and a hair-cut, TWO BITS!

? *Forget the sound of a rhythm pattern?* **You Can Look It Up** *in the* **Rhythm Pattern Dictionary** *on pages 46 and 47.*

Rhythmic Flashcard Reading Option for *Old King Cole*

R-2

R-1

R-19 *NEW*

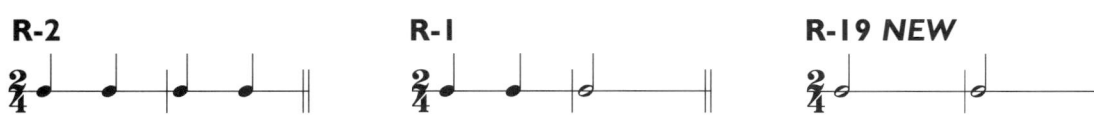

Melodic Ear-to-Hand Training and Assessment for *Old King Cole*.

TEXT: "Listen and Play What You Hear. The Starting Tone is G."

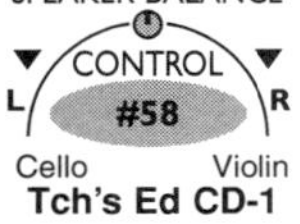

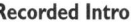

SPEAKER BALANCE
CONTROL
#58
L
R
Cello
Violin

Tch's Ed CD-1

Recorded Intro

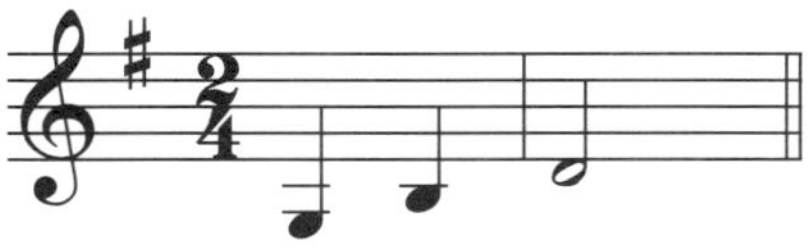

Recorded Model or (Tch Demo)

Student Response (Pizz. or Arco)

VN.
VA.
VC.
D-B.

VN.
VA.
VC.
D-B.

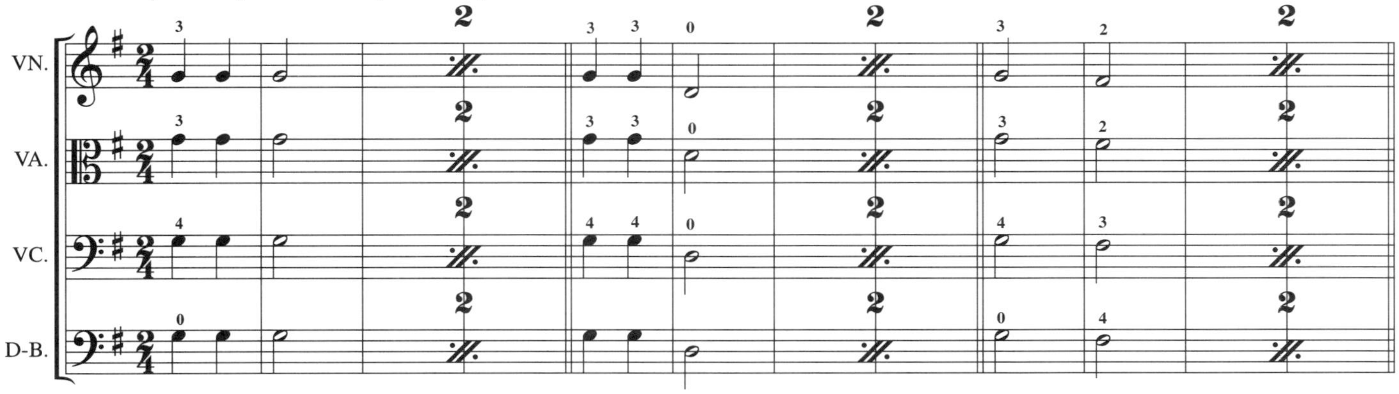

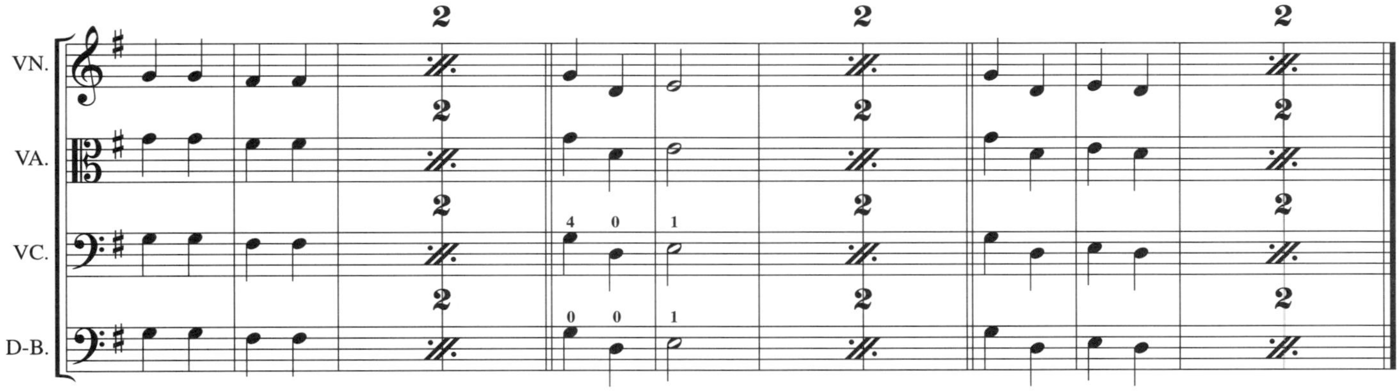

Rhythmic Flashcard Reading Option for *Jacob Drink, Accompaniments, and Obligato*

R-10 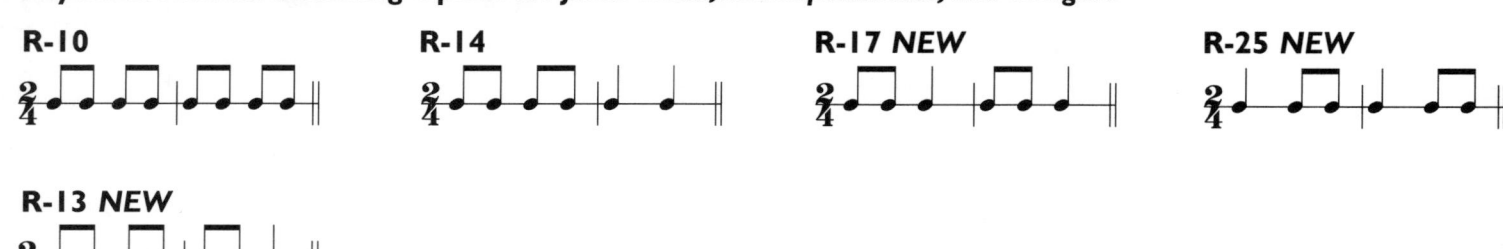 **R-14** **R-17 *NEW*** **R-25 *NEW***

R-13 *NEW*

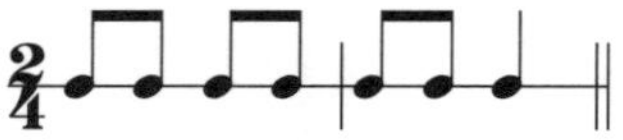

Rhythmic Flashcard Reading Option for *Shave and a Haircut*

R-15 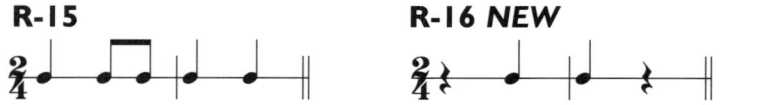 **R-16 *NEW***

Rhythmic, Bowing, and Articulation Ear-to-Hand Training and Assessment for *Jacob Drink.*
TEXT: "Listen and Play What You Hear. The Starting Tone is G."

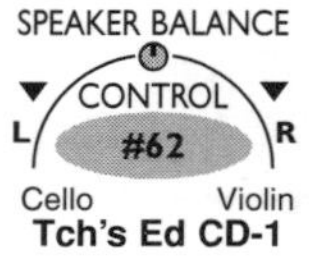

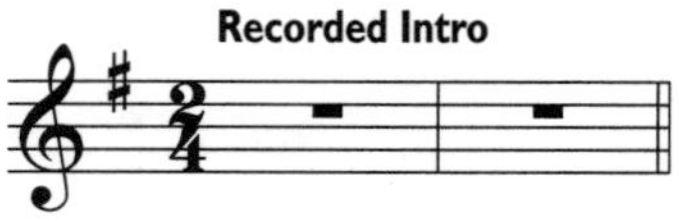

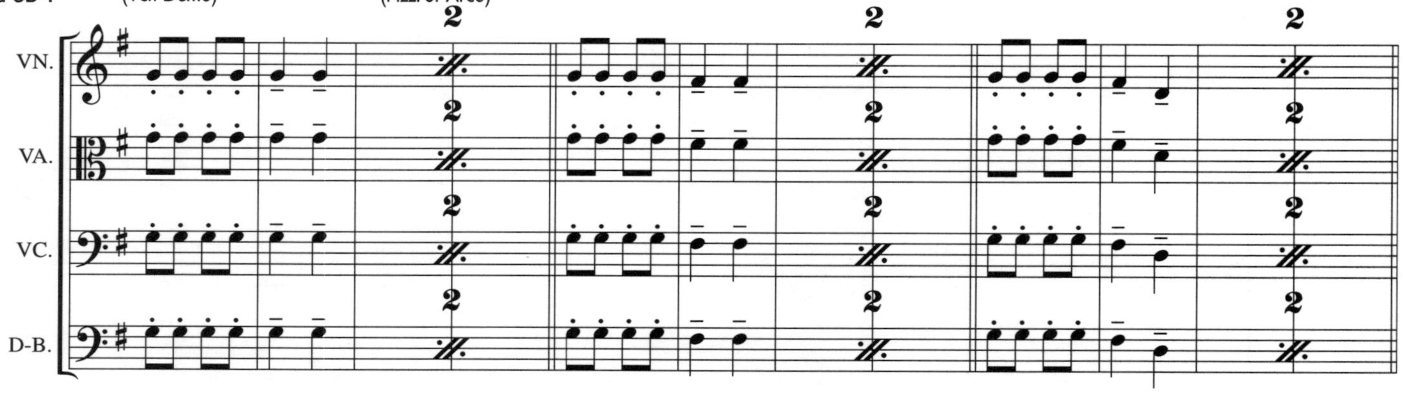

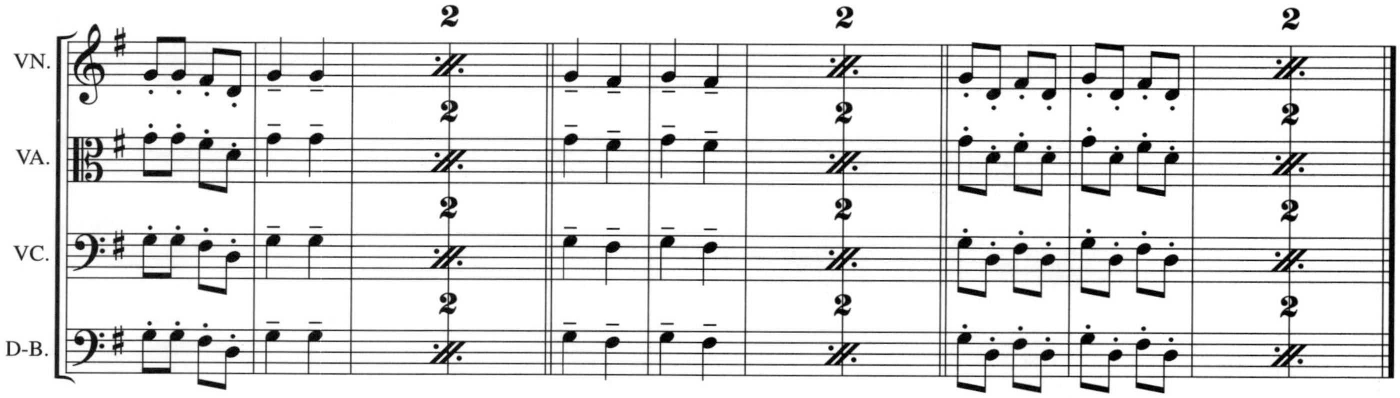

SOUND AND SILENCE - AN EXPRESSIVE ELEMENT OF MUSIC IMPROVISATION

Extended Accom.

#57

Tch's Ed CD-1

Return to
DOWN BY THE STATION - Jazz Style

Procedure 1. Direct students to "Use only the tones D, E, and F♯."

Procedure 2. Teach everyone an 8-beat riff (melodic ostinato).

(**NOTE:** Riffs may be improvised and taught to the class by the teacher or by students)

Riff 1 in a swinging style

(Example of the use of sound as the primary expressive element)

Riff 2 in a swinging style

(Example of the use of both sound and silence as expressive elements)

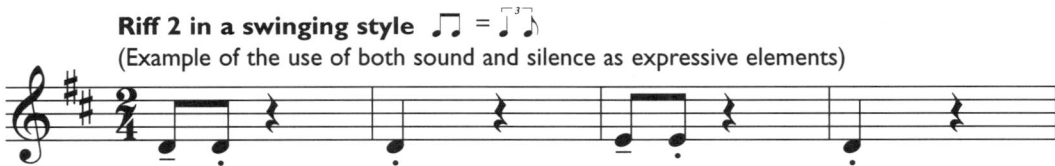

Procedure 3. Direct students to "Repeat the riff until the music ends."

(For an interesting effect, perform Riff 1 and Riff 2 simultaneously)

Procedure 4. When individual students are chosen or volunteer, suggest that they:

A. "Play the riff."

B. "Improvise a rhythmic variation employing both sound and silence, or"

C. "Improvise a rhythmic/melodic variation employing both sound and silence."

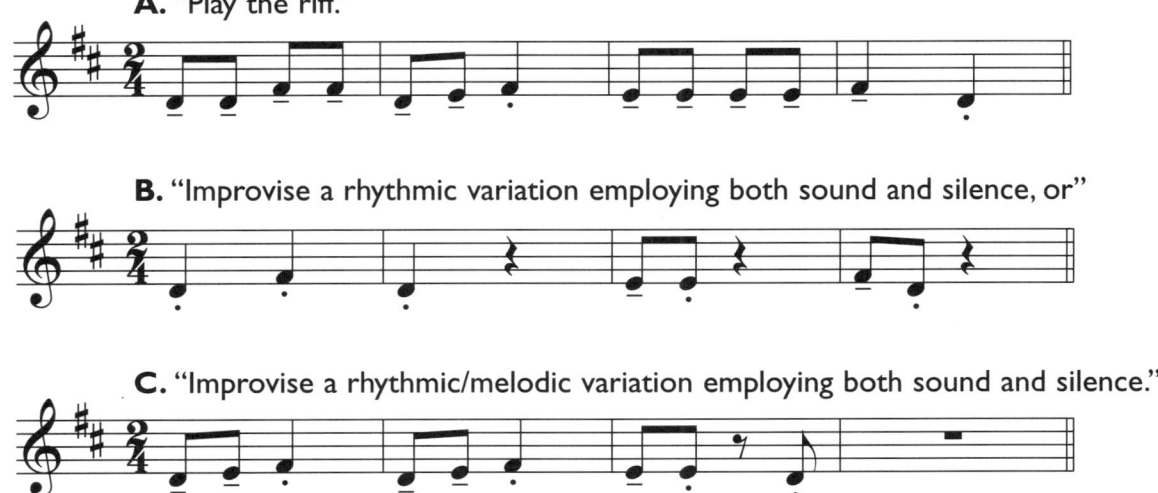

Optional Procedure 5. Direct students to simultaneously improvise variations using both sound and silence as expressive elements.

NEW NOTE

ALTERNATIVE FINGERINGS

Violin — G — 3

Viola — G — 3

Cello — G — 4

Bass — G — 0

F# — 2

G — 4 on D string

1 **Old King Cole**

Moderato

Adaptation of an Old Folk Tune

VN.

Old King Cole's a mer - ry soul, mer - ry soul is he, is he.
Has his pipe and has his bowl, has his fid - 'lers three, all three.

VA.

VC.

D-B.

VN.

Dance with fid - 'lers, dance with fid - 'lers, dance with fid - 'lers three, three.

VA.

VC.

D-B.

(4)

2 **Jacob Drink** (SOLO, ENSEMBLE 2-5 PARTS)

With enthusiasm

Polish Folk Song

VN.

VA.

VC.

D-B.

(4   2   0)

Violin #59 Tch's Ed CD-1

Bass #60 Tch's Ed CD-1

Accom. #61 Tch's Ed CD-1

Violin #63 Tch's Ed CD-1

Cello #64 Tch's Ed CD-1

Accom. #65 Tch's Ed CD-1

3 **Variation on** *Jacob Drink*

Accom.
#65
Tch's Ed CD-1

4 **Accompaniment Number One to** *Jacob Drink*

Accom.
#65
Tch's Ed CD-1

5 **Accompaniment Number Two to** *Jacob Drink*

Accom.
#65
Tch's Ed CD-1

6 ⭐ **Obbligato to** *Jacob Drink*

Accom.
#65
Tch's Ed CD-1

7 **Shave and a Haircut**

As quickly as possible   Early American

STUDENT CD

STACCATO *— A style of playing that makes use of separation between notes.*

Violin Cello
Solo Trk 16
Accom. Trk 16-2

1 Bile 'em Cabbage Down

FULL SCORE ON P. 10-C

Lively

Fiddler's Tune

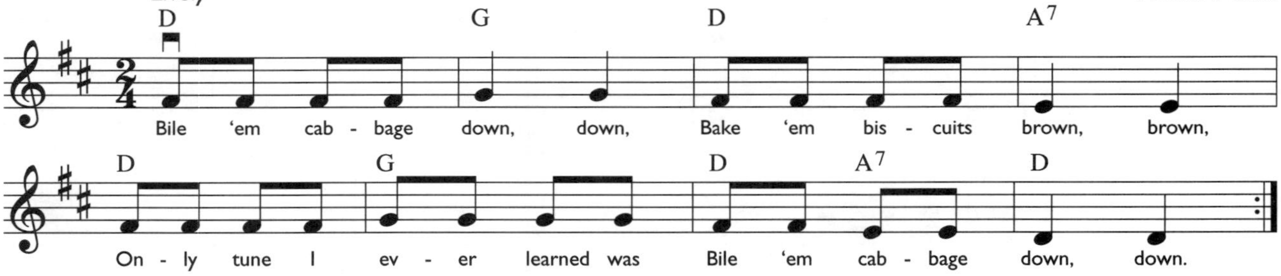
D G D A7
Bile 'em cab - bage down, down, Bake 'em bis - cuits brown, brown,
D G D A7 D
On - ly tune I ev - er learned was Bile 'em cab - bage down, down.

Violin Cello
Solo Trk 17
Accom. Trk 17-2

2 Juba

FULL SCORE ON P. 10-C

Playfully

African-American Folk Song

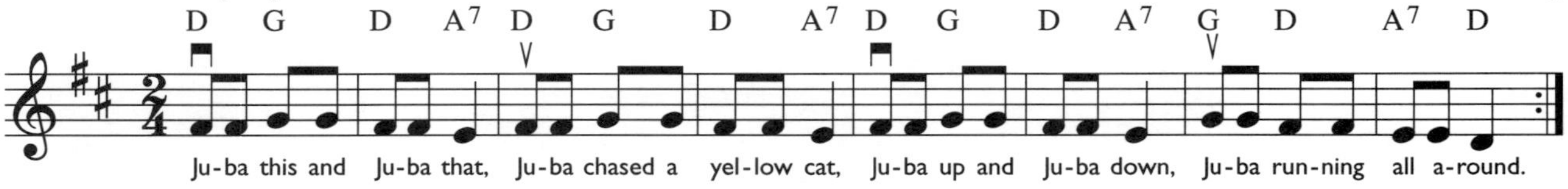
D G D A7 D G D A7 D G D A7 G D A7 D
Ju-ba this and Ju-ba that, Ju-ba chased a yel-low cat, Ju-ba up and Ju-ba down, Ju-ba run-ning all a-round.

Accom. Trk 17-2

3 Variation on *Juba*

FULL SCORE ON P. 10-D

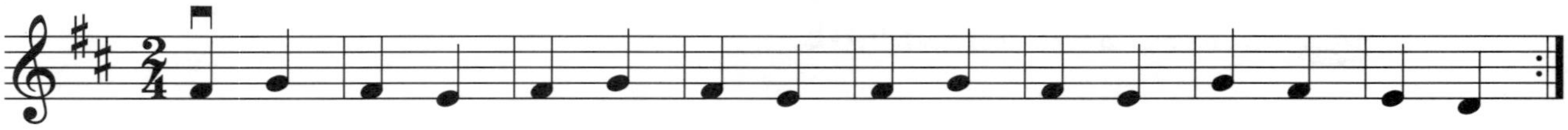

IMPROVISATION *— The art of creating music spontaneously, during performance; also a form of composition.*

RHYTHMIC IMPROVISATION *— The act of expressing one's own rhythmic ideas while maintaining the basic melodic character of the piece.*

Accom. Trk 17-2

★ SOLO — Improvise Rhythmic Variations on *Juba*

Violin Bass
Solo Trk 18
Accom. Trk 18-2

4 Cobbler, Cobbler

FULL SCORE ON P. 10-D

Rhythmically

Jamaican Street Song

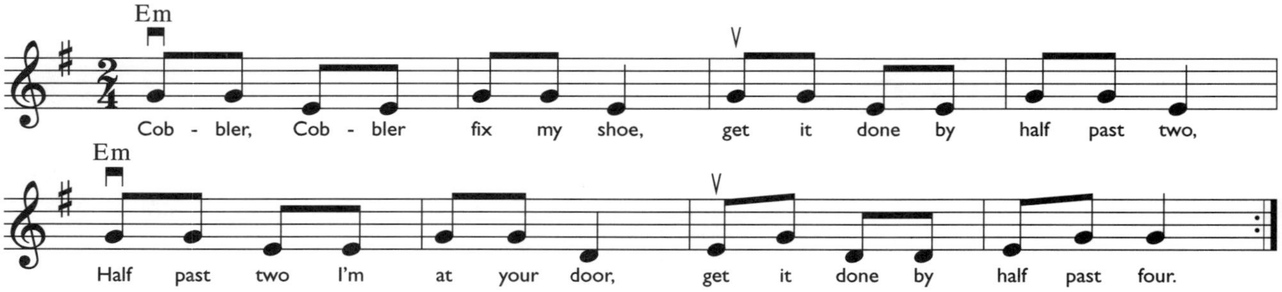
Em
Cob - bler, Cob - bler fix my shoe, get it done by half past two,
Em
Half past two I'm at your door, get it done by half past four.

Accom. Trk 18-2

5 Variation on *Cobbler, Cobbler*

FULL SCORE ON P. 10-E

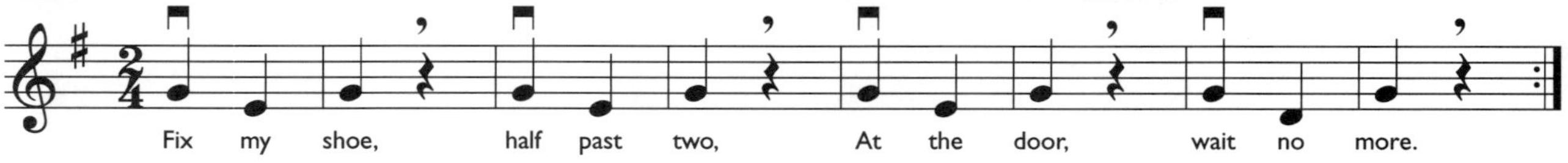
Fix my shoe, half past two, At the door, wait no more.

Accom. Trk 18-2

6 ★ SOLO — Improvise Rhythmic Variations on *Cobbler, Cobbler*

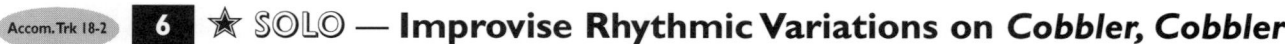

Rhythmic Flashcard Reading Option for *Bile 'em Cabbage Down*

R-14   **R-10**

Rhythmic Flashcard Reading Option for *Juba* **and** *Variation on Juba*

R-13   **R-2**

Rhythmic Flashcard Reading Option for *Cobbler, Cobbler* **and** *Variation on Cobbler, Cobbler*

R-13   **R-8**

SPECIAL OPTIONS FOR MUSICAL CREATIVITY

SPECIAL OPTION: IMPROVISE RHYTHMIC VARIATIONS ON *JUBA* "BY EAR"

PRINCIPLE #1: *Keep it Simple (Too many options can inhibit creativity).*

Procedure 1. Direct students to "Use the same pitches, but vary the rhythm pattern."

Extended Accom.
#72
Tch's Ed CD-1

Example:

SPECIAL OPTION: CREATE A FIDDLING STYLE "BY EAR" - SONGS ON PAGES 6, 7, 8, 9, AND 10

Procedure 1. Direct students to "Create a country fiddle sound by adding an open A string (simple double stop)."

Procedure 1a (bass). Direct students to "Play the melody on the D string and add an open A string below."

Example: Bile 'em Cabbage Down - with open string (violin)

Example: Bile 'em Cabbage Down - with open string (bass)

SPECIAL OPTION: CREATE AN OPEN STRING BASS LINE "BY EAR" - SONGS ON PAGES 6, 7, 8, 9, AND 10

Procedure 1. Direct students to "Listen to the melody, and create a new part using open D, A, and G that sounds good to you."

Example: Bile 'em Cabbage Down - with open string bass line

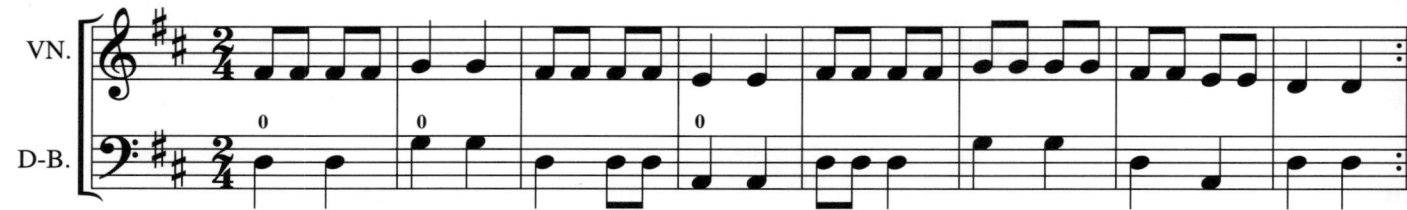

CREATING A SAFE ENVIRONMENT FOR SPONTANEOUS MUSIC MAKING

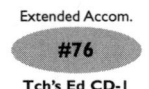

Extended Accom.
#76
Tch's Ed CD-1

Cobbler, Cobbler

PRINCIPLE #1: *Keep it Simple (Too many options can inhibit creativity).*

Procedure 1. Direct students to "Use the tones G, E, and D."

PRINCIPLE #2: *Keep Everyone Involved (Peer observation can be intimidating).*

Procedure 2a. Direct students to simultaneously improvise rhythmic variations on *Cobbler, Cobbler.*

Procedure 2b. Teach everyone an 8-beat riff (melodic ostinato).
(**Note:** Riffs may be improvised and taught to the class by the teacher or by the students.)

Example:

Procedure 3. Direct students to "Repeat the riff until the music ends."

PRINCIPLE #3: *Allow for Self-Selection of Tasks (Absence of options can stifle creativity).*

Procedure 4. When individual students are chosen or volunteer, suggest that they:

A. "Play the riff."

B. "Improvise rhythmic variations on the riff."

STACCATO — *A style of playing that makes use of separation between notes.*

1 Bile 'em Cabbage Down

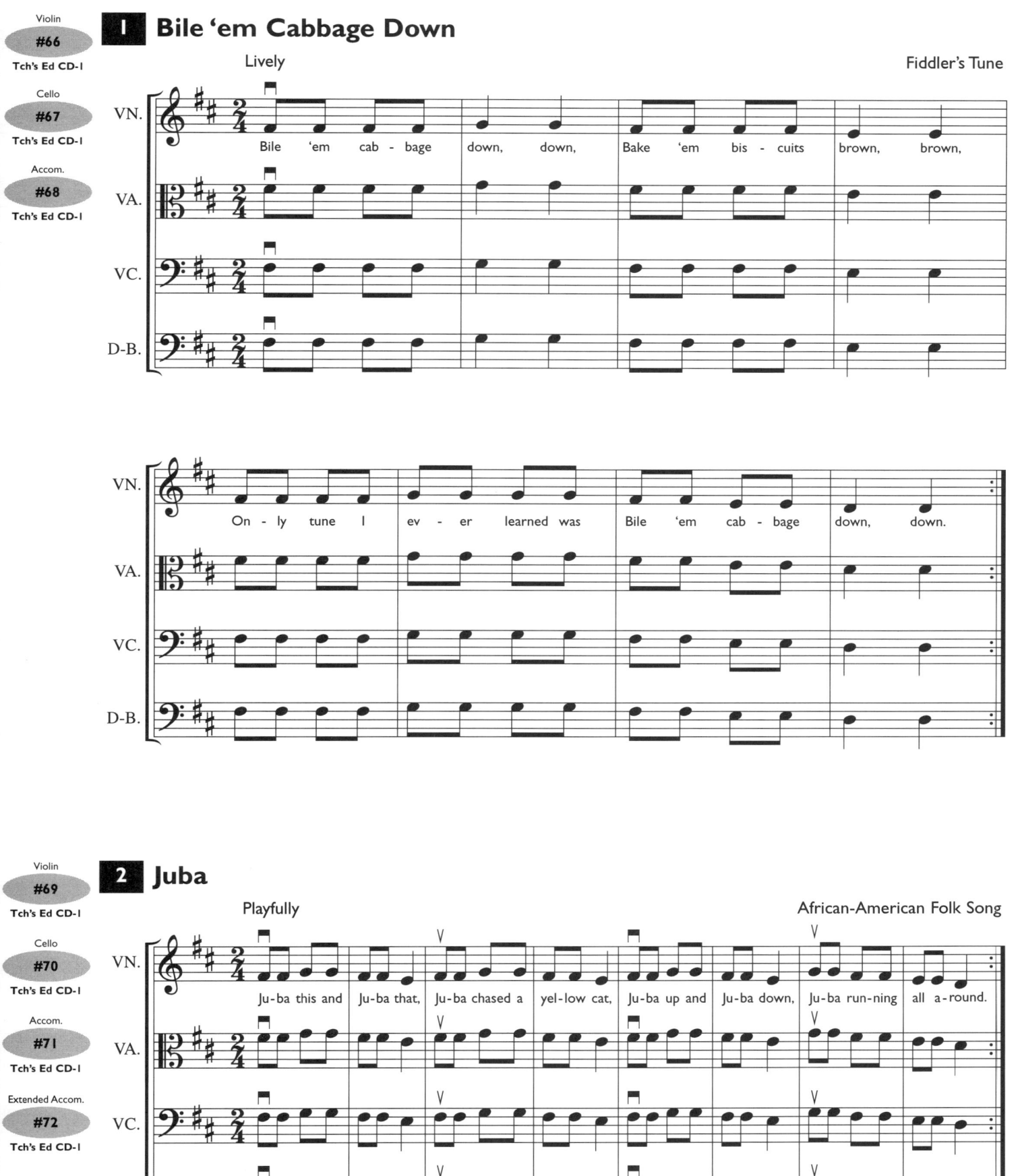

Violin #66 Tch's Ed CD-1
Cello #67 Tch's Ed CD-1
Accom. #68 Tch's Ed CD-1

Lively

Fiddler's Tune

Bile 'em cab-bage down, down, Bake 'em bis-cuits brown, brown,

On-ly tune I ev-er learned was Bile 'em cab-bage down, down.

2 Juba

Violin #69 Tch's Ed CD-1
Cello #70 Tch's Ed CD-1
Accom. #71 Tch's Ed CD-1
Extended Accom. #72 Tch's Ed CD-1

Playfully

African-American Folk Song

Ju-ba this and Ju-ba that, Ju-ba chased a yel-low cat, Ju-ba up and Ju-ba down, Ju-ba run-ning all a-round.

Accom.
#71
Tch's Ed CD-1

Extended Accom.
#72
Tch's Ed CD-1

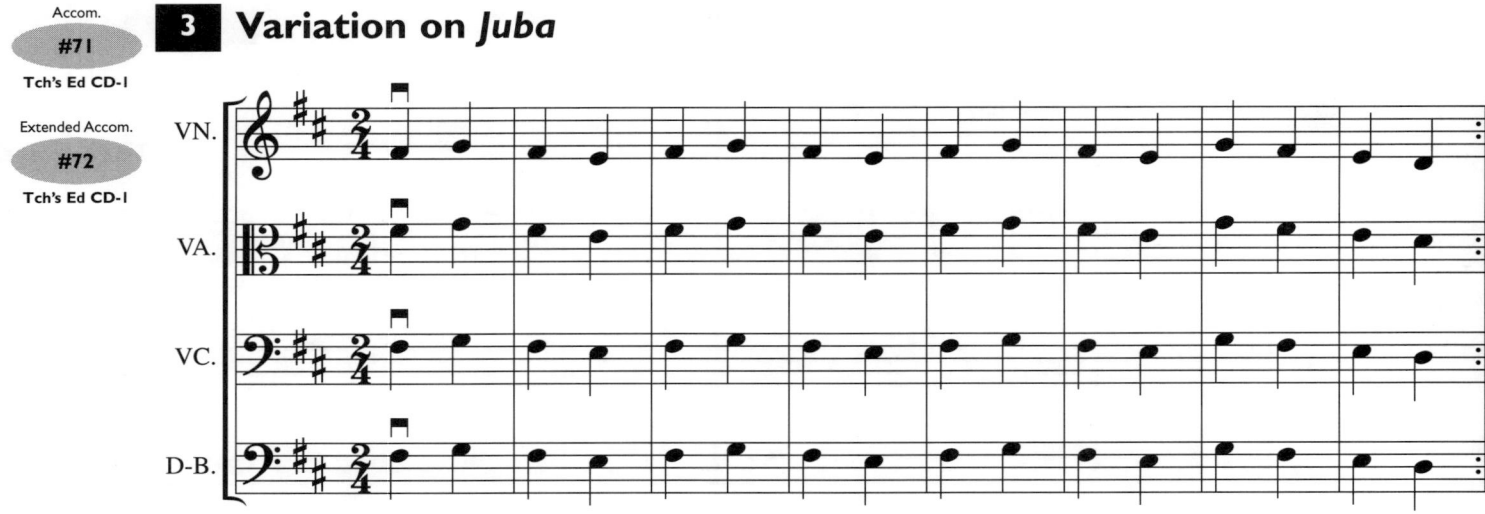

3 Variation on *Juba*

VN.
VA.
VC.
D-B.

IMPROVISATION — *The art of creating music spontaneously, during performance; also a form of composition.*

RHYTHMIC IMPROVISATION — *The act of expressing one's own rhythmic ideas while maintaining the basic melodic character of the piece.*

★ SOLO — Improvise Rhythmic Variations on *Juba*

Extended Accom.
#72
Tch's Ed CD-1

Violin
#73
Tch's Ed CD-1

Bass
#74
Tch's Ed CD-1

Accom.
#75
Tch's Ed CD-1

Extended Accom.
#76
Tch's Ed CD-1

4 Cobbler, Cobbler

Rhythmically

Jamaican Street Song

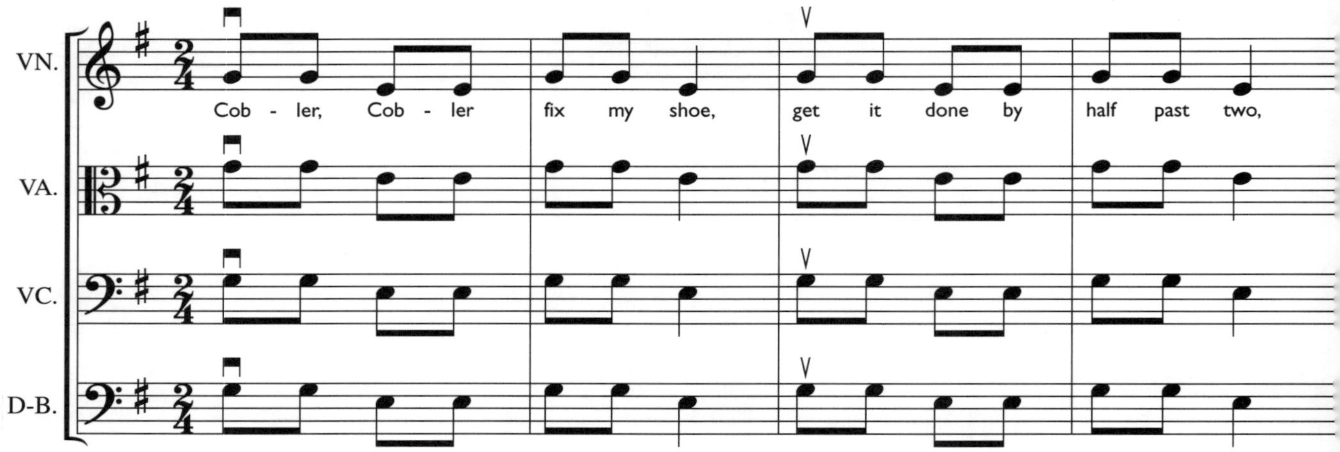
VN.
Cob - ler, Cob - ler fix my shoe, get it done by half past two,
VA.
VC.
D-B.

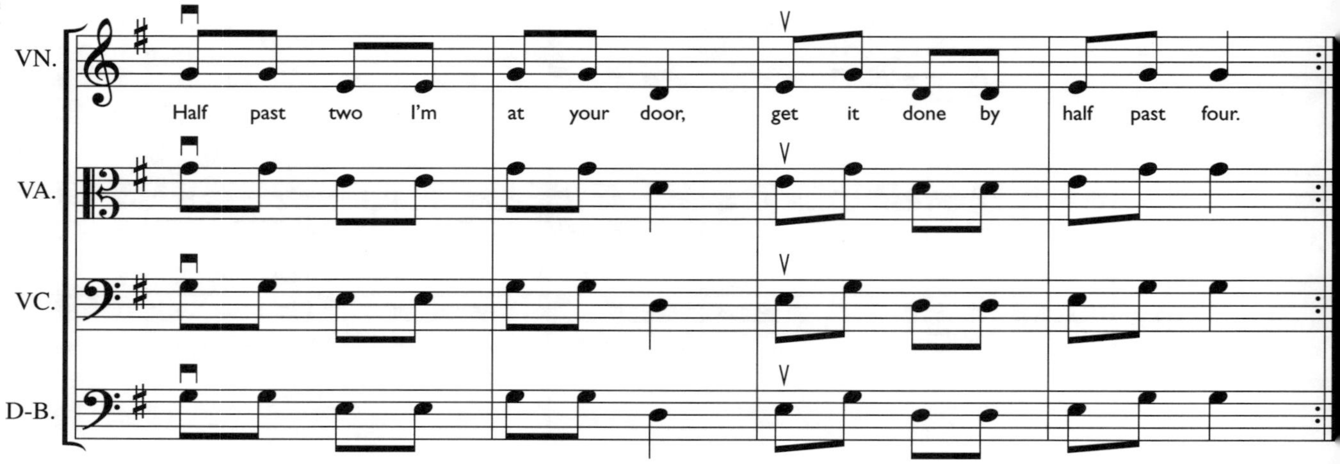
VN.
Half past two I'm at your door, get it done by half past four.
VA.
VC.
D-B.

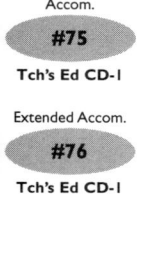

5 **Variation on *Cobbler, Cobbler***

Fix my shoe, half past two, At the door, wait no more.

6 ★ SOLO — **Improvise Rhythmic Variations on *Cobbler, Cobbler***

LULLABY — *A cradle song, usually sung by a mother to soothe or quiet an infant before bedtime.*

STUDENT CD

Viola
Cello
Solo Trk 19
Accom. Trk 19-2

1 Fais do do

FULL SCORE ON P. 11-C

Legato

French Lullaby

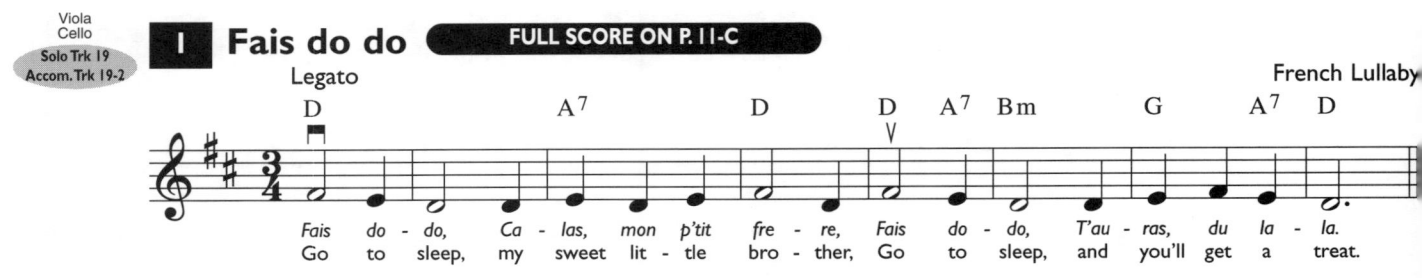

WALTZ — *A 19th century dance in triple meter.*

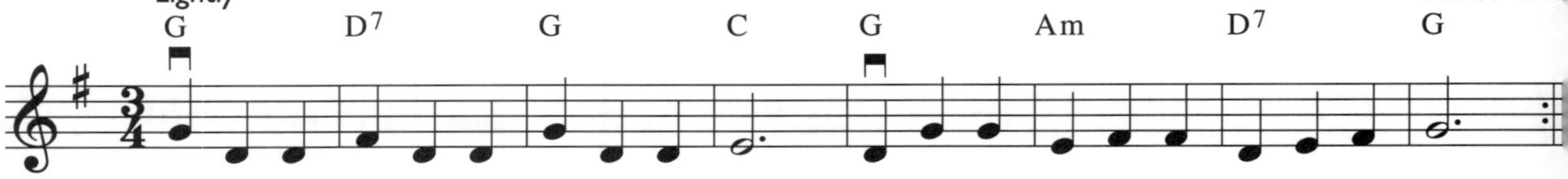

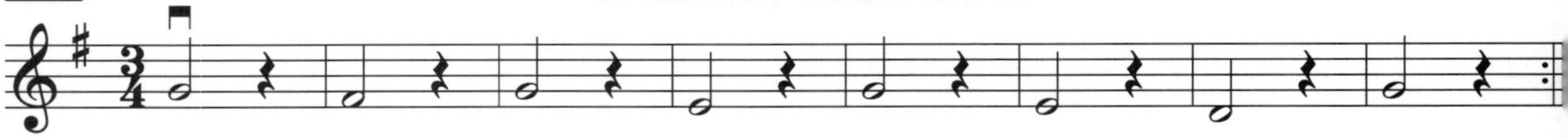

Violin
Bass
Solo Trk 20
Accom. Trk 20-2

2 Waltz

FULL SCORE ON P. 11-C

Lightly

Dance Tune

Accom. Trk 20-2

3 Waltz Variation One

FULL SCORE ON P. 11-C

Accom. Trk 20-2

4 Waltz Variation Two

FULL SCORE ON P. 11-D

Accom. Trk 20-2

5 Waltz Variation Three

FULL SCORE ON P. 11-D

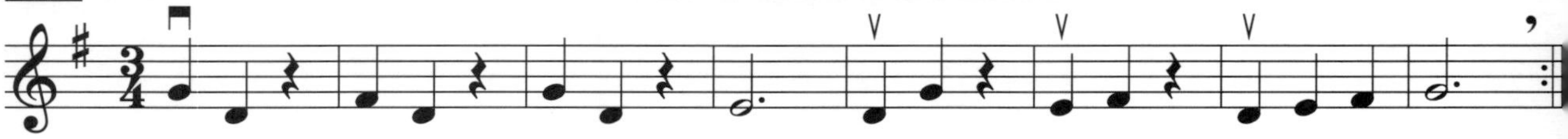

BRANLE — *A popular French dance of the 16th century in which all of the motions of the lead couple are imitated.*

Violin
Cello
Solo Trk 21
Accom. Trk 21-2

6 Champaigne Branle

FULL SCORE ON P. 11-D

Lively

16th century French Dance Tune
Claude Gervaise

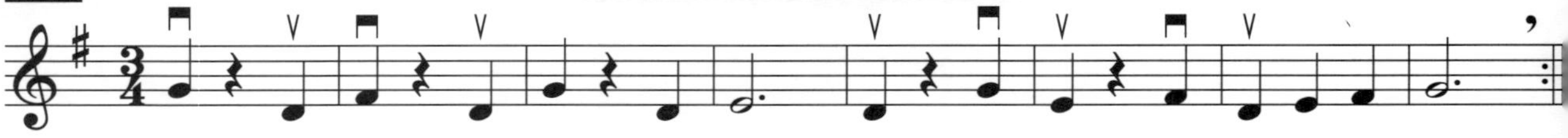

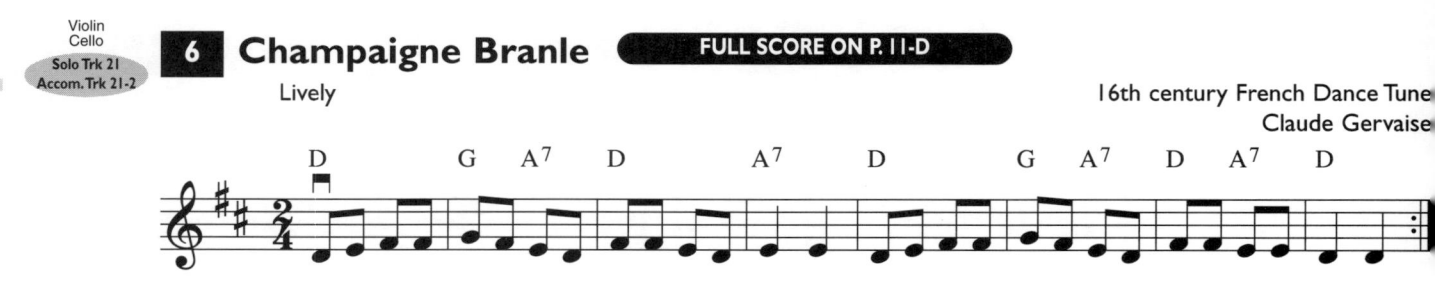

Rhythmic Reading Exercise

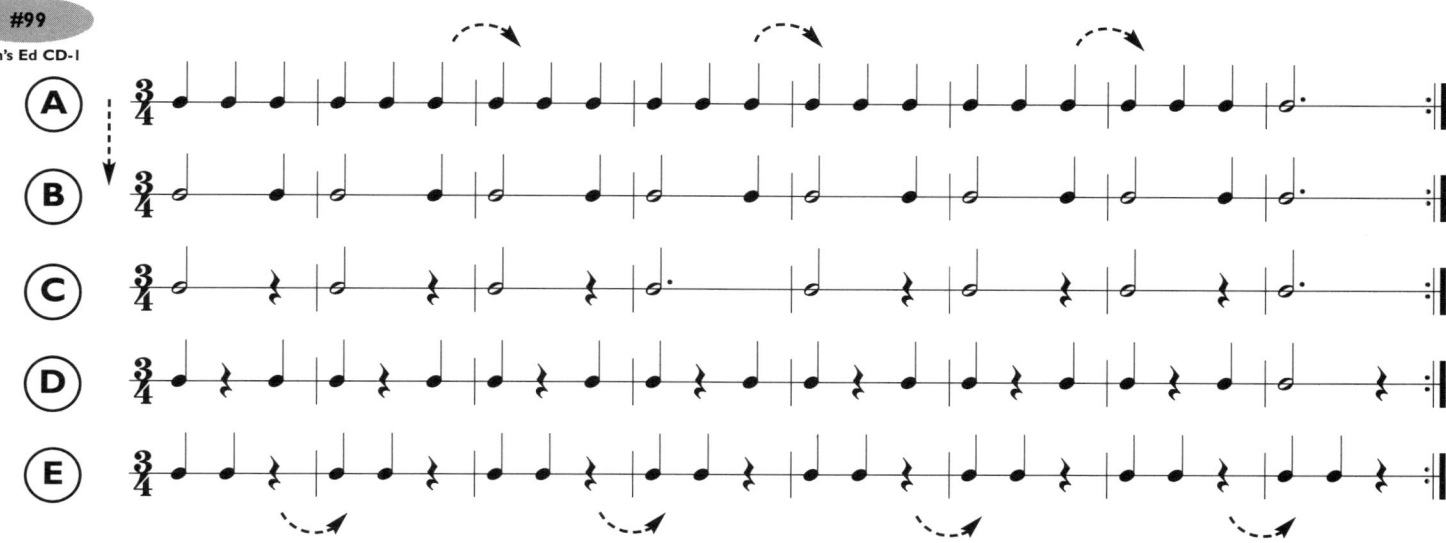

RHYTHMIC ROUND – A specially composed series of rhythmic patterns that allows two or more individuals to create interesting rhythmic effects by starting the round at different times. After the first individual or group begins, the second group enters when the first group gets to number 2.

Rhythmic Reading Round One

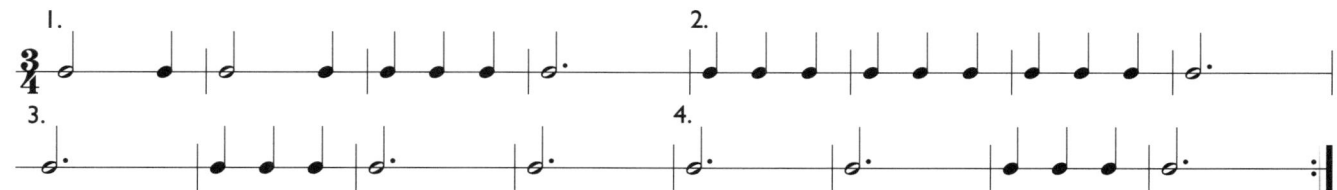

Rhythmic Reading Round Two

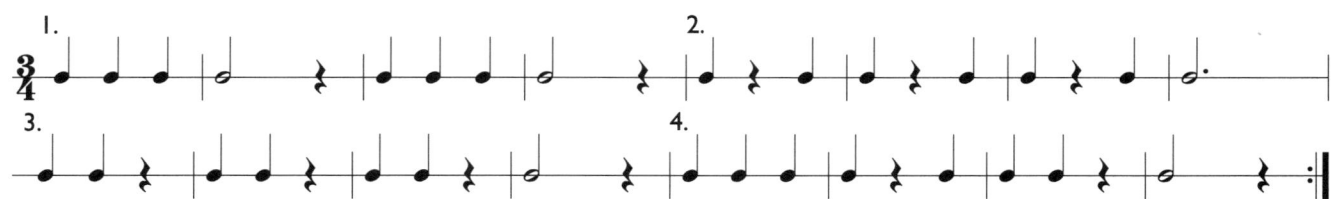

Compose a Rhythmic Round in Three Quarter Measure Signature

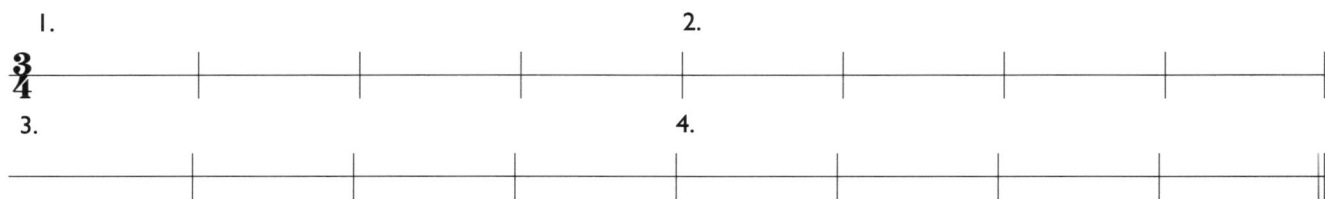

MUSICAL DYNAMICS - AN EXPRESSIVE ELEMENT FOR MUSIC IMPROVISATION

Extended Accom.
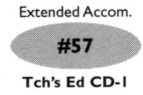
#57

Tch's Ed CD-1

Down By the Station (JAZZ STYLE)

Procedure 1: Direct students to use the tones D, E, and F#.

Procedure 2: Teach everyone an 8-beat riff (melodic ostinato).
(Note: Riffs may be improvised and taught to the class by the teacher or by students.)

Riff 1 in a swinging style
(Example of the use of subdivision as an expressive element)

Riff 2 in a swinging style
(Example of the use of sound and silence as an expressive element)

Procedure 3: Direct students to "Repeat the riff until the music ends."
(Note: For an interesting effect, perform Riff 1 and Riff 2 simultaneously.)

Procedure 4: When individual students are chosen or volunteer, suggest that they:

A. "Play the riff,"

B. "Improvise a rhythmic variation on the riff employing musical dynamics, or"

C. "Improvise a rhythmic/melodic variation on the riff employing musical dynamics."

MORE OPTIONS FOR SPONTANEOUS AND CREATIVE MUSIC MAKING

Option 1: Ask for student volunteers to improvise their own riffs.

Direct the class to replicate student riffs or to improvise rhythmic/melodic variations.

Option 2: Encourage students to notate their improvised riffs.
(Refer to page 41-1 for Principles of Music Notation)

LULLABY — *A cradle song, usually sung by a mother to soothe or quiet an infant before bedtime.*

WALTZ — *A 19th century dance in triple meter.*

4 **Waltz Variation Two**

Accom. #82 Tch's Ed CD-1

4 **Waltz Variation Three**

Accom. #82 Tch's Ed CD-1

BRANLE — *A popular French dance of the 16th century in which all of the motions of the lead couple are imitated.*

6 **Champaigne Branle**

Lively

16th century French Dance Tune
Claude Gervaise

Violin. #83 Tch's Ed CD-1

Cello. #84 Tch's Ed CD-1

Accom. #85 Tch's Ed CD-1

BLANK PAGE

TONALITY — *A characteristic of Western music, referring to the relationship of pitches to a specific tonal center. If DO is the tonal center, the tonality is Major; if LA is the tonal center, the tonality is Minor.*

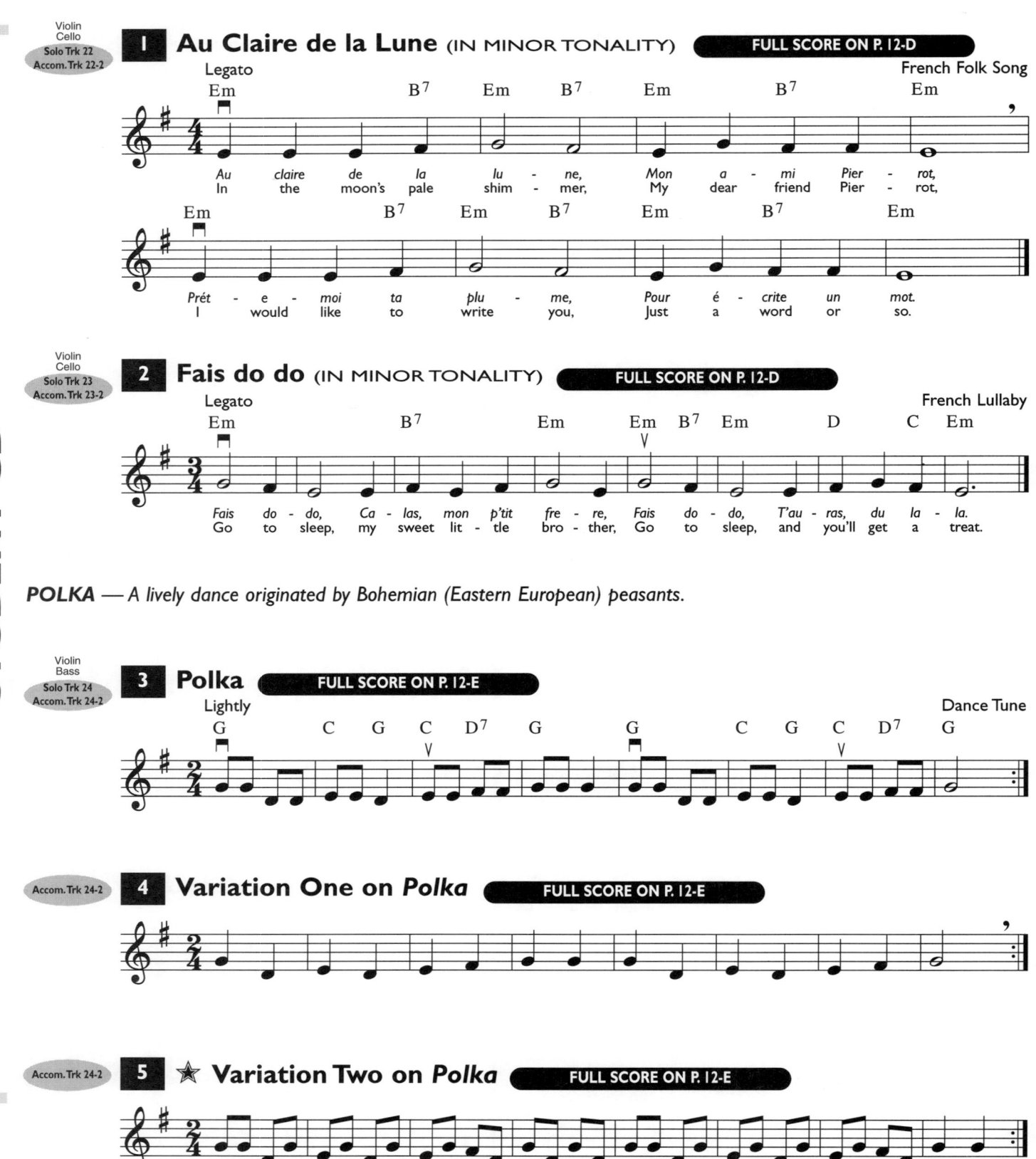

*Forget the meaning of something? **You Can Look It Up** in the **Music Terms Dictionary** on pages 42, 43, 44, and 45.*

Rhythmic Flashcard Reading Option for *Polka,* **Variation One on** *Polka,* **and** *Variation Two on Polka*

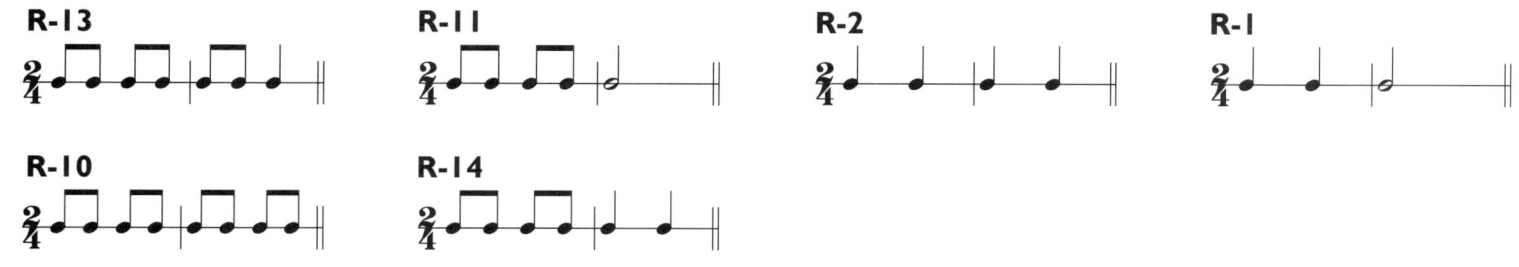

R-13 R-11 R-2 R-1

R-10 R-14

SPECIAL OPTIONS FOR AURAL AND TECHNICAL DEVELOPMENT

PERFORM FAMILIAR MUSIC IN OTHER KEYS, IN OTHER POSITIONS "BY EAR"

AU CLAIRE DE LA LUNE and FAIS DO DO (IN MINOR TONALITY)

APPLY FAMILIAR MELODIC AND RHYTHMIC PATTERNS AS WE EXPLORE THE FINGERBOARD "BY EAR"

PRINCIPLE #1: *Keep it Simple.*

Procedure 1 (Violin, Viola, Cello). Transpose to a new key. Direct students to "Play the melody on a different starting note."

Procedure 1 (Bass). Introduce the 2nd finger "by ear." Direct students to "Begin on an open string and use 1st and 2nd finger to play the melody."

Procedure 1a (Bass). Shift and transpose on a single string. Direct students to "Begin on a first or fourth finger, and shift on one string to play the melody."

Procedure 2 (All instruments). Find the same notes in a different octave or position. Direct students to "Find another place on your instrument where the melody sounds the same."

Accom.
#92
Tch's Ed CD-1

Au Claire de la Lune (IN G MINOR "BY EAR" - STARTING ON G)
EXAMPLE:

Fais do do (IN G MINOR "BY EAR" - STARTING ON B♭)

EXAMPLE:

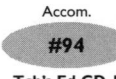

Au Claire de la Lune (IN A MINOR "BY EAR" - STARTING ON A)

EXAMPLE:

Fais do do (IN A MINOR "BY EAR" - STARTING ON C)

EXAMPLE:

Accom.
#96
Tch's Ed CD-1

Au Claire de la Lune (IN D MINOR "BY EAR" - STARTING ON D)
EXAMPLE:

Accom.
#97
Tch's Ed CD-1

Fais do do (IN D MINOR "BY EAR" - STARTING ON F)
EXAMPLE:

ADDITIONAL OPTION FOR TECHNICAL DEVELOPMENT

- In D minor and A minor, introduce low 2nd finger for violin and viola, 2nd finger for cello
- In E minor, introduce low 2nd finger on the E string for violin

TONALITY — *A characteristic of Western music, referring to the relationship of pitches to a specific tonal center. If DO is the tonal center, the tonality is Major; if LA is the tonal center, the tonality is Minor.*

Violin
#86
Tch's Ed CD-1

Cello
#87
Tch's Ed CD-1

Accom.
#88
Tch's Ed CD-1

1 Au Claire de la Lune (IN MINOR TONALITY)

Legato

French Folk Song

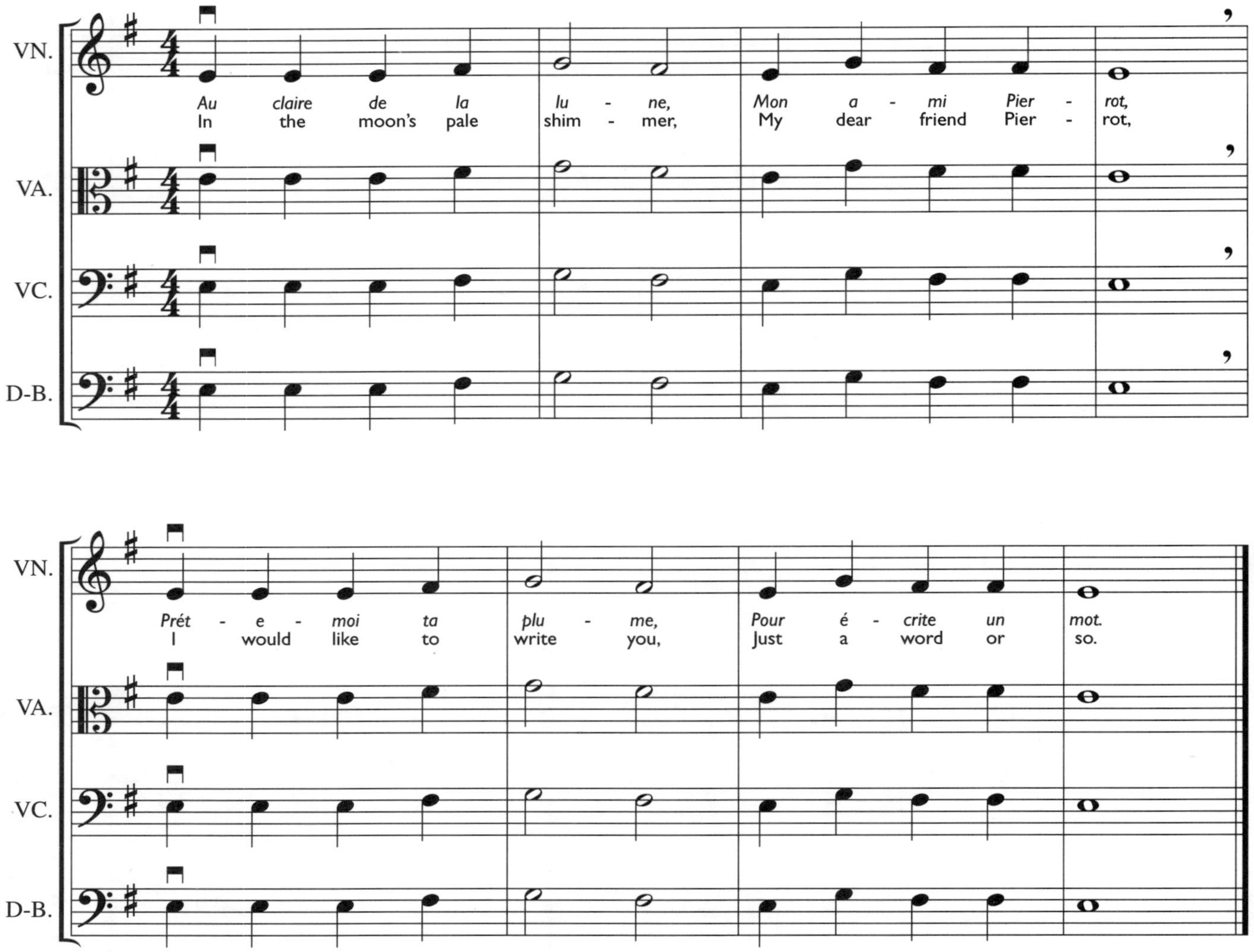

Violin
#89
Tch's Ed CD-1

Cello
#90
Tch's Ed CD-1

Accom.
#91
Tch's Ed CD-1

2 Fais do do (IN MINOR TONALITY)

Legato

French Lullaby

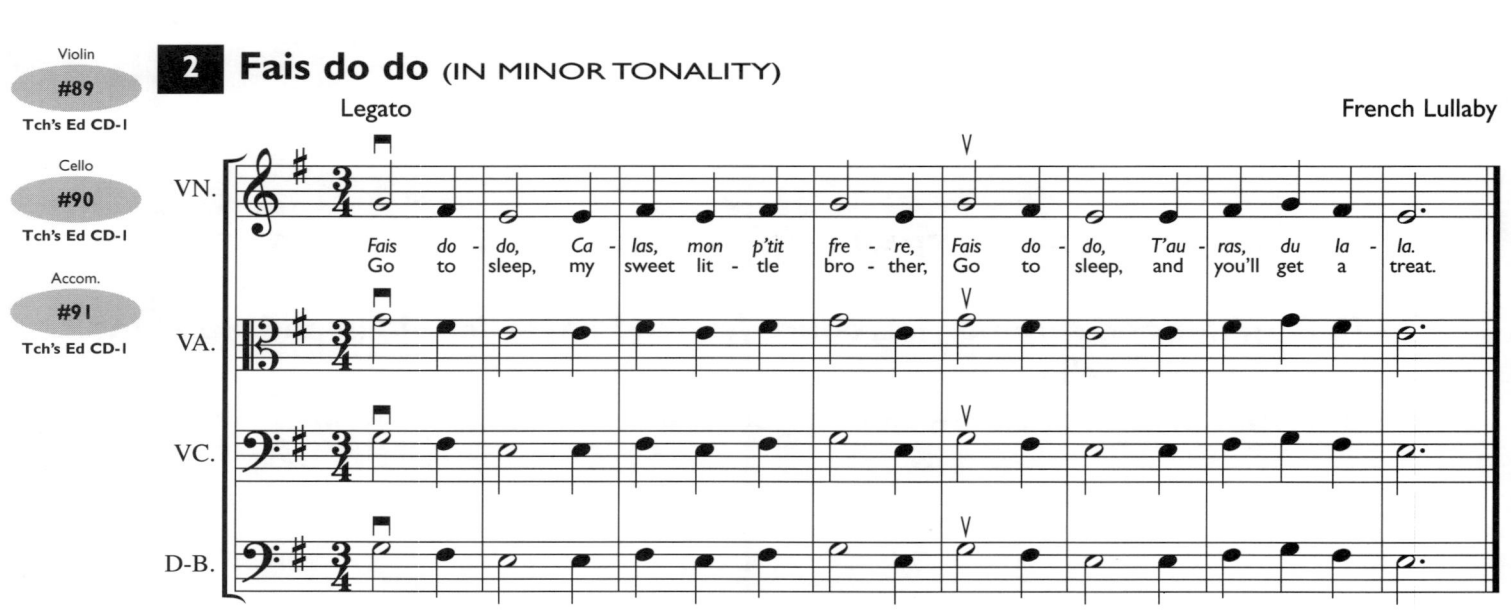

POLKA — *A lively dance originated by Bohemian (Eastern European) peasants.*

3 **Polka**

Lightly   Dance Tune

4 **Variation One on *Polka***

5 ☆ **Variation Two on *Polka***

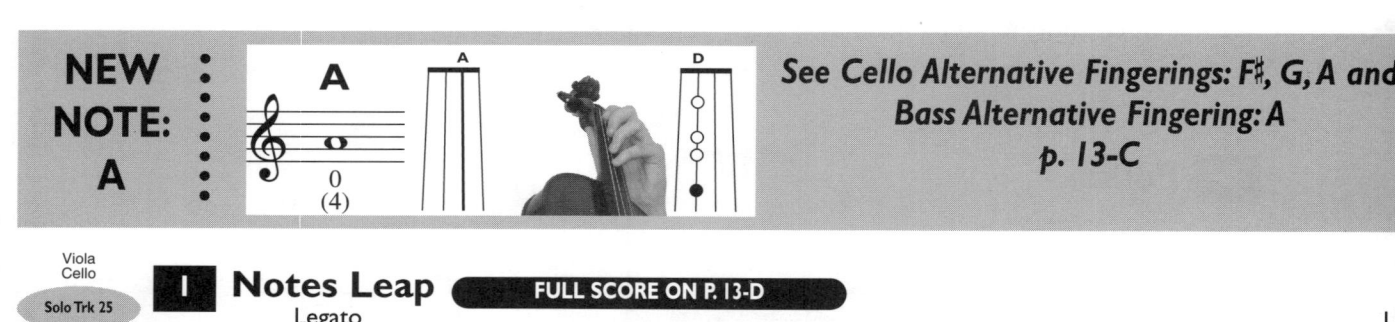

NEW NOTE: A

See Cello Alternative Fingerings: F♯, G, A and
Bass Alternative Fingering: A
p. 13-C

Viola
Cello
Solo Trk 25

SPEAKER BALANCE
CD Trk 5
Accom.

1 Notes Leap   **FULL SCORE ON P. 13-D**

Legato

D A⁷ D   D A⁷ D   D   A⁷ D

Notes leap up, notes leap down, notes are found all o - ver town.

CD Trk 26
Violin
Bass   Accom.

2 Hush My Baby   **FULL SCORE ON P. 13-D**

Legato   Tradition

D Em F♯m   D Em F♯m   D Em F♯m   F♯m Em D

Hush my ba - by, Hush my ba - by, Hush my ba - by, don't you cry.

BALLAD — *A short, simple song in narrative or descriptive form, sometimes set to a romantic or historical poem.*

CD Trk 27
Violin
Cello   Accom.

3 Cowboy Ballad   **FULL SCORE ON P. 13-D**

D Em⁷ D Em⁷ D Em⁷ F♯m   D Em⁷ D Em⁷ D Em⁷ D

Cow - boy, cow - boy rid - ing West, Clip - clop, clip - clop, need to rest.
Git - up, git - up, move a - long. Hear me sing my sad old song.

MARCH — *Music for a procession or a parade.*

CD Trk 28
Violin
Cello   Accom.

4 Practice Every Day March   **FULL SCORE ON P. 13-E**

D   A⁷   D   D   A⁷ D A⁷   D

Prac - tice eve - ry day. If you do you'll learn to play.

HYMN — *A song of worship.*

CD Trk 29
Viola
Cello   Accom.

5 Vesper Hymn   **FULL SCORE ON P. 13-E**

Legato   Russian Folk Tun
Text by Thomas Moor

D   A⁷   D   A⁷   D   A⁷   D A⁷ D

Hark! The Ves - per Hymn is steal - ing o'er the wa - ters soft and clear.

D   A⁷   D   A⁷   D   A⁷   D A⁷ D

Near - er yet and near - er peal - ing. Soft it breaks up - on the ear.

Rhythmic Flashcard Reading Option for *Notes Leap, Hush My Baby, Cowboy Ballad, and Practice Every Day March*

R-1   **R-2**   **R-19**

Rhythmic Flashcard Reading Option for *Vesper Hymn*

R-3   **R-4**

Melodic Ear-to-Hand Training and Assessment for *Notes Leap, Hush My Baby, Cowboy Ballad, and Practice Every Day March.*

TEXT: "Listen and Play What You Hear. The Starting Tone is D."

Recorded Intro

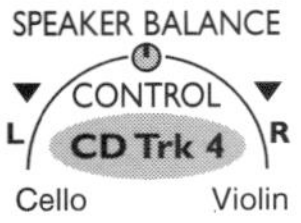

SPEAKER BALANCE
CONTROL
L   R
CD Trk 4
Cello   Violin

Recorded Call   Student Response

VN.

VA.

VC.

D-B.

SPECIAL PROJECTS FOR EXTENDING TECHNIQUE

- Violin and Viola: Use the 4th finger instead of the open A string
- Cello: Use the 4th finger (2nd position) instead of the open A string

REMINDERS FOR ALL INSTRUMENTS

- Leave the left hand fingers down forming a "tunnel" while you bow the higher string
- Make the string change part of a large smooth curve in the right hand

RHYTHMIC SUBDIVISION - AN EXPRESSIVE ELEMENT FOR MUSIC IMPROVISATION

Extended Accom.
#57
Tch's Ed CD-1

Down By the Station (JAZZ STYLE)

Procedure 1: Direct students to use the tones D, E, F♯, G and A.

Procedure 2: Teach everyone an 8-beat riff (melodic ostinato).
(Note: Riffs may be improvised and taught to the class by the teacher or by students.)

Riff 1 in a swinging style
(Example of the use of subdivision as an expressive element)

Riff 2 in a swinging style
(Example of the use of sound and silence as an expressive element)

Procedure 3: Direct students to "Continue the riff until the music ends."
(Note: For an interesting effect, perform Riff 1 and Riff 2 simultaneously.)

Procedure 4: When individual students are chosen or volunteer, suggest that they:

A. "Play the riff,"

B. "Improvise a rhythmic variation on the riff employing musical dynamics, or"

C. "Improvise a rhythmic/melodic variation on the riff employing rhythmic subdivision."

MORE OPTIONS FORSPONTANEOUS AND CREATIVE MUSIC MAKING

Option 1: Ask for student volunteers to improvise their own riffs.

Direct the class to replicate student riffs or to improvise rhythmic/melodic variations.

Option 2: Encourage students to notate their improvised riffs.
(Refer to page 41-1 for Principles of Music Notation)

NEW NOTE

ALTERNATIVE FINGERINGS

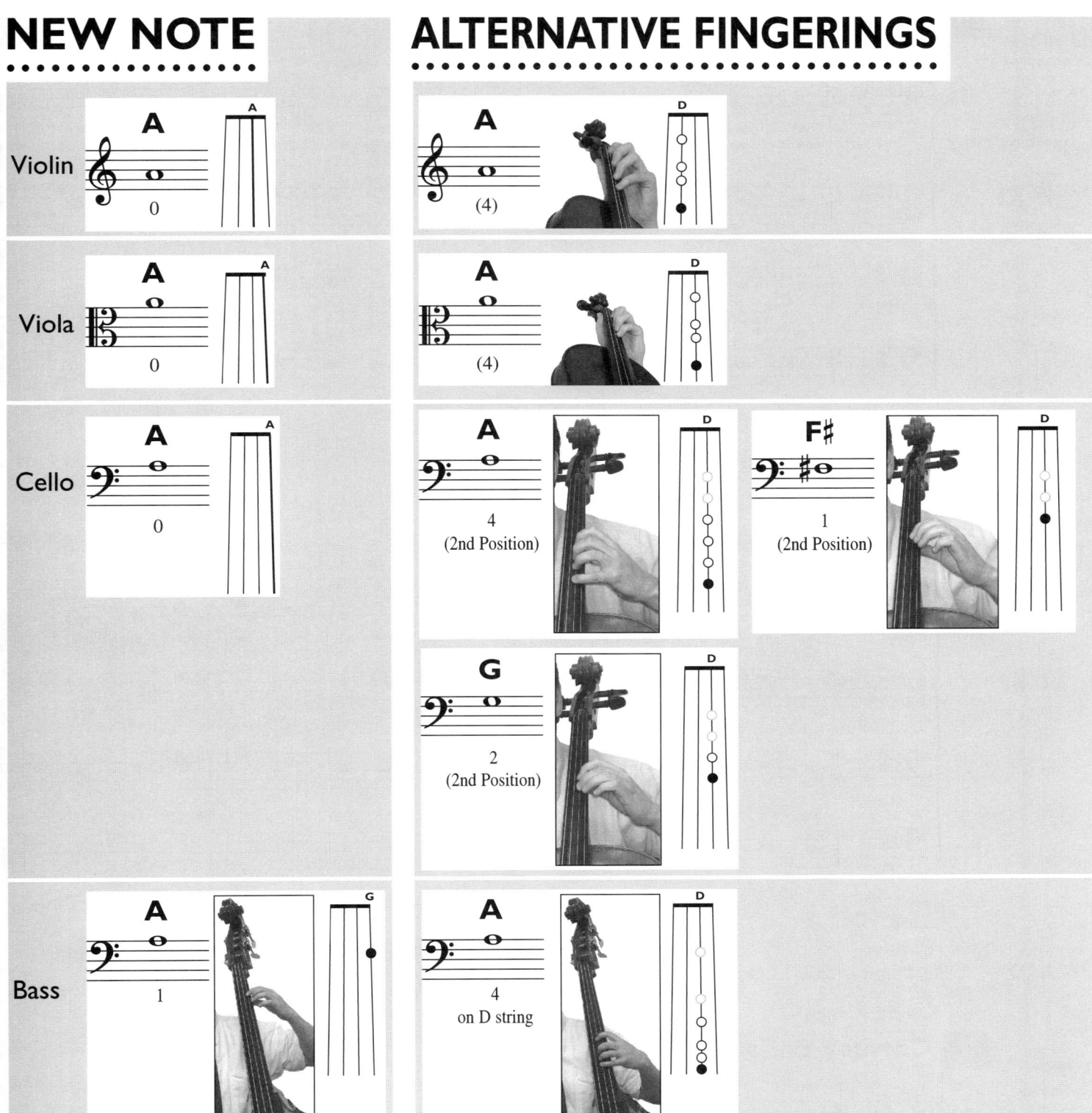

Viola
#5
Tch's Ed CD-2

Cello
#6
Tch's Ed CD-2

Accom.
#7
Tch's Ed CD-2

1 Notes Leap

U.S.

Notes leap up, notes leap down, notes are found all o - ver town.

Violin
#8
Tch's Ed CD-2

Bass
#9
Tch's Ed CD-2

Accom.
#10
Tch's Ed CD-2

2 Hush My Baby

Traditional

Hush my ba - by, Hush my ba - by, Hush my ba - by, don't you cry.

BALLAD — *A short, simple song in narrative or descriptive form, sometimes set to a romantic or historical poem.*

Violin
#11
Tch's Ed CD-2

Cello
#12
Tch's Ed CD-2

Accom.
#13
Tch's Ed CD-2

3 Cowboy Ballad

U.S.

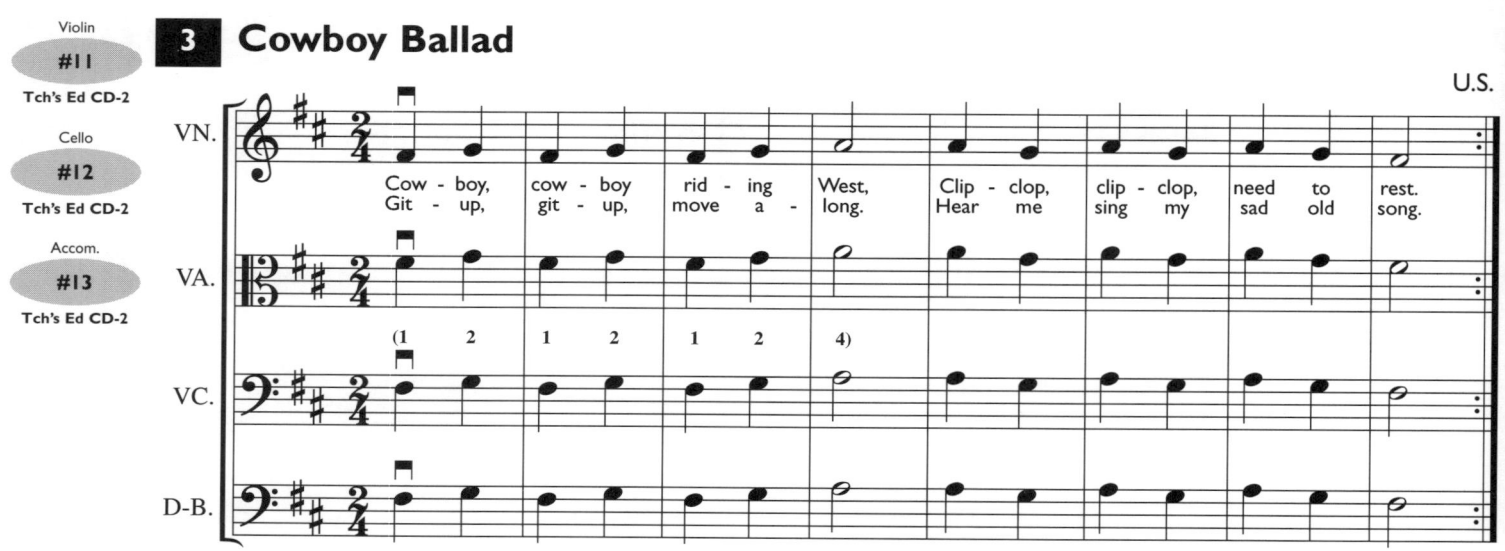

Cow - boy, cow - boy, rid - ing West, Clip - clop, clip - clop, need to rest.
Git - up, git - up, move a - long. Hear me sing my sad old song.

MARCH — *Music for a procession or a parade.*

4 **Practice Every Day March**

U.S.

Violin
#14
Tch's Ed CD-2

Cello
#15
Tch's Ed CD-2

Accom.
#16
Tch's Ed CD-2

VN.

Prac - tice eve - ry day. If you do you'll learn to play.

VA.

VC.

(1   2   4)

D-B.

HYMN — *A song of worship.*

5 **Vesper Hymn**

Viola
#17
Tch's Ed CD-2

Cello
#18
Tch's Ed CD-2

Accom.
#19
Tch's Ed CD-2

Russian Folk Tune
Text by Thomas Moore

Legato

VN.

Hark! The Ves - per Hymn is steal - ing o'er the wa - ters soft and clear.

VA.

VC.

D-B.

VN.

Near - er yet and near - er peal - ing. Soft it breaks up - on the ear.

VA.

VC.

D-B.

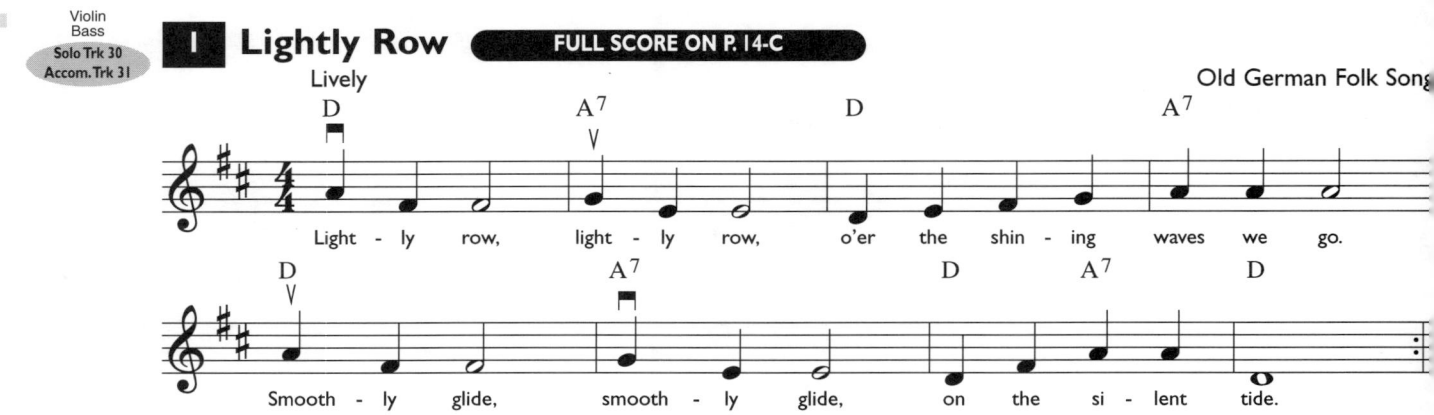

1   Lightly Row   FULL SCORE ON P. 14-C

Violin
Bass
Solo Trk 30
Accom. Trk 31

Lively

Old German Folk Song

Light - ly row, light - ly row, o'er the shin - ing waves we go.

Smooth - ly glide, smooth - ly glide, on the si - lent tide.

COUNTRY SWING — *A blend of Western, bluegrass, and swing styles originating in Texas during the 1940s.*

Violin
Cello
Solo Trk 32
Accom. Trk 32-2

2   ★ SOLO Lightly Row (COUNTRY SWING STYLE - "BY EAR" STARTING ON D)

Viola
Cello
Solo Trk 33
Accom. Trk 33-2

3   ★★ SOLO Lightly Row (QUICK TIME)   FULL SCORE ON P. 14-C

Light - ly row, light - ly row, o'er the shin - ing waves we go.

Smooth - ly glide, smooth - ly glide, on the si - lent tide.

DIXIELAND JAZZ — *An early style of African-American jazz music originating in New Orleans.*

AURAL TRANSCRIPTION — *Learning to play recorded music "by ear" without the aid of music notation. Also, the transfer of music heard to music notation.*

SPECIAL PROJECT — **Learn to Play a Song "By Ear"**

Violin
Cello
Solo Trk 34
Accom. Trk 35

4   ★★★ SOLO — **Play *Oh When the Saints Go Marching In*** (STARTING ON D)

FULL SCORE ON P. 14-D

LISTEN AND PLAY — *A procedure requiring musical discrimination and memorization skills to perceive and accurately replicate a musical model.*

LISTEN AND
PLAY
Trk 36
Trk 36-2
Trk 36-3

5   Rain, Rain (FIRST LISTEN, THEN PLAY)   FULL SCORE ON P. 14-E

Expressively

Traditional

Play only on repeat

Rain, Rain, go a - way, come a - gain some oth - er day.

LISTEN AND
IMPROVISE
Trk 36
Trk 36-2
Trk 36-3

6   ★ SOLO — **Listen and Improvise Variations on *Rain, Rain* "By Ear"**

Use the tones D, E, G, and A:

Rhythmic Flashcard Reading Option for *Lightly Row* **and** *Lightly Row (Quick Time)*

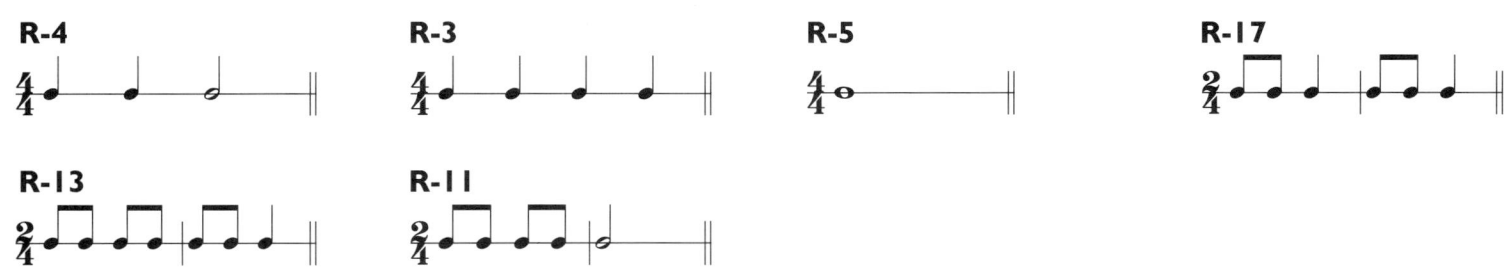

R-4   R-3   R-5   R-17

R-13   R-11

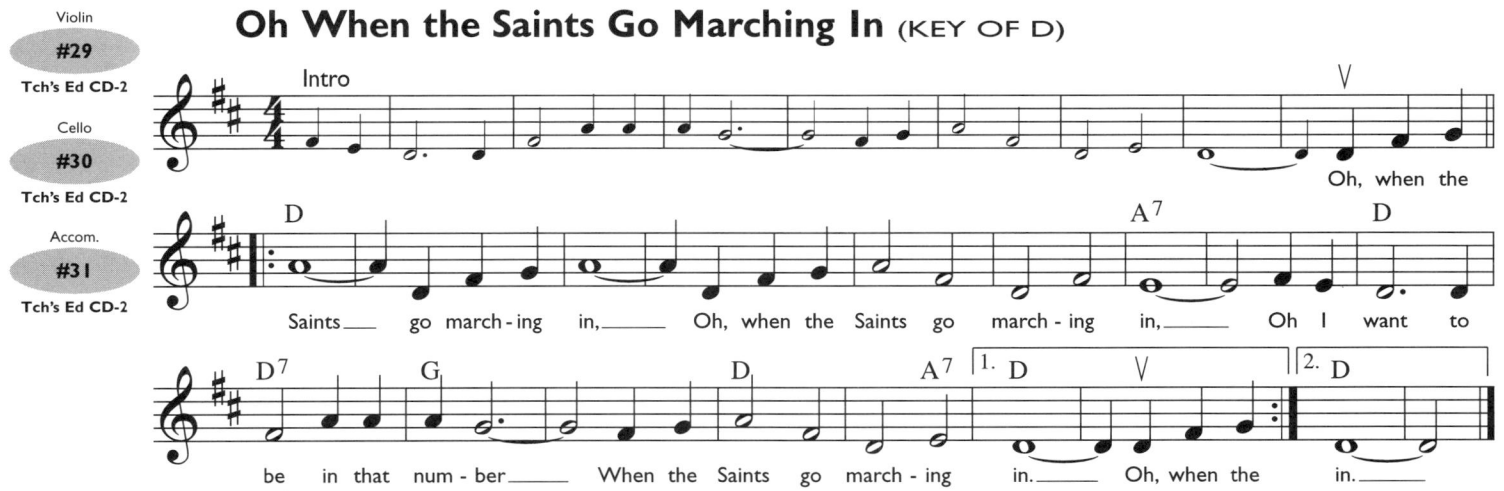

Oh When the Saints Go Marching In (KEY OF D)

Violin
#29
Tch's Ed CD-2

Cello
#30
Tch's Ed CD-2

Accom.
#31
Tch's Ed CD-2

Intro

D

Saints___ go march-ing in,___ Oh, when the Saints go march-ing in,___ Oh I want to

D⁷   G   D   A⁷   1. D   2. D

be in that num-ber___ When the Saints go march-ing in.___ Oh, when the in.___

Rhythmic Flashcard Reading Option for *Rain, Rain*

R-20 *NEW*   R-13

#32 Violin
#32-2 Viola
#32-3 Viola
#32
Tch's Ed CD-2

#33 Cello
#33-2 Bass
#33-3 Cello
#33
Tch's Ed CD-2

A SPECIAL OPTION FOR SPONTANEOUS MUSIC MAKING

LISTEN AND IMPROVISE MELODIC VARIATIONS

RAIN, RAIN

PRINCIPLE #1: *Keep it Simple (Too many options can inhibit creativity).*

> **Procedure 1.** Direct students to "Use only the tones E, D, (E), G, and A."

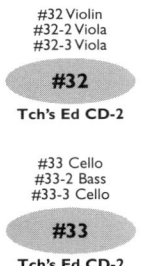

PRINCIPLE #2: *Keep Everyone Involved (Peer observation can be intimidating).*

> **Procedure 2a.** Direct students to "Use the same rhythm patterns, but different pitches to *Rain, Rain*."

> **Procedure 2b.** Direct students to "Listen to the model, and either echo or improvise a response."

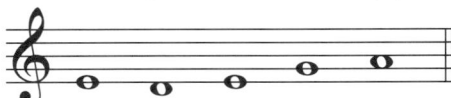

Example: Student Response (Improvised)

STRUCTURAL ELEMENTS OF MUSIC IMPROVISATION AND COMPOSITION

1. REPETITION

(Repetition creates structure and predictability.)

2. VARIATION

(Variation generates interest.)

RAIN, RAIN

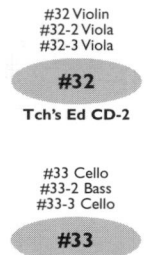

#32 Violin
#32-2 Viola
#32-3 Viola

#32

Tch's Ed CD-2

#33 Cello
#33-2 Bass
#33-3 Cello

#33

Tch's Ed CD-2

Procedure. Direct students to "Use only the tones G, E, D, (E), (G), and A to improvise and compose.*"

* See page 41-1 for Principles of Music Notation

THE TUNE

| Basic | Melodic Repetition | Melodic Variation | Melodic Repetition |
| Pattern | Rhythmic Variation | Rhythmic Variation | Rhythmic Repetition |

VARIATION 1

| Basic | Melodic Variation | Melodic Variation | Melodic Variation |
| Pattern | Rhythmic Repetition | Rhythmic Variation | Rhythmic Repetition |

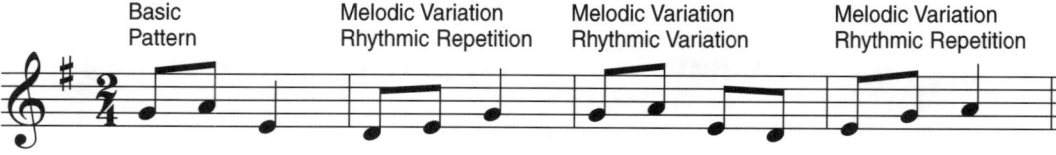

VARIATION 2

| Basic | Melodic Repetition | Melodic Variation | Melodic Repetition |
| Pattern | Rhythmic Repetition | Rhythmic Repetition | Rhythmic Variation |

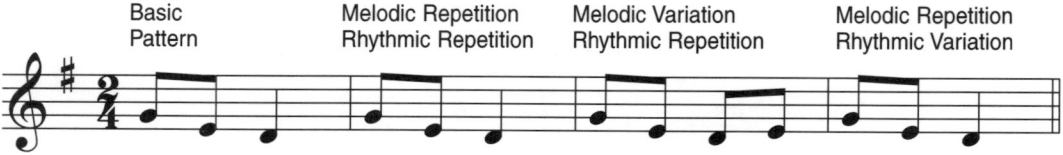

VARIATION 3

| Basic | Melodic Repetition | Melodic Repetition | Melodic Variation |
| Pattern | Rhythmic Repetition | Rhythmic Repetition | Rhythmic Variation |

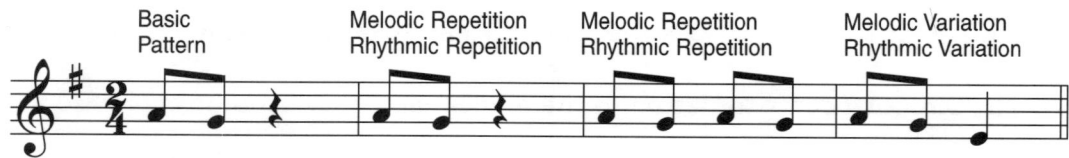

1 **Lightly Row**

Lively

Old German Folk Song

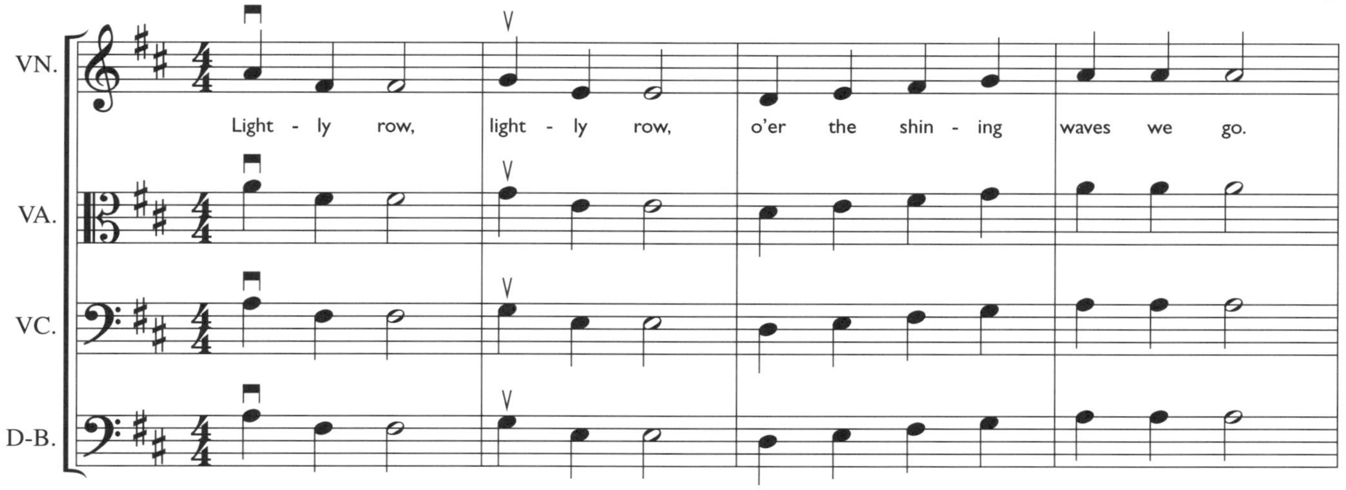

Violin
#20
Tch's Ed CD-2

Bass
#21
Tch's Ed CD-2

Accom.
#22
Tch's Ed CD-2

VN.

Light - ly row, light - ly row, o'er the shin - ing waves we go.

VA.

VC.

D-B.

VN.

Smooth - ly glide, smooth - ly glide, on the si - lent tide.

VA.

VC.

D-B.

COUNTRY SWING — *A blend of Western, bluegrass, and swing styles originating in Texas during the 1940s.*

Violin
#23
Tch's Ed CD-2

Cello
#24
Tch's Ed CD-2

Accom.
#25
Tch's Ed CD-2

2 ★ SOLO **Lightly Row** (COUNTRY SWING STYLE - "BY EAR" STARTING ON D)

Viola
#26
Tch's Ed CD-2

Cello
#27
Tch's Ed CD-2

Accom.
#28
Tch's Ed CD-2

3 ★★ SOLO **Lightly Row** (QUICK TIME)

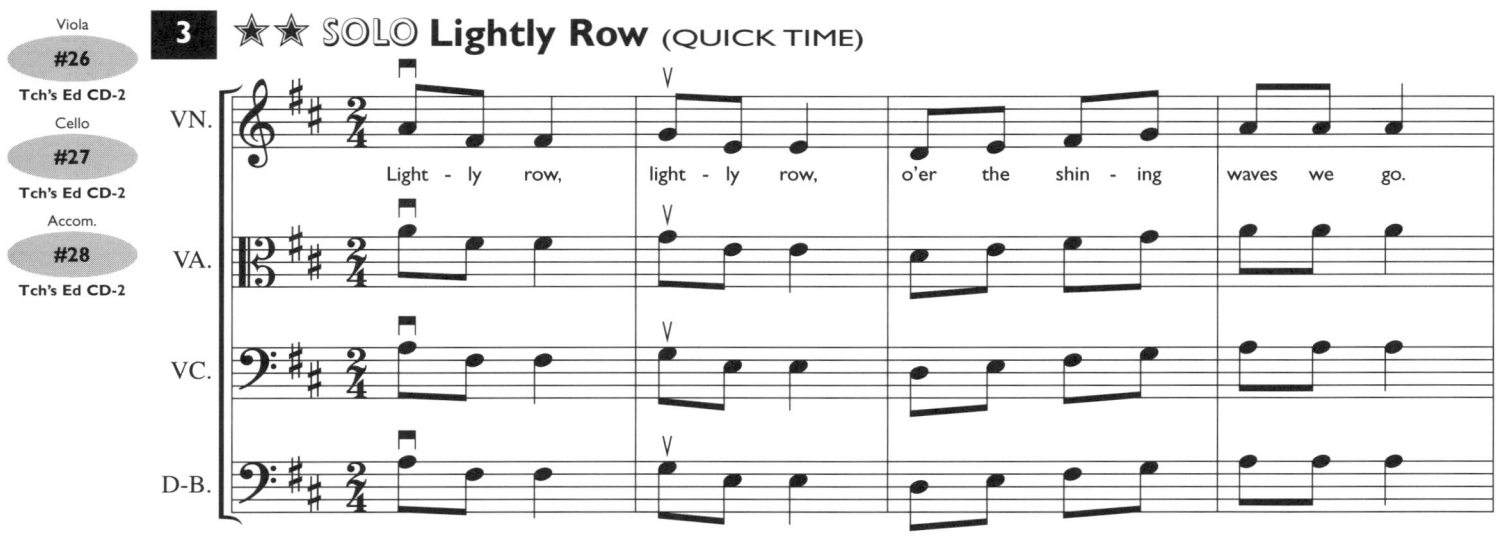

VN.

Light - ly row, light - ly row, o'er the shin - ing waves we go.

VA.

VC.

D-B.

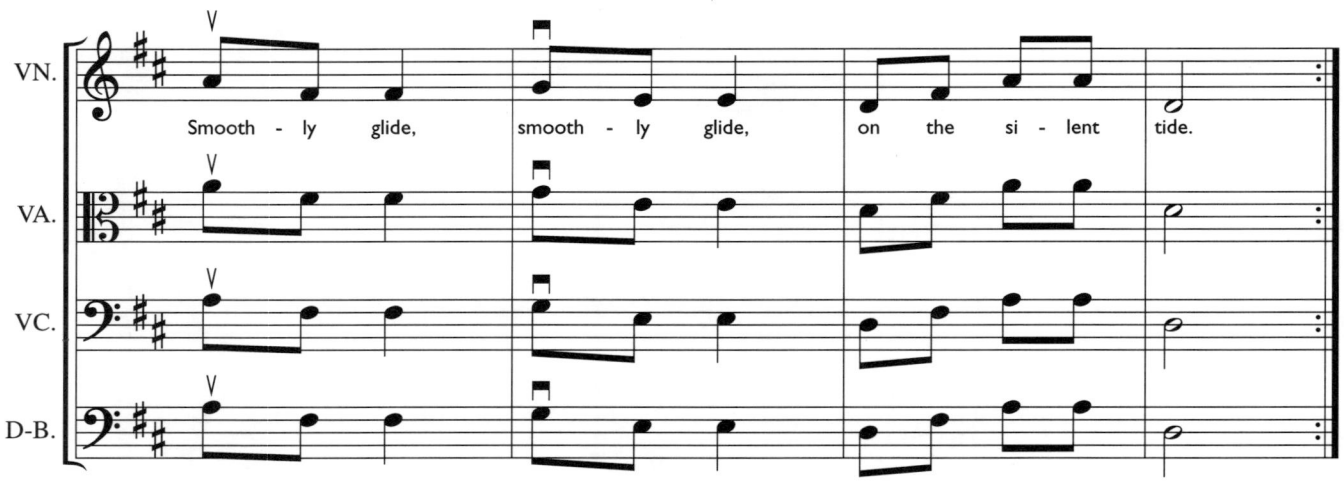

VN.
VA.
VC.
D-B.
Smooth - ly glide, smooth - ly glide, on the si - lent tide.

DIXIELAND JAZZ *— An early style of African-American jazz music originating in New Orleans.*

AURAL TRANSCRIPTION *— Learning to play recorded music "by ear" without the aid of music notation. Also, the transfer of music heard to music notation.*

SPECIAL PROJECT — Learn to Play a Song "By Ear"

Violin
#29
Tch's Ed CD-2

Cello
#30
Tch's Ed CD-2

Accom.
#31
Tch's Ed CD-2

4 ★★★ SOLO — Play *Oh When the Saints Go Marching In* (STARTING ON D)

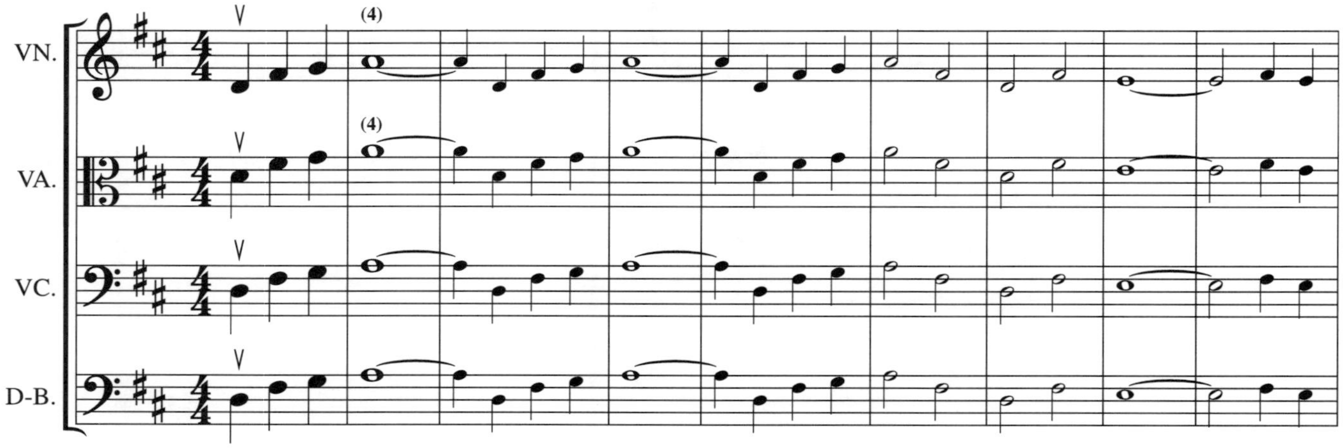
VN.
VA.
VC.
D-B.
(4)
(4)

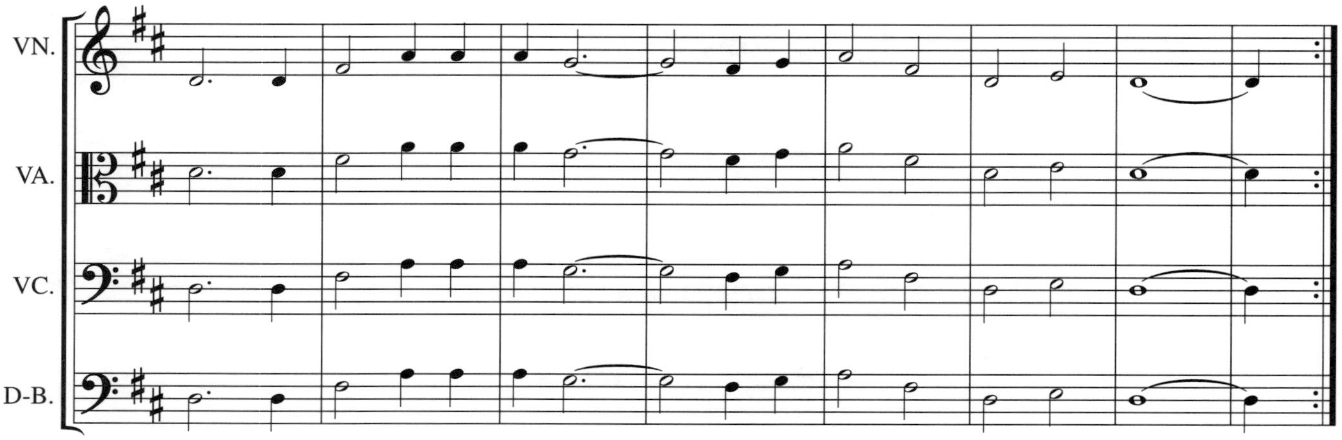
VN.
VA.
VC.
D-B.

LISTEN AND PLAY — *A procedure requiring musical discrimination and memorization skills to perceive and accurately replicate a musical model.*

#32 Violin
#32-2 Viola
#32-3 Viola

#32

Tch's Ed CD-2

#33 Cello
#33-2 Bass
#33-3 Cello

#33

Tch's Ed CD-2

5 **Rain, Rain** (FIRST LISTEN, THEN PLAY)

Expressively

Traditional

Rain, Rain, go a-way, come a-gain some oth-er day.

6 ★ SOLO — **Listen and Improvise Variations on *Rain, Rain* "By Ear"**

Use the tones D, E, G, and A:

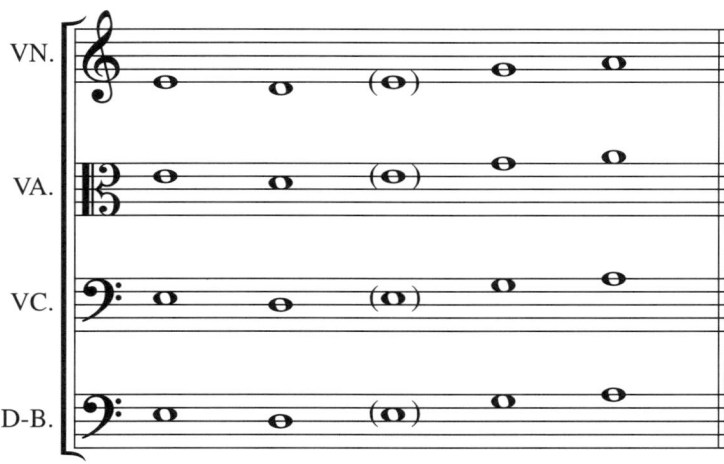

NEW NOTE: B

B
1
A

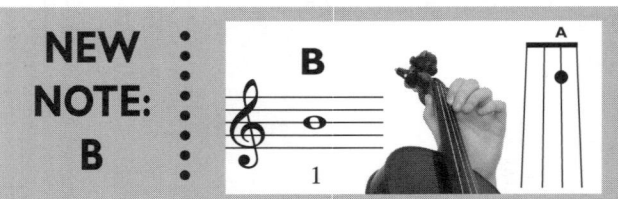

See Bass Alternative Fingerings: A, B p. 15-A

D.C. AL FINE — *An abbreviation for* Da Capo al Fine *which means go back to the beginning and end at the* Fine.

STUDENT CD

Violin Cello Solo Trk 37 Accom. Trk 39

Viola Bass Solo Trk 38 Accom. Trk 39

1 Twinkle, Twinkle, Little Star

FULL SCORE ON P. 15-A

French Folk Tune
Text by Jane and Ann Taylor (1806)

Smoothly

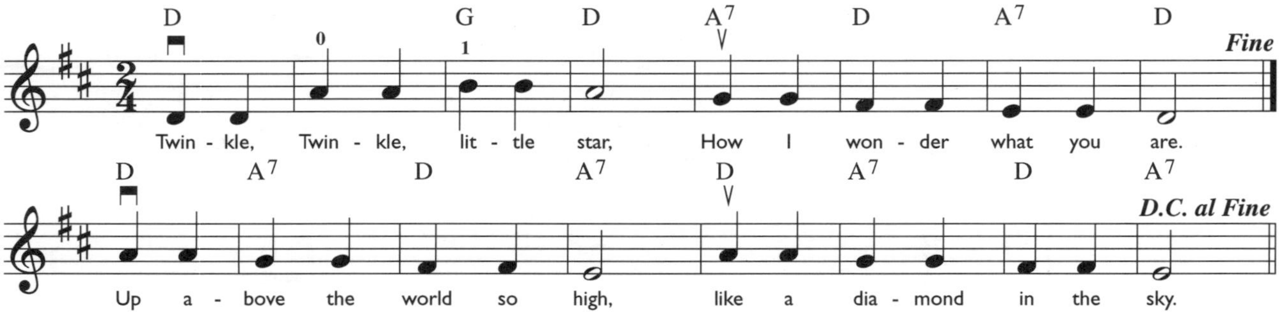
D G D A7 D A7 D
0
1
Fine
Twin - kle, Twin - kle, lit - tle star, How I won - der what you are.
D A7 D A7 D A7 D A7
D.C. al Fine
Up a - bove the world so high, like a dia - mond in the sky.

Violin Cello Solo Trk 37

Viola Bass Solo Trk 38

2 Harmony Part One to *Twinkle, Twinkle, Little Star*

Softly and smoothly

FULL SCORE ON P. 15-B

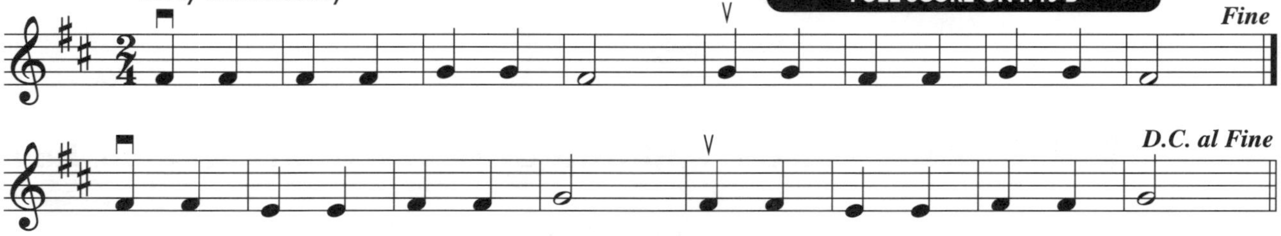
Fine
D.C. al Fine

Violin Cello Solo Trk 37

Viola Bass Solo Trk 38

3 Harmony Part Two to *Twinkle, Twinkle, Little Star*

Softly and smoothly

FULL SCORE ON P. 15-C

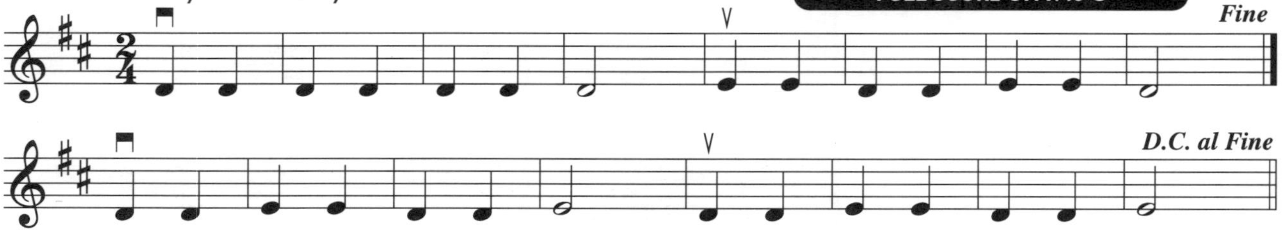
Fine
D.C. al Fine

SWING STYLE — *A type of Big Band jazz of the late 1930s and 1940s.*

Violin Cello Solo Trk 40 Accom. Trk 41

4 ★★ SOLO — Twinkle, Twinkle, Little Star (SWING STYLE - "BY EAR" STARTING ON D)

5 We Are Met (4 PART ROUND)

FULL SCORE ON P. 15-C

Expressively

Samuel Webbe (c. 1680)

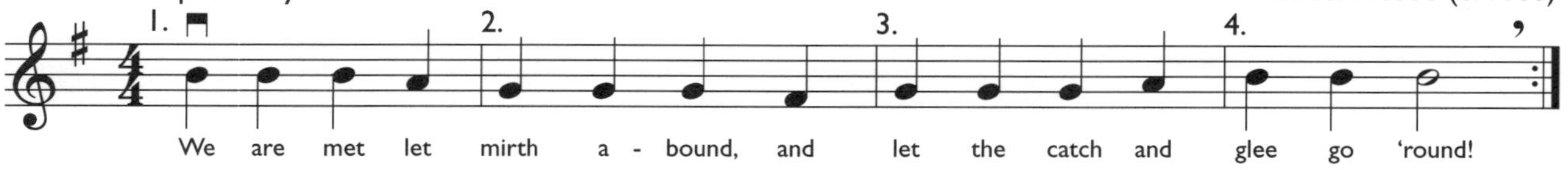
1.
2.
3.
4.
We are met let mirth a - bound, and let the catch and glee go 'round!

NEW NOTE

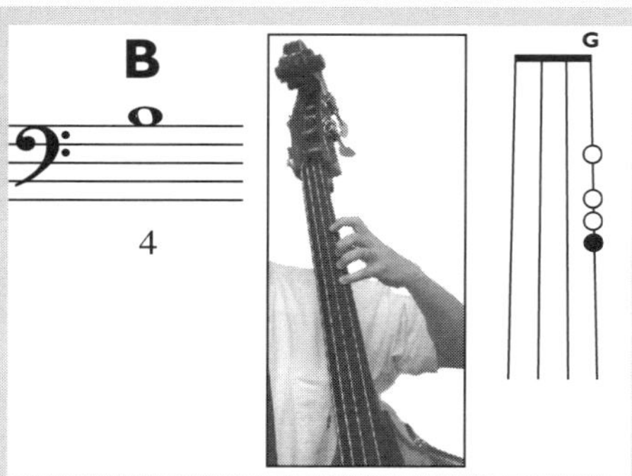

ALTERNATIVE FINGERINGS

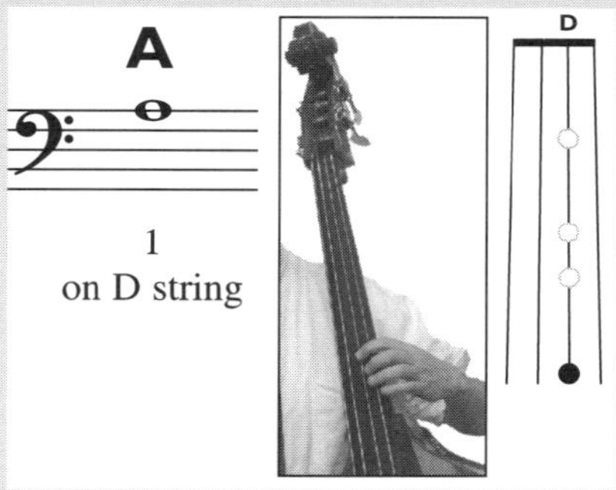

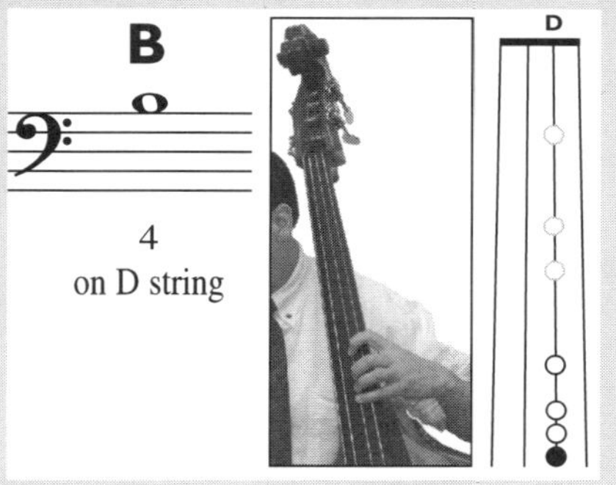

Violin	 B (1)	
Viola	 B (1)	
Cello	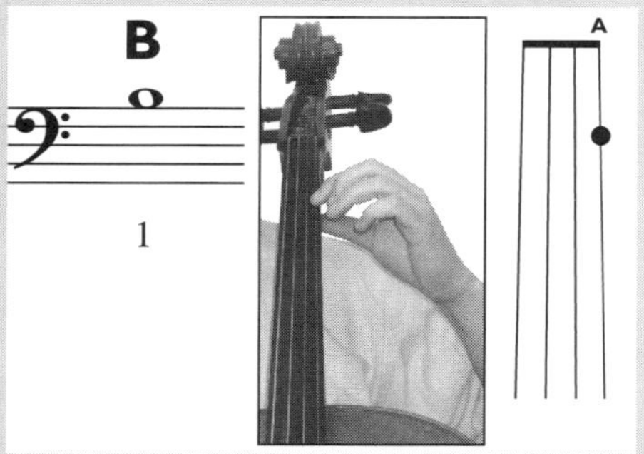 B (1)	
Bass	B (4)	A (1 on D string) — B (4 on D string)

D.C. AL FINE — *An abbreviation for* Da Capo al Fine *which means go back to the beginning and end at the* Fine.

1 Twinkle, Twinkle, Little Star

French Folk Tune
Text by Jane and Ann Taylor (1806)

Smoothly

Twin - kle, Twin - kle, lit - tle star, How I won - der what you are.

Violin #34 — Tch's Ed CD-2
Viola #35 — Tch's Ed CD-2
Cello #36 — Tch's Ed CD-2
Bass #37 — Tch's Ed CD-2
Accom. #38 — Tch's Ed CD-2

VN.
VA.
VC.
D-B.

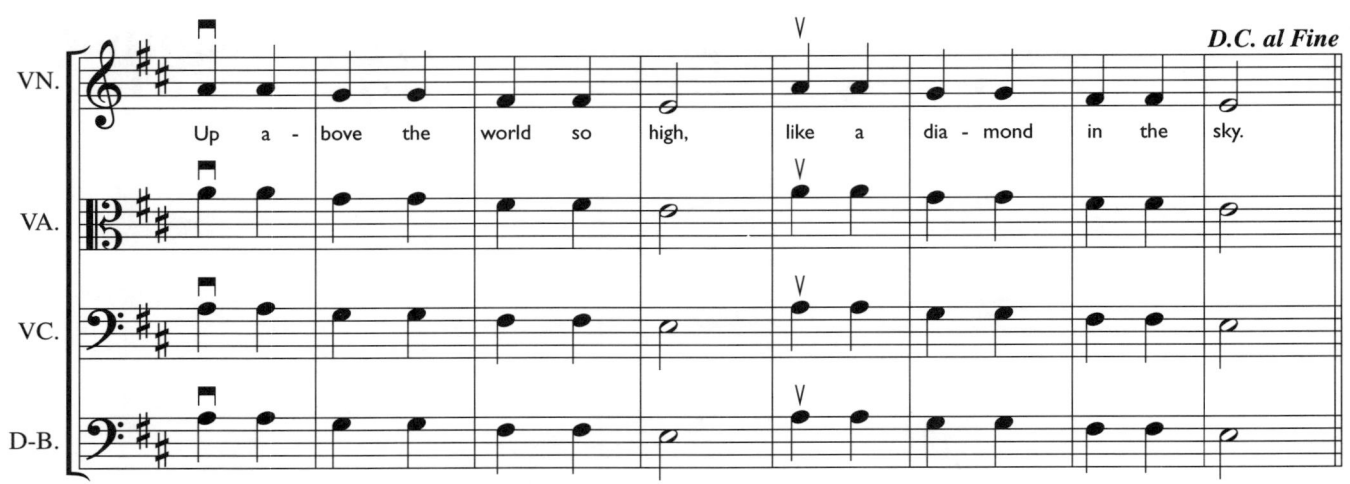

D.C. al Fine

Up a - bove the world so high, like a dia - mond in the sky.

2 **Harmony Part One to** *Twinkle, Twinkle, Little Star*

Accom.
#38
Tch's Ed CD-2

Softly and smoothly

Fine

D.C. al Fine

3 Harmony Part Two to *Twinkle, Twinkle, Little Star*

SWING STYLE — *A type of Big Band jazz of the late 1930s and 1940s.*

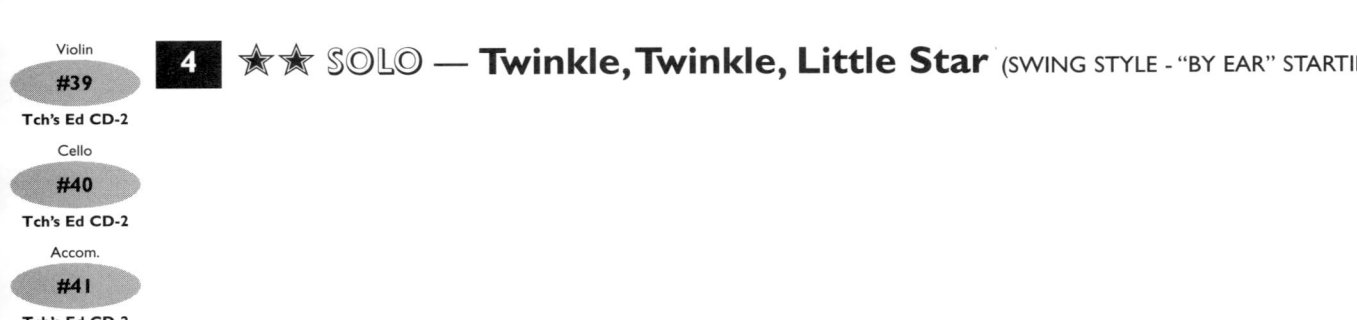

4 ★★ SOLO — **Twinkle, Twinkle, Little Star** (SWING STYLE - "BY EAR" STARTING ON D)

5 **We Are Met** (4 PART ROUND)

Samuel Webbe (c. 1680)

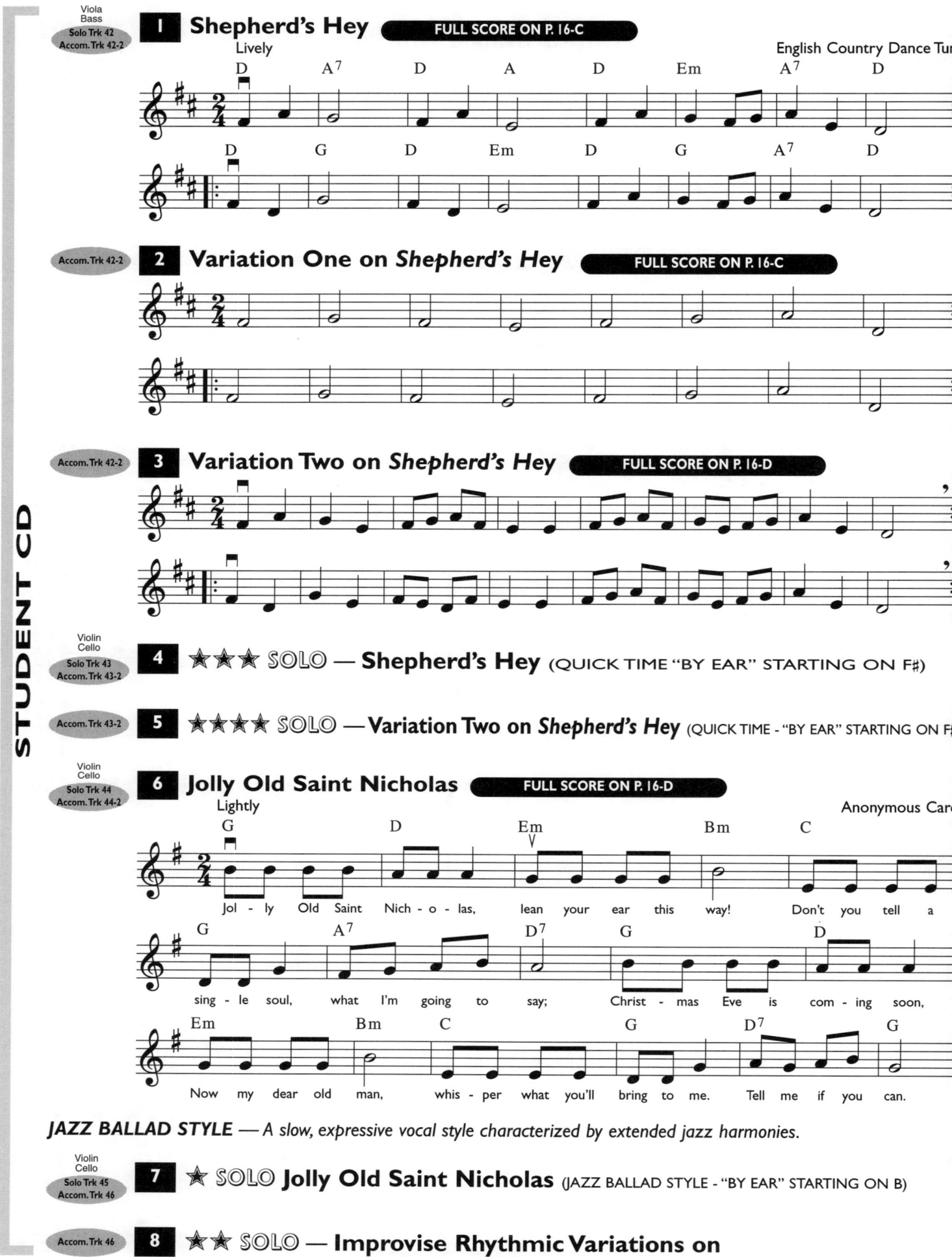

STUDENT CD

JAZZ BALLAD STYLE — A slow, expressive vocal style characterized by extended jazz harmonies.

Rhythmic Flashcard Reading Option for *Shepherd's Hey,* *Variation One,* **and** *Variation Two*

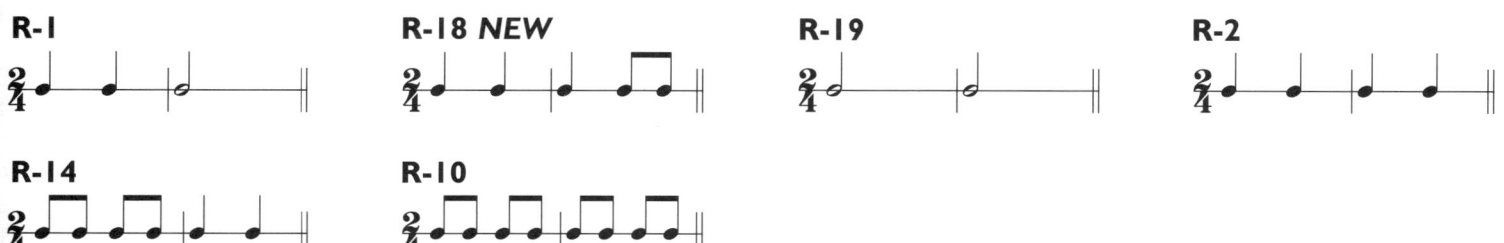

R-1   **R-18** *NEW*   **R-19**   **R-2**

R-14   **R-10**

Rhythmic Flashcard Reading Option for *Jolly Old Saint Nicholas*

R-13   **R-11**

Rhythmic Round

1.   2.   3.   4.

Rhythmic Reading Exercise (SEE PAGE 8-A FOR PROCEDURE)

A SPECIAL OPTION FOR SPONTANEOUS MUSIC MAKING
IMPROVISE RHYTHMIC VARIATIONS (see page 10-A)
JOLLY OLD SAINT NICHOLAS (JAZZ BALLAD STYLE "BY EAR" STARTING ON B)

Accom.
#53

Tch's Ed CD-2

TRACKING THE BLUES IN D

Estended Accom.

#5

Tch's Ed CD-I

or

Estended Accom.

#33

Tch's Ed CD-3

Blues in D "Call and Response" (AS PERFORMED BY THE TEACHER)

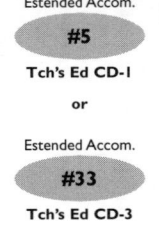

In a swinging style

Intro

TEACHER CALL	STUDENT RESPONSE	TEACHER CALL	STUDENT RESPONSE
D^7	Imitated or Improvised	D^7	
CALL G^7	RESPONSE	CALL D^7	RESPONSE
CALL A^7	RESPONSE	CALL D^7	RESPONSE
CALL D^7	RESPONSE	CALL D^7	RESPONSE
CALL G^7	RESPONSE	CALL D^7	RESPONSE
CALL A^7	RESPONSE	CALL D^7	RESPONSE

1 **Shepherd's Hey**

Lively

English Country Dance Tune

Viola
#42
Tch's Ed CD-2

Bass
#43
Tch's Ed CD-2

Accom.
#44
Tch's Ed CD-2

2 **Variation One on *Shepherd's Hey***

Accom.
#44
Tch's Ed CD-2

Accom.
#44
Tch's Ed CD-2

3 **Variation Two on** *Shepherd's Hey*

Violin
#45
Tch's Ed CD-2

Cello
#46
Tch's Ed CD-2

Accom.
#47
Tch's Ed CD-2

4 ★★★ SOLO — **Shepherd's Hey** (QUICK TIME "BY EAR" STARTING ON F♯)

Accom.
#47
Tch's Ed CD-2

5 ★★★★ SOLO — **Variation Two on** *Shepherd's Hey* (QUICK TIME - "BY EAR" STARTING ON F♯)

Violin
#48
Tch's Ed CD-2

Cello
#49
Tch's Ed CD-2

Accom.
#50
Tch's Ed CD-2

6 **Jolly Old Saint Nicholas**

Anonymous Carol

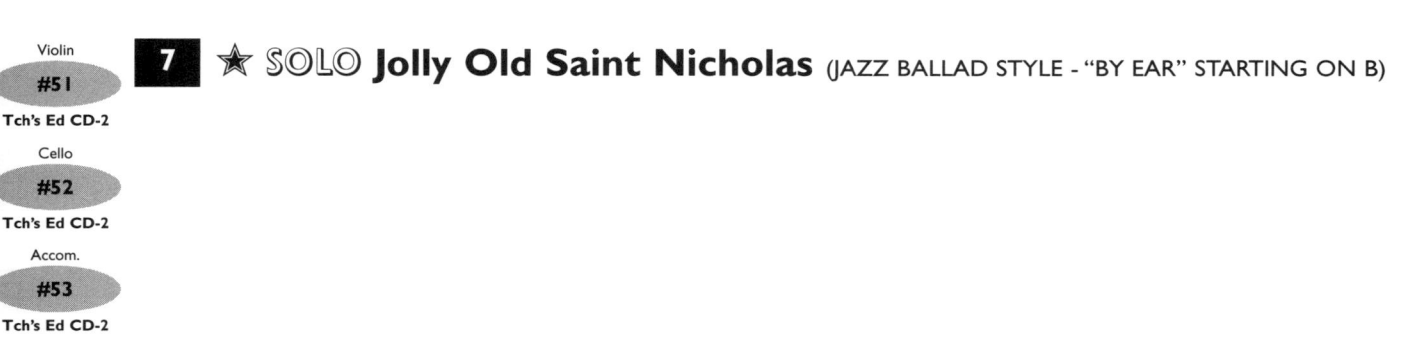

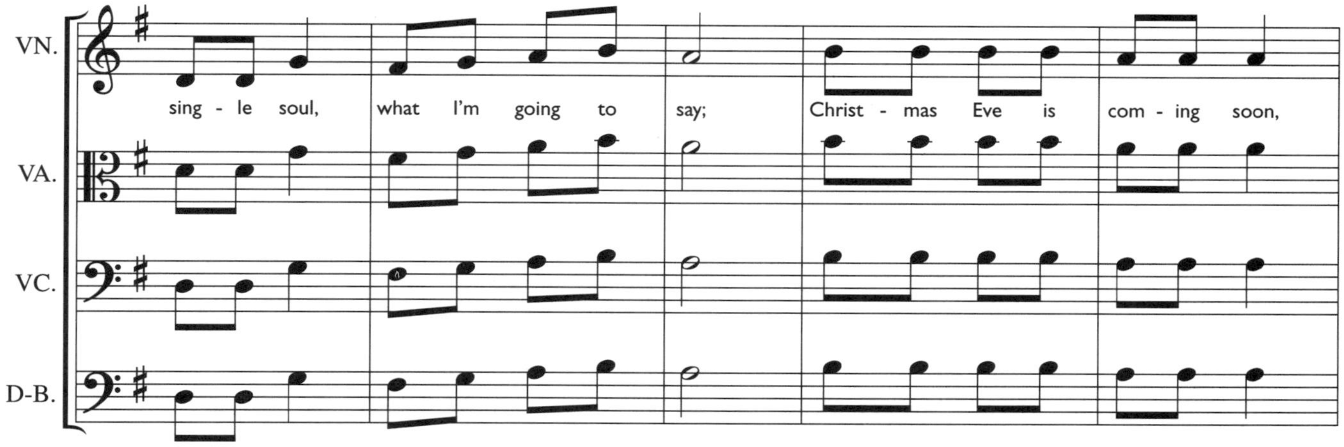
VN.
sing - le soul, what I'm going to say; Christ - mas Eve is com - ing soon,
VA.
VC.
D-B.

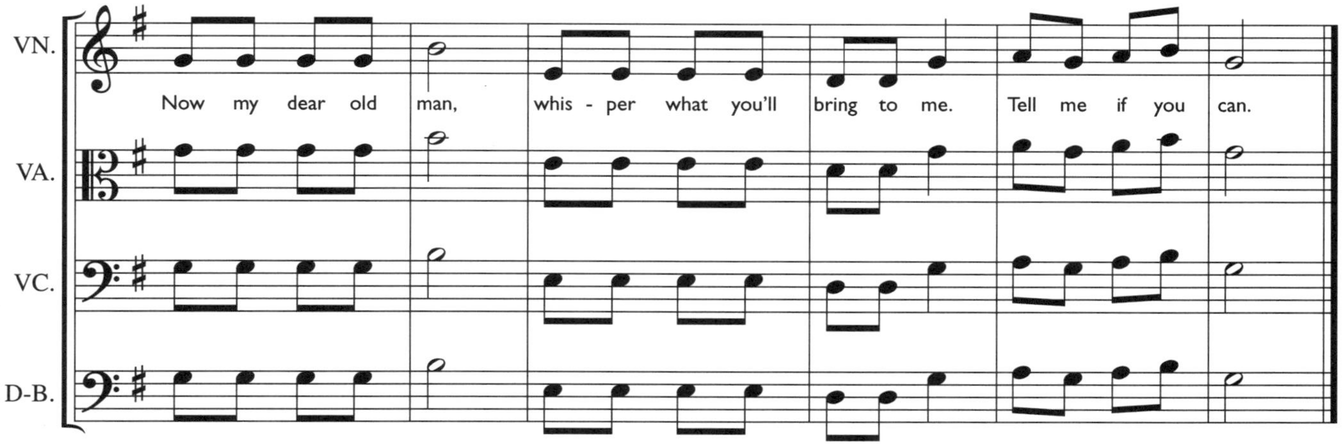
VN.
Now my dear old man, whis - per what you'll bring to me. Tell me if you can.
VA.
VC.
D-B.

***JAZZ BALLAD STYLE** — A slow, expressive vocal style characterized by extended jazz harmonies.*

Violin
#51
Tch's Ed CD-2
Cello
#52
Tch's Ed CD-2
Accom.
#53
Tch's Ed CD-2

7 ★ SOLO Jolly Old Saint Nicholas (JAZZ BALLAD STYLE - "BY EAR" STARTING ON B)

Accom.
#53
Tch's Ed CD-2

8 ★★ SOLO — Improvise Rhythmic Variations on *Jolly Old Saint Nicholas* (JAZZ BALLAD STYLE)

STUDENT CD

Violin
Cello
Solo Trk 47
Accom. Trk 47-2

1 By the Fireside (SOLO, DUET, TRIO, OR QUARTET)

FULL SCORE ON P. 17-C

U.S.

Lightly

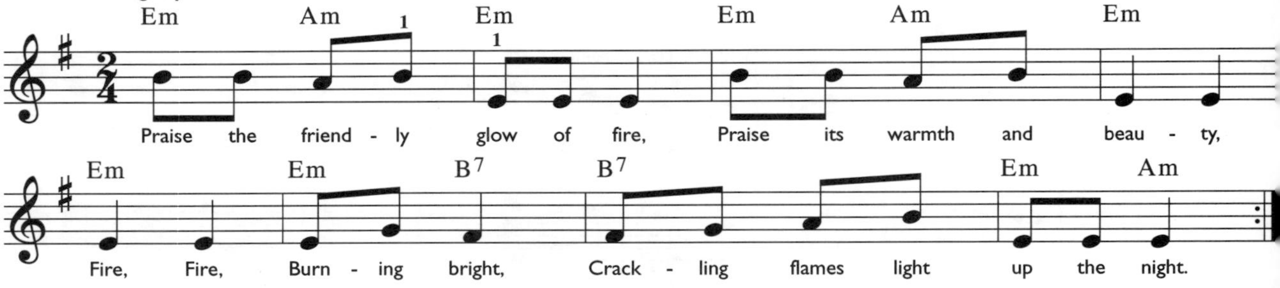
Em Am 1 Em 1 Em Am Em
Praise the friend - ly glow of fire, Praise its warmth and beau - ty,
Em Em B7 B7 Em Am
Fire, Fire, Burn - ing bright, Crack - ling flames light up the night.

Violin
Cello
Solo Trk 47

2 Accompaniment One to *By the Fireside*

FULL SCORE ON P. 17-C

Lightly

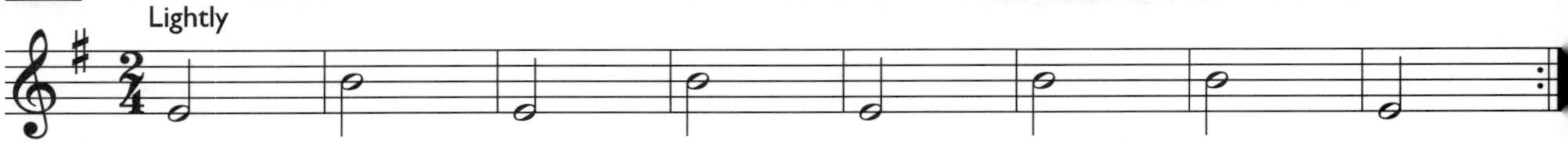

Violin
Cello
Solo Trk 47

3 Accompaniment Two to *By the Fireside*

FULL SCORE ON P. 17-D

Softly and lightly

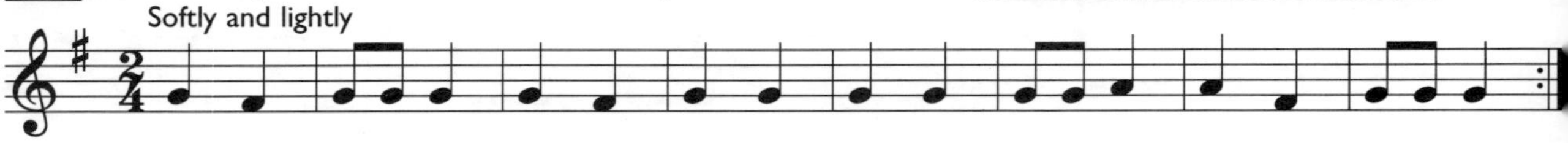

Violin
Cello
Solo Trk 47

4 ★ Obbligato to *By the Fireside*

FULL SCORE ON P. 17-D

Softly and lightly

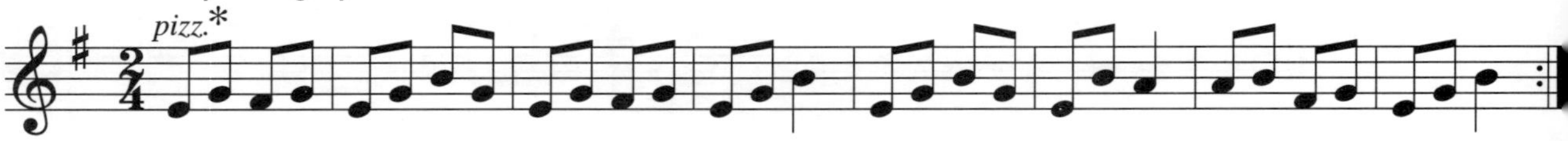
pizz.*

TENUTO — *A term used to indicate a sustained (connected) style of articulation. Horizontal dashes above or below a series of notes also indicate tenuto.*

TIE — *A curved line connecting two or more notes of the same pitch, resulting in one longer tone.*

Viola
Bass
Solo Trk 48
Accom. Trk 48-2

5 The Birch Tree (THEME FROM THE FOURTH SYMPHONY)

Russian Folk Song
Tchaikovsky (1840-1893)

FULL SCORE ON P. 17-D

Tenuto

Em B7 Em B7 Em Em B7 Em B7 Em
B7 B7 Em B7 B7 Em

SPECIAL PROJECT — Learn a Song "By Ear"

SPEAKER BALANCE
Trk 6 or 8
R
Accom.

6 ★★ SOLO — London Bridge is Falling Down ("BY EAR" STARTING ON A)

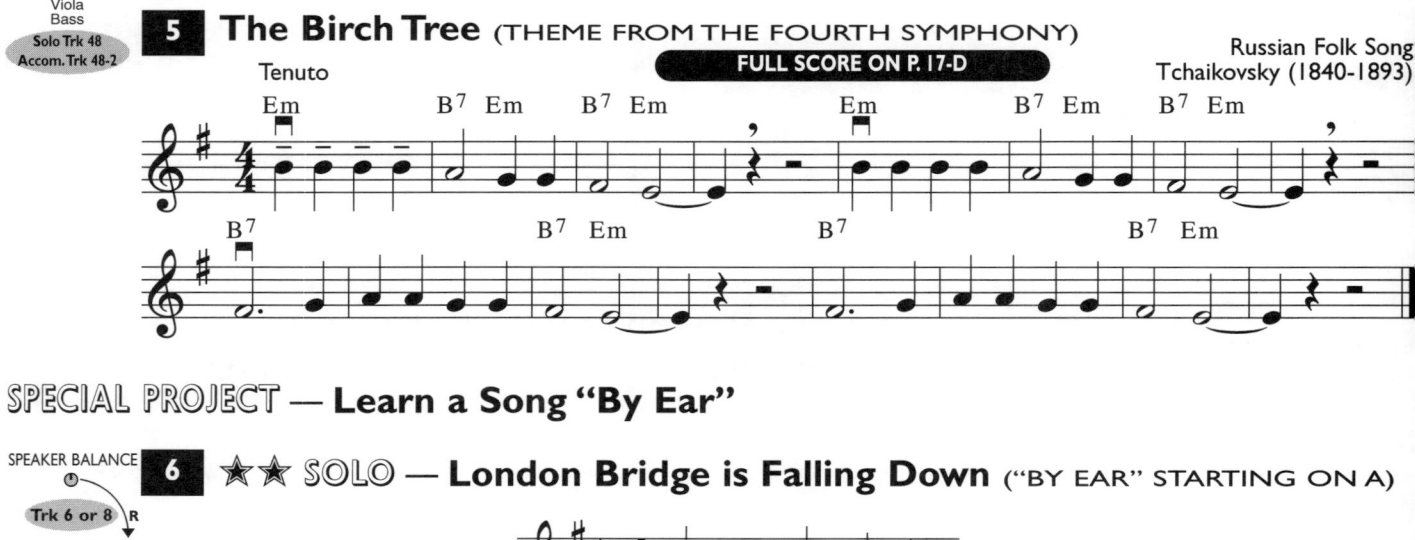

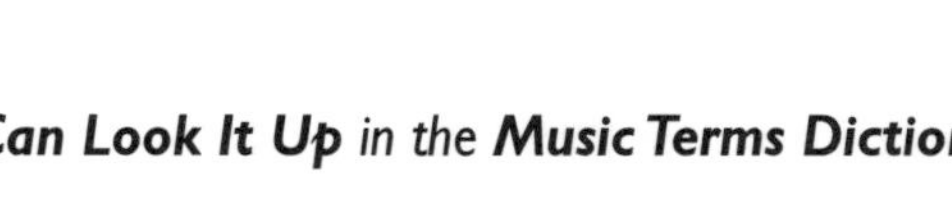

? * *Forget the meaning of something? **You Can Look It Up** in the **Music Terms Dictionary** on pages 42, 43, 44, and 45.*

Rhythmic Flashcard Reading Option for *By the Fireside, Accompaniments,* **and** *Obbligato*

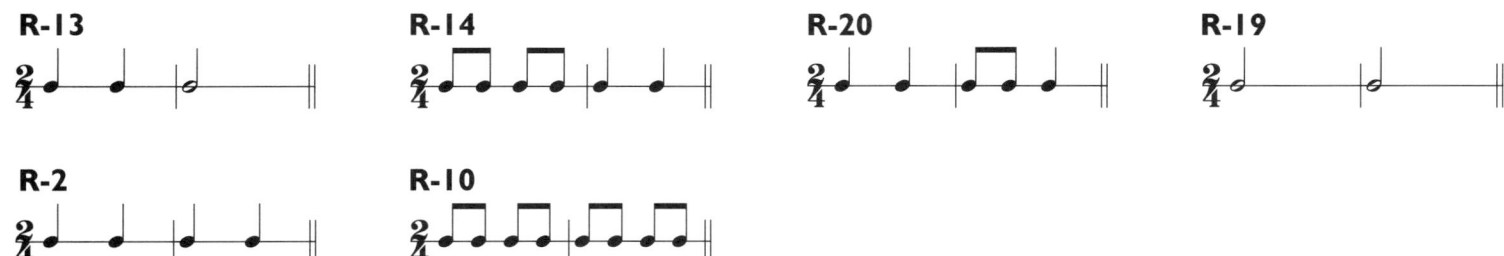

R-13   R-14   R-20   R-19

R-2   R-10

Accom.
#29 or #34
Tch's Ed CD-1

London Bridge is Falling Down (IN D MAJOR - STARTING ON A)

Lon - don Bridge is fall - ing down, fall - ing down, fall - ing down,

Lon - don Bridge is fall - ing down, my fair la - dy.

ADDITIONAL OPTIONS FOR AURAL AND CREATIVE MUSICIANSHIP

London Bridge is Falling Down ("BY EAR")

- **Improvise an open string harmony part "By Ear"**
- **Improvise rhythmic variations on** *London Bridge is Falling Down*
- **Improvise melodic variations on** *London Bridge is Falling Down*
- **Create a group arrangement using student-created variations**
- **Vary articulations to play in multiple musical styles**

A SPECIAL INDIVIDUALIZED OPTION FOR SPONTANEOUS MUSIC MAKING

Return to COBBLER, COBBLER

THE MUSICAL PARAPHRASE – An improvised conversation between two performers. The conversation begins with a 4-beat improvised "Call." The "Response" is a 4-beat restatement (paraphrase) of the "Call" using a slightly different combination of tones, rhythms, and/or articulations.

Extended Accom.
#76
Tch's Ed CD-1

Direct students to employ one of the following options:

A. "Use the tones G, E, and D."   or   **B.** "Use the tones B, A, G, E, and D."

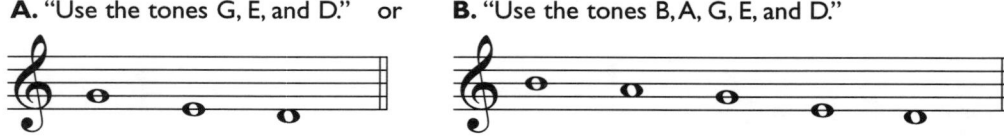

EXAMPLE OF OPTION A:
    Teacher: "The Starting Note is G."

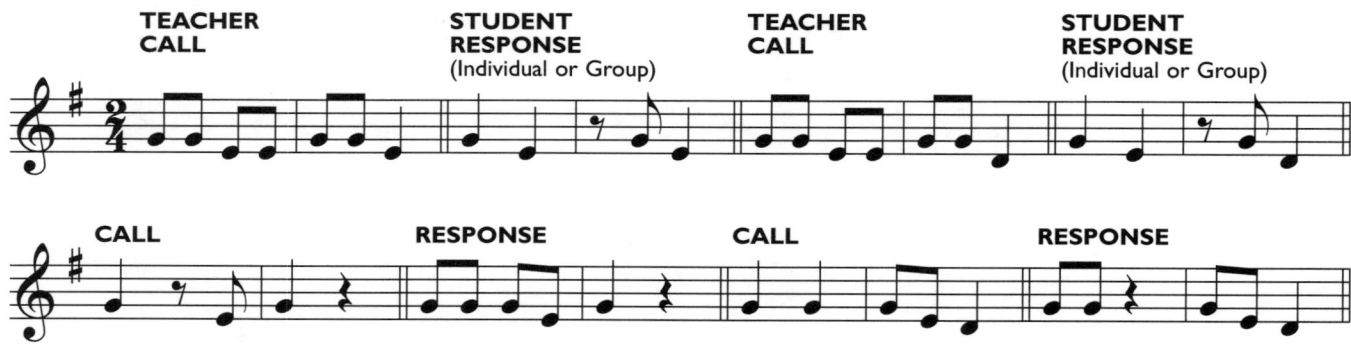

EXAMPLE OF OPTION B:
    Teacher: "The Starting Note is G."

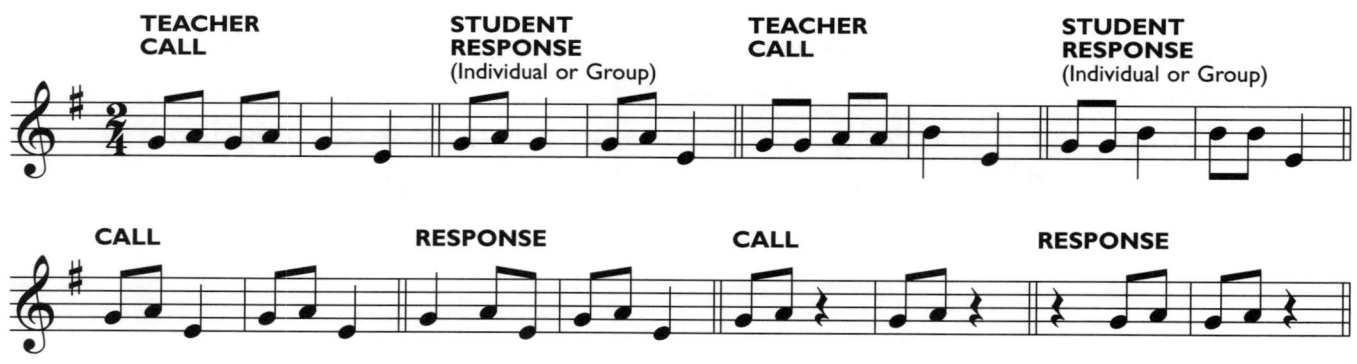

ANOTHER OPTION FOR SPONTANEOUS AND CREATIVE MUSIC MAKING

- **Ask for volunteers to lead the class with their own improvised calls**
- **Direct the class or individual volunteers to follow with musical paraphrases**

1 By the Fireside (SOLO, DUET, TRIO, OR QUARTET)

U.S.

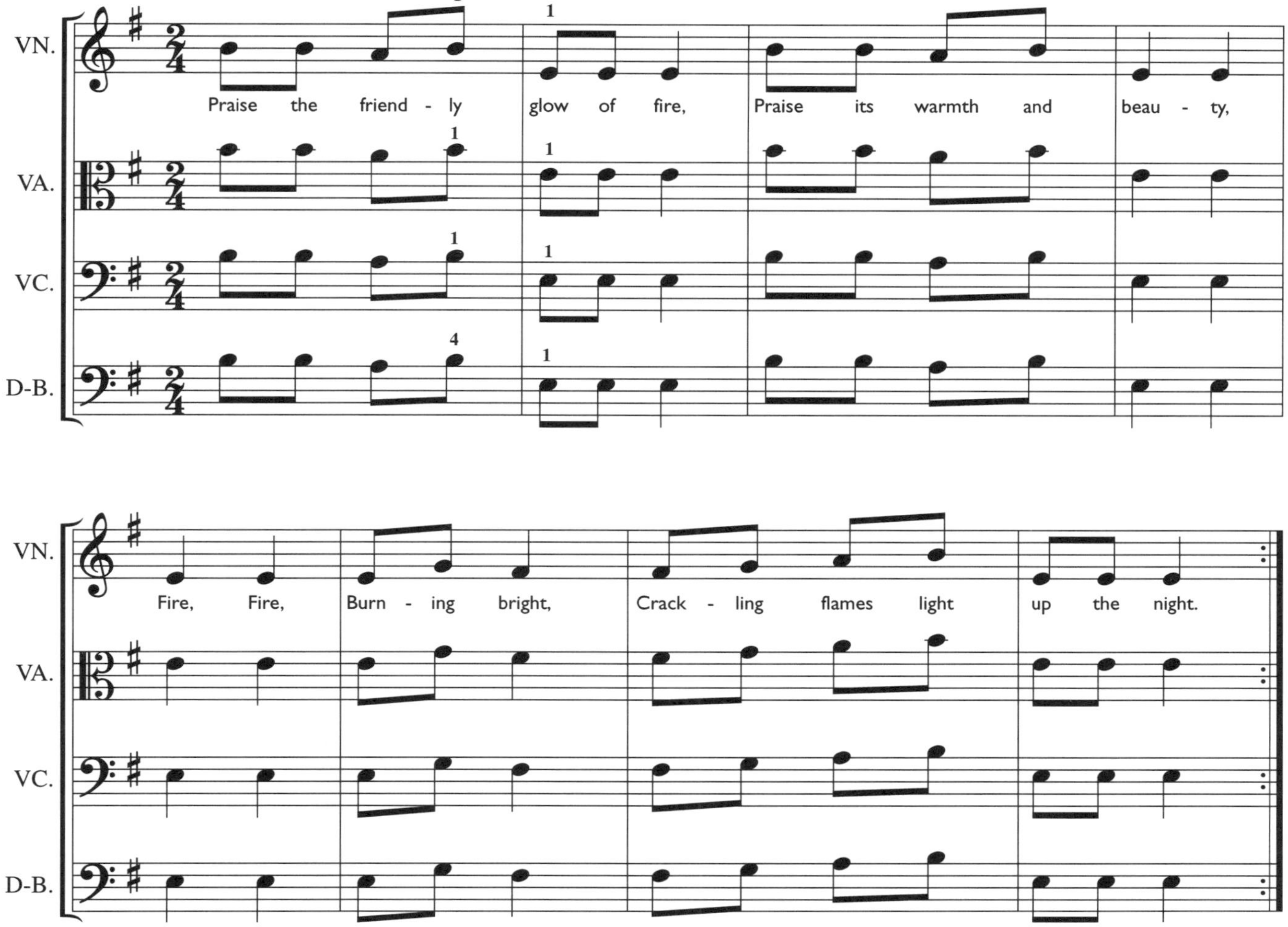

Lightly

VN.

Praise the friend - ly glow of fire, Praise its warmth and beau - ty,

VA.

VC.

D-B.

VN.

Fire, Fire, Burn - ing bright, Crack - ling flames light up the night.

VA.

VC.

D-B.

2 Accompaniment One to By the Fireside

Lightly

VN.

VA.

VC.

D-B.

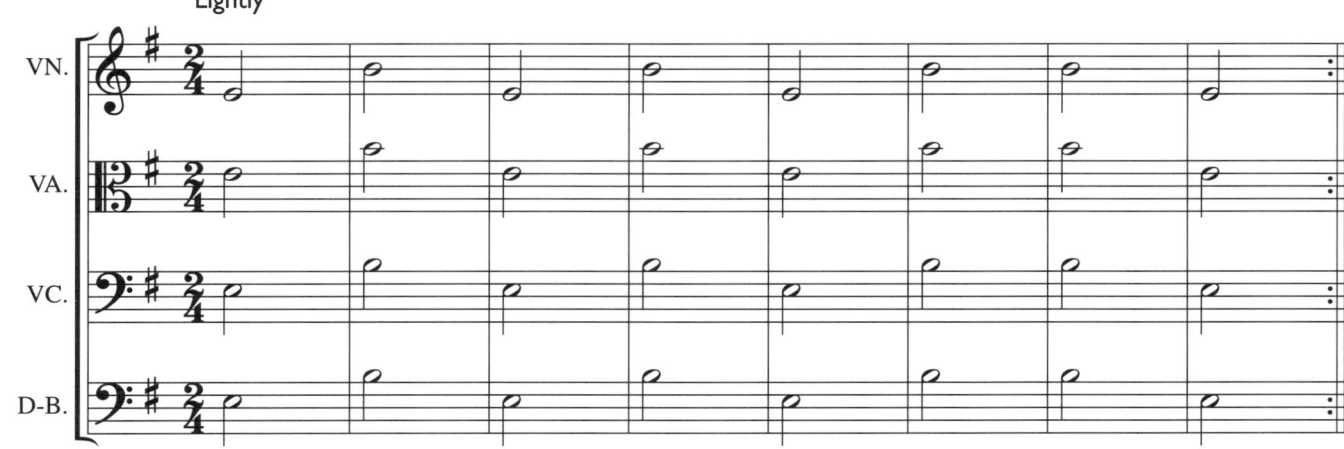

3 **Accompaniment Two to *By the Fireside***

Violin
#54
Tch's Ed CD-2

Cello
#55
Tch's Ed CD-2

Softly and lightly

VN.

VA.

VC.

D-B.

4 ★ **Obbligato to *By the Fireside***

Violin
#54
Tch's Ed CD-2

Cello
#55
Tch's Ed CD-2

Softly and lightly

VN.

VA.

VC.

D-B.

TENUTO — *A term used to indicate a sustained (connected) style of articulation. Horizontal dashes above or below a series of notes also indicate tenuto.*

TIE — *A curved line connecting two or more notes of the same pitch, resulting in one longer tone.*

5 **The Birch Tree** (THEME FROM THE FOURTH SYMPHONY)

Russian Folk Song
Tchaikovsky (1840-1893)

Viola
#57
Tch's Ed CD-2

Bass
#58
Tch's Ed CD-2

Accom.
#59
Tch's Ed CD-2

Tenuto

VN.

VA.

VC.

D-B.

SPECIAL PROJECT — Learn a Song "By Ear"

Accom.
#29 or #34
Tch's Ed CD-1

6 ★★ SOLO — **London Bridge is Falling Down** ("BY EAR" STARTING ON A)

NEW NOTES: C♯, D

C♯

D

ACCENT (>) — A symbol to indicate special stress or emphasis upon a note.

MARTELÉ — A term describing an accented style of bowing. The arm and hand provide weight to the bow before the beginning of a tone, gripping the string, and release the weight as the bow is moved.

1 Scotland's Burning (FOUR PART ROUND)   **FULL SCORE ON P. 18-D**

2 Variation on Scotland's Burning   **FULL SCORE ON P. 18-E**

STUDENT CD

SPEAKER BALANCE
CONTROL
L CD Trk 49 R
Violin   Accom.
Cello

3 Old King Cole   **FULL SCORE ON P. 18-E**

? *Forget the meaning of something?* **You Can Look It Up** *in the* **Music Terms Dictionary** *on pages 42, 43, 44, and 45.*

Rhythmic Flashcard Reading Option for *Scotland's Burning*

R-10

R-2

Rhythmic Flashcard Reading Option for *Old King Cole*

R-2

R-1

R-19

Melodic Ear-to-Hand Training and Assessment for *Scotland's Burning* and *Old King Cole*.

TEXT: "Listen and Play What You Hear. The Starting Tone is D."

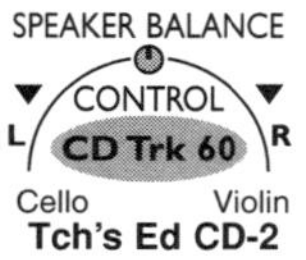

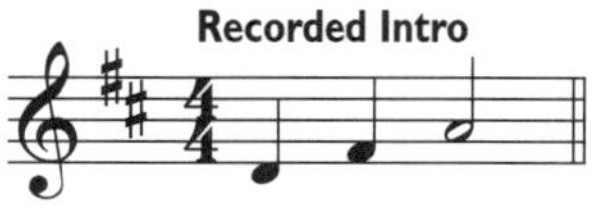

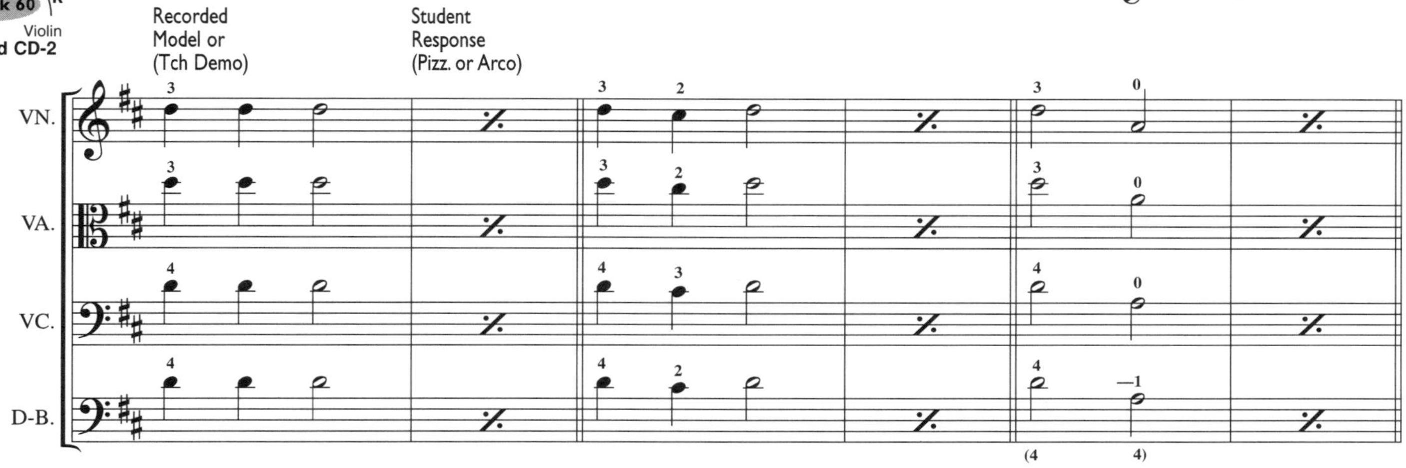

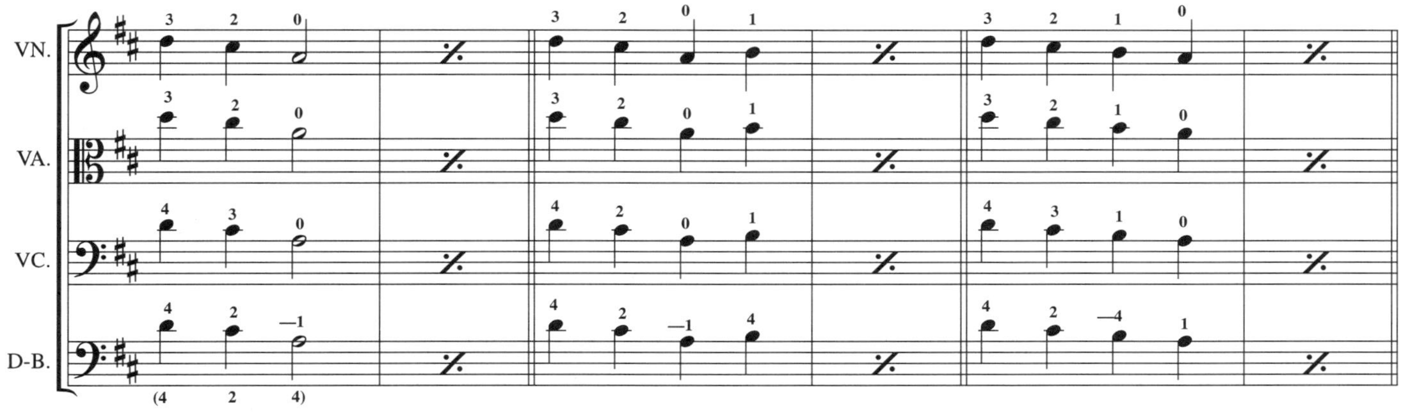

Rhythmic, Bowing, and Articulation Ear-to-Hand Training and Assessment on *Scotland's Burning and Old King Cole.*
TEXT: "Listen and Play What You Hear. The Starting Tone is D."

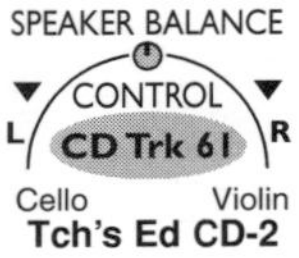

Recorded Intro

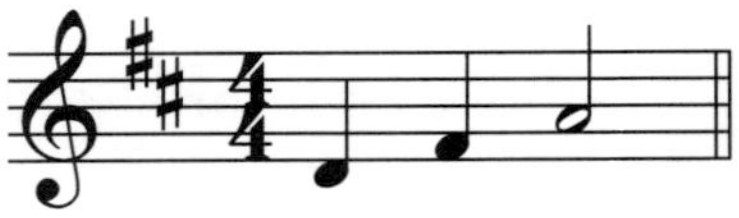

Recorded Model or (Tch Demo)

Student Response

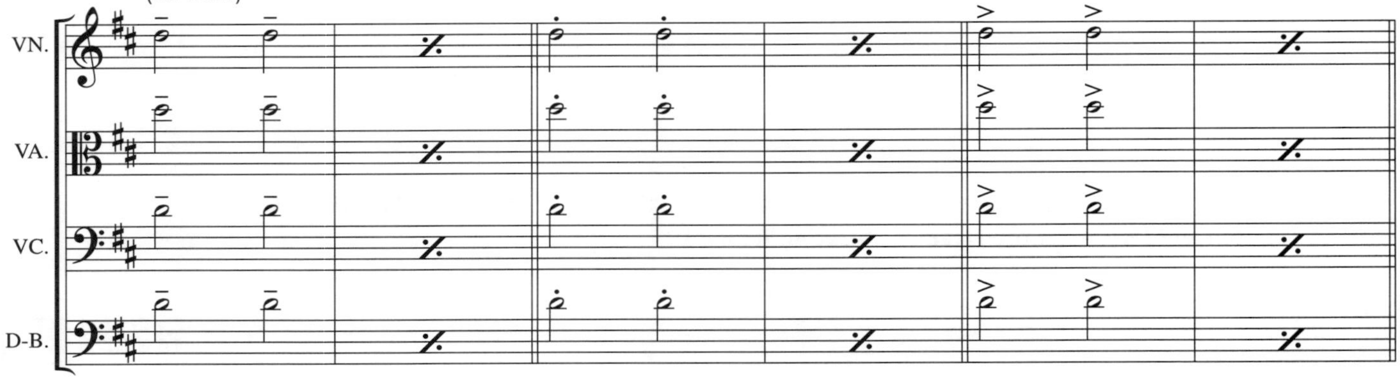

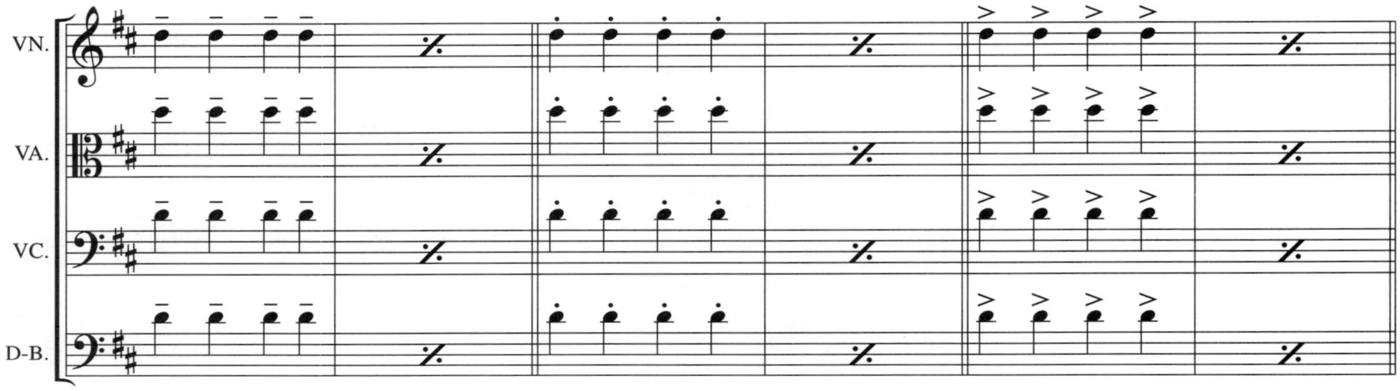

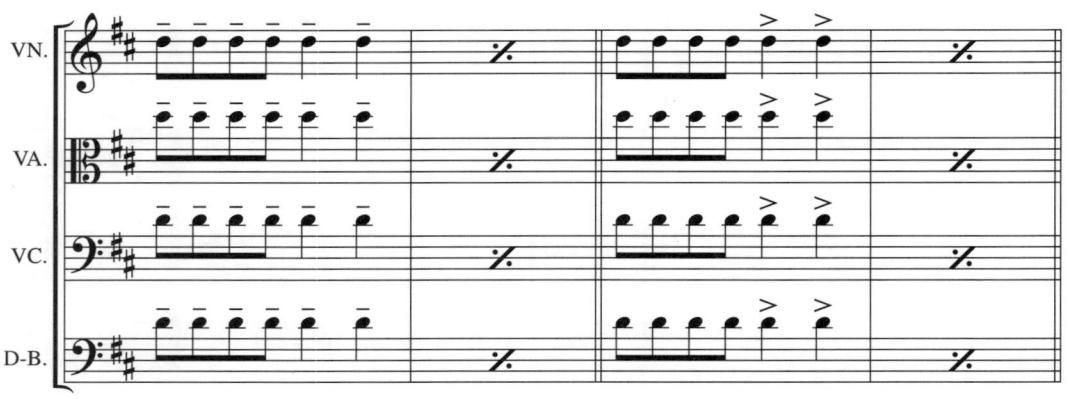

COOL JAZZ (VOCAL CALL AND RESPONSE - TEACHER CALL, STUDENT RESPONSE - IN A SWINGING STYLE)

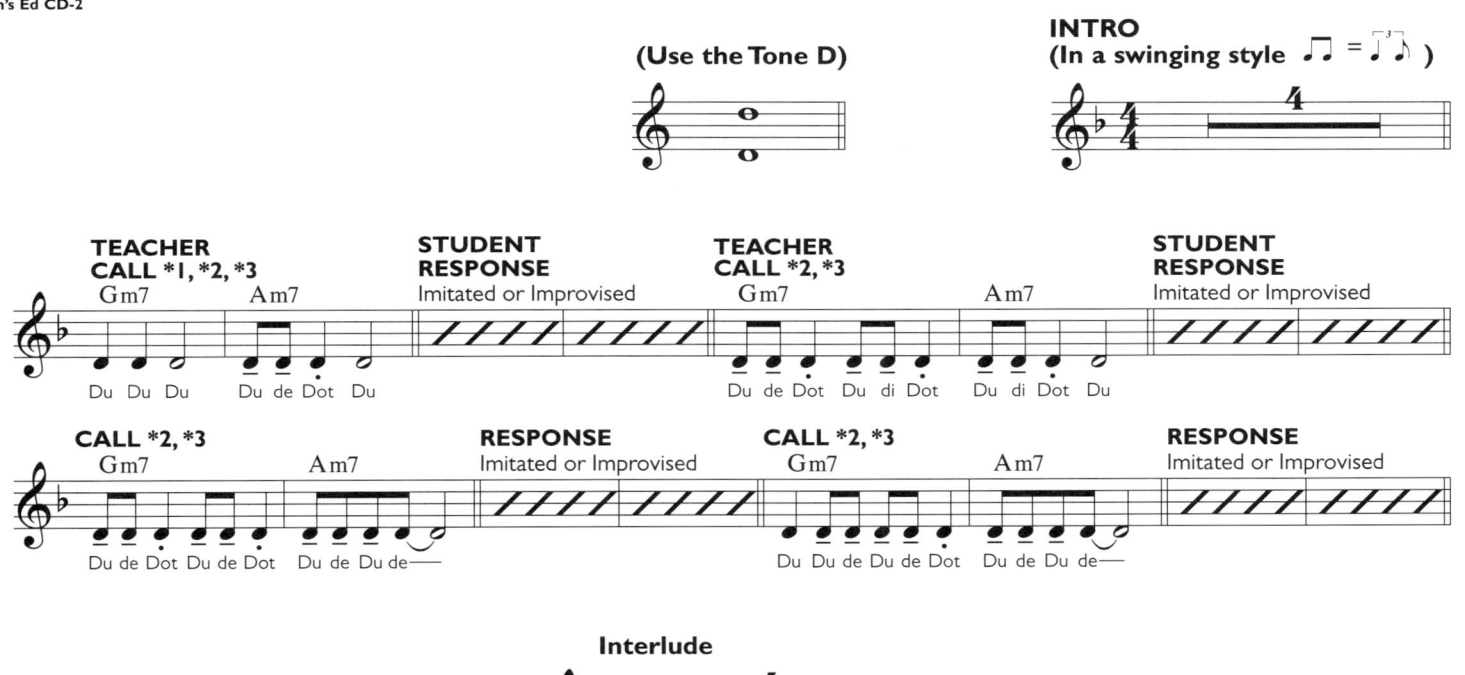

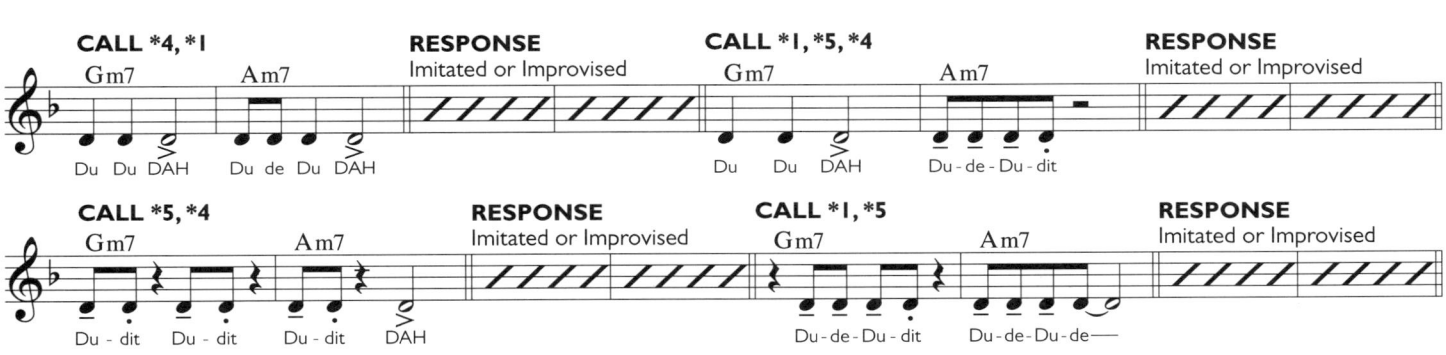

* 1. *Du* and *de* — normal articulation with a slight separation between tones
  Du as in "due;" de as in "day"
* 2. *Du—* and *de—* — connected style of articulation
* 3. *Dot* — slightly sharper articulation with a quick release of the tone
* 4. *DAH* — strong accent with a sharp release of the tone
* 5 *du—dit* — fully extended tone (du—) to a short tone with a quick release (dit)

ANOTHER OPTION FOR SPONTANEOUS AND CREATIVE MUSIC MAKING

- Ask for volunteers to lead the class with their own improvised calls (Vocal or instrumental)

- Direct the class to follow with imitated or improvised responses

* *Do It! Improvise* (CD Backgrounds and Scale Notations for Entry-Level Music Improvisation - MLR 422) Albert Blaser and James Froseth, © 1994 GIA Publications Inc., 7404 South Mason Avenue, Chicago, IL 60638

NEW NOTES

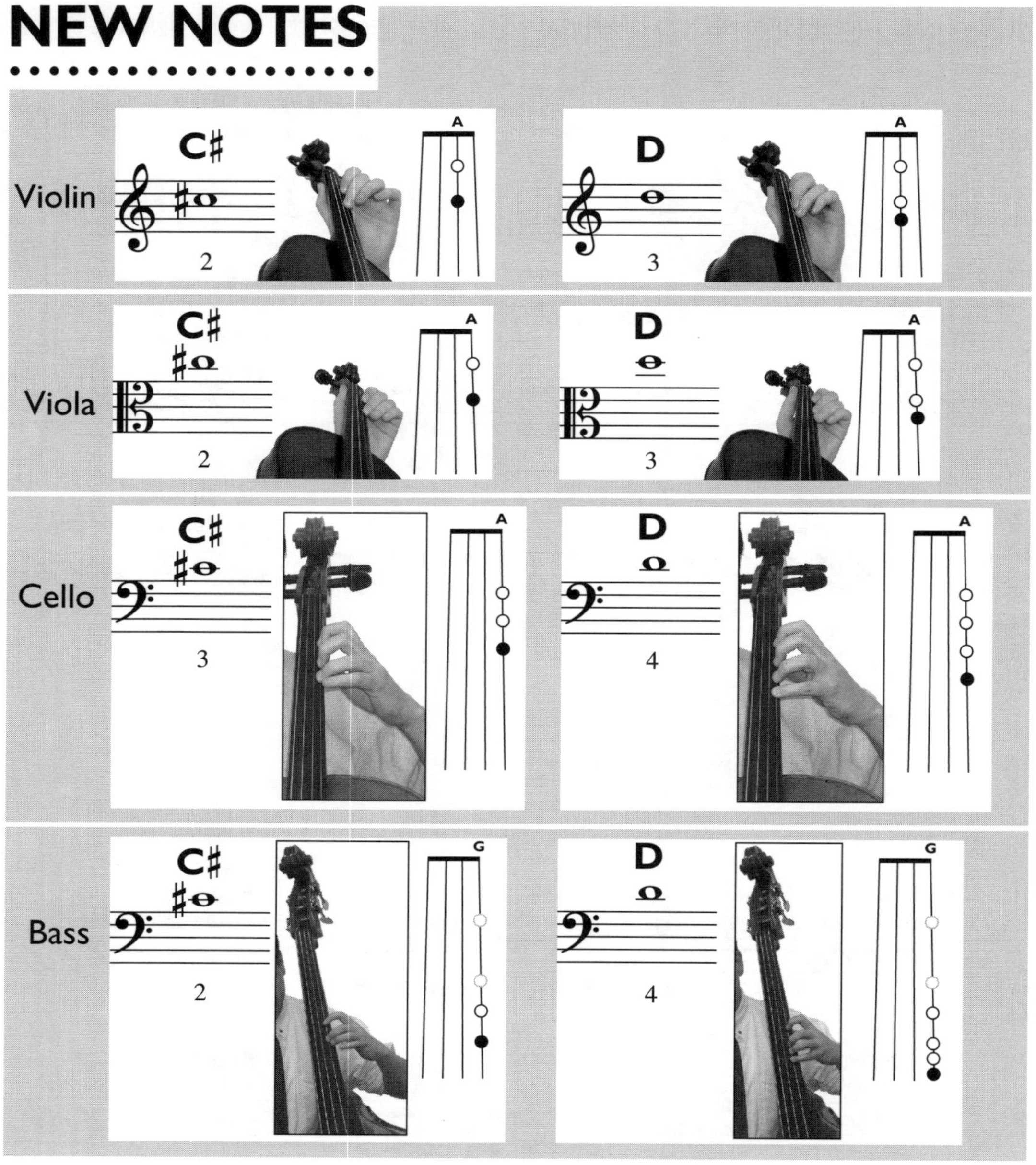

	C#	D
Violin		
Viola		
Cello		
Bass		

ACCENT (>) — *A symbol to indicate special stress or emphasis upon a note.*

MARTELÉ — *A term describing an accented style of bowing. The arm and hand provide weight to the bow before the beginning of a tone, gripping the string, and release the weight as the bow is moved.*

1 Scotland's Burning (FOUR PART ROUND)

Brightly

Traditional

VN. Scot - land's burn - ing, Scot - land's burn - ing. Look out, look out,

2 **Variation on *Scotland's Burning***

3 **Old King Cole**

Moderato

Adaptation of an Old Folk Tune

HOOKED BOW *— Linking two down bows or two up bows together by stopping the bow and continuing in the same direction.*

STUDENT CD

1 **Dance in the Circle** (D MAJOR SCALE SONG)   FULL SCORE ON P. 19-D

Viola
Bass
Solo Trk 50
Accom. Trk 50-2

Legato   Louisiana Folk Song

2 **French Folk Song**   FULL SCORE ON P. 19-D

Violin
Cello
Solo Trk 51
Accom. Trk 52

Legato

PICK-UP NOTE *— One or more notes that come before the first full measure of a piece.*

UPPER HALF (U.H.) *— Play one or more notes from the middle to the tip of the bow.*

LOWER HALF (L.H.) *— Play one or more notes from the frog to the middle of the bow.*

WHOLE BOW (W.B.) *— Play one or more notes from the frog to the tip of the bow.*

SPEAKER BALANCE
CONTROL
L   CD Trk 53   R
Violin   Accom.
Cello

3 **On Top of Old Smokey**   FULL SCORE ON P. 19-E

Moderato   Adaptation of an Old Folk Tune

On   top   of   old   Smo - key,   all   cov - ered   with   snow,____

lost   my   true   lov - er,   for   court - ing   too   slow.____

Rhythmic Round

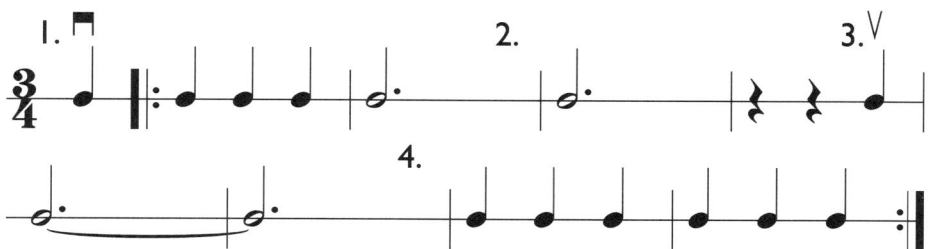

Rhythmic Reading Exercise

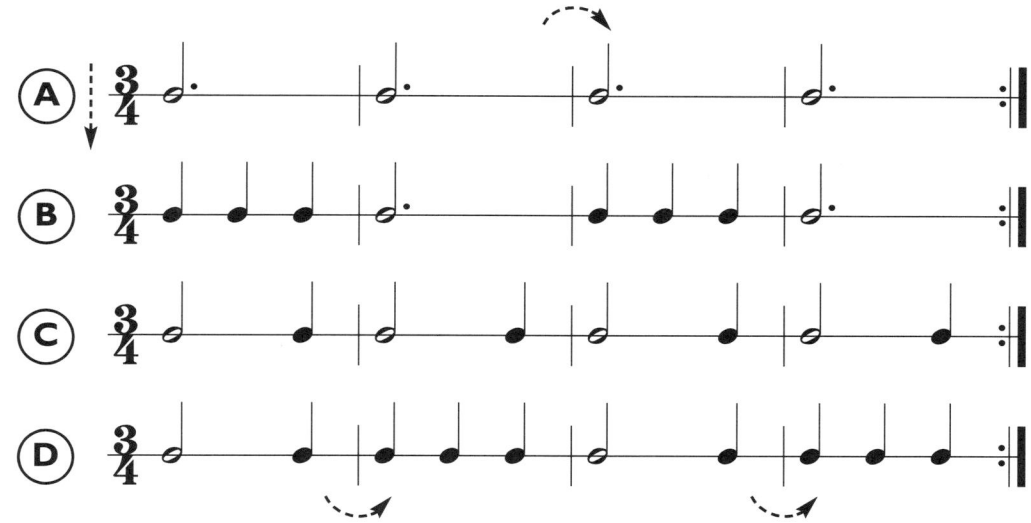

A SPECIAL OPTION FOR ENSEMBLE INTONATION TRAINING

CENTER MELODIC AND HARMONIC PITCHES "BY EAR"

Procedure 1. Direct students to "Play the D major scale without repeating the top note."

> **Procedure 1a.** Direct students to match their pitches carefully - hold each note until signal.

> **Procedure 1b.** Allow students to listen and signal when they think the group is "in tune."

Procedure 2. Direct students to "Play the D major scale as a round, without repeating the top note."

> **Procedure 2a.** Direct students to match their pitches carefully - hold each note until signal.

> **Procedure 2b.** Allow students to listen and signal when they think the group is "in tune."

Procedure 3. Create variations on the scale round.

> **Procedure 3a.** Use 3 parts to create triads, 4 parts to create diatonic 7th chords.

> **Procedure 3b.** Use different sections entering at various times to create chord inversions.

> **Procedure 3c.** Use different dynamics, pizzicato, and rhythmic variations.

See pages 41-J, K, L, and M for one-octave major and minor scales.

A SPECIAL OPTION FOR ENSEMBLE INTONATION TRAINING

HARMONIZE TONIC AND DOMINANT "BY EAR"

Return to DOWN BY THE STATION

Procedure 1. Direct students to "Using only open D and A, discover an open-string harmony part that sounds good to you."

Procedure 1a. Play teacher or recorded model several times, allowing students to explore.

Procedure 1b. Teacher or individual student can model the open-string harmony part:

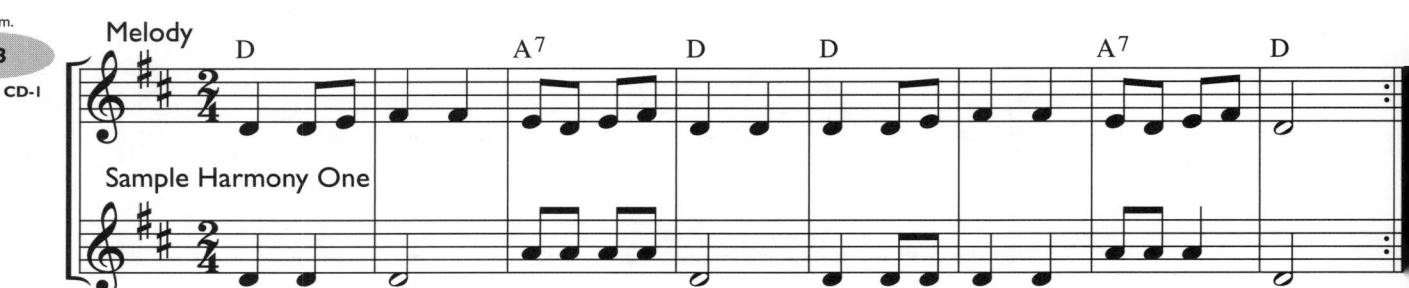

Procedure 1c. Allow students to play either the melody or the open-string harmony part.

Procedure 2. Direct students to "Using only D and C♯, discover a second harmony part that sounds good to you." (Remind students that these pitches sound and feel "close together.")

Procedure 2a. Play teacher or recorded model several times, allowing students to explore.

Procedure 2b. Teacher or individual student can model the second harmony part:

Procedure 2c. Allow students to play either the melody, open-string, or second harmony part.

Procedure 3. Direct students to "Using only F♯ and G, discover a third harmony part that sounds good to you." (Remind students that these pitches sound and feel "close together.")

Procedure 3a. Play teacher or recorded model several times, allowing students to explore.

Procedure 3b. Teacher or individual student can model the third harmony part:

Procedure 3c. Allow students to play either the melody, open-string, second, or third harmony part.

Procedure 4. Create a group arrangement of *Down By the Station*.

Procedure 4a. Decide on sections to play melody and harmony parts.

Procedure 4b. Decide on dynamic levels, pizzicato, and other musical elements.

Procedure 4c. Decide on number of repetitions - allow for student solos.

Procedure 4d. Allow for rhythmic improvisation.

Procedure 5. Use this option with other tunes easily harmonized with D and A⁷ chords:

Twinkle, Twinkle Little Star
Lightly Row
Au Claire de la Lune
Oh When the Saints Go Marching In
Mary Had a Little Lamb
Rocket Cruiser
Notes
Hot Cross Buns

HOOKED BOW — *Linking two down bows or two up bows together by stopping the bow and continuing in the same direction.*

Viola #65 Tch's Ed CD-2
Bass #66 Tch's Ed CD-2
Accom. #67 Tch's Ed CD-2

1 Dance in the Circle (D MAJOR SCALE SONG)

Legato

Louisiana Folk Song

Violin #68 Tch's Ed CD-2
Cello #69 Tch's Ed CD-2
Accom. #70 Tch's Ed CD-2

2 French Folk Song

Legato

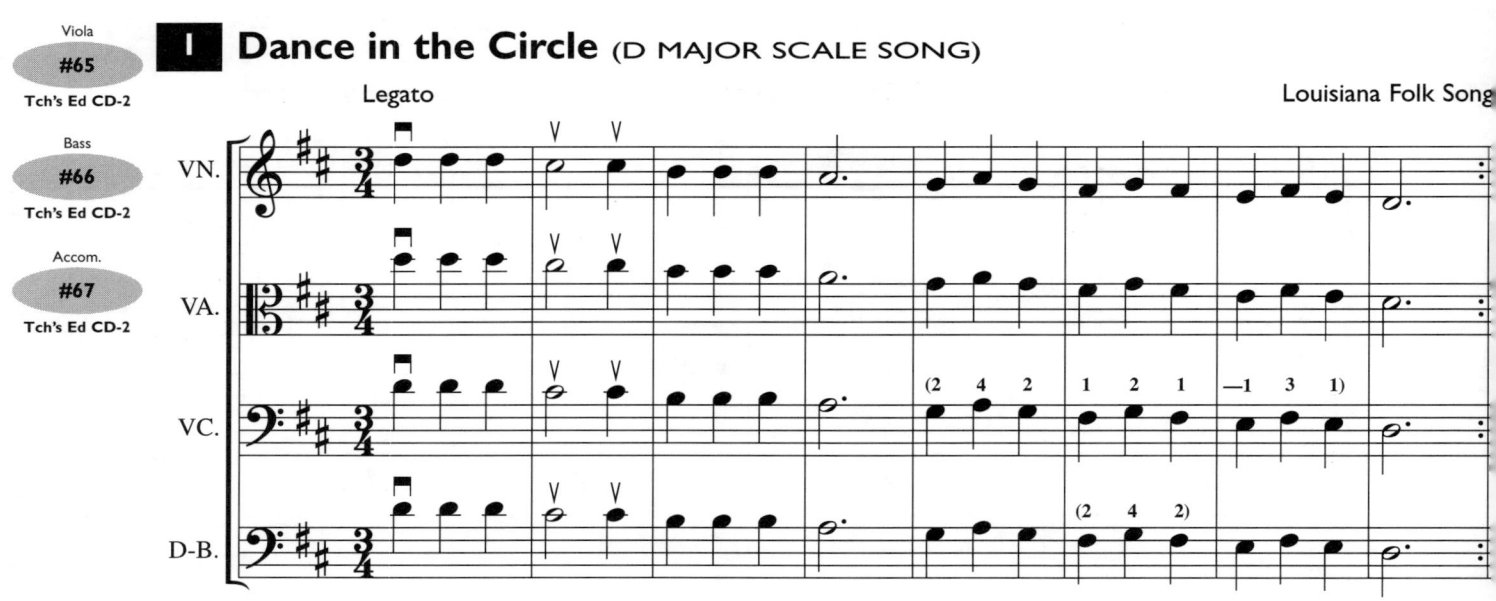

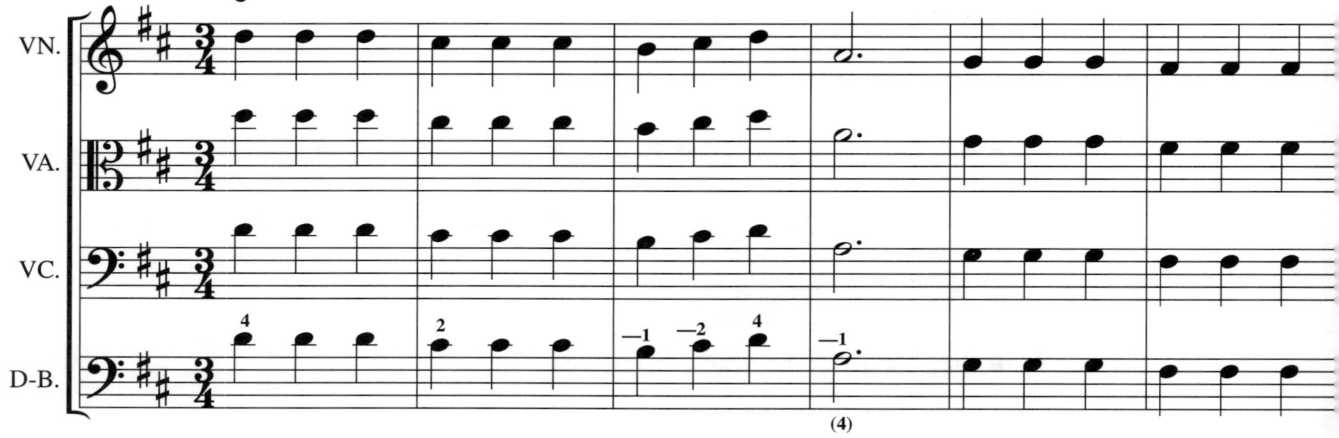

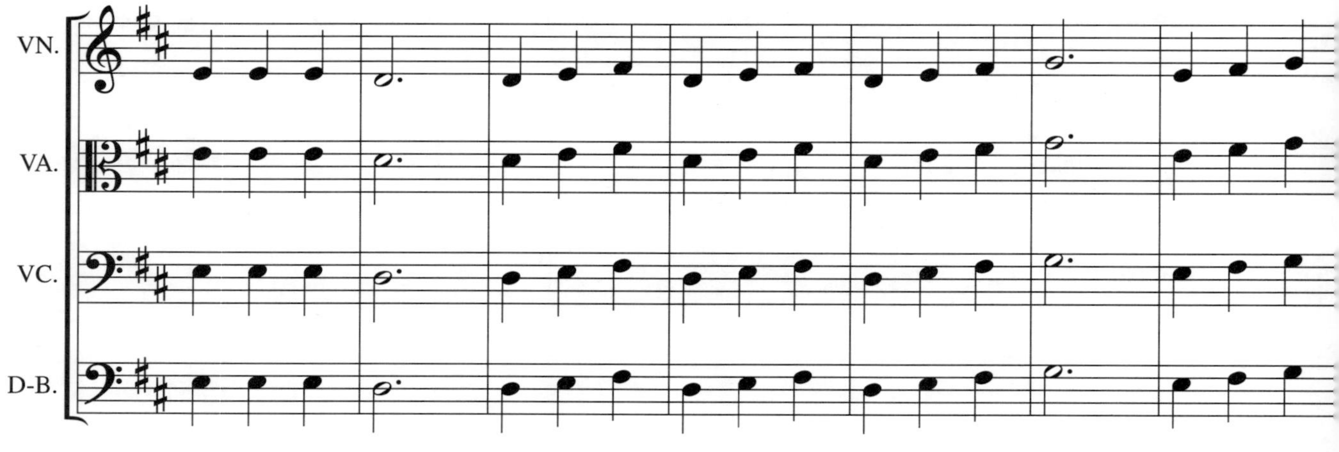

VN.
VA.
VC.
D-B.

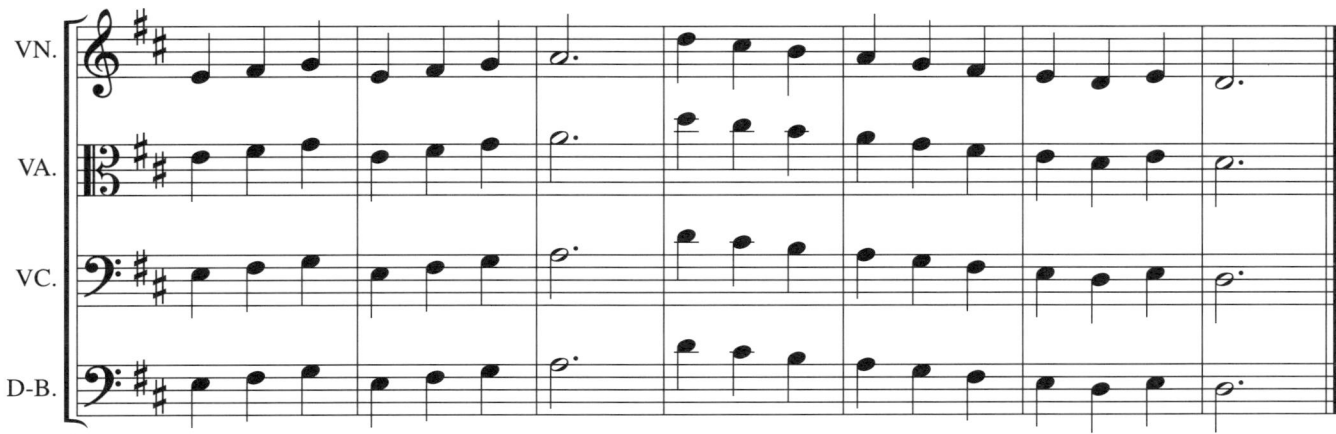

PICK-UP NOTE — *One or more notes that come before the first full measure of a piece.*

UPPER HALF (U.H.) — *Play one or more notes from the middle to the tip of the bow.*

LOWER HALF (L.H.) — *Play one or more notes from the frog to the middle of the bow.*

WHOLE BOW (W.B.) — *Play one or more notes from the frog to the tip of the bow.*

Violin
#71
Tch's Ed CD-2

Cello
#72
Tch's Ed CD-2

Accom.
#73
Tch's Ed CD-2

3 On Top of Old Smokey

Moderato

Adaptation of an Old Folk Tune

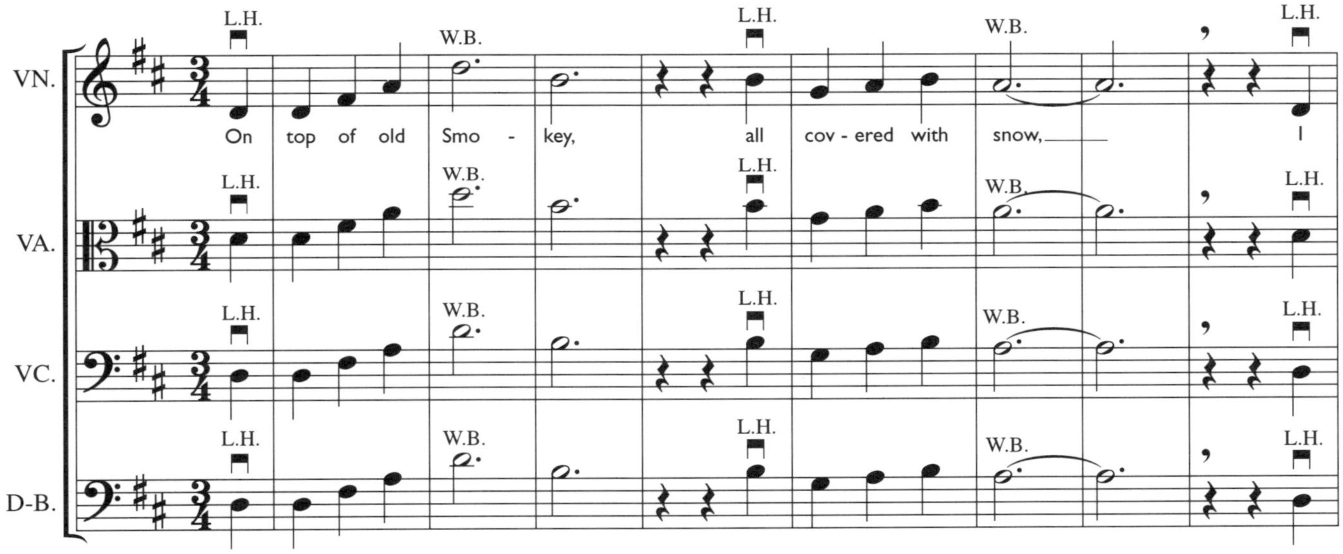
VN.
VA.
VC.
D-B.
L.H.
W.B.
On top of old Smo - key, all cov - ered with snow, I

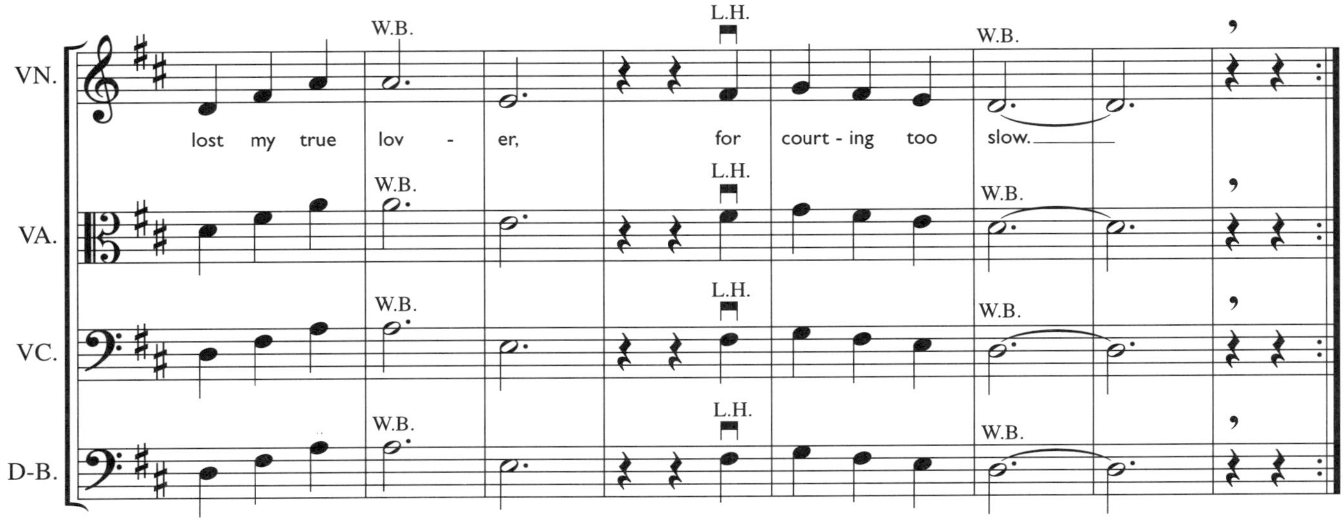
VN.
VA.
VC.
D-B.
L.H.
W.B.
lost my true lov - er, for court - ing too slow.

See Bass New Notes: C♯, B, A - p. 20-B

Violin page 20

SLUR — *A curved line* above or below two or more notes of different pitch to indicate no change of bow direction, resulting in a continuous, smooth style of articulation.

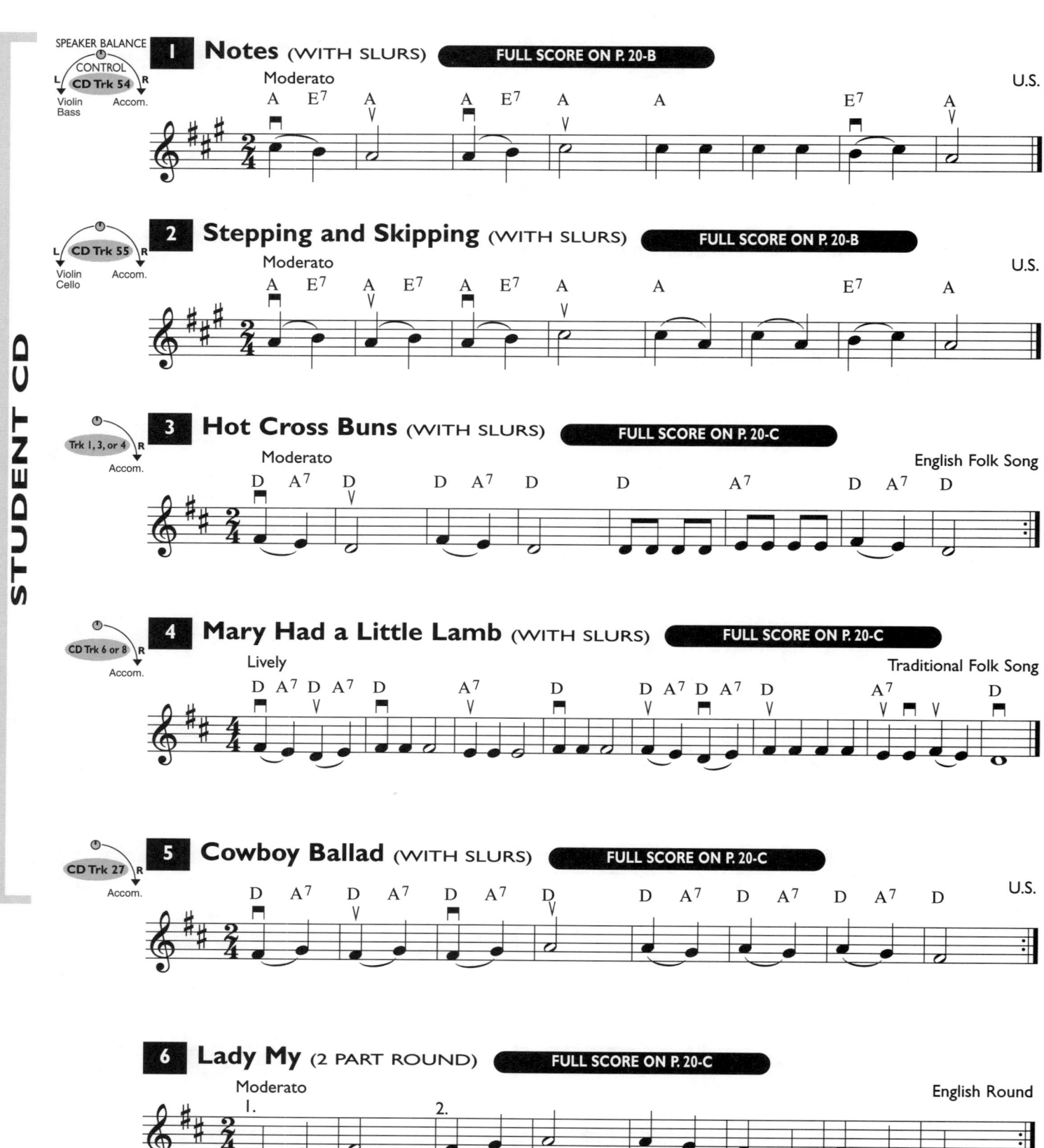

1 **Notes** (WITH SLURS) FULL SCORE ON P. 20-B

2 **Stepping and Skipping** (WITH SLURS) FULL SCORE ON P. 20-B

3 **Hot Cross Buns** (WITH SLURS) FULL SCORE ON P. 20-C

4 **Mary Had a Little Lamb** (WITH SLURS) FULL SCORE ON P. 20-C

5 **Cowboy Ballad** (WITH SLURS) FULL SCORE ON P. 20-C

6 **Lady My** (2 PART ROUND) FULL SCORE ON P. 20-C

STUDENT CD

Melodic and Bowing Ear-to-Hand Training and Assessment for *Notes, Stepping and Skipping, Hot Cross Buns,* and *Mary Had a Little Lamb (WITH SLURS).* TEXT: "Listen and Play What You Hear. The Starting Tone is F♯."

SPEAKER BALANCE CONTROL
L CD Trk 74 R
Cello Violin
Tch's Ed CD-2

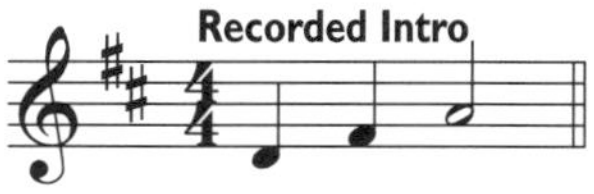

Recorded Call or (Tch Demo)

Student Response

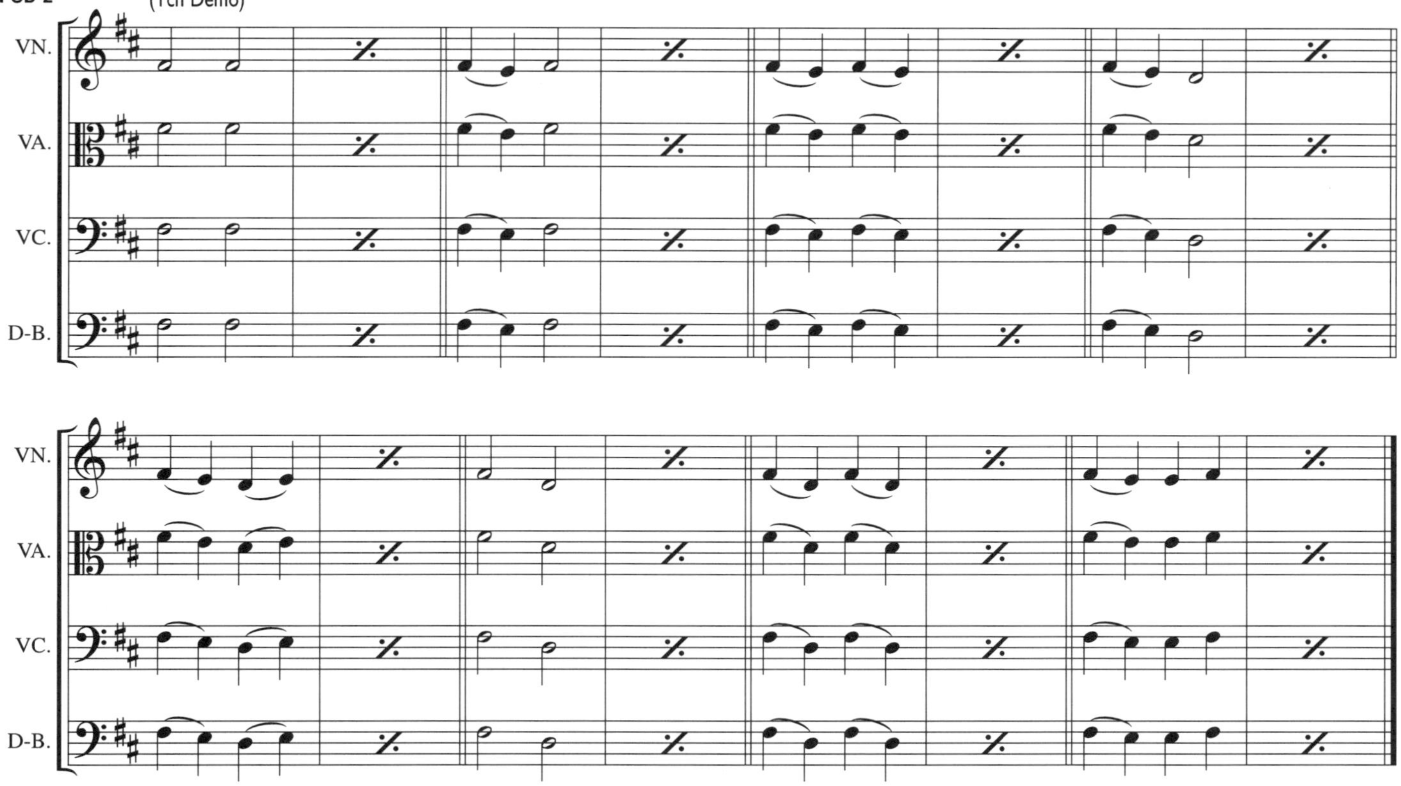

Melodic and Bowing Ear-to-Hand Training and Assessment for *Cowboy Ballad (WITH SLURS).*

TEXT: "Listen and Play What You Hear. The Starting Tone is F♯."

Violin
#75
Tch's Ed CD-2

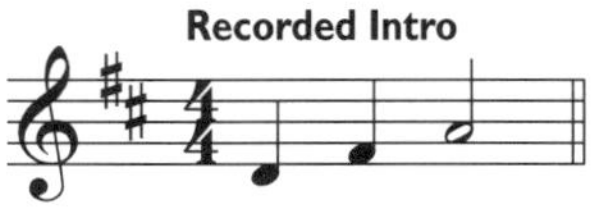

Recorded Model or (Tch Demo)

Student Response

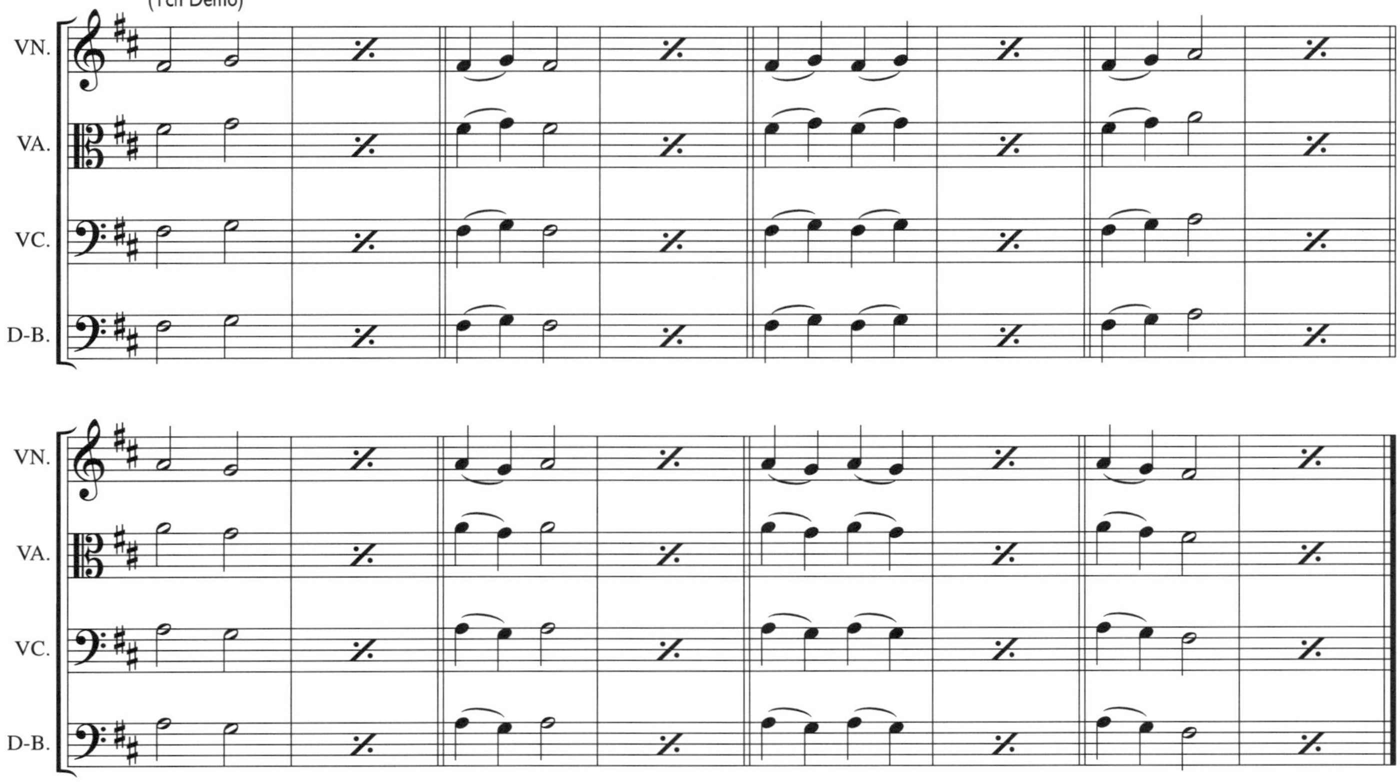

NEW NOTES

Bass

C# 4

B 1

A 0

SLUR — *A curved line* ⌒ *above or below two or more notes of different pitch to indicate no change of bow direction, resulting in a continuous, smooth style of articulation.*

Violin
#76
Tch's Ed CD-2

Bass
#77
Tch's Ed CD-2

Accom.
#78
Tch's Ed CD-2

1 **Notes** (WITH SLURS)

Moderato

U.S.

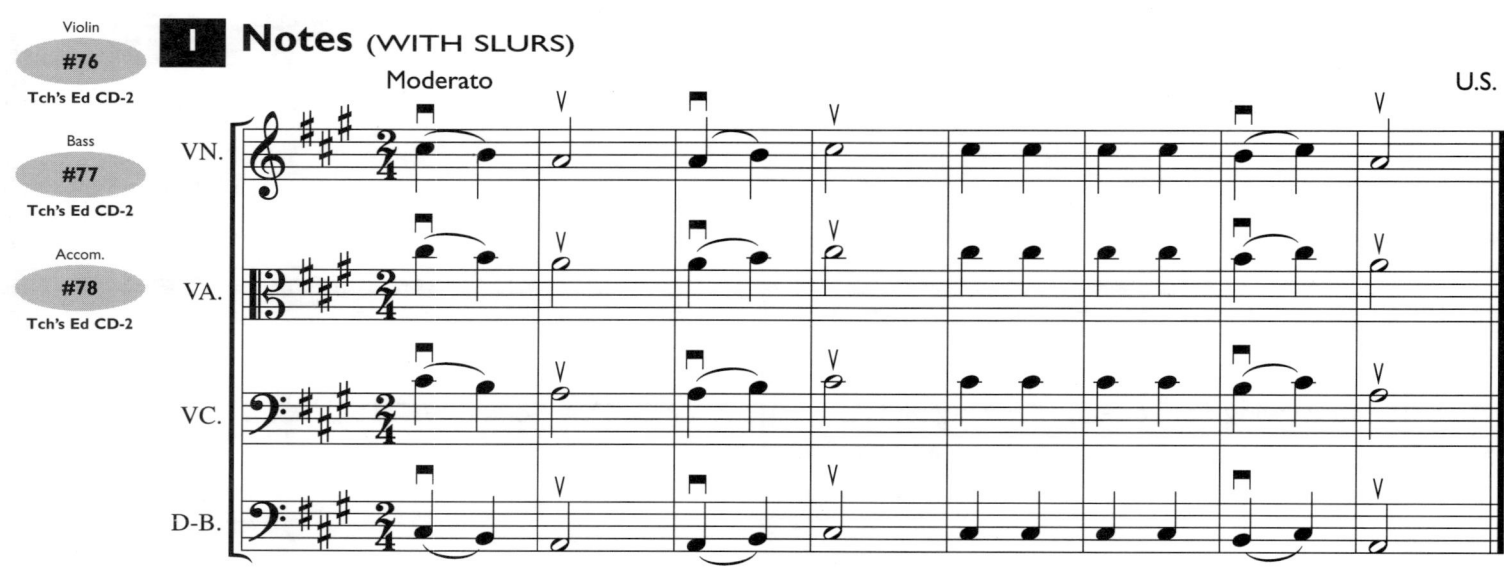

Violin
#79
Tch's Ed CD-2

Cello
#80
Tch's Ed CD-2

Accom.
#81
Tch's Ed CD-2

2 **Stepping and Skipping** (WITH SLURS)

Moderato

U.S.

1 **Shepherd's Hey** (WITH SLURS) — FULL SCORE ON P. 21-B

Accom. Trk 42-2 or 43-2

English Country Dance Tune

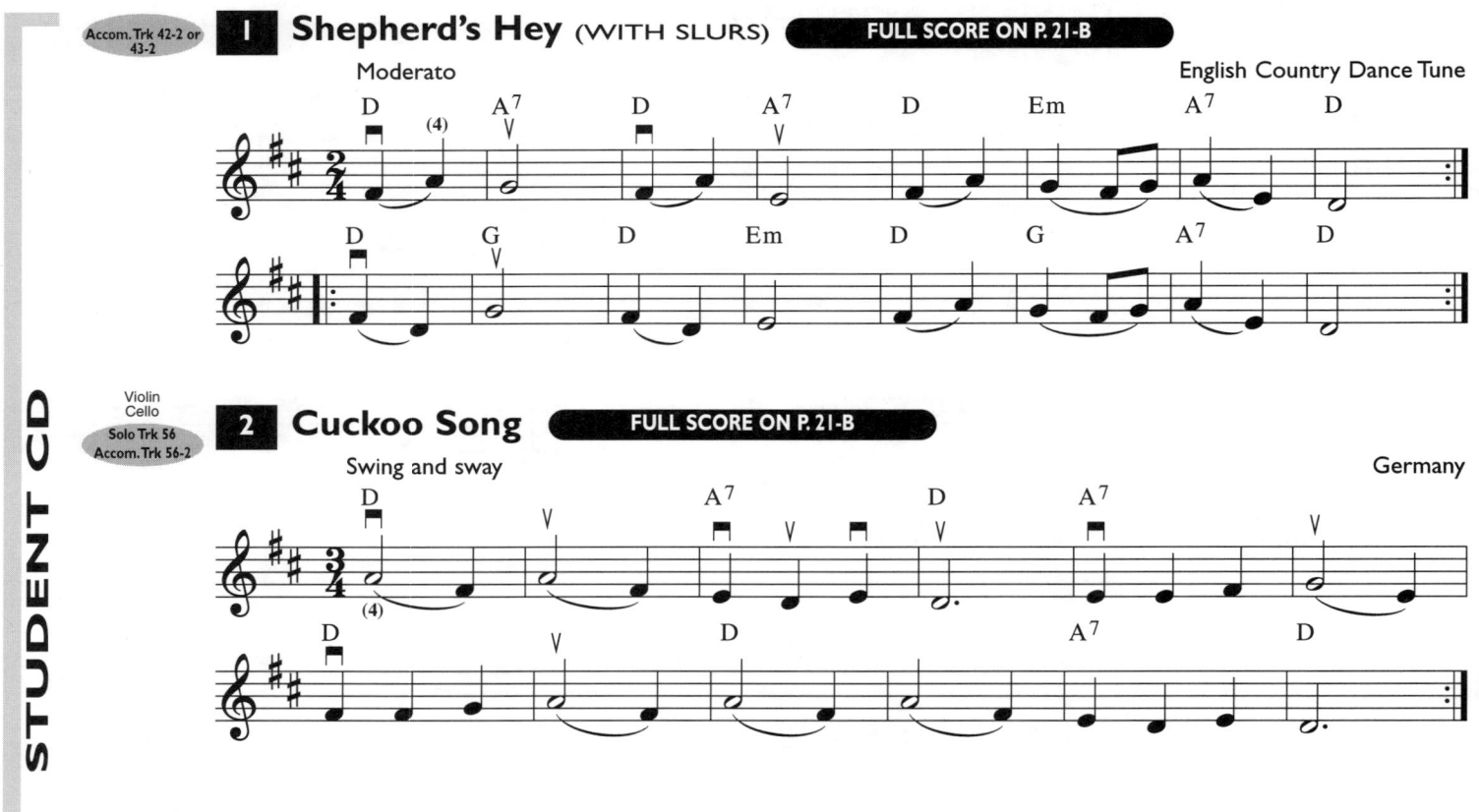

2 **Cuckoo Song** — FULL SCORE ON P. 21-B

Violin
Cello
Solo Trk 56
Accom. Trk 56-2

Germany

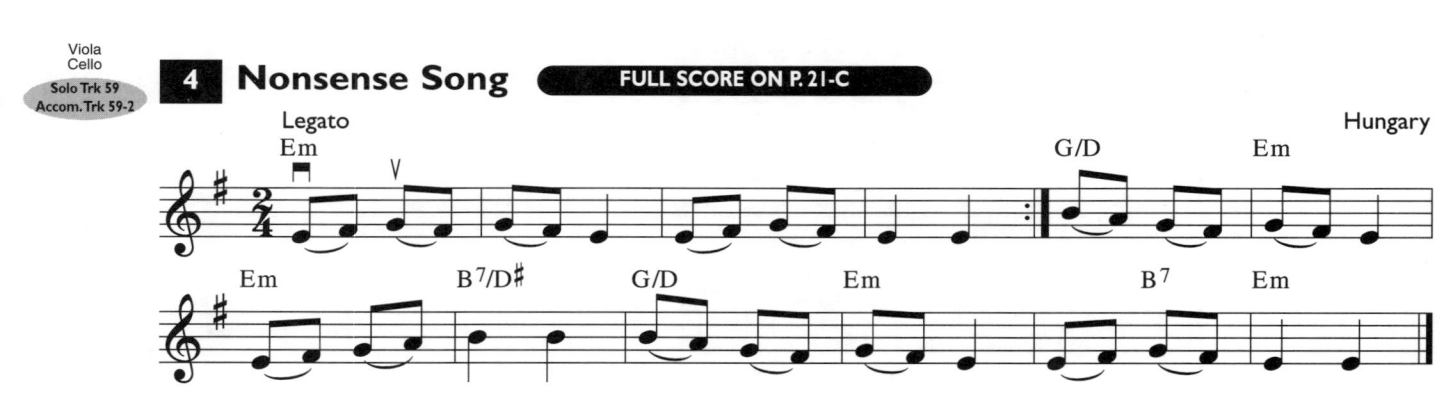

JAZZ WALTZ — *An adaptation of jazz harmonies to 3/4 time characterized by a hard driving bass line and swinging drums, especially in the ride cymbal.*

3 ☆ SOLO — **Cuckoo Song** (JAZZ WALTZ STYLE - "BY EAR" STARTING ON A)

Violin
Cello
Solo Trk 57
Accom. Trk 58

4 **Nonsense Song** — FULL SCORE ON P. 21-C

Viola
Cello
Solo Trk 59
Accom. Trk 59-2

Hungary

5 **S'evivon Round (Spin, My Top)** — FULL SCORE ON P. 21-D

Hebrew Song

CREATING COMPOSITIONS FROM A SINGLE MUSICAL IDEA
WITH THE STRUCTURAL ELEMENTS OF REPETITION AND VARIATION

Motif (Motive) - A short melodic pattern; a musical idea of two or more notes.

RAIN, RAIN (AN EXAMPLE OF A TUNE BASED UPON A SINGLE MUSICAL IDEA)

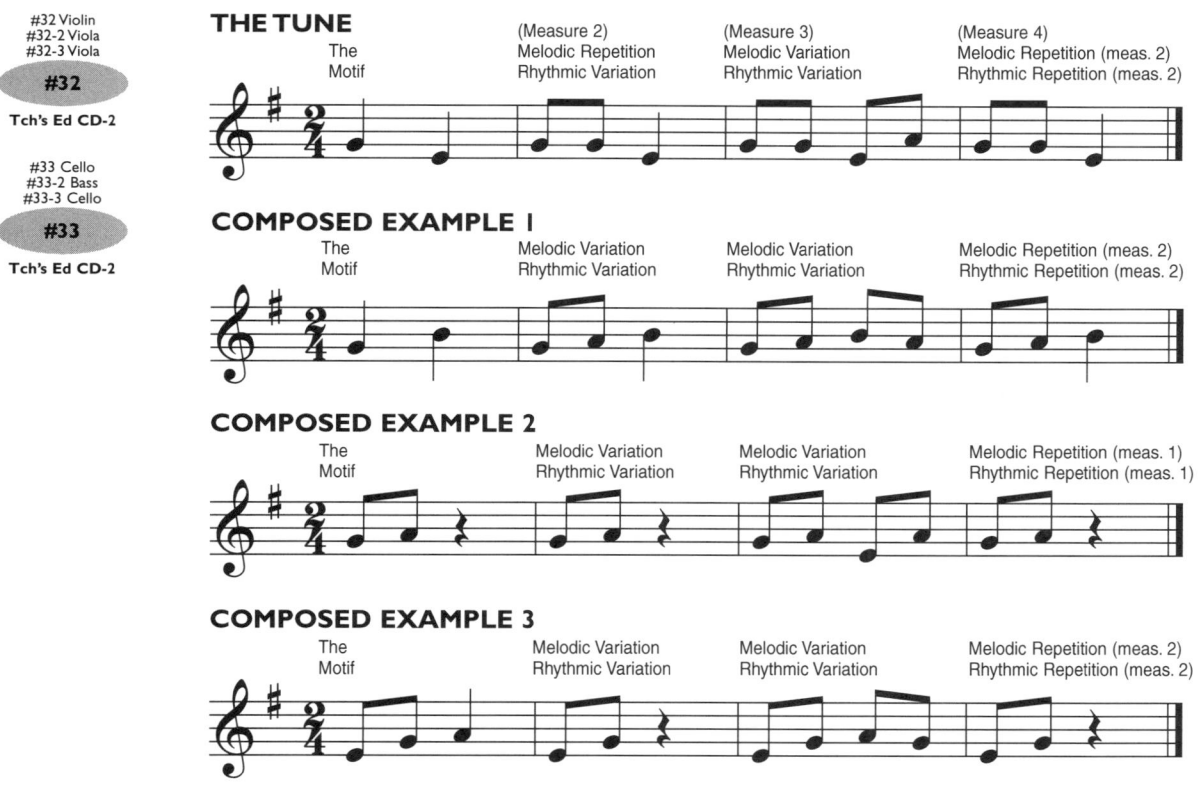

#32 Violin
#32-2 Viola
#32-3 Viola

#32

Tch's Ed CD-2

#33 Cello
#33-2 Bass
#33-3 Cello

#33

Tch's Ed CD-2

SPECIAL PROJECT — COMPOSE YOUR OWN TUNE FROM A SINGLE MUSICAL IDEA

Procedure 1. Compose a one-measure (two-beat) motif.
Direct students to use the tones D, E, G, A, B, and D.

My Motif

Procedure 2. Compose three one-measure (two-beat) segments that employ the Structural Elements of Repetition and Variation.

MY COMPOSITION

My Motif	Segment One	Segment Two	Segment Three

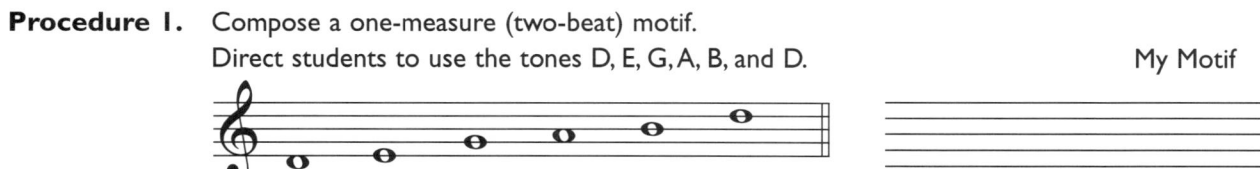

1 **Shepherd's Hey** (WITH SLURS)

Moderato

English Country Dance Tune

Accom.
#44
Tch's Ed CD-2

Accom. - Quick Time
#47
Tch's Ed CD-2

2 **Cuckoo Song**

Swing and sway

Germany

Violin
#82
Tch's Ed CD-2

Cello
#83
Tch's Ed CD-2

Accom.
#84
Tch's Ed CD-2

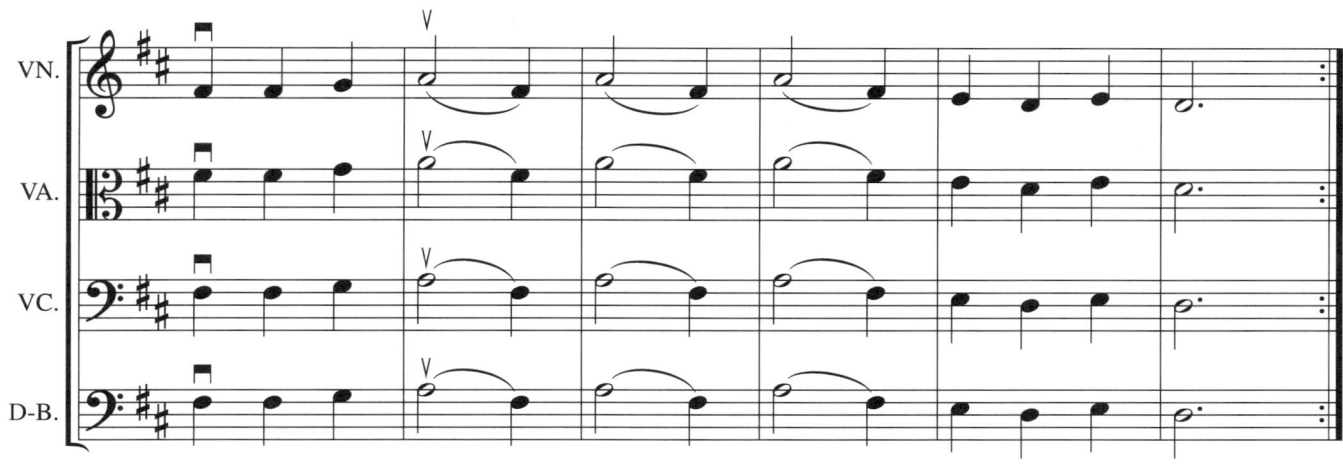

JAZZ WALTZ — *An adaptation of jazz harmonies to 3/4 time characterized by a hard driving bass line and swinging drums, especially in the ride cymbal.*

Violin
#85
Tch's Ed CD-2

Cello
#86
Tch's Ed CD-2

Accom.
#87
Tch's Ed CD-2

3 ★ SOLO — **Cuckoo Song** (JAZZ WALTZ STYLE - "BY EAR" STARTING ON A)

Viola
#88
Tch's Ed CD-2

Cello
#89
Tch's Ed CD-2

Accom.
#90
Tch's Ed CD-2

4 **Nonsense Song**

Legato

Hungary

5 ## S'evivon Round (Spin, My Top)

Not too slowly

Hebrew Song

S'e - vi - von, sov, sov, sov, Ha - nu - kah_____ hu hag tov,
Spin, my top 'round and 'round. Ha - nu - kah_____ days we love,

Ha - nu - kah, hu hag tov, s'e - vi - von, sov, sov, sov.
Glow - ing lights, joy - ful sounds, spin, my top 'round and 'round.

BLANK PAGE

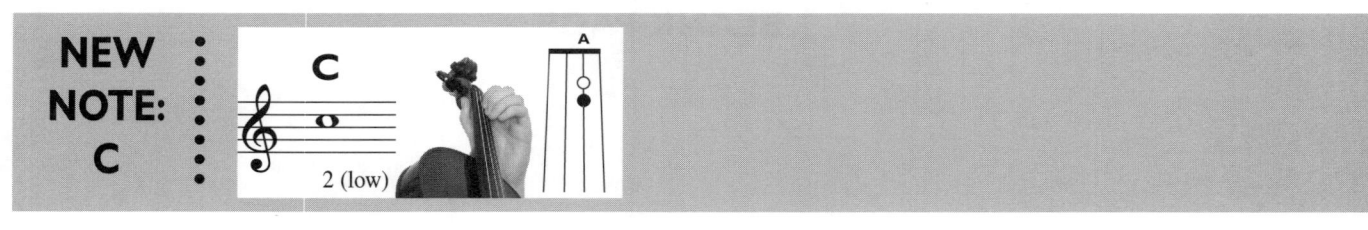

NEW NOTE: C

C
2 (low)

Violin
Cello
Solo Trk 60
Accom. Trk 60-2

1 **Juba**   FULL SCORE ON P. 22-C

Playfully   African-American Folk Song

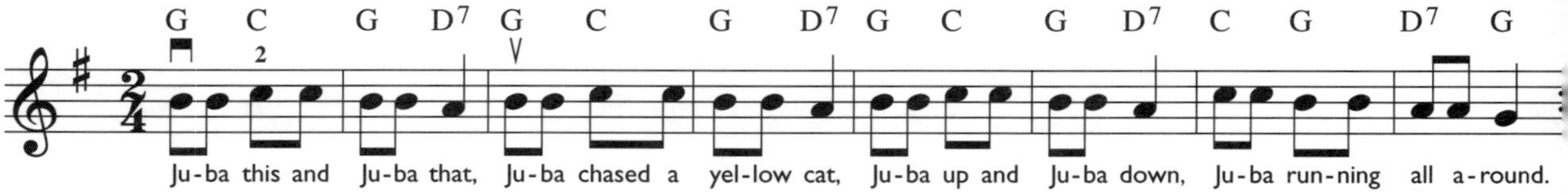

G C   G D⁷ G C   G D⁷ G C   G D⁷ C G   D⁷ G

Ju-ba this and Ju-ba that, Ju-ba chased a yel-low cat, Ju-ba up and Ju-ba down, Ju-ba run-ning all a-round.

Accom. Trk 60-2

2 **Variation on** *Juba*   FULL SCORE ON P. 22-D

Violin
Cello
Solo Trk 61
Accom. Trk 61-2

3 **A Paris**   FULL SCORE ON P. 22-D

Moderato   Old French Tune

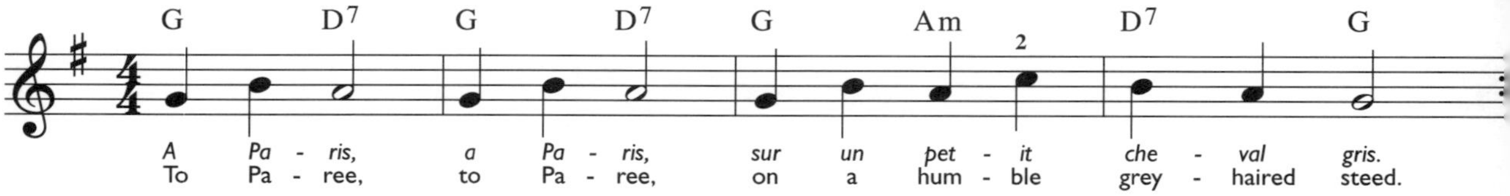

G   D⁷   G   D⁷   G   Am   D⁷   G

A   Pa - ris,   a   Pa - ris,   sur un pet - it che - val gris.
To   Pa - ree,   to   Pa - ree,   on   a   hum - ble grey - haired steed.

See Bass Alternative Fingerings: C, G - p. 22-D

SPEAKER BALANCE
CONTROL
L CD Trk 62 R
Violin   Accom.
Cello

4 **Cobbler, Cobbler**   FULL SCORE ON P. 22-E

Rhythmically   Jamaican Street Song

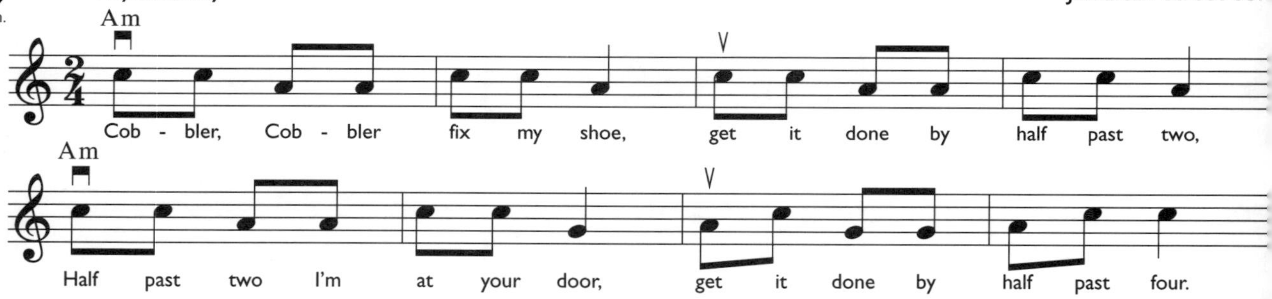

Am

Cob - bler, Cob - bler fix my shoe, get it done by half past two,

Am

Half past two I'm at your door, get it done by half past four.

CD Trk 62 R
Accom.

5 ★★★ SOLO — **Improvise Melodic Variations on** *Cobbler, Cobbler*
FULL SCORE ON P. 22-E

A C D (C A) G E

Use Tones of the A Minor Pentatonic Scale:

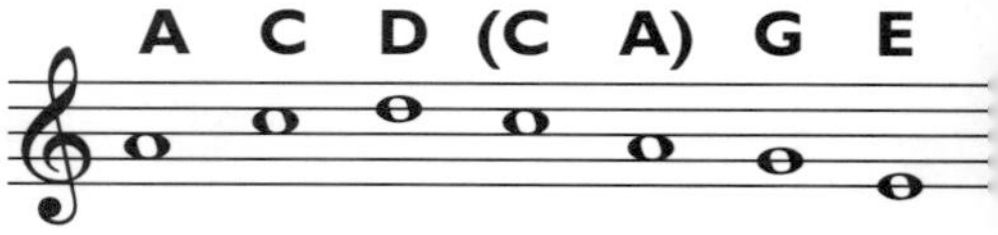

A SPECIAL OPTION FOR SPONTANEOUS MUSIC MAKING

COBBLER, COBBLER

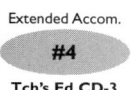

Extended Accom.

#4

Tch's Ed CD-3

Procedure 1. Direct students to employ one of the following options:

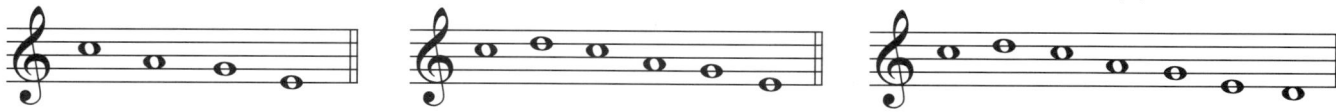

"Use the tones C, A, G, and E"   or   "Use the tones C, D, (C), A, G, and E"   or   "Use the tones C, D, (C), A, G, E, and D."

Procedure 2. Teach everyone an 8-beat riff (melodic ostinato).
(**NOTE:** Riffs may be improvised and taught to the class by the teacher or by students)

Riff 1

Riff 2

Procedure 3. Direct students to "Repeat the riff until the music ends."
(For an interesting effect, perform Riff 1 and Riff 2 simultaneously)

Procedure 4. When individual students are chosen or volunteer, suggest that they:

A. "Play the riff."
Example:

B. "Improvise an 8-beat rhythmic variation on the riff, or"
Example:

C. "Improvise an 8-beat rhythmic/melodic variation on the riff."
Example:

Optional Procedure 5. Direct students to simultaneously improvise variations using both sound and silence as expressive elements.

"COOL JAZZ"

A SPECIAL OPTION FOR SPONTANEOUS MUSIC MAKING
from the CD
DO IT! IMPROVISE *

Procedure 1. Teach students to play a musical riff (ostinato) in a swinging style (♫ = ♩♪)

Procedure 2. Direct students to "Continue the riff until the music ends"
(For an interesting effect, perform Riff 1 and Riff 2 simultaneously)

Procedure 3. When individual students are chosen or volunteer, suggest that they:

A. "Play the riff"

B. "Improvise a rhythmic variation on the riff, or"

C. "Improvise a rhythmic/melodic variation on the riff"

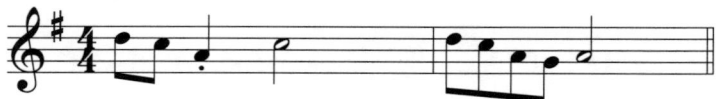

Procedure 4. Encourage students to notate their best improvised riffs (See page 41-F for Cool Jazz Composition Worksheet)

* *Do It! Improvise* (CD Backgrounds and Scale Notations for Entry-Level Music Improvisation - MLR 422) Albert Blaser and James Froseth, © 1994 GIA Publications Inc., 7404 South Mason Avenue, Chicago, IL 60638

NEW NOTES

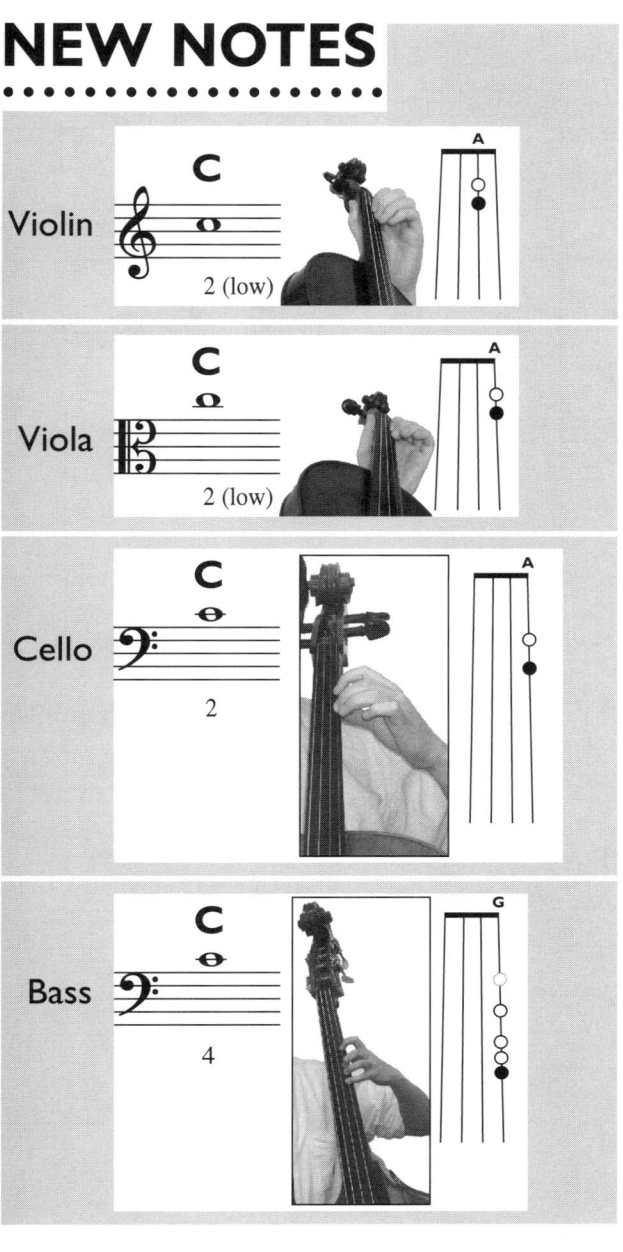

Violin — C — 2 (low)

Viola — C — 2 (low)

Cello — C — 2

Bass — C — 4

Violin
#91
Tch's Ed CD-2

Cello
#92
Tch's Ed CD-2

Accom.
#93
Tch's Ed CD-2

1 Juba

Playfully

African-American Folk Song

VN. — Ju-ba this and Ju-ba that, Ju-ba chased a yel-low cat, Ju-ba up and Ju-ba down, Ju-ba run-ning all a-round.

VA.

VC.

D-B.

2 **Variation on *Juba***

3 **A Paris**

Moderato

Old French Tune

A Pa - ris, a Pa - ris, sur un pet - it che - val gris.
To Pa - ree, to Pa - ree, on a hum - ble grey - haired steed.

ALTERNATIVE FINGERINGS

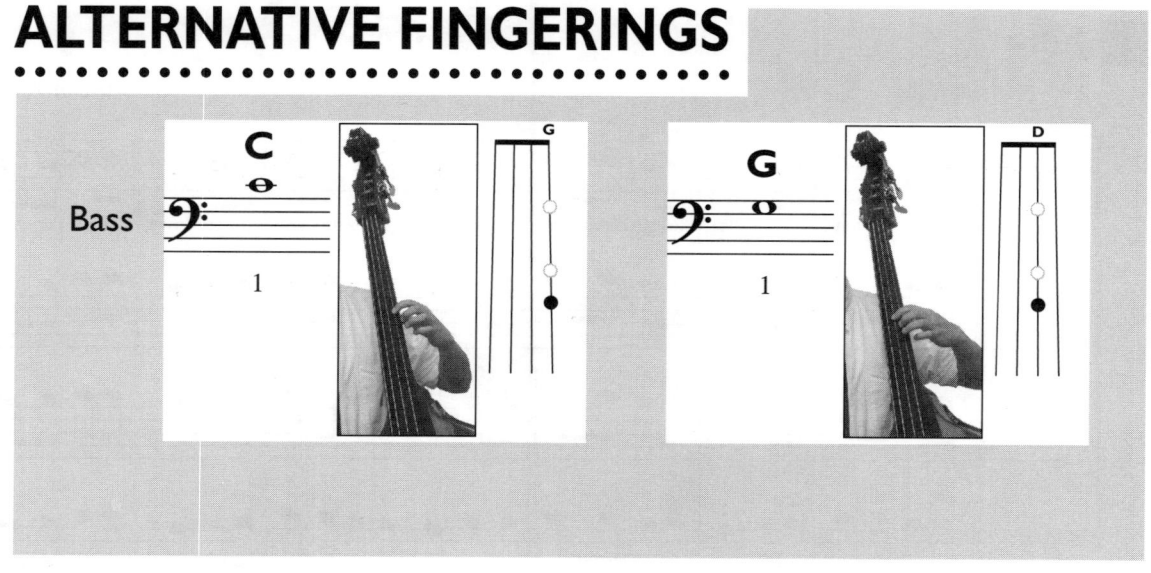

Violin
#1
Tch's Ed CD-3

Cello
#2
Tch's Ed CD-3

Accom.
#3
Tch's Ed CD-3

Extended Accom.
#4
Tch's Ed CD-3

4 Cobbler, Cobbler

Rhythmically

Jamaican Street Song

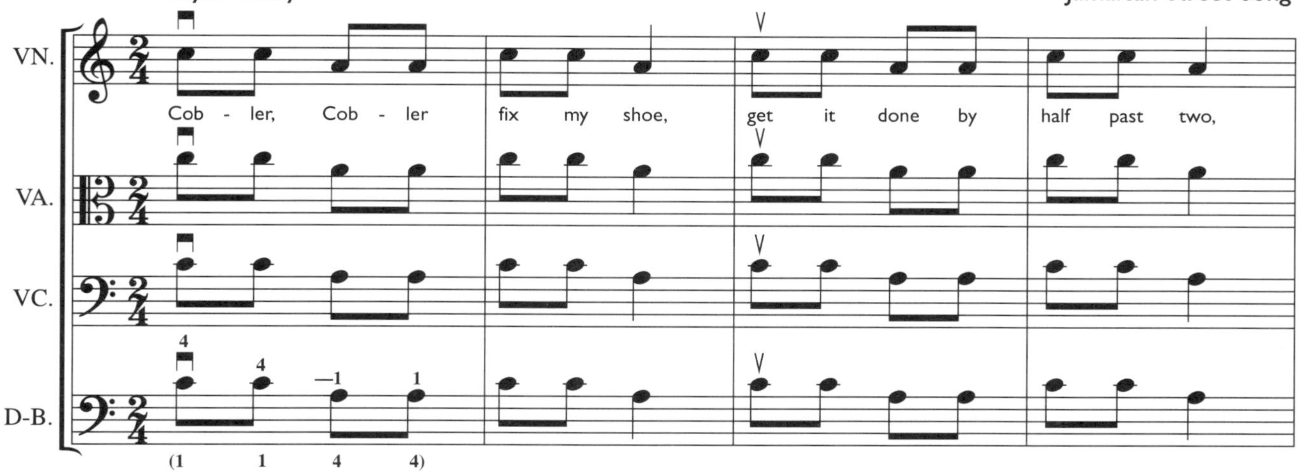

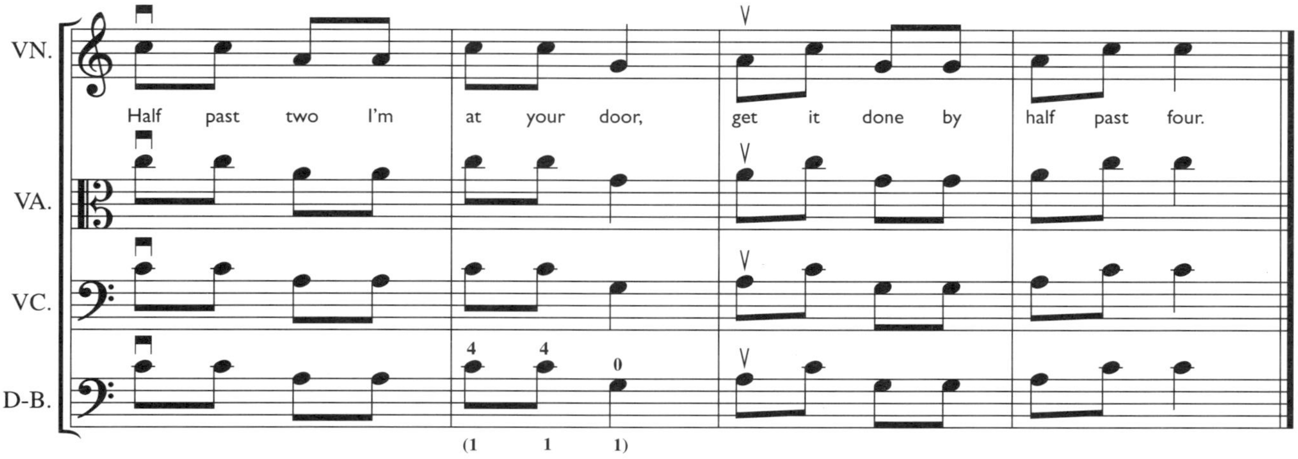

VN.
Cob - ler, Cob - ler fix my shoe, get it done by half past two,
VA.
VC.
D-B.
4 4 –1 1
(1 1 4 4)

VN.
Half past two I'm at your door, get it done by half past four.
VA.
VC.
D-B.
4 4 0
(1 1 1)

5 ★★★ SOLO — Improvise Melodic Variations on *Cobbler, Cobbler*

Use Tones of the A Minor Pentatonic Scale: A, C, D, (C), (A), G, and E

VN.
VA.
VC.
D-B.

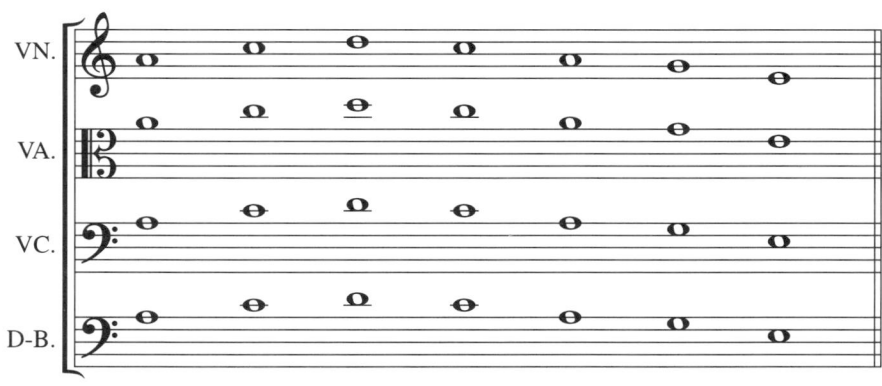

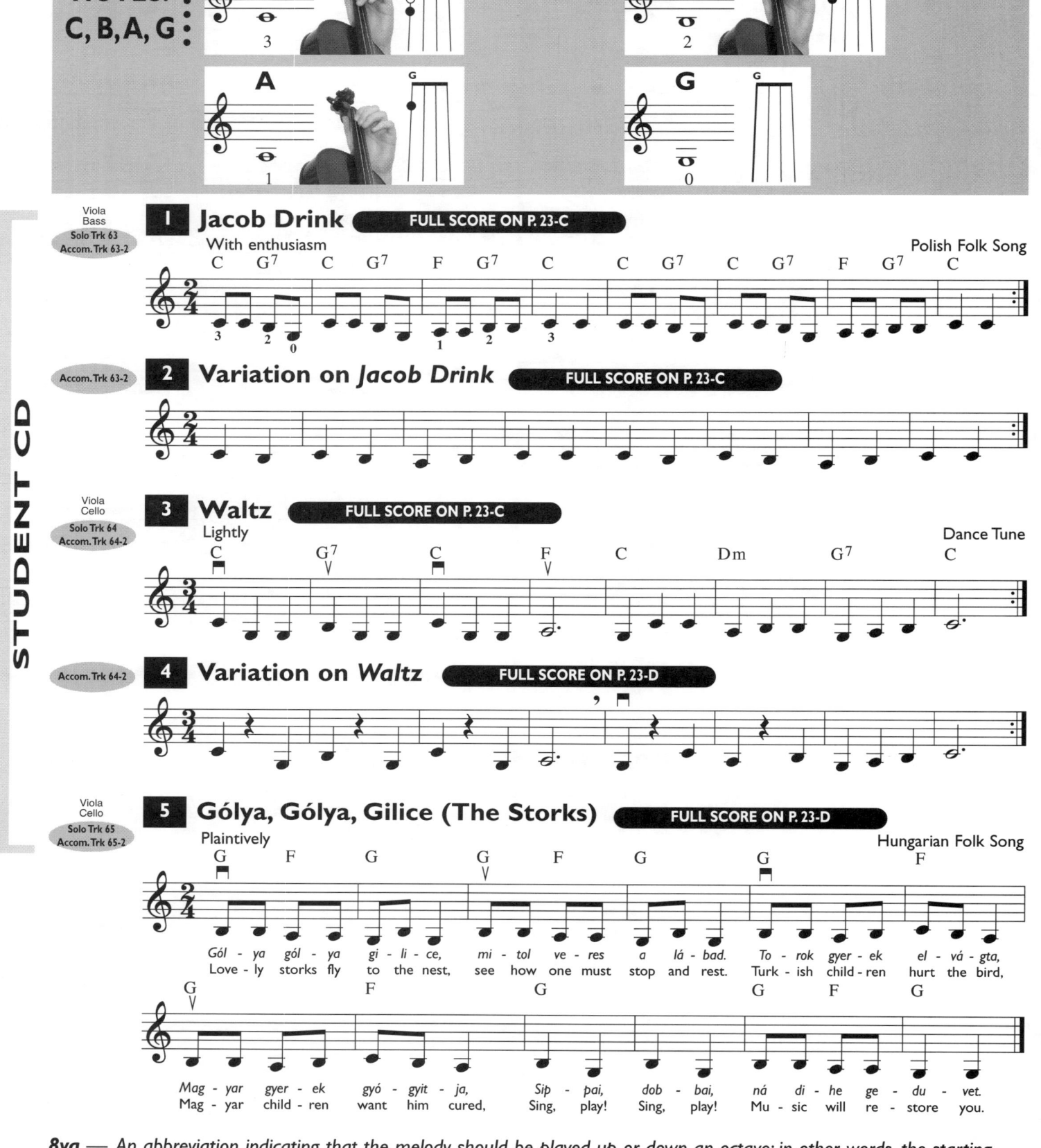

8va — *An abbreviation indicating that the melody should be played up or down an octave; in other words, the starting note is eight pitches higher or lower than notated. Pitch names remain the same.*

SPECIAL PROJECT — ★ **Learn to Play Songs on Page 22 8va Lower "By Ear"**

SPECIAL PROJECT — ★ **Learn to Play Songs on Page 23 8va Higher "By Ear"**

Rhythmic Flashcard Reading Review Option for *Golya, Golya, Gilice*

R-13   **R-2**   **R-14**

Rhythm Round

Rhythmic Reading Exercise

SPECIAL CREATIVE MUSICIANSHIP OPTION

COMPOSE A RHYTHMIC ROUND*

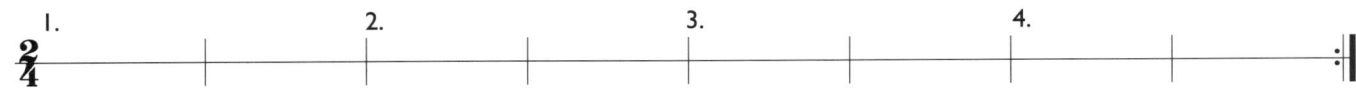

See page 41-1 for Principles of Music Notation

NEW NOTES

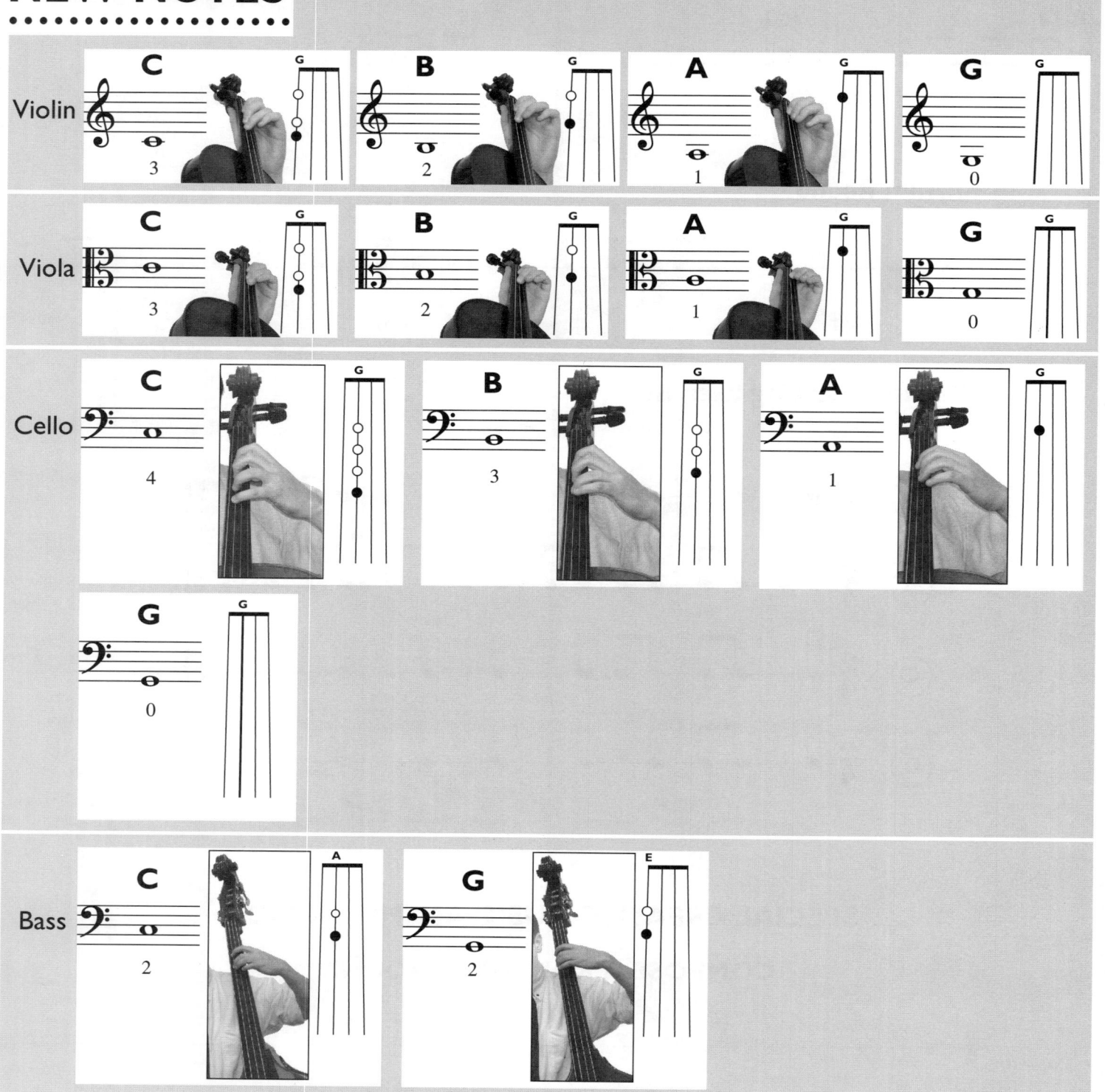

1 Jacob Drink

With enthusiasm

Polish Folk Song

2 Variation on *Jacob Drink*

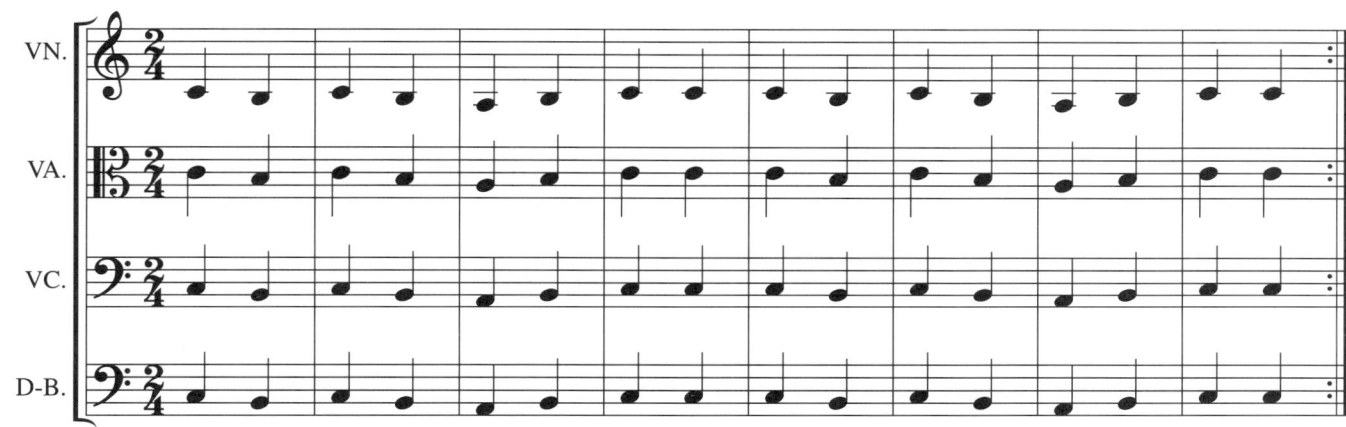

3 Waltz

Lightly

Dance Tune

Accom. **#10** Tch's Ed CD-3

4 Variation on *Waltz*

VN.
VA.
VC.
D-B.

Viola **#11** Tch's Ed CD-3

Cello **#12** Tch's Ed CD-3

Accom. **#13** Tch's Ed CD-3

5 Gólya, Gólya, Gilice (The Storks)

Plaintively

Hungarian Folk Song

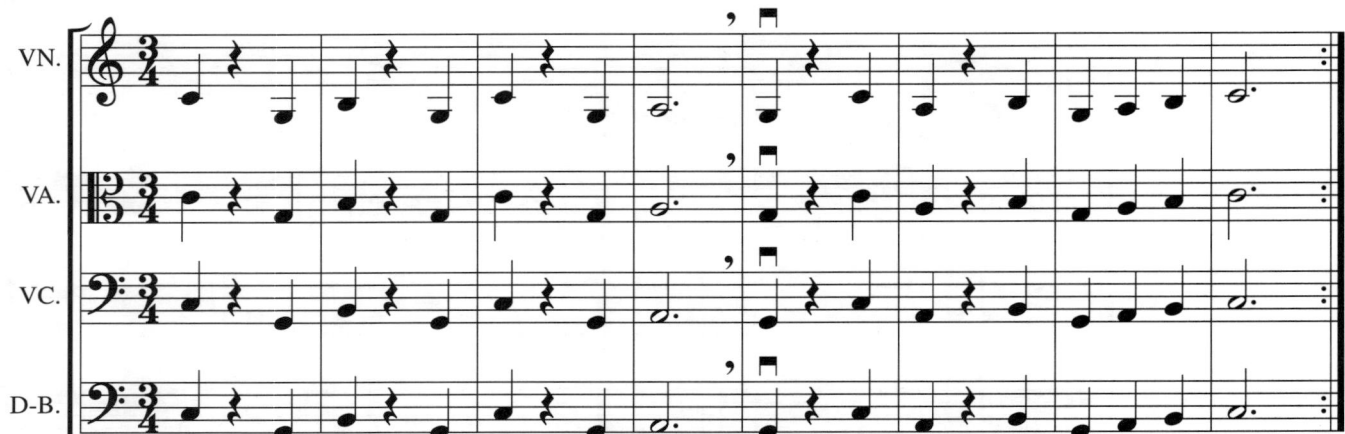

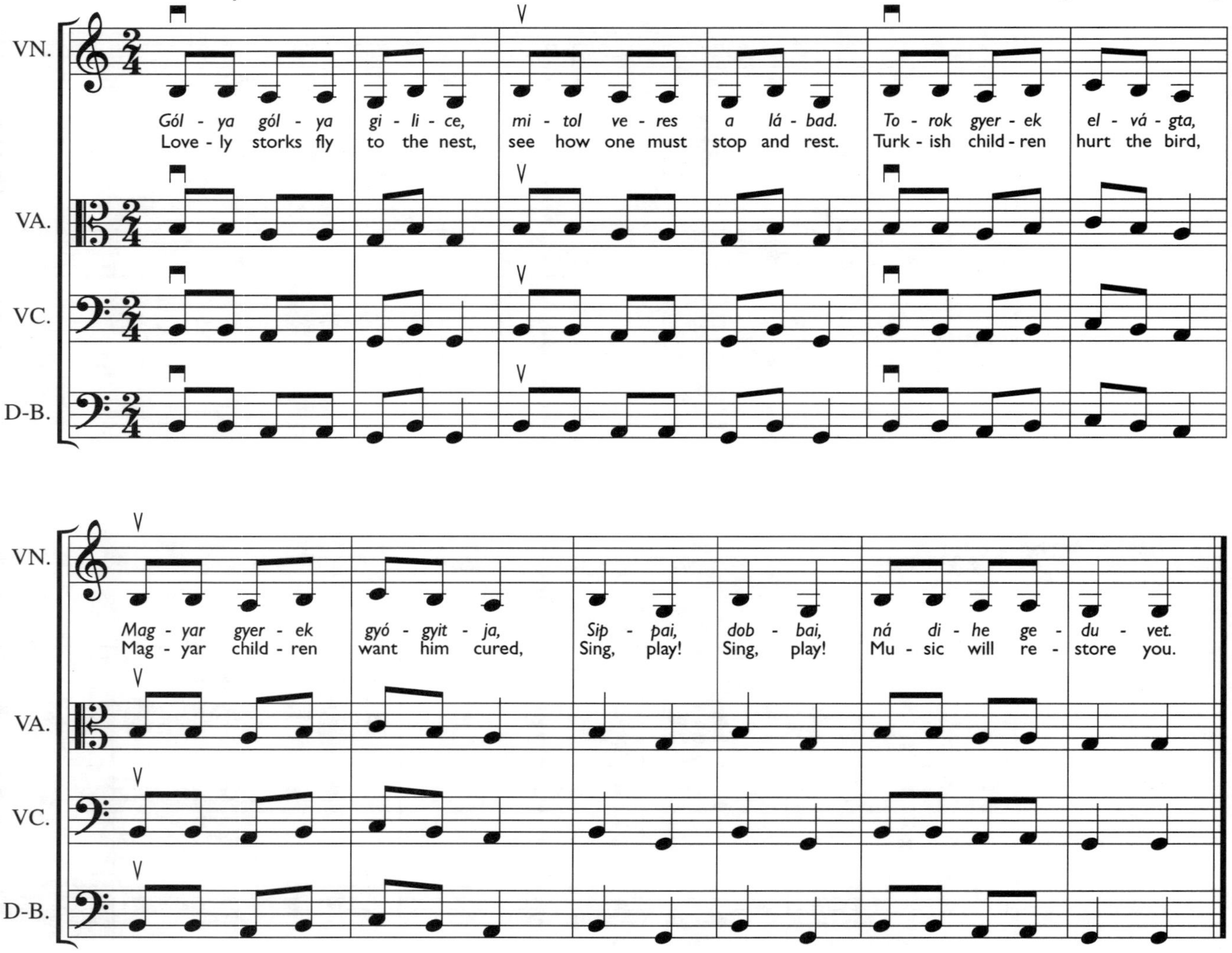
VN.
VA.
VC.
D-B.
Gól - ya gól - ya gi - li - ce, mi - tol ve - res a lá - bad. To - rok gyer - ek el - vá - gta,
Love - ly storks fly to the nest, see how one must stop and rest. Turk - ish child - ren hurt the bird,
Mag - yar gyer - ek gyó - gyit - ja, Sip - pai, dob - bai, ná di - he ge - du - vet.
Mag - yar child - ren want him cured, Sing, play! Sing, play! Mu - sic will re - store you.

8va — *An abbreviation indicating that the melody should be played up or down an octave; in other words, the starting note is eight pitches higher or lower than notated. Pitch names remain the same.*

SPECIAL PROJECT — ★ **Learn to Play Songs on Page 22 8va Lower "By Ear"**

Transpose songs on P. 22 down an octave (violin, viola, cello: to the G string, bass: to the A and E strings) "by ear."

Juba (IN G MAJOR - DOWN AN OCTAVE "BY EAR")

African-American Folk Song

Variation on *Juba* (IN G MAJOR - DOWN AN OCTAVE "BY EAR")

A Paris (IN G MAJOR - DOWN AN OCTAVE "BY EAR")

Old French Tune

Accom.
#3
Tch's Ed CD-3

Cobbler, Cobbler (IN A MINOR - DOWN AN OCTAVE "BY EAR")

Jamaican Street Song

Rhythmically

SPECIAL PROJECT — ★ Learn to Play Songs on Page 23 8va Higher "By Ear"

Transpose songs on P. 23 up an octave (violin, viola, cello: to the D and A strings, bass: to the G string) "by ear."

Accom.
#7
Tch's Ed CD-3

Jacob Drink (IN C MAJOR - UP AN OCTAVE "BY EAR")

Polish Folk Song

With enthusiasm

Accom.
#7
Tch's Ed CD-3

Variation on *Jacob Drink* (IN C MAJOR - UP AN OCTAVE "BY EAR")

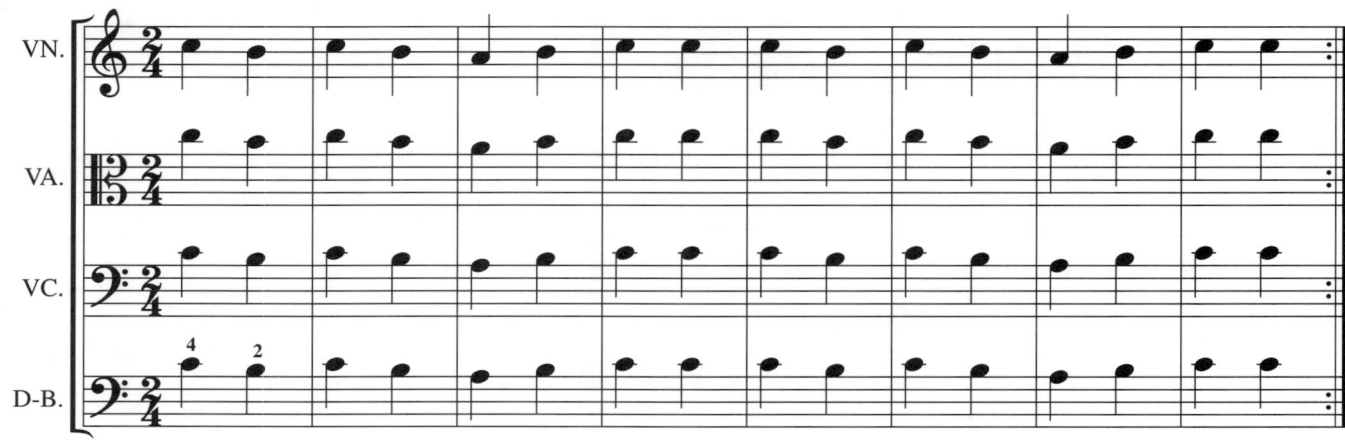

Accom.
#10
Tch's Ed CD-3

Waltz (IN C MAJOR - UP AN OCTAVE "BY EAR")

Lightly

Dance Tune

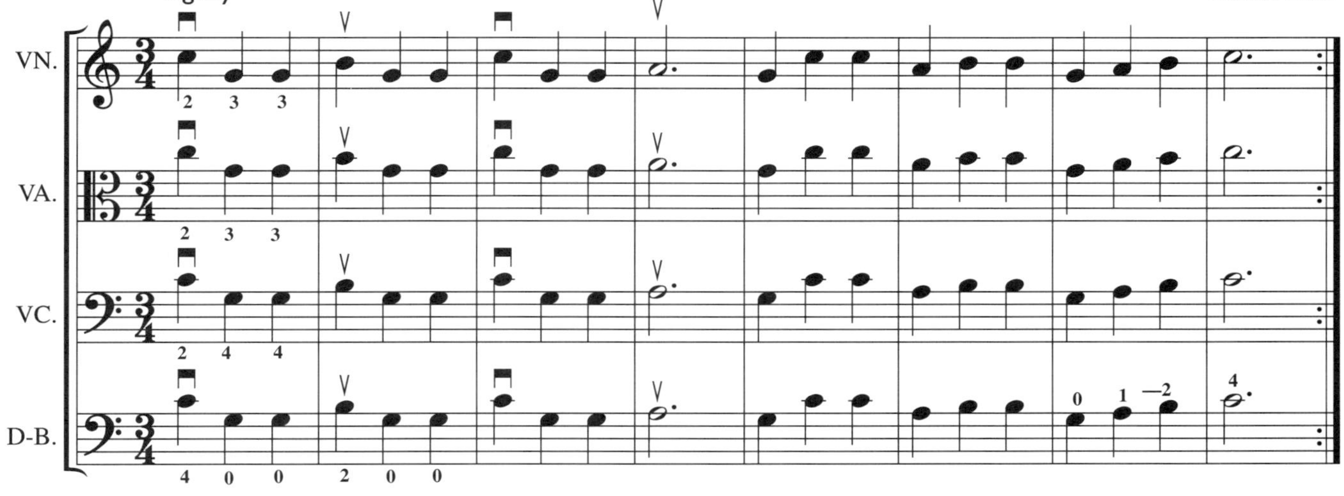
VN.
VA.
VC.
D-B.

Accom.
#10
Tch's Ed CD-3

Variation on *Waltz* (IN C MAJOR - UP AN OCTAVE "BY EAR")

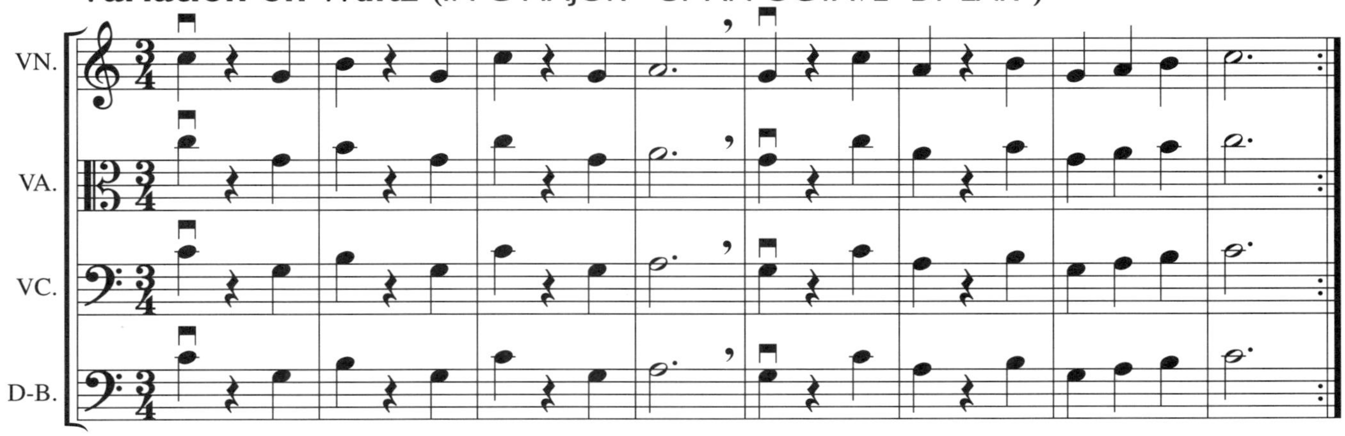
VN.
VA.
VC.
D-B.

#13
Tch's Ed CD-3

Gólya, Gólya, Gilice (The Storks) (IN G MIXOLYDIAN - UP AN OCTAVE "BY EAR")

Plaintively

Hungarian Folk Song

VN.
VA.
VC.
D-B.

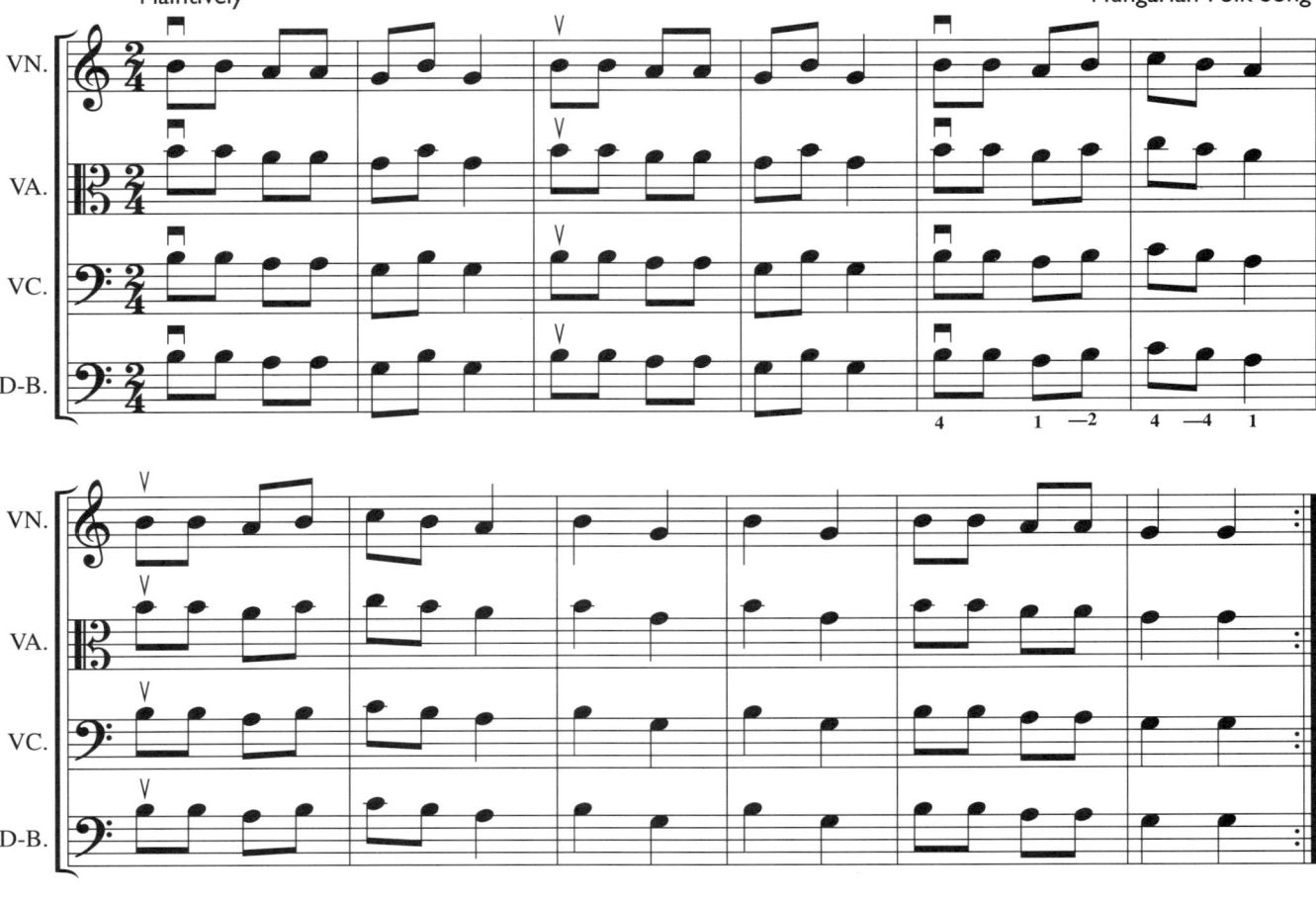

VN.
VA.
VC.
D-B.

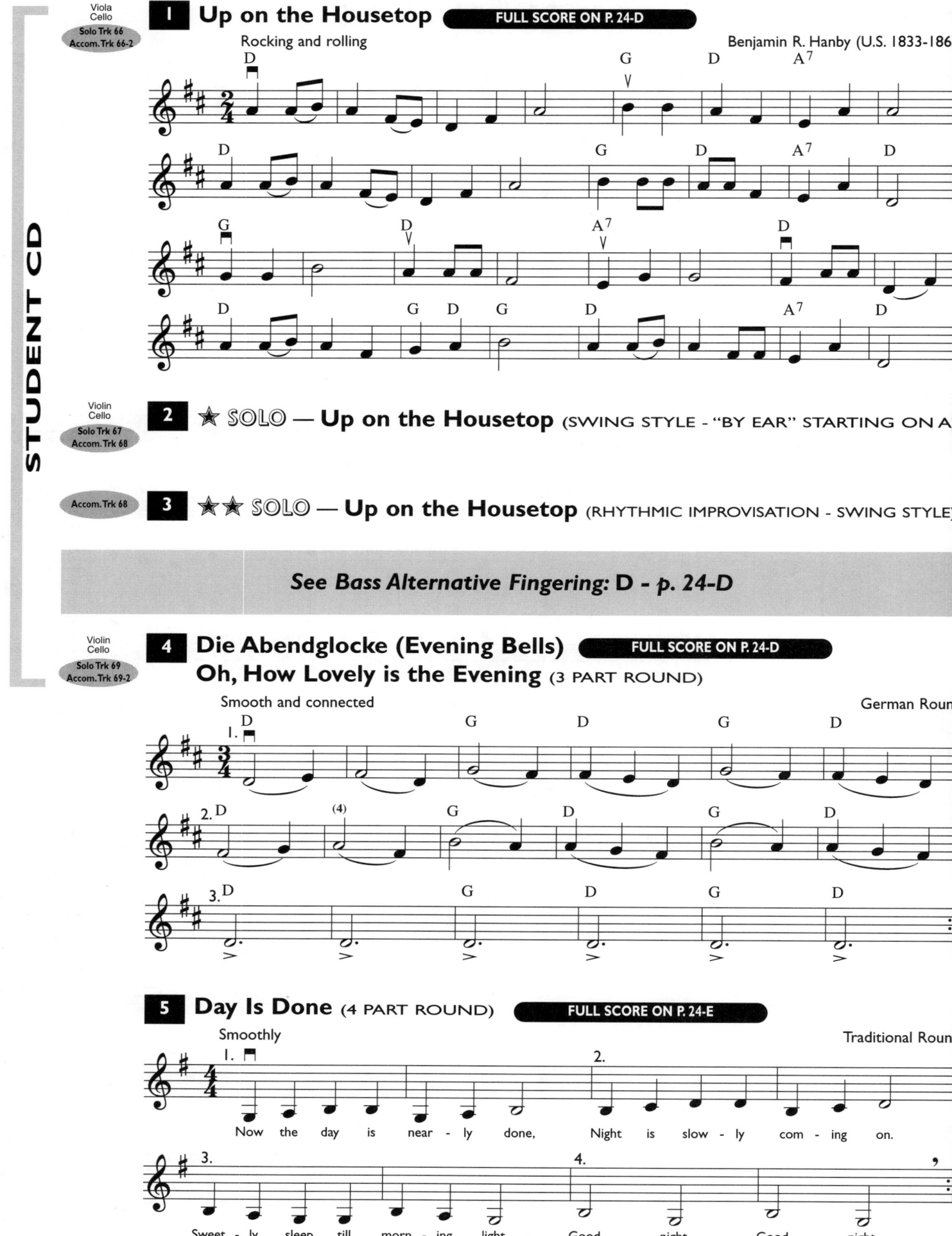

Rhythmic Flashcard Reading Option for *Up On the Housetop*

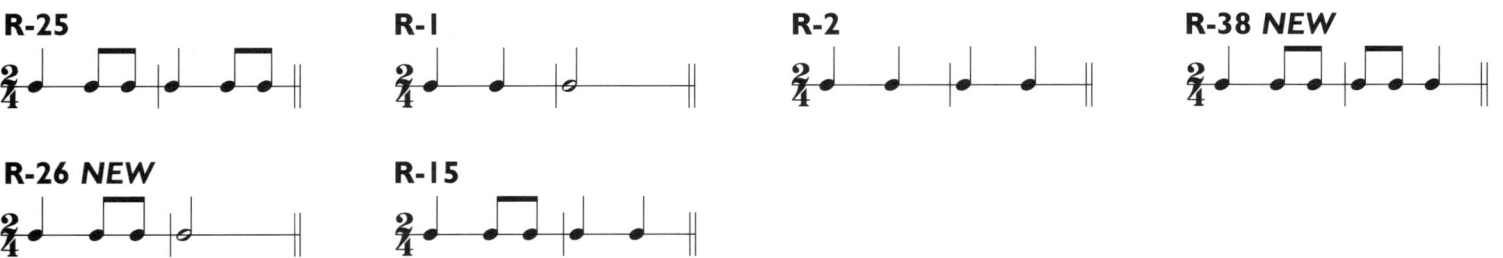

R-25 R-1 R-2 R-38 *NEW*

R-26 *NEW* R-15

Rhythmic Reading Exercise

(A) (B) (C) (D)

Rhythmic Reading Round

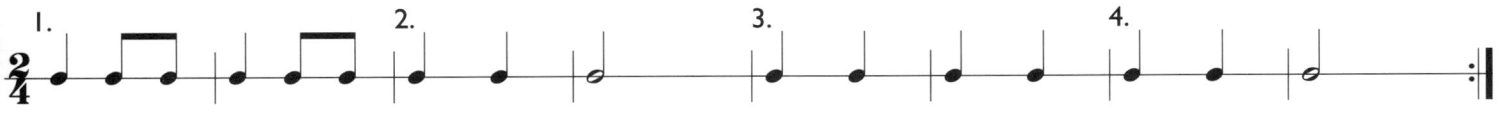

1. 2. 3. 4.

SPECIAL OPTION FOR TECHNICAL DEVELOPMENT

INTRODUCE "CLOSED" D OPTION FOR ALL INSTRUMENTS

- **Violin, viola use 4th finger on the G string instead of open D**

- **Cello use 4th finger, second position, on the G string OR 1st finger, 4th position, on the G string instead of open D**

- **Bass use 4th finger, second position, on the A string instead of open D**

- **Alternate closed and open D's for the last measures of** *Die Abendglocke*

A SPECIAL INDIVIDUALIZED OPTION FOR SPONTANEOUS MUSIC MAKING

Return to COBBLER, COBBLER

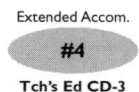

Extended Accom.
#4
Tch's Ed CD-3

THE MUSICAL PARAPHRASE — An improvised conversation between two performers. The conversation begins with a 4-beat improvised "Call." The "Response" is a 4-beat restatement (paraphrase) of the "Call" using a slightly different combination of tones, rhythms, and/or articulations.

Direct students to employ one of the following options:

A. "Use the tones C, A, and G." or   **B.** "Use the tones D, C, A, and G." or   **C.** "Use the tones D, C, A, G, E, and D."

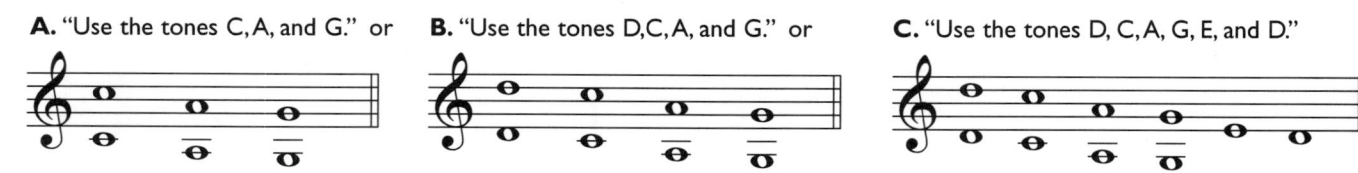

EXAMPLE OF OPTION A:

Teacher: "The Starting Note is C."

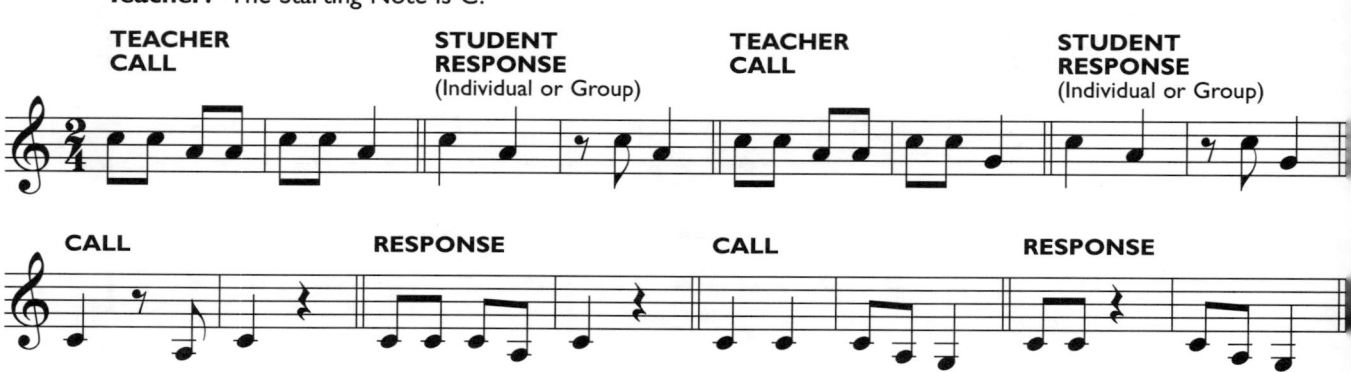

EXAMPLE OF OPTION B:

Teacher: "The Starting Note is C."

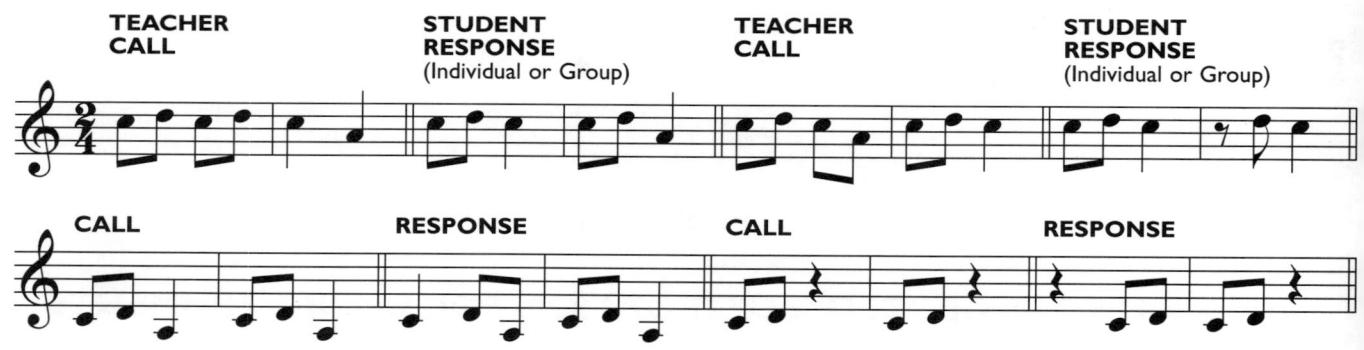

EXAMPLE OF OPTION C:

Teacher: "The Starting Note is C."

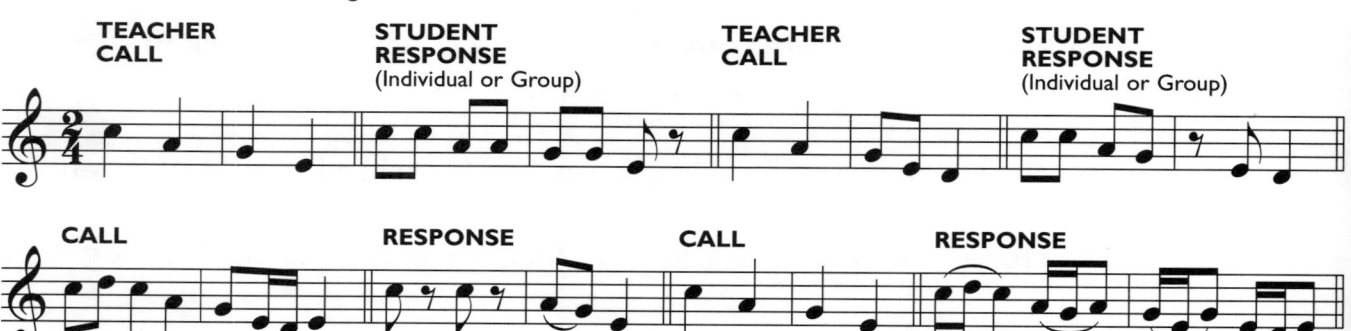

Up on the Housetop

Rocking and rolling

Benjamin R. Hanby (U.S. 1833-1867)

2 ★ SOLO — **Up on the Housetop** (SWING STYLE - "BY EAR" STARTING ON A)

Violin
#17
Tch's Ed CD-3

3 ★★ SOLO — **Up on the Housetop** (RHYTHMIC IMPROVISATION - SWING STYLE)

Cello
#18
Tch's Ed CD-3

Accom.
#19
Tch's Ed CD-3

ALTERNATIVE FINGERING

Violin
#20
Tch's Ed CD-3

4 **Die Abendglocke (Evening Bells)**
Oh, How Lovely is the Evening (3 PART ROUND)

Cello
#21
Tch's Ed CD-3

Accom.
#22
Tch's Ed CD-3

Smooth and connected   German Round

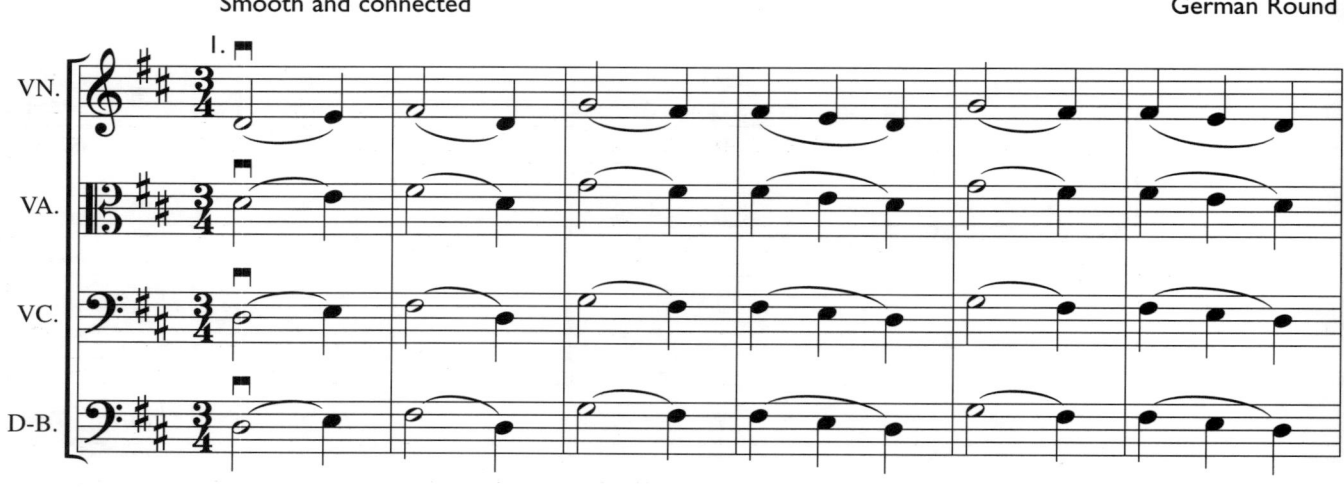

5 ## Day Is Done (4 PART ROUND)

Smoothly

Traditional Round

Now the day is near - ly done, Night is slow - ly com - ing on.

Sweet - ly sleep till morn - ing light. Good night. Good night.

SPICCATO — *A bowing style that allows the bow to spring or bounce away from the string between notes. The first of a series of spiccato strokes usually begins on the string. A dot (.) over or under a note can indicate a spiccato stroke.*

STUDENT CD

Accom. Trk 31

1 **Lightly Bounce the Bow to Lightly Row** — FULL SCORE ON P. 25-B

Accom. Trk 31

FULL SCORE ON P. 25-B

2 **Variation One on** *Lightly Bounce the Bow to Lightly Row*

Accom. Trk 31

FULL SCORE ON P. 25-C

3 **Variation Two on** *Lightly Bounce the Bow to Lightly Row*

Violin
Bass
Solo Trk 70
Accom. Trk 70-2

4 **Norwegian Dance** — FULL SCORE ON P. 25-D

Lively

Scandinavian Folk Tune

BOUFFONS — *Costumed dancers of the 15th and 16th centuries.*

Violin
Cello
Solo Trk 71
Accom. Trk 71-2

5 **Bouffons** — FULL SCORE ON P. 25-D

Briskly

Thoinot Arbeau (ca. 1519-1595)

Rhythmic Flashcard Reading Option for *Norwegian Dance*

A SPECIAL OPTION FOR INDIVIDUAL AND ENSEMBLE TECHNICAL DEVELOPMENT
APPLY RHYTHMIC SUBDIVISION AND SPICCATO BOWING TO A FAMILIAR TUNE ("BY EAR")

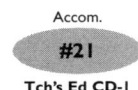

HOT CROSS BUNS

Procedure 1. Direct students to "Play the melody or use rhythmic subdivision."

      Procedure 1a. Direct students to "Use the spiccato bowing on the subdivisions."
           (If playing without accompaniment, tempo can be modified to ease bowing.)

Example:

Procedure 2. Assign sections or groups of students either the melody or the subdivided variation
      (on the string or spiccato).

Example:

Procedure 3. Create an ensemble arrangement by alternating sections or groups of students on
      the melody and subdivided variation.

      Procedure 3a. Teacher or student volunteers can suggest other musical variations,
           such as pizzicato, dynamics, legato, and octave transposition.

APPLY THIS PROCEDURE TO FAMILIAR TUNES SUCH AS:

Mary Had a Little Lamb
Notes
Down By the Station
Stepping and Skipping
Au Claire de la Lune
Old King Cole
Lightly Row
Shepherd's Hey

25-B

SPICCATO — *A bowing style that allows the bow to spring or bounce away from the string between notes. The first of a series of spiccato strokes usually begins on the string. A dot (.) over or under a note can indicate a spiccato stroke.*

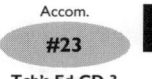

1 **Lightly Bounce the Bow to Lightly Row**

2 **Variation One on *Lightly Bounce the Bow to Lightly Row***

3 **Variation Two on** *Lightly Bounce the Bow to Lightly Row*

Violin
#24
Tch's Ed CD-3

Bass
#25
Tch's Ed CD-3

Accom.
#26
Tch's Ed CD-3

4 Norwegian Dance

Lively

Scandanavian Folk Tune

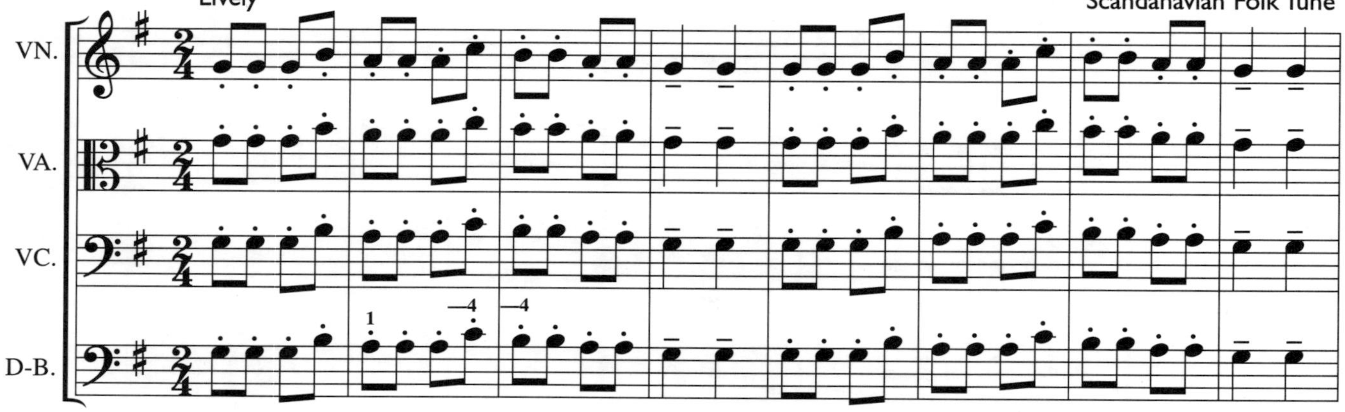

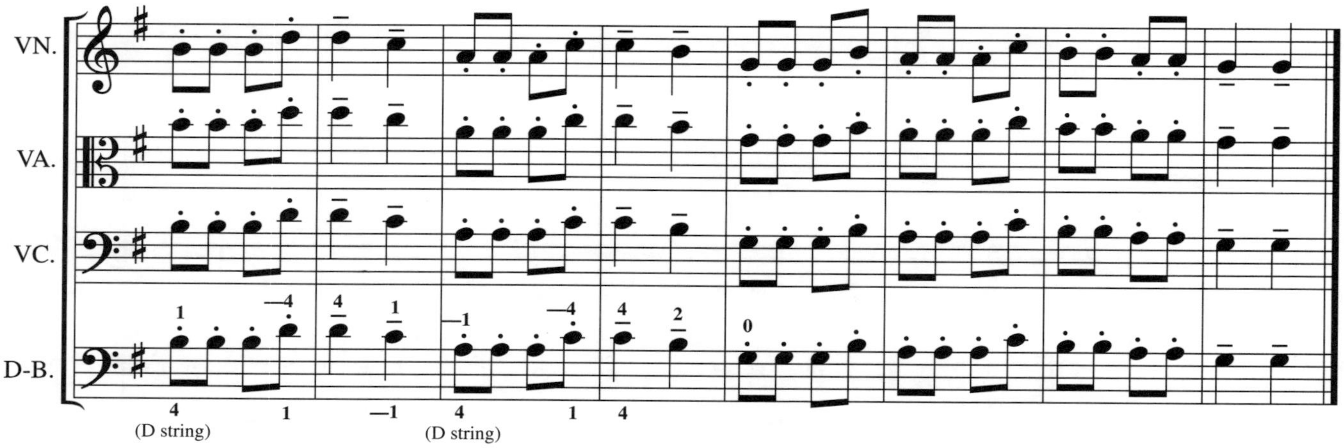

***BOUFFONS** — Costumed dancers of the 15th and 16th centuries.*

Violin
#27
Tch's Ed CD-3

Cello
#28
Tch's Ed CD-3

Accom.
#29
Tch's Ed CD-3

5 Bouffons

Briskly

Thoinot Arbeau (ca. 1519-1595)

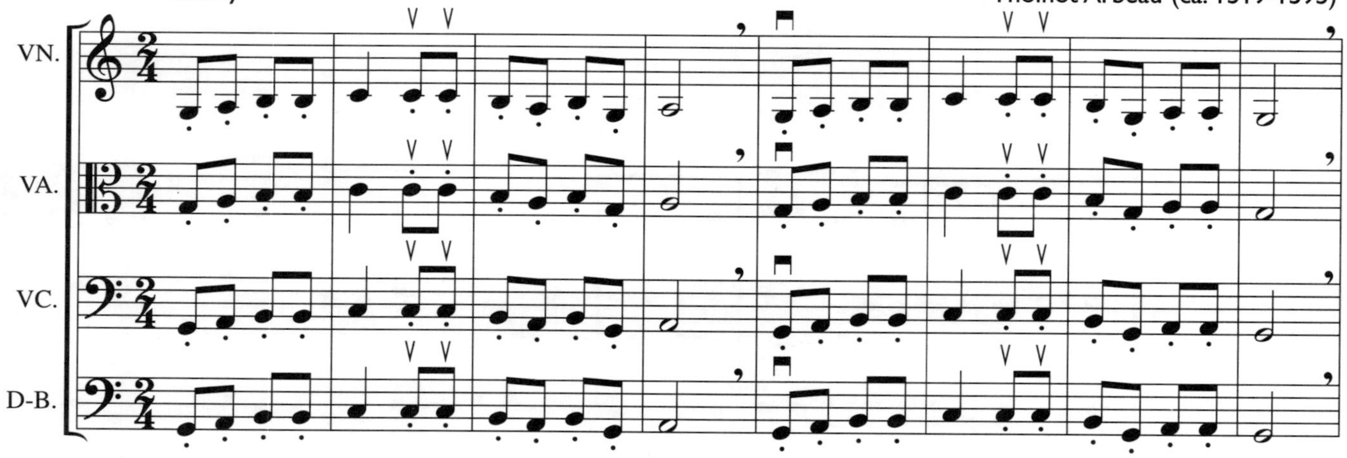

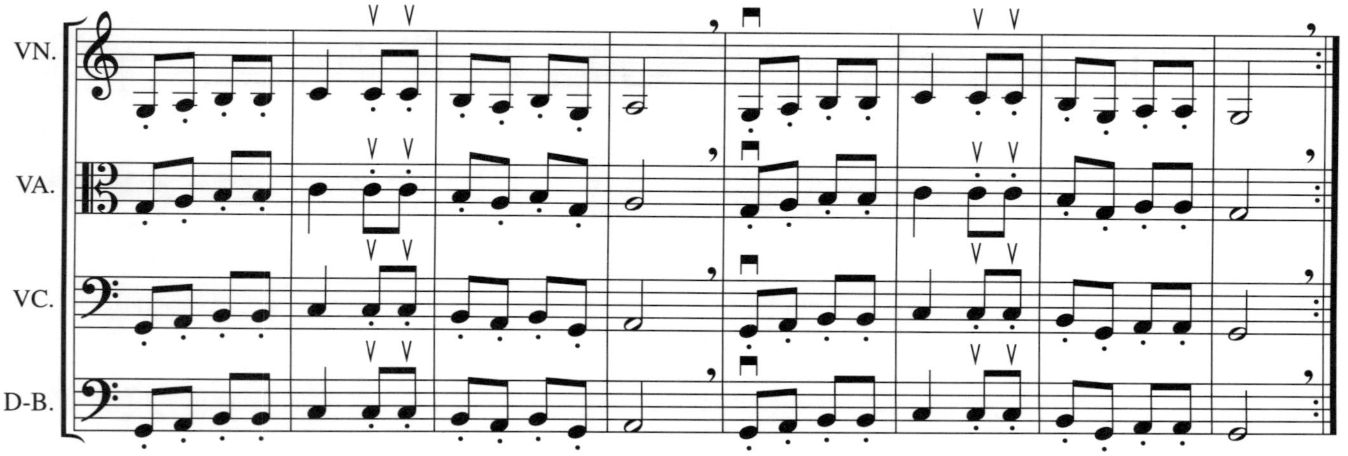

BLANK PAGE

1 **Round Evening** FULL SCORE ON P. 26-F

U.S.

Smoothly

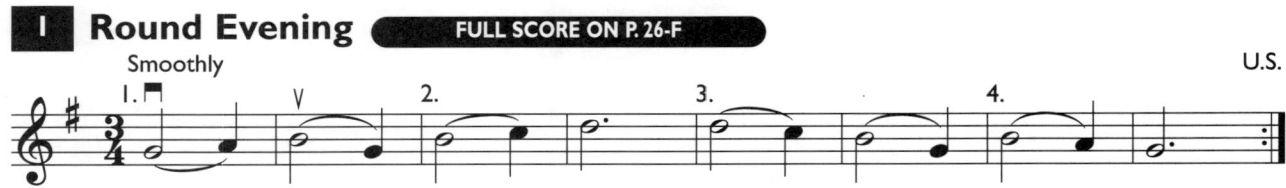

2 **Round Evening Two** FULL SCORE ON P. 26-F

U.S.

Smoothly

SPEAKER BALANCE
CONTROL
L CD Trk 72 R
Viola   Accom.
Cello

3 **The Blues in D** FULL SCORE ON P. 26-F

U.S.

In a swinging style

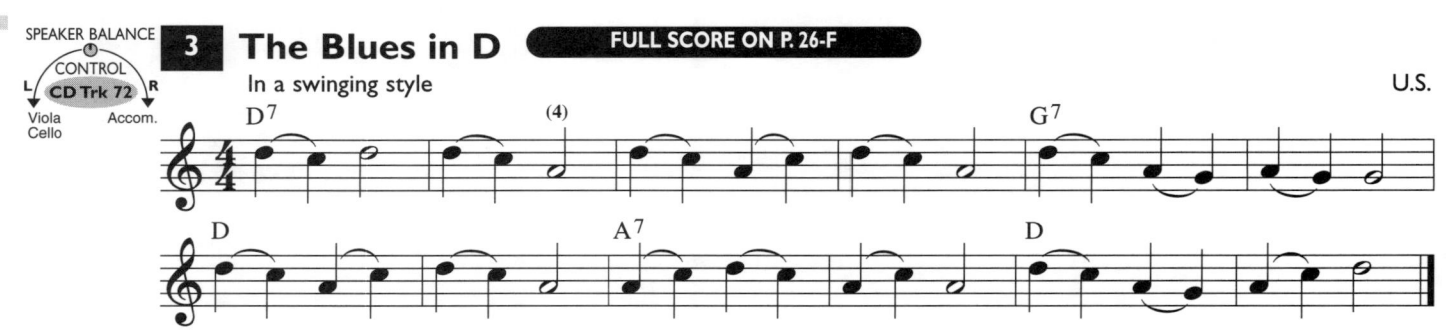

CALL AND RESPONSE — *A musical alternation between two performers or a performer and a group of performers.*
The musical response to the call can be imitated or improvised.

L Call and Resp. R
Trk 73
Violin   Accom.
Cello

4 ★ SOLO — **The Blues in D** (IMITATIVE CALL AND RESPONSE - "BY EAR" STARTING ON D)

EXAMPLE: Call   **Response (Imitated)**

AS NOTATED ON P. 26-A

L Call and Resp. R
Trk 73
Violin   Accom.
Cello

5 ★★ SOLO — **The Blues in D** (IMITATIVE CALL AND RESPONSE - "BY EAR" STARTING ON D)

EXAMPLE: Call   **Response (Improvised)**

AS NOTATED ON P. 26-A

CD Trk 73 R
Accom.

6 ★★★ SOLO — **Improvise Over the 12 Bar Blues in D "By Ear"**

Use Tones of the D Mixolydian Scale:

FULL SCORE ON P. 26-H

STUDENT CD

Blues in D CALL AND RESPONSE (AS RECORDED ON STUDENT CD TRACK 73)

Intro:

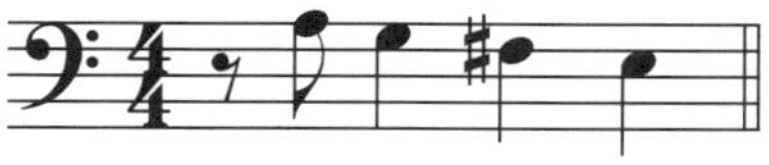

Swing style

Recorded Call   **Student Response**

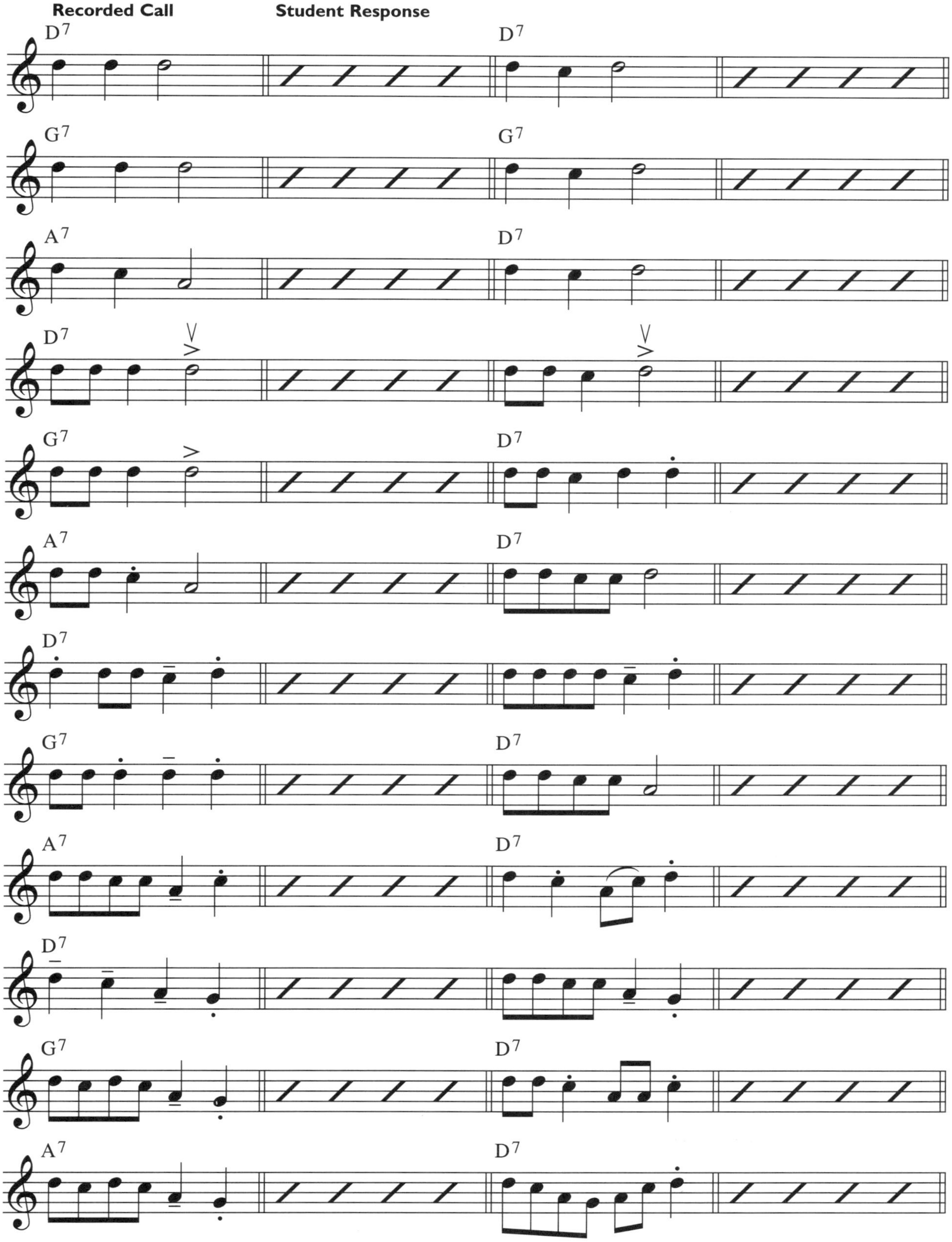

A SPECIAL INDIVIDUALIZED OPTION FOR SPONTANEOUS MUSIC MAKING

BLUES IN D
Vocal Call and Response
(Teacher Call - Student Response)

Extended Accom.
#33
Tch's Ed CD-3

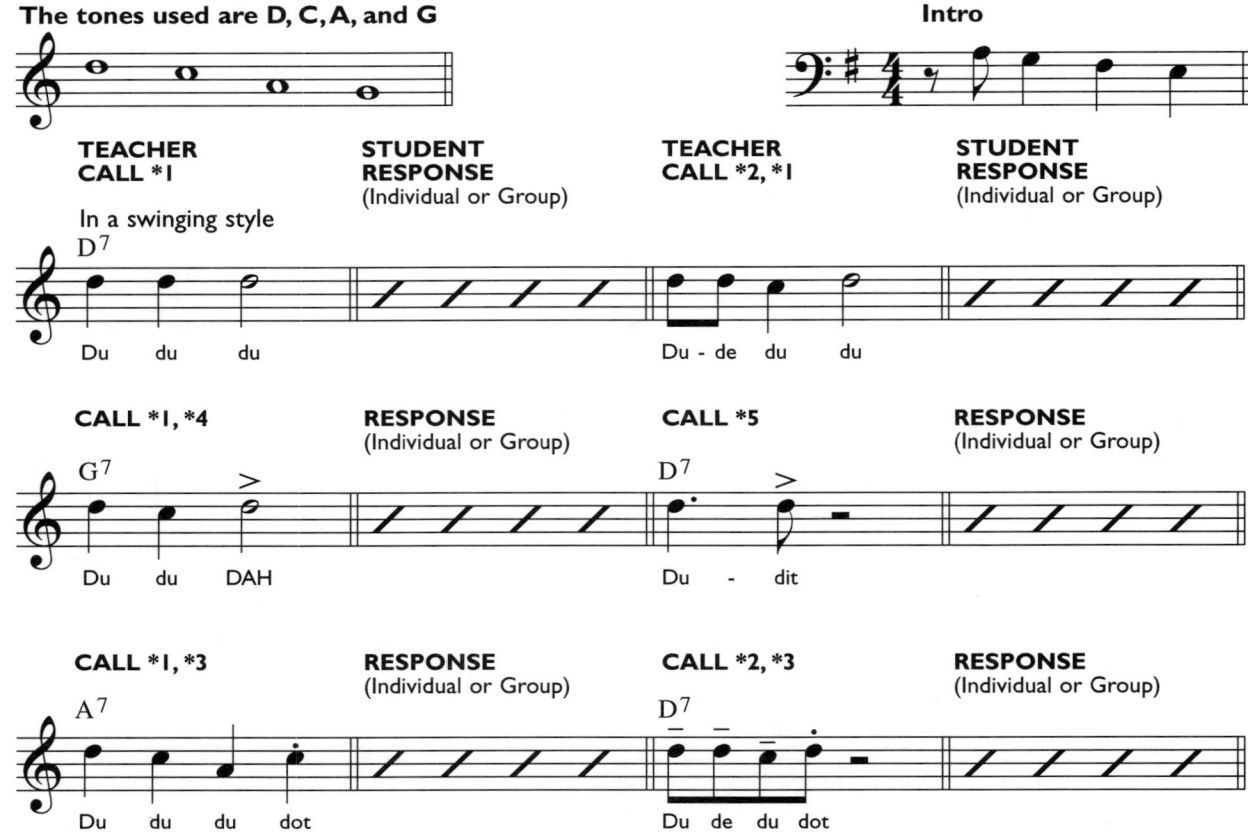

* 1. *Du* and *de*   normal articulation with a slight separation between tones
   Du as in "due;" de as in "day"
* 2. *Du—* and *de—*   connected style of articulation
* 3. *Dot*   slightly sharper articulation with a quick release of the tone
* 4. *DAH*   strong accent with a sharp release of the tone
* 5 *du—dit*   fully extended tone (du—) to a short tone with a quick release (dit)

ANOTHER OPTION FOR SPONTANEOUS AND CREATIVE MUSIC MAKING

• **Ask for volunteers to lead the class with their own improvised calls (Vocal or instrumental)**

• **Direct the class to follow with imitated or improvised responses**

CREATING A SAFE ENVIRONMENT FOR SPONTANEOUS MUSIC MAKING

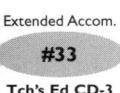

Extended Accom.
#33
Tch's Ed CD-3

Blues in D

PRINCIPLE #1: *Keep it Simple (Too many options can inhibit creativity).*

   Procedure 1. Direct students to "Use the tones D, C, A, and G."

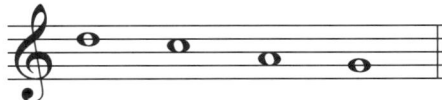

PRINCIPLE #2: *Keep Everyone Involved (Peer observation can be intimidating).*

   Procedure 2. Teach everyone an 8-beat riff (melodic ostinato).
   (**Note:** Riffs may be improvised and taught to the class by the teacher or by the students.)

   Example:

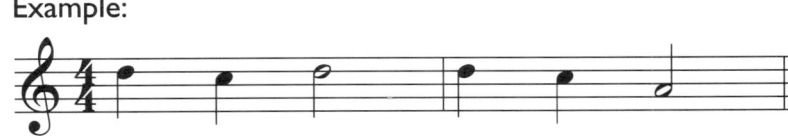

   Procedure 3. Direct students to "Repeat the riff until the music ends."

PRINCIPLE #3: *Allow for Self-Selection of Tasks (Absence of opinions can stifle creativity).*

   Procedure 4. When individual students are chosen or volunteer, suggest that they:

      A. "Play the riff (in a swinging style)."

      B. "Improvise a rhythmic variation on the riff, or"

      C. "Improvise a rhythmic/melodic variation on the riff."

PRINCIPLE #4: *Avoid Common Creativity Killers Including Expressions of Approval or Disapproval, Surveillance, Evaluation, Reward Systems, and Competition.*

FIRST STEPS TO MUSIC COMPOSITION
CREATING COMPOSITIONS BY NOTATING AND COMBINING IMPROVISED RIFFS

Extended Accom.
#33

Tch's Ed CD-3

Blues in D

Procedures:

A. Provide students with opportunities to improvise musical riffs over recorded background music. (Riffs are usually four- or eight-beat melodic patterns that are repeated over and over the background music while others improvise.) (See example below.)

B. Teach students music manuscript skills necessary to notate their best improvised riffs.

C. Combine several riffs to compose a 12-bar blues melody. (See example below.)

D. Combine musically compatible riffs to compose two- and three-part pieces.

EXAMPLE OF PROCEDURE A AND B, ABOVE

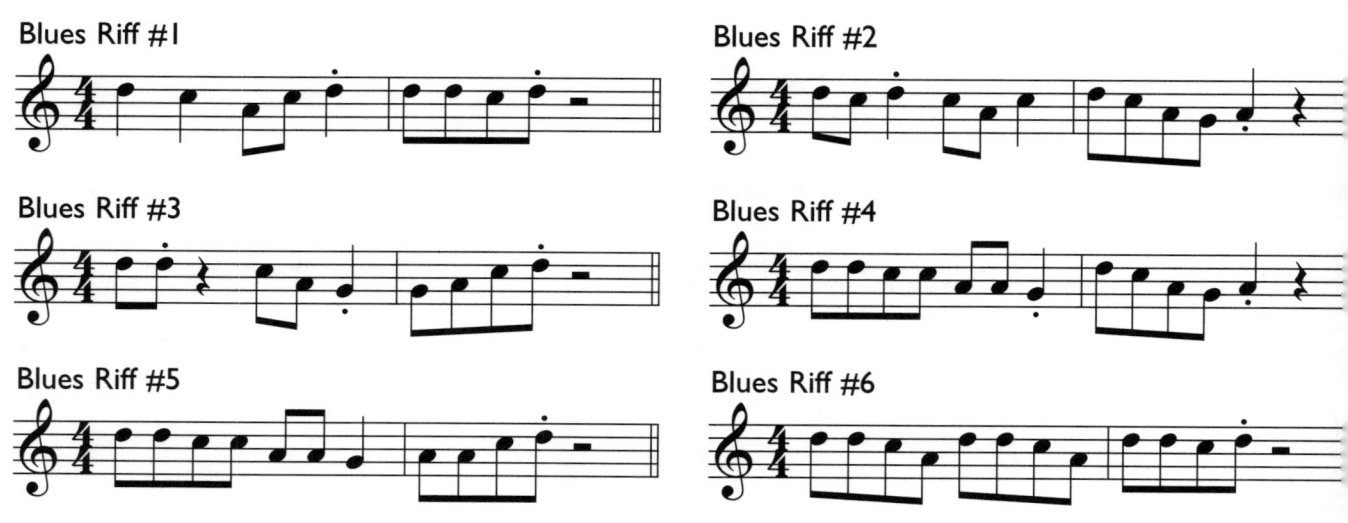

My Blues in D (EXAMPLE OF POCEDURE C, ABOVE)

See page 41-G for Blues in D Composition Worksheet

BLUES SHOWCASE
- Ensemble Arrangement -
(With Group Call and Response and Accompanied Improvisation)

GROUP ONE:

Option 1. Play the riff 12 times. Then, play the ending tone.
Option 2. Improvise one bar "Calls" or "Responses" with another player (6 "Calls" or 6 "Responses").
Option 3. Improvise two bar "Calls" or "Responses" with another player (3 "Calls" or 3 "Responses").
Option 4. Share two bar solos with other members of the ensemble.

GROUP TWO:

Option 1. Play the riff 12 times. Then, play the ending tone.
Option 2. Improvise one bar "Calls" or "Responses" with another player (6 "Calls" or 6 "Responses").
Option 3. Improvise two bar "Calls" or "Responses" with another player (3 "Calls" or 3 "Responses").
Option 4. Share two bar solos with other members of the ensemble.

1 **Round Evening**

Smoothly

U.S.

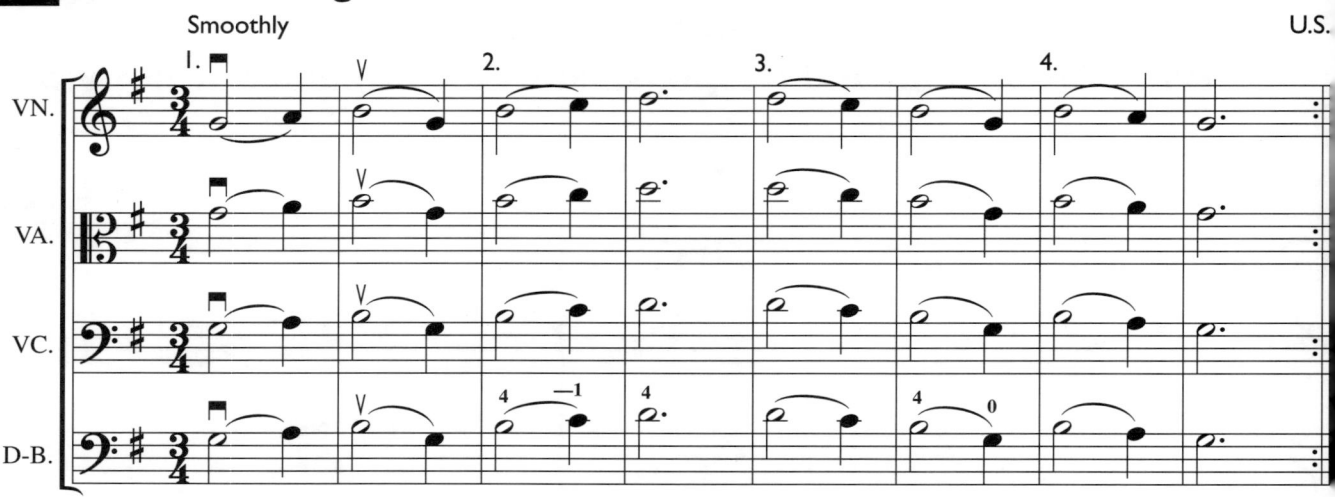

2 **Round Evening Two**

Smoothly

U.S.

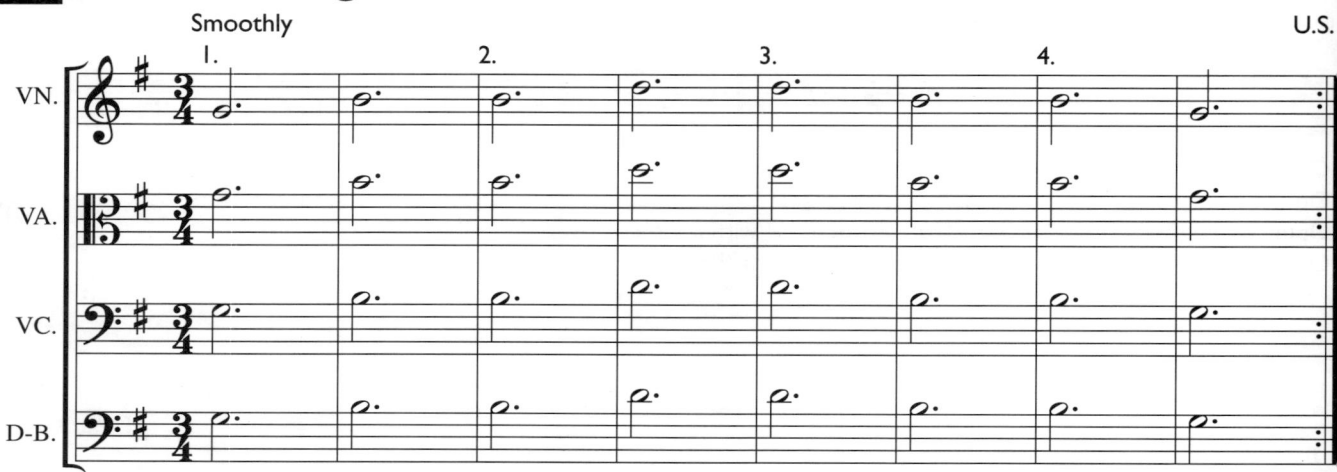

Viola
#30
Tch's Ed CD-3

Cello
#31
Tch's Ed CD-3

Extended Accom.
#32
Tch's Ed CD-3

3 **The Blues in D**

In a swinging style

U.S.

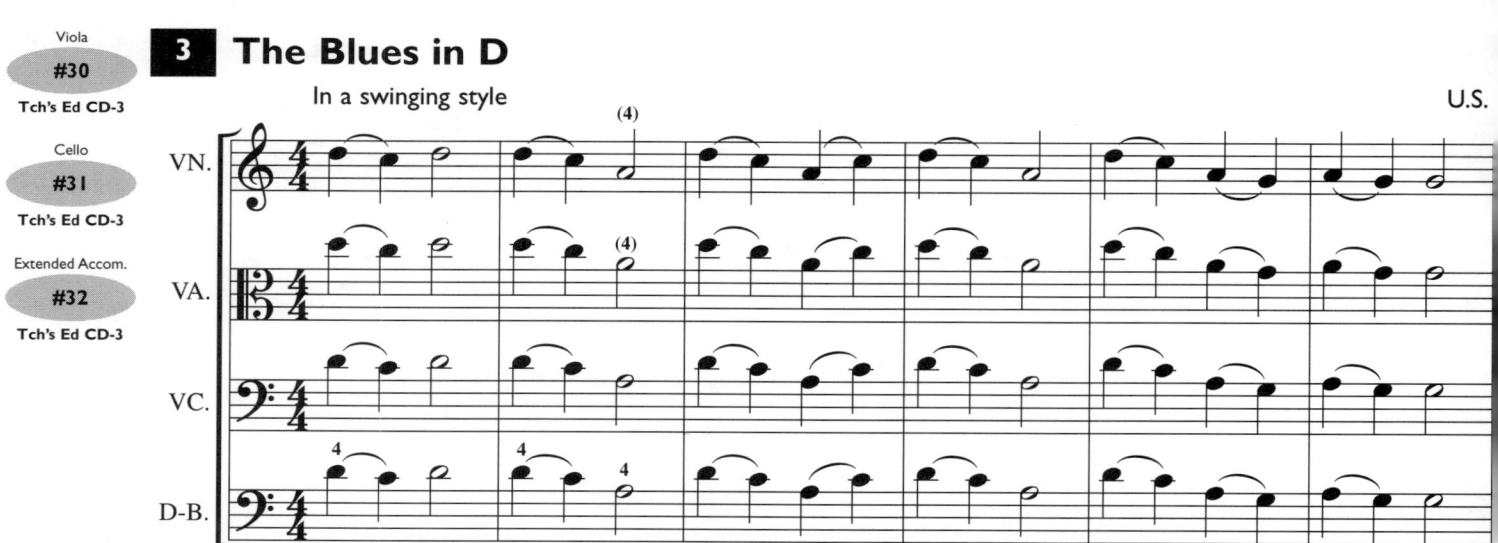

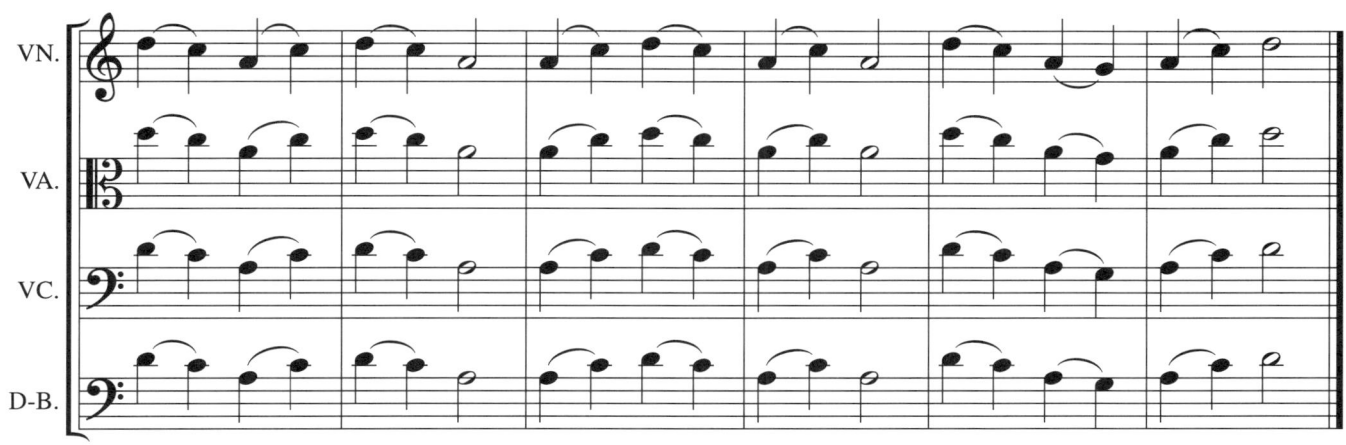

CALL AND RESPONSE — *A musical alternation between two performers or a performer and a group of performers. The musical response to the call can be imitated or improvised.*

Violin
#32

Tch's Ed CD-3

4 ★ SOLO — **The Blues in D** (IMITATIVE CALL AND RESPONSE - "BY EAR" STARTING ON D)

EXAMPLE: Call   Response (Imitated)

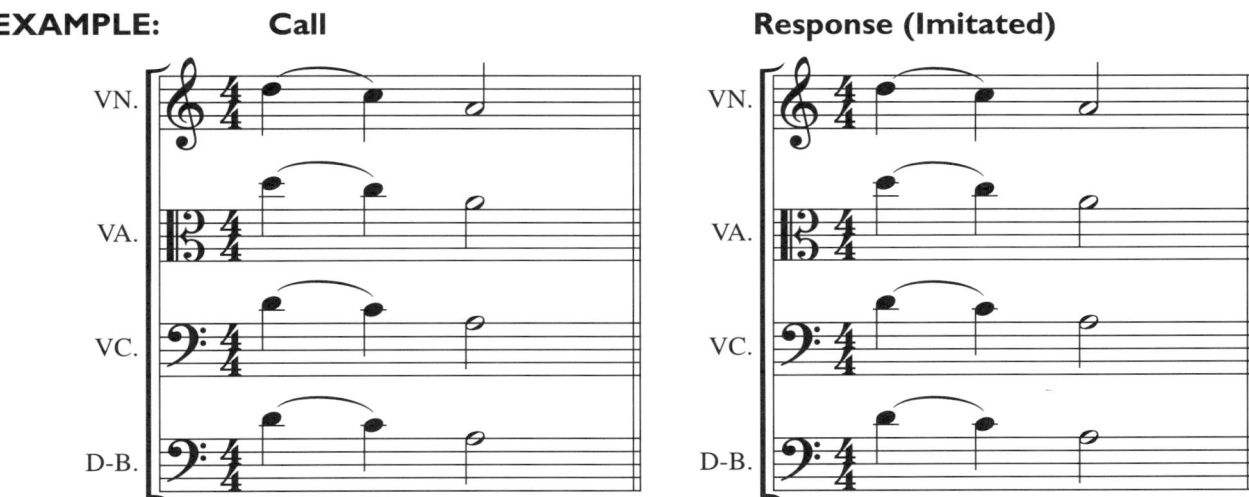

5 ★★ SOLO — **The Blues in D** (IMITATIVE CALL AND RESPONSE - "BY EAR" STARTING ON D)

EXAMPLE: Call   Response (Improvised)

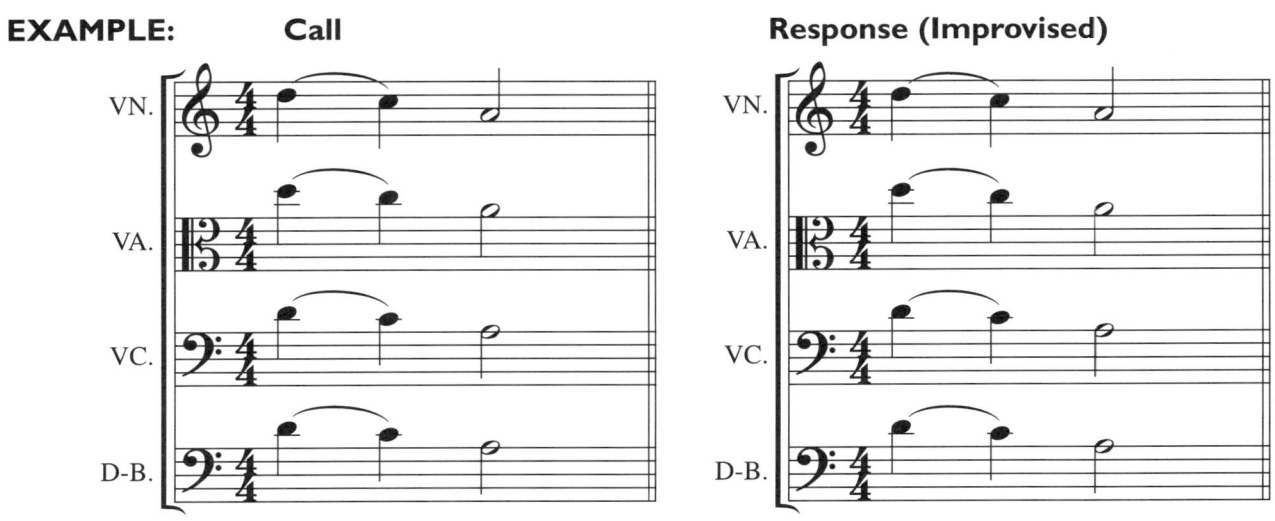

Extended Accom.
#33
Tch's Ed CD-3

6 ★★★ SOLO — **Improvise Over the 12 Bar Blues in D "By Ear"**

Use Tones of the D Mixolydian Scale:

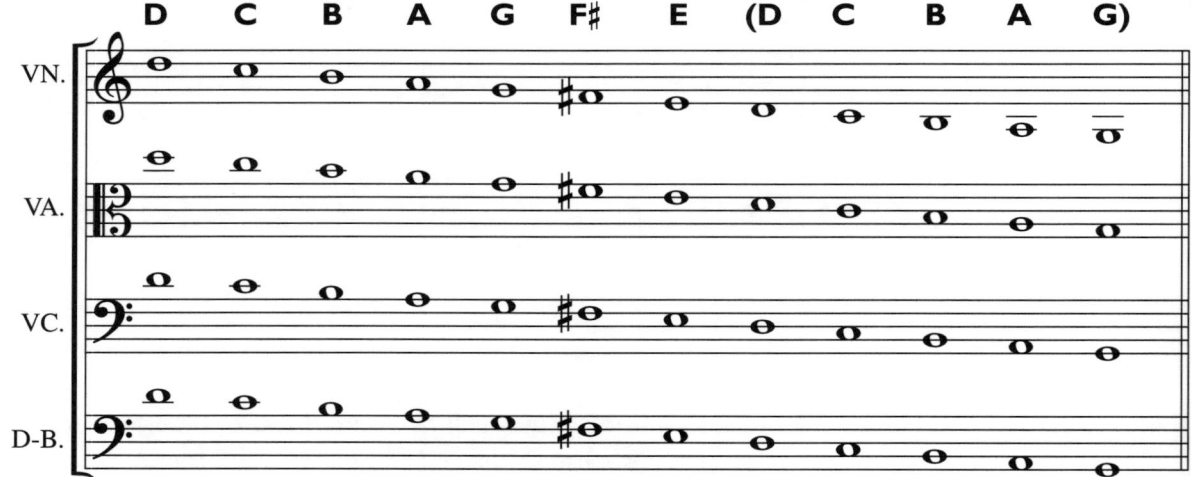

BLANK PAGE

NEW NOTE: F

F

2 (low)

See Bass Alternative Fingering: F and Viola/Cello New Notes: F, E, D, C
p. 27-G

STUDENT CD

Violin / Cello
Solo Trk 74
Accom. Trk 74-2

1 **Shoheen Sho**   FULL SCORE ON P. 27-H

Gently   Welsh Folk Song

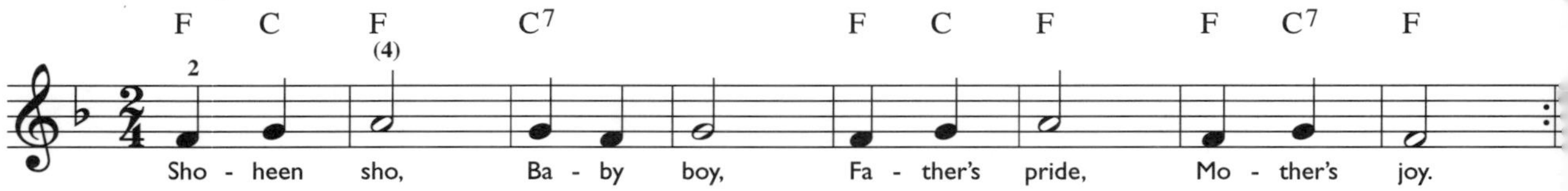

F   C   F   C⁷   F   C   F   F   C⁷   F
(4)

Sho - heen sho,   Ba - by boy,   Fa - ther's pride,   Mo - ther's joy.

Viola-8va lower / Bass
Solo Trk 75
Accom. Trk 75-2

2 **Intry Mintry**   FULL SCORE ON P. 27-H

Playfully   Game Song

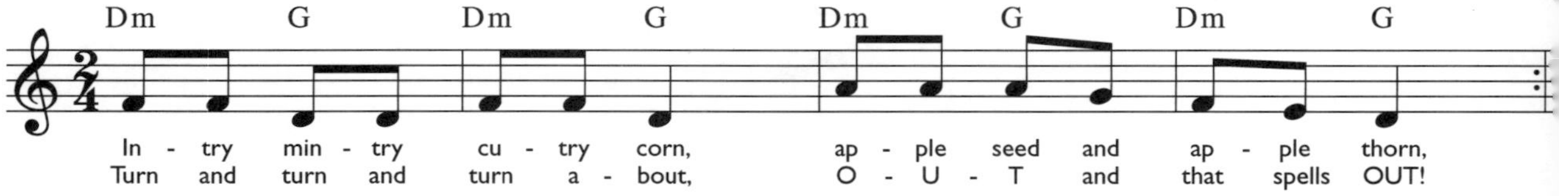

Dm   G   Dm   G   Dm   G   Dm   G

In - try min - try cu - try corn,   ap - ple seed and ap - ple thorn,
Turn and turn and turn a - bout,   O - U - T and that spells OUT!

Accom. Trk 75-2

3 ★ SOLO — **Improvise Rhythmic Variations on** *Intry Mintry*

Accom. Trk 75-2

4 ★★ SOLO — **Improvise Melodic Variations on** *Intry Mintry*

Use Tones of the D Minor Pentatonic Scale: D   F   G   A   C   D

FULL SCORE ON P. 27-H

Accom. Trk 75-2

5 ★★★ SOLO — **Improvise Melodic Variations on** *Intry Mintry*

Use Tones of the D Dorian Scale: D   E   F   G   A   B   C   D

FULL SCORE ON P. 27-I

SEA CHANTY —*A song sung by sailors to coordinate their movements while working.*

Viola / Cello
Solo Trk 76
Accom. Trk 76-2

6 **Yangtze Boatman Chanty**   FULL SCORE ON P. 27-I

Slowly   Sea Chanty

Dm   Gm   Dm   Gm   Dm   Gm   A⁷   Dm

INTRY MINTRY
Vocal Call and Response
(Teacher Call - Student Response)

*1. *Du and de*   normal articulation with a slight separation between tones
Du as in "due," de as in "day"

*2. *Du– and de–* connected style of articulation

*3. *Dot*   slightly sharper articulation with a quick release of the tone

*4. *DAH*   strong accent with a sharp release of the tone (martelé stroke)

*5. *du–dit*   fully extended tone (du–) to a short tone with a quick release (dit)

ANOTHER OPTION FOR SPONTANEOUS AND CREATIVE MUSIC MAKING

- **Ask for volunteers to lead the class with their own improvised calls.**
  (Vocal or instrumental)
- **Direct the class to follow with imitated or improvised responses.**

AN OPTION FOR SPONTANEOUS MUSIC MAKING

INTRY MINTRY

Extended Accom.
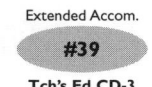
#39
Tch's Ed CD-3

Procedure 1. Direct students to employ one of the following two options:

A. "Use the tones of the D Minor Pentatonic Scale:
D, C, A, G, F, D, C, and **D**"

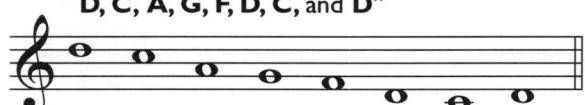

B. "Use the tones of the D Dorian Scale:
D, C, B, A, G, F, E, D, C, and **D**"

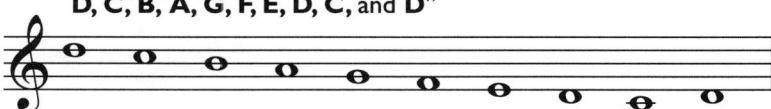

Procedure 2. Teach everyone an 8-beat riff (melodic ostinato).

Procedure 3. Direct students to "Repeat the riff until the music ends."

Example 1:

Example 2:

Procedure 4. When individual students are chosen or volunteer, suggest that they:

A. "Play the riff."

B. "Improvise rhythmic variations on the riff, or"

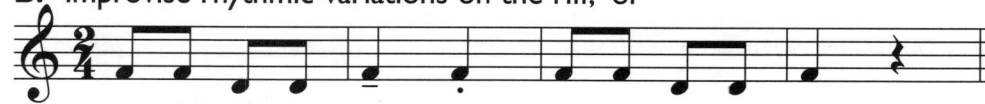

C. "Improvise rhythmic/melodic variations on the riff."

ANOTHER OPTION FOR SPONTANEOUS MUSIC MAKING

INTRY MINTRY

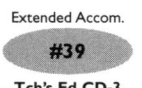

Extended Accom.
#39
Tch's Ed CD-3

Procedure 1. Direct students to use the tones of the D Dorian Scale:

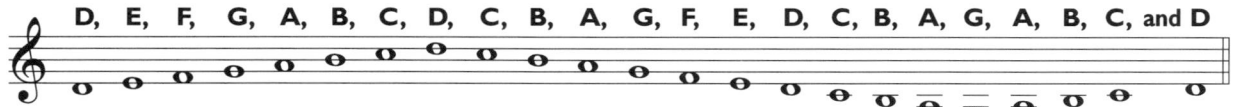

D, E, F, G, A, B, C, D, C, B, A, G, F, E, D, C, B, A, G, A, B, C, and D

Procedure 2. Teach everyone an 8-beat riff (melodic ostinato).

Procedure 3. Direct students to "Repeat the riff until the music ends."

Example 1:

Example 2:

Procedure 4. When individual students are chosen or volunteer, suggest that they:

A. "Play the riff."

B. "Improvise rhythmic variations on the riff, or"

C. "Improvise rhythmic/melodic variations on the riff."

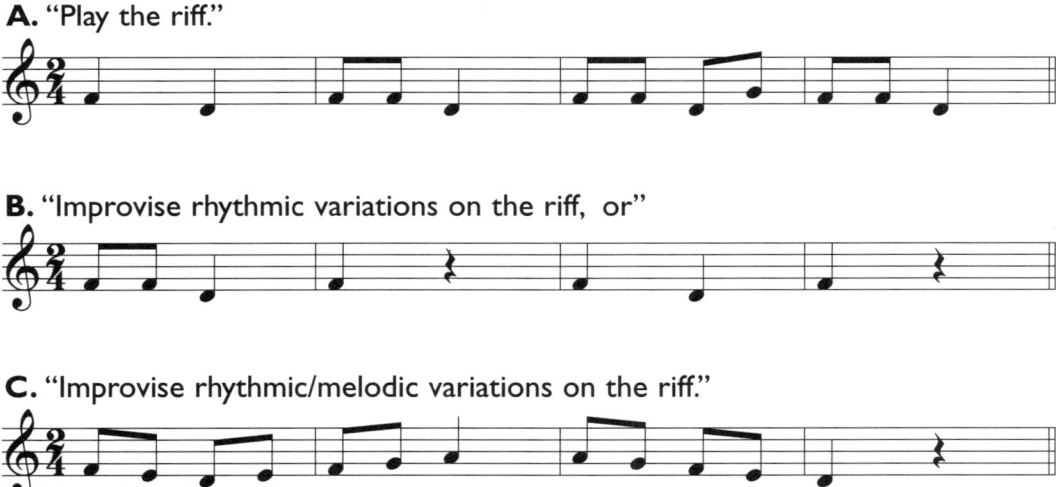

Accom.
#98

Tch's Ed CD-2

COOL JAZZ — (INSTRUMENTAL CALL AND RESPONSE - TEACHER CALL, STUDENT RESPONSE - IN A SWINGING STYLE)

"Use the notes D, C, (D), F, and G"   **"The starting tone is D"**    **INTRO**
(In a swinging style ♫ = ♪♪)

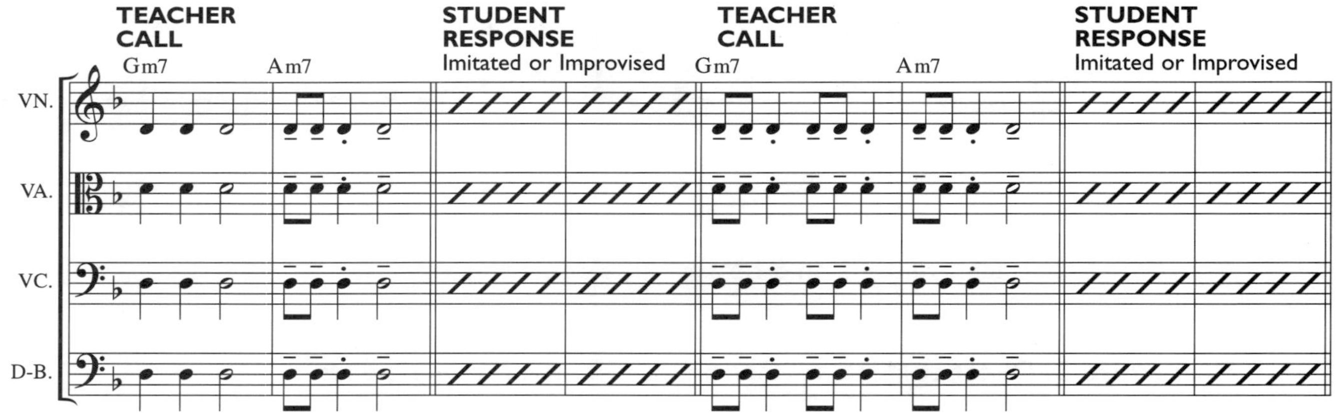

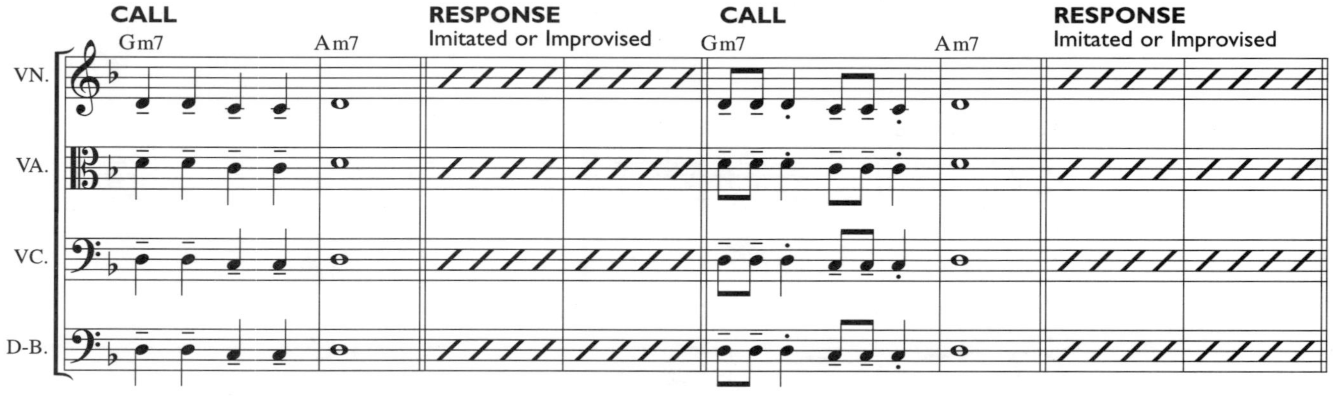

COOL JAZZ – Teacher Call and Student Response (CONTINUED)

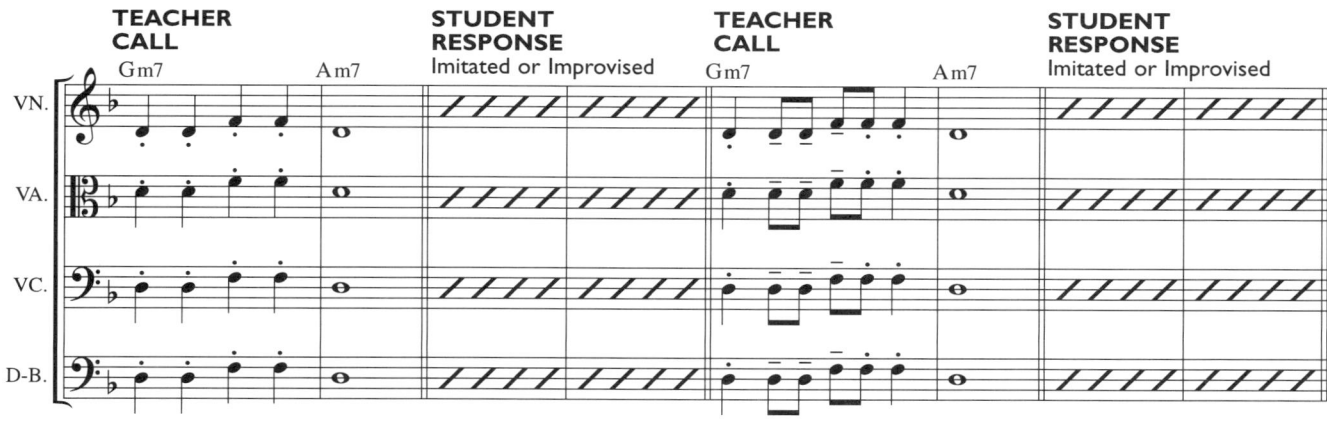

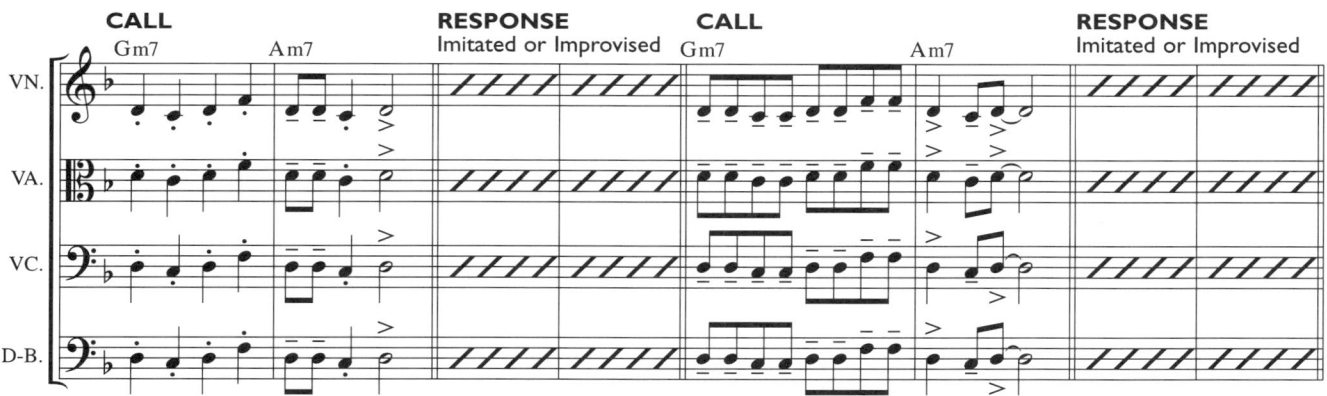

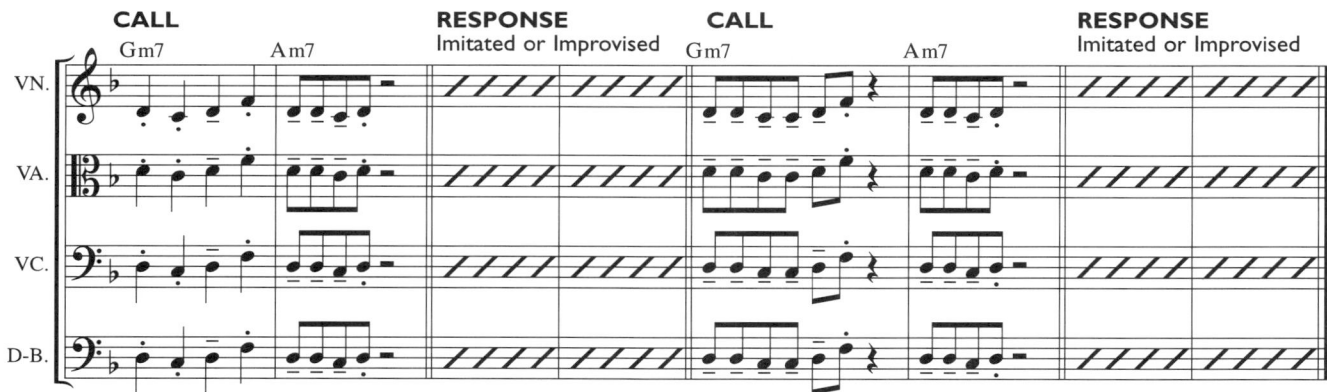

ANOTHER OPTION FOR SPONTANEOUS MUSIC MAKING
from the CD
DO IT! IMPROVISE *

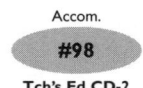

Accom.
#98

Tch's Ed CD-2

"COOL JAZZ"

Procedure 1. Direct students to use the tones D, C, (D), and F.

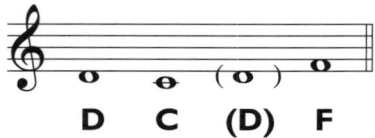

D   C   (D)   F

Procedure 2. Teach students to play a musical riff (ostinato).

Riff #1

Du – dit   Dot   Du – de – Du – dit

Riff #2

Du   Du de Du——Dot   Du   Du   Du——Dot

Procedure 3. Direct students to "Continue the riff until the music ends."

Procedure 4. When individual students are chosen or volunteer, suggest that they:
(For an interesting effect, perform Riff 1 and Riff 2 simultaneously.)

A. "Play the riff,"

B. "Improvise a rhythmic variation on the riff, or"

C. "Improvise a rhythmic/melodic variation on the riff."

Procedure 5. Encourage students to notate their best improvised riffs. (See page 41-A)

* *Do It! Improvise* (CD Backgrounds and Scale Notations for Entry-Level Music Improvisation - MLR 422) Albert Blaser and James Froseth, © 1994 GIA Publications Inc., 7404 South Mason Avenue, Chicago, IL 60638

NEW NOTES

Violin

F
2 (low)

Viola

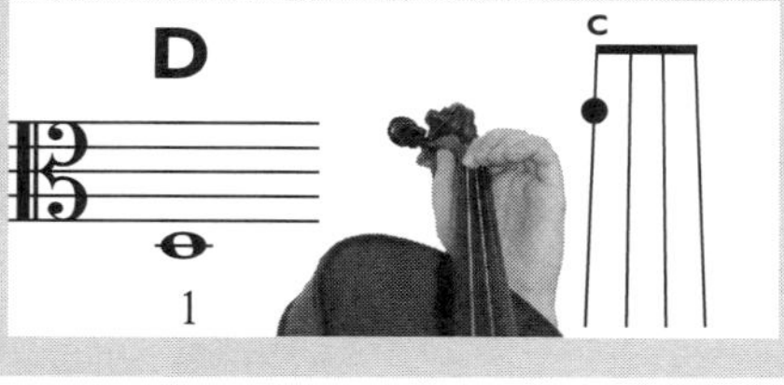

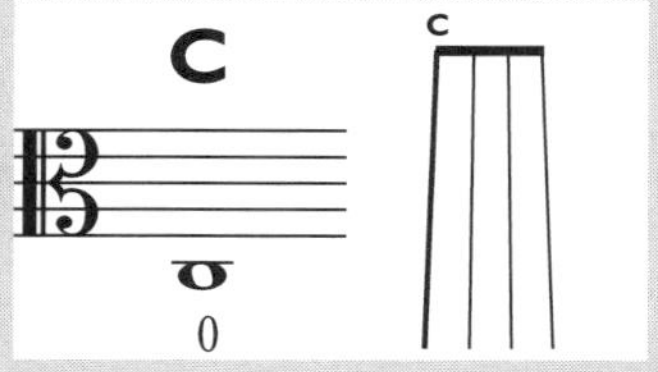

F
2 (low)

F
3

E
2

D
1

C
0

Cello

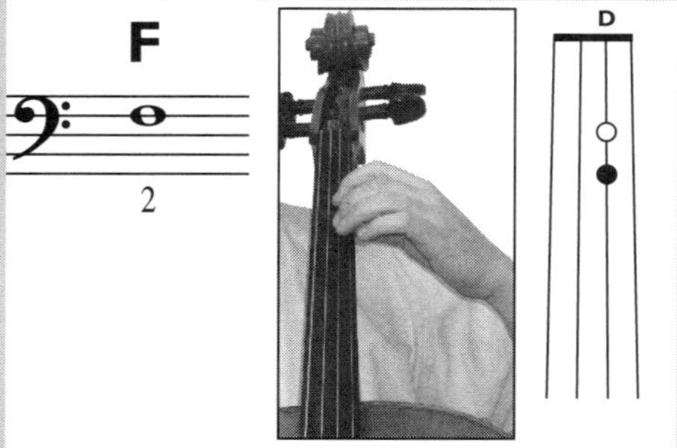

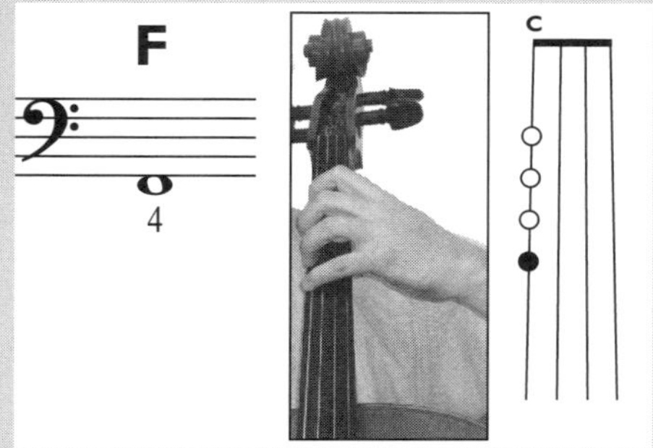

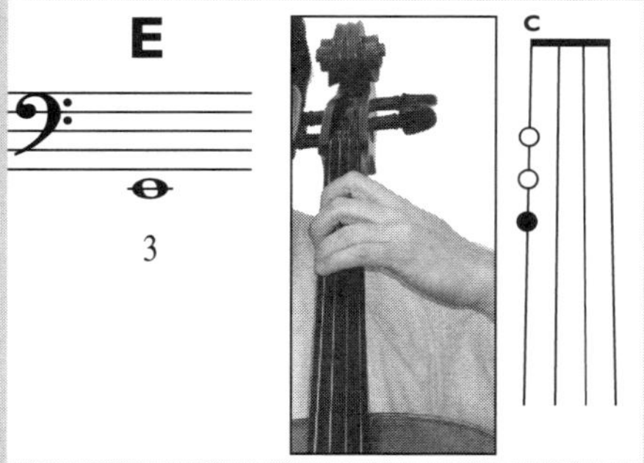

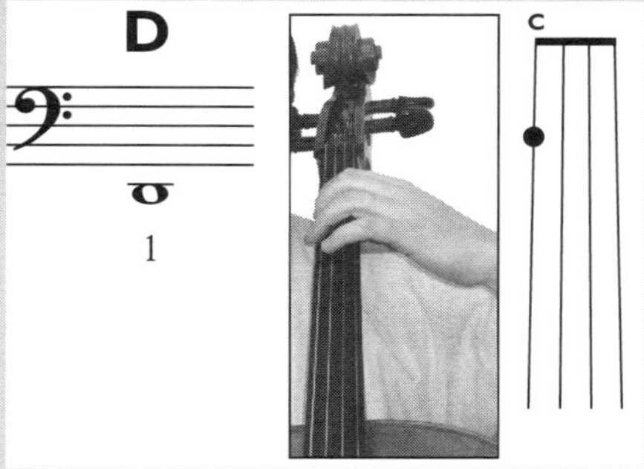

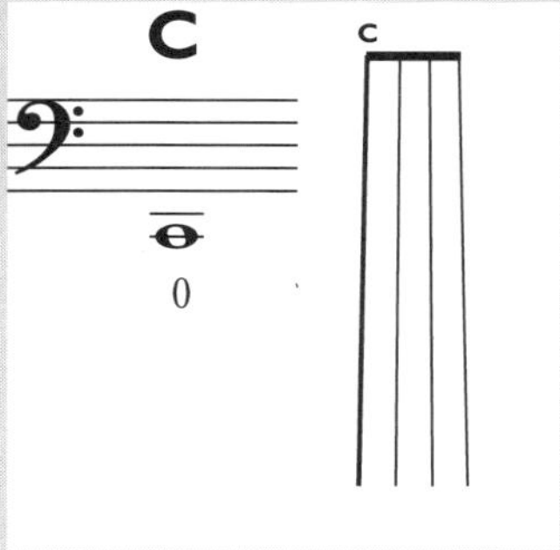

F
2

F
4

E
3

D
1

C
0

Bass

F
2

ALTERNATIVE FINGERING

Bass

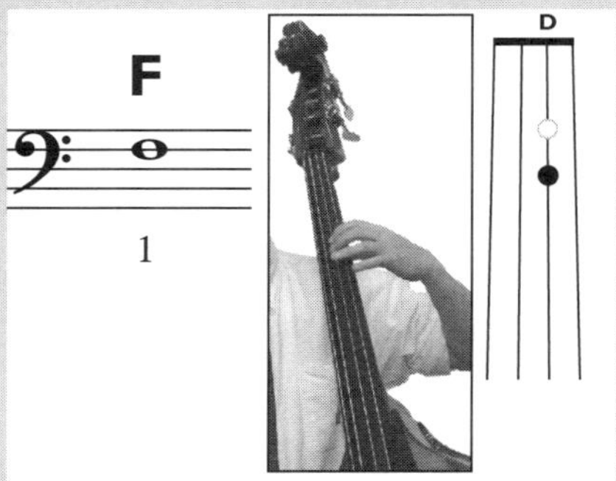

F
1

1 Shoheen Sho

Welsh Folk Song

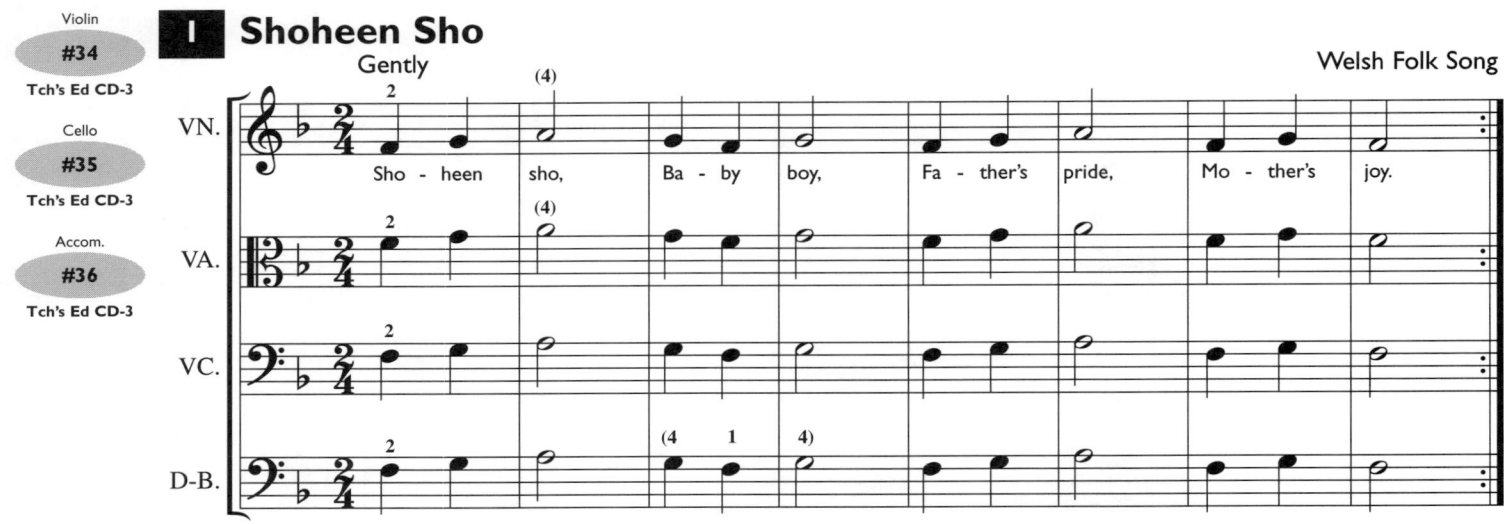

Violin
#34
Tch's Ed CD-3

Cello
#35
Tch's Ed CD-3

Accom.
#36
Tch's Ed CD-3

Sho - heen sho, Ba - by boy, Fa - ther's pride, Mo - ther's joy.

2 Intry Mintry

Game Song

Viola
#37
Tch's Ed CD-3

Bass
#38
Tch's Ed CD-3

Extended Accom.
#39
Tch's Ed CD-3

In - try min - try cu - try corn, ap - ple seed and ap - ple thorn,
Turn and turn and turn a - bout, O - U - T and that spells OUT!

Cued notes do not appear in the Student Text. See Special Project below.

SPECIAL PROJECT — ☆ (Viola and Cello) Learn to Play *Intry Mintry* 8va Higher "By Ear"
(See score above)

3 ☆ SOLO — Improvise Rhythmic Variations on *Intry Mintry*

4 ☆☆ SOLO — Improvise Melodic Variations on *Intry Mintry*

Extended Accom.
#39
Tch's Ed CD-3

Use Tones of the D Minor Pentatonic Scale: D F G A C D

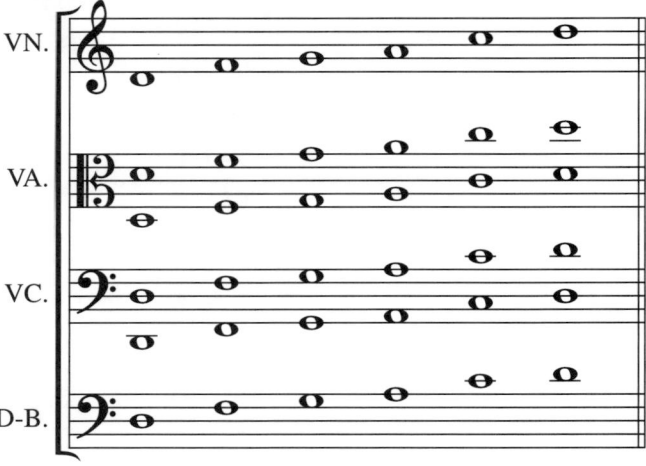

5 ★★★ SOLO — **Improvise Melodic Variations on** *Intry Mintry*

Use Tones of the D Dorian Scale: D   E   F   G   A   B   C   D

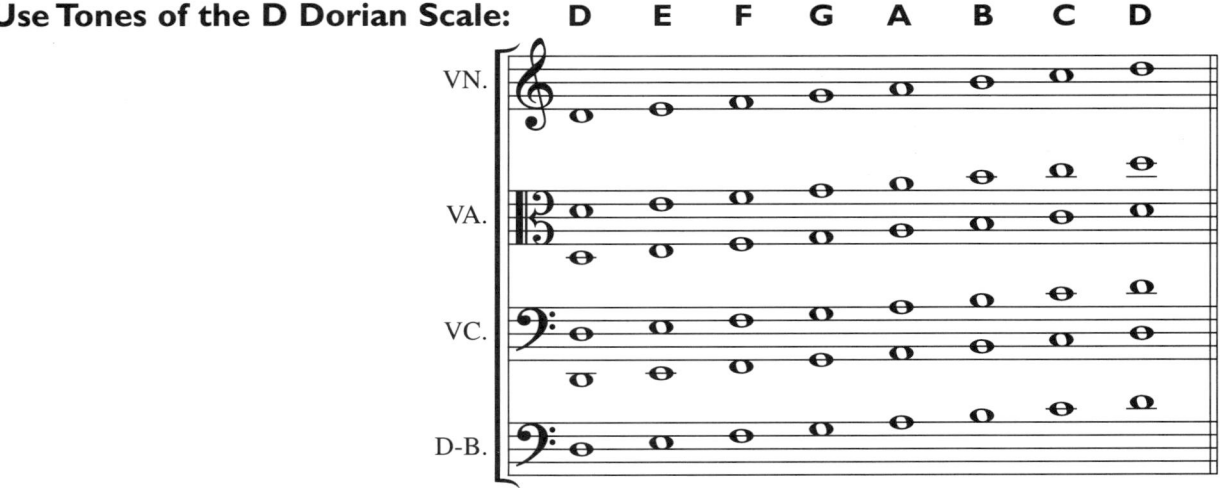

SEA CHANTY —*A song sung by sailors to coordinate their movements while working.*

Viola
#41
Tch's Ed CD-3

Cello
#42
Tch's Ed CD-3

Accom.
#43
Tch's Ed CD-3

6 **Yangtze Boatman Chanty**

Sea Chanty

* Cued notes do not appear in the Student Text. See Special Project below.

SPECIAL PROJECT — ★ **(Viola and Cello) Learn to Play** *Yangtze Boatman Chanty*
8va Lower "By Ear" (See score above)

Some Folks Do (SOLO OR DUET)   FULL SCORES ON PP. 28-I and 28-J   Adapted from Stephen C. Foster (1825-1864)

Whimsically
Play lower octave on repeat

1A

Some folks like to sigh, some folks do, some folks do.

1B *pizz.*

Some folks like to lie, that's not me or you.

Silent, Silent (SOLO OR DUET)   FULL SCORES ON PP. 28-K and 28-L   German Lullaby

Legato

2A

Si - lent, Si - lent, make no sound at all. Now I lay the child to sleep,

2B

Love and peace his soul to keep. Si - lent, Si - lent, make no sound at all.

3 SPECIAL PROJECT — ★ **Learn to Play** *Silent, Silent* **8va Lower "By Ear"**

4 Lady My (2 PART ROUND)   FULL SCORE ON P. 28-L   English Round

Moderato

La - dy My, can't you see, John fell off the white oak tree.

Rhythmic Flashcard Reading Option for *Some Folks Do*

R-11  **R-17**  **R-2**  **R-1**

Rhythmic Flashcard Reading Option for *Silent, Silent*

R-2  **R-11**  **R-13**

Rhythmic Flashcard Reading Option for *Lady My*

R-1 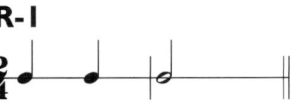 **R-2**

A SPECIAL OPTION FOR ENSEMBLE INTONATION TRAINING
HARMONIZE TONIC AND DOMINANT "BY EAR" - SOME FOLKS DO (KEY OF G MAJOR)
Return to procedures on pages 19-B and 19-C

Procedure 1. Direct students to "Using only open G and D discover an open-string harmony part that sounds good to you."

Procedure 1a. Play teacher or recorded model several times, allowing students to explore.

Procedure 1b. Teacher or individual student can model the open-string harmony part:

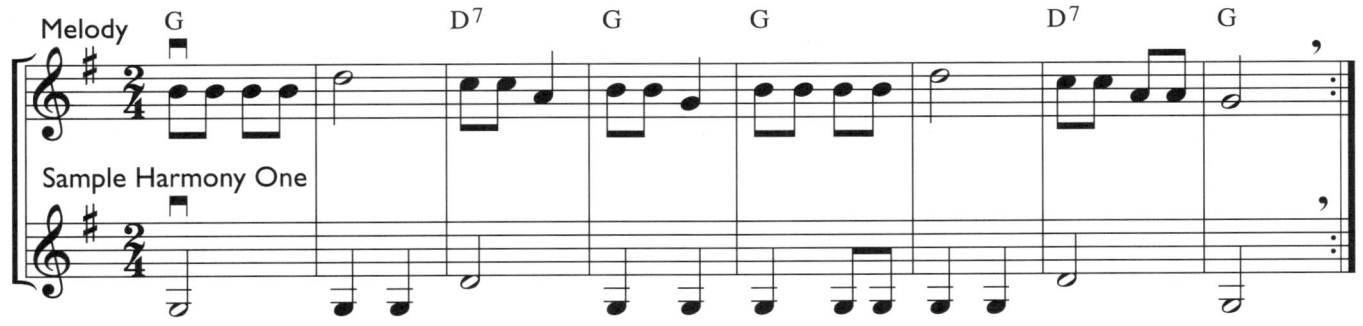

Procedure 1c. Allow students to play either the melody or the open-string harmony part.

Procedure 2. Direct students to "Using only G and F♯, discover a second harmony part that sounds good to you." (Remind students that these pitches sound and feel "close together.")

Procedure 2a. Play teacher or recorded model several times, allowing students to explore.

Procedure 2b. Teacher or individual student can model the second harmony part:

Procedure 2c. Allow students to play the melody, open-string, or second harmony part.

Procedure 3. Direct students to "Using only B and C, discover a third harmony part that sounds good to you." (Remind students that these pitches sound and feel "close together.")

Procedure 3a. Play teacher or recorded model several times, allowing students to explore.

Procedure 3b. Teacher or individual student can model the third harmony part:

Procedure 3c. Allow students to play the melody, open-string, second, or third harmony part.

Procedure 4. Create a group arrangement of *Some Folks Do*

    Procedure 4a. Decide on sections to play melody, harmony, and duet parts.

    Procedure 4b. Decide on dynamic levels, pizzicato, and other musical elements.

    Procedure 4c. Decide on number of repetitions - allow for student solos.

    Procedure 4d. Allow for rhythmic improvisation.

Procedure 5. Use this option with other tunes easily harmonized with G and D^7 chords:

Silent, Silent
Lady My
Bingo
Raindrops
Sur la Pont d'Avignon
Amazing Grace

A SPECIAL OPTION FOR SPONTANEOUS MUSIC MAKING

Return to DOWN BY THE STATION

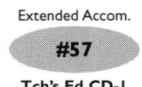

Extended Accom.
#57
Tch's Ed CD-1

Procedure 1. Direct students to employ one of the following options:

A. "Use the tones D, E, and F"   or **B.** "Use the tones D, E, F, F♯, G, and A"

   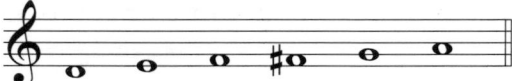

Procedure 2. Teach everyone an 8-beat riff (melodic ostinato).
        (**Note:** *Riffs may be improvised and taught to the class by the teacher or by the students.*)

Procedure 3. Direct students to "Repeat the riff until the music ends."
        (*For an interesting effect, perform Riff 1 and Riff 2 simultaneously.*)

Procedure 4. When individual students are chosen or volunteer, suggest that they:

A. "Play the riff."

B. "Improvise rhythmic variations on the riff, or"

C. "Improvise an 8-beat rhythmic variation on *Down By the Station*."

A SPECIAL OPTION FOR SPONTANEOUS MUSIC MAKING

Return to DOWN BY THE STATION

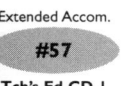

Extended Accom.
#57
Tch's Ed CD-1

Procedure 1. Direct students to use the tones of the D Minor Pentatonic Scale.

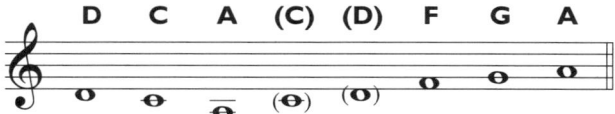

Procedure 2. Teach everyone an 8-beat riff (melodic ostinato).

Procedure 3. Direct students to "Repeat the riff until the music ends."
(For an interesting effect, perform Riff 1 and Riff 2 simultaneously.)

Procedure 4. When individual students are chosen or volunteer, suggest that they:

A. "Play the riff."

B. "Improvise rhythmic variations on the riff, or"

C. "Improvise an 8-beat rhythmic/melodic variation on the riff."

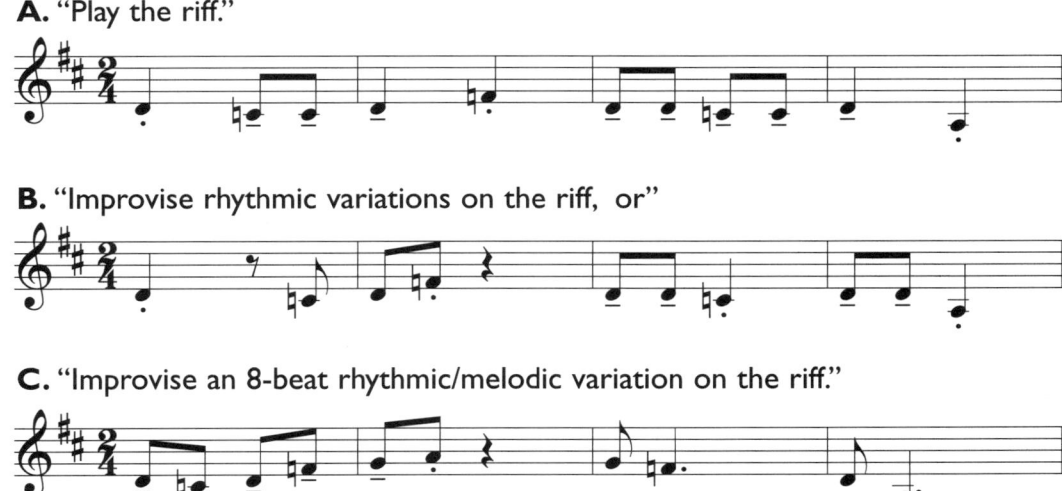

A SPECIAL INDIVIDUALIZED OPTION FOR SPONTANEOUS MUSIC MAKING

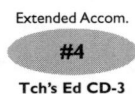

Extended Accom.

#4

Tch's Ed CD-3

COBBLER, COBBLER

MUSICAL DIALOGUE – *An improvised conversation between two performers. A performer initiates a "Dialogue" with a 4-beat improvised "Statement" or a 4-beat improvised "Question." A second performer responds with a 4-beat improvised "Answer," a 4-beat improvised "Statement," or a 4-beat improvised "Question."*

A musical "Statement" usually starts on the resting tone and always ends on the resting tone. (C is the resting tone for Cobbler, Cobbler)

A musical "Answer" usually starts on a tone other than the resting tone and always ends on the resting tone.

A musical "Question" can begin on any tone but always ends on a tone other than the resting tone.

Direct students to employ one of the following options:

A. "Use the tones C, A, and G" or   **B.** "Use the tones D, C, A, and G" or   **C.** "Use the tones D, C, A, G, E, and D"

 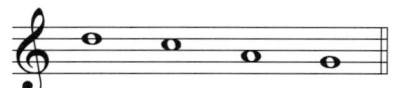 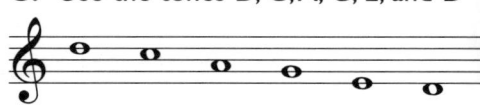

EXAMPLE OF OPTION A:

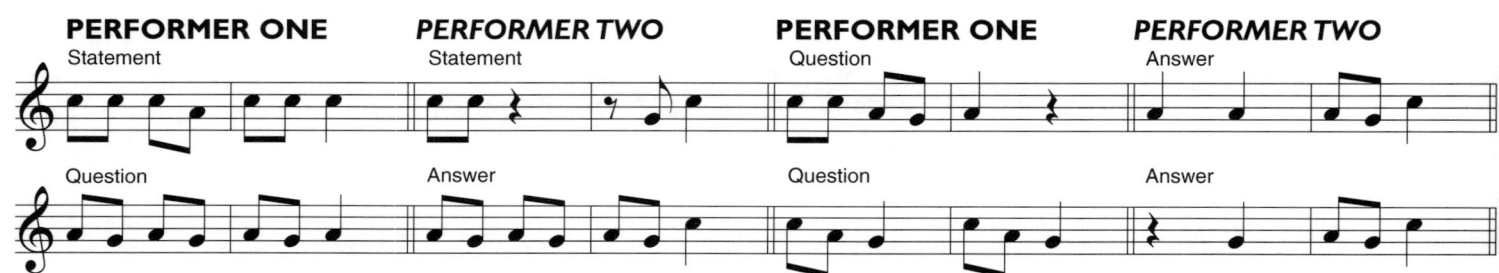

EXAMPLE OF OPTION B:

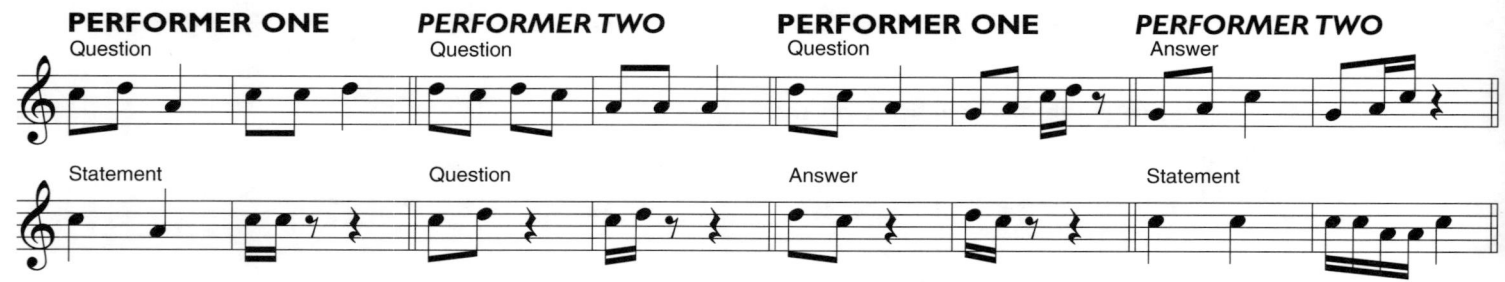

EXAMPLE OF OPTION C:

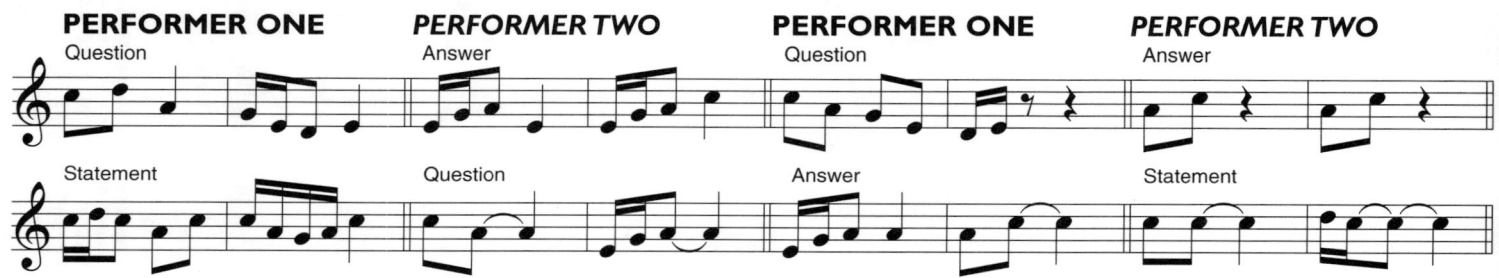

Accom. #98

Tch's Ed CD-2

COOL JAZZ – Teacher Call and Student Response (IN A SWINGING STYLE)

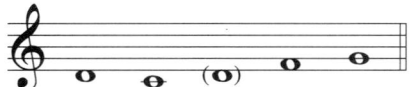

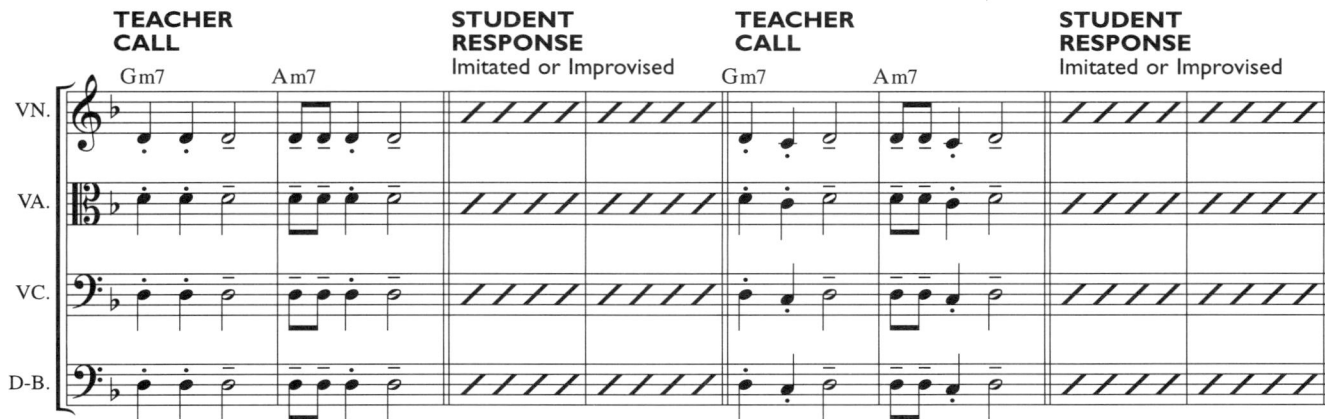

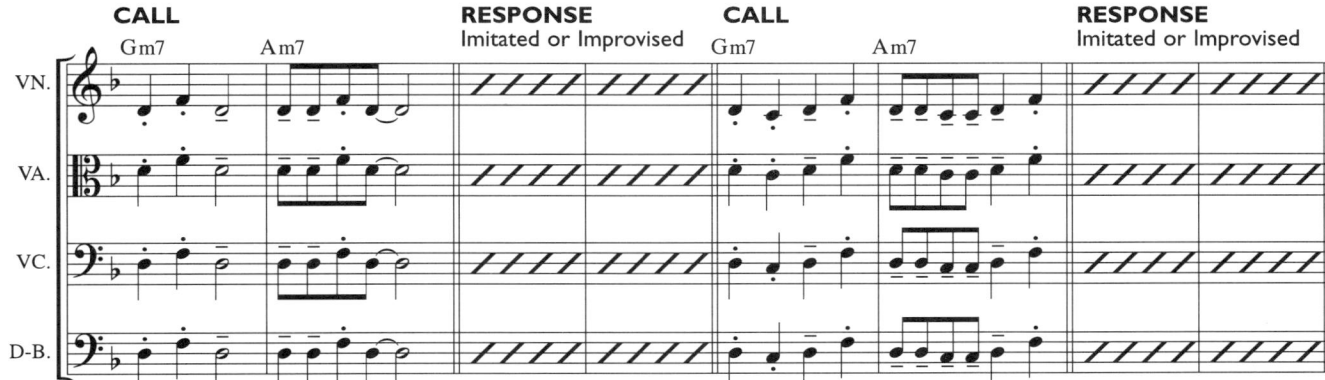

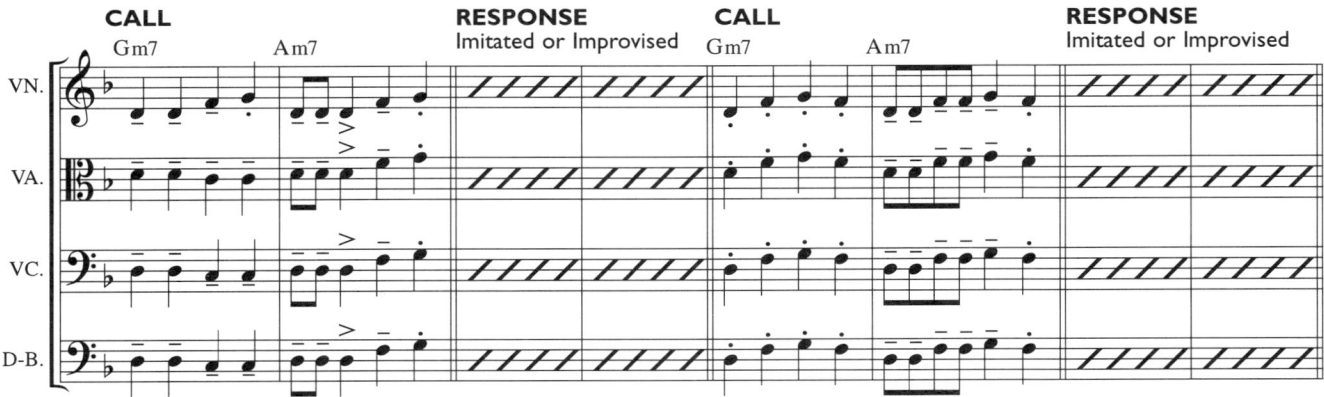

COOL JAZZ – Teacher Call and Student Response (CONTINUED)

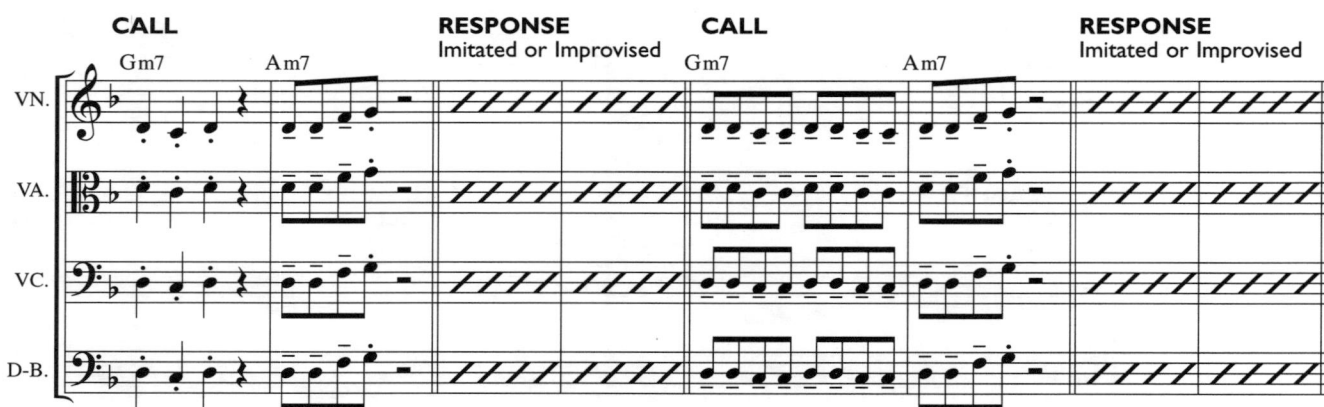

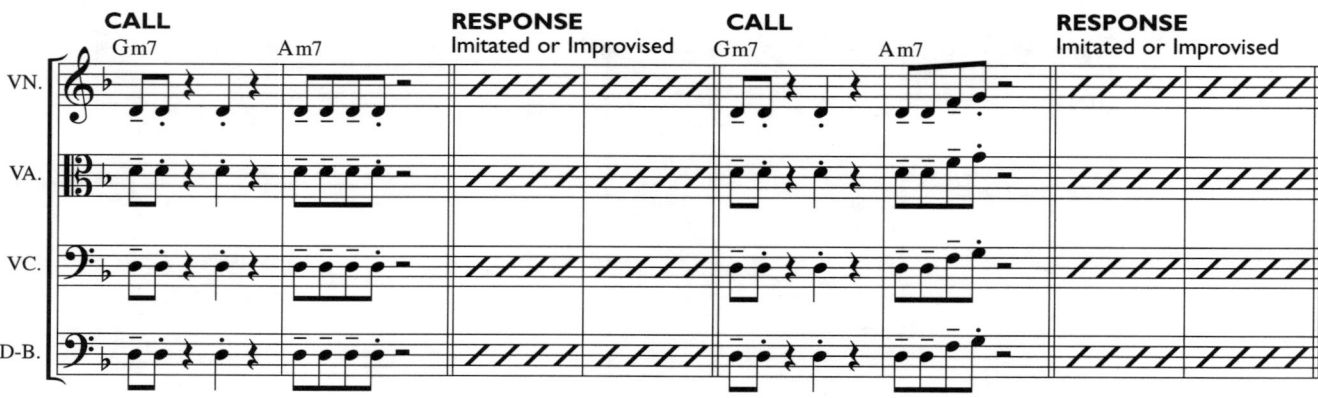

1A **Some Folks Do** (SOLO OR DUET - PART A)

Adapted from
Stephen C. Foster (1825-1864)

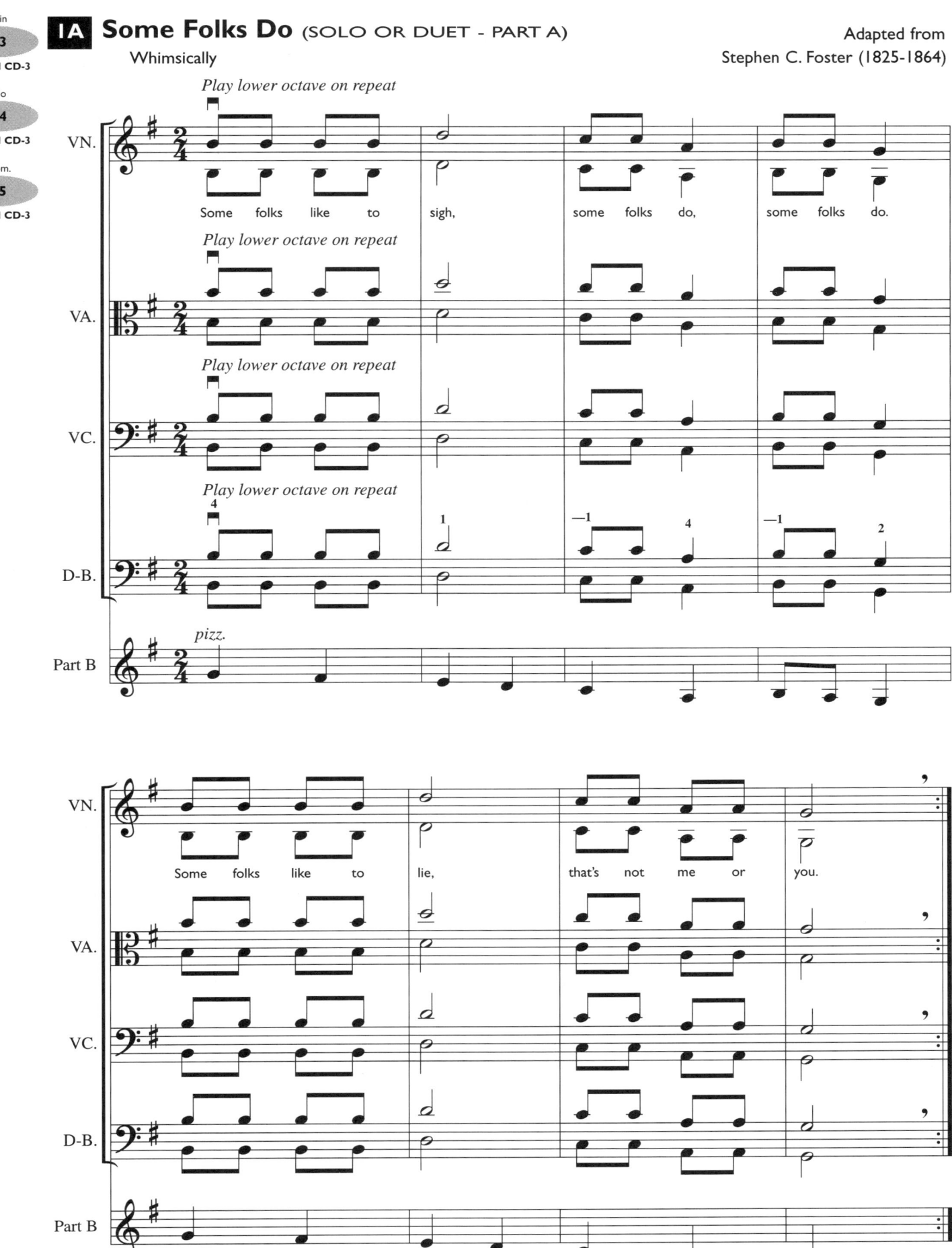

Violin
#43
Tch's Ed CD-3

Cello
#44
Tch's Ed CD-3

Accom.
#45
Tch's Ed CD-3

1B **Some Folks Do** (SOLO OR DUET - PART B)

Adapted from
Stephen C. Foster (1825-1864)

Whimsically

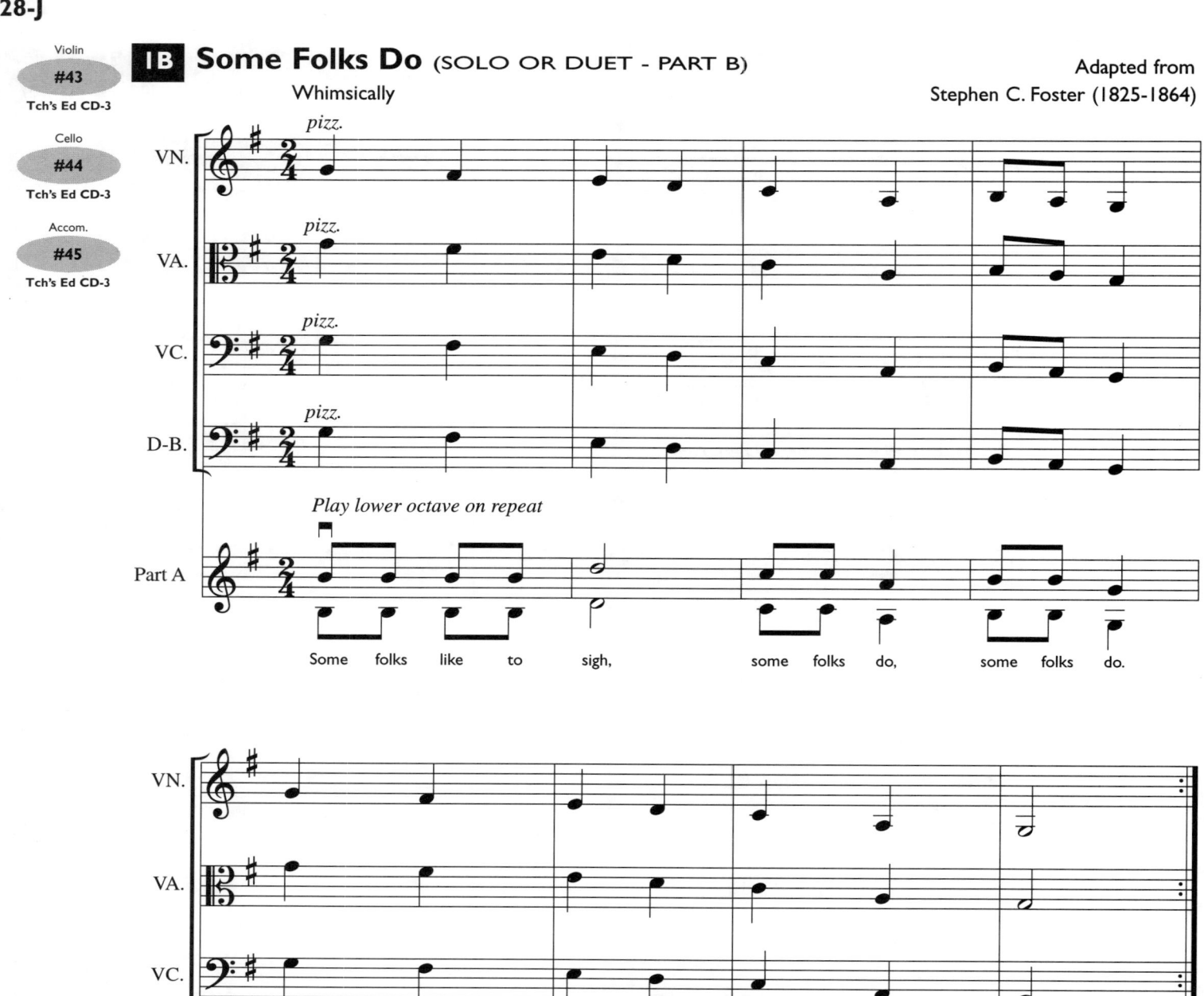

Some folks like to sigh, some folks do, some folks do.

Some folks like to lie, that's not me or you.

2A Silent, Silent (SOLO OR DUET - PART A)

German Lullaby

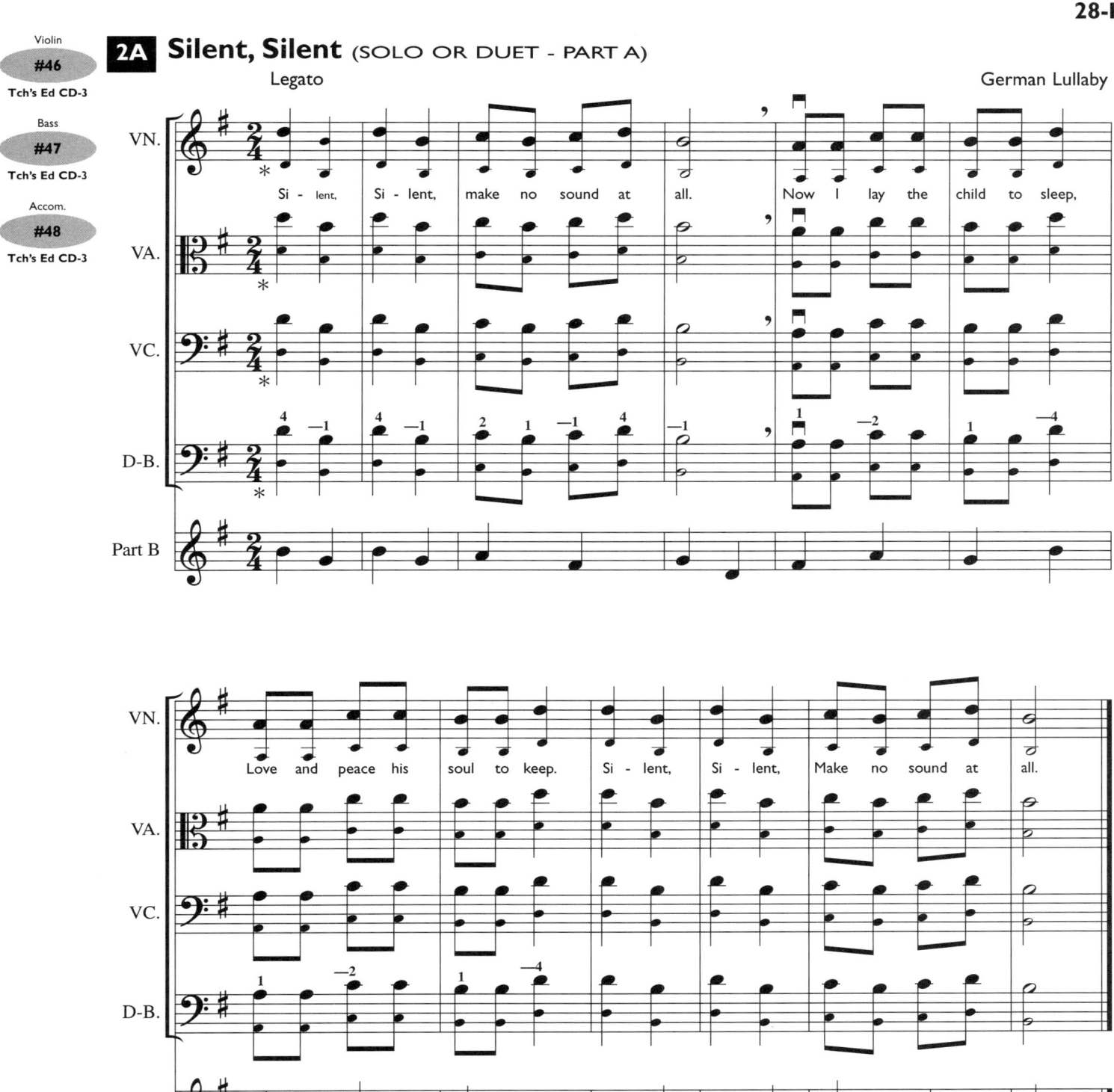

Silent, Silent, make no sound at all. Now I lay the child to sleep,

Love and peace his soul to keep. Silent, Silent, Make no sound at all.

* Cued notes do not appear in the Student Text. See Special Project on page 28-L.

2B **Silent, Silent** (SOLO OR DUET - PART B)

German Lullaby

Violin
#46
Tch's Ed CD-3

Bass
#47
Tch's Ed CD-3

Accom.
#48
Tch's Ed CD-3

Legato

VN.

VA.

VC.

D-B.

Part A

Si - lent, Si - lent, make no sound at all. Now I lay the child to sleep,

VN.

VA.

VC.

D-B.

Part A

Love and peace his soul to keep. Si - lent, Si - lent, Make no sound at all.

3 SPECIAL PROJECT — ★ **Learn to Play** *Silent, Silent* **8va Lower "By Ear"**
(See score on page 28-K)

4 **Lady My** (2 PART ROUND)

Moderato

English Round

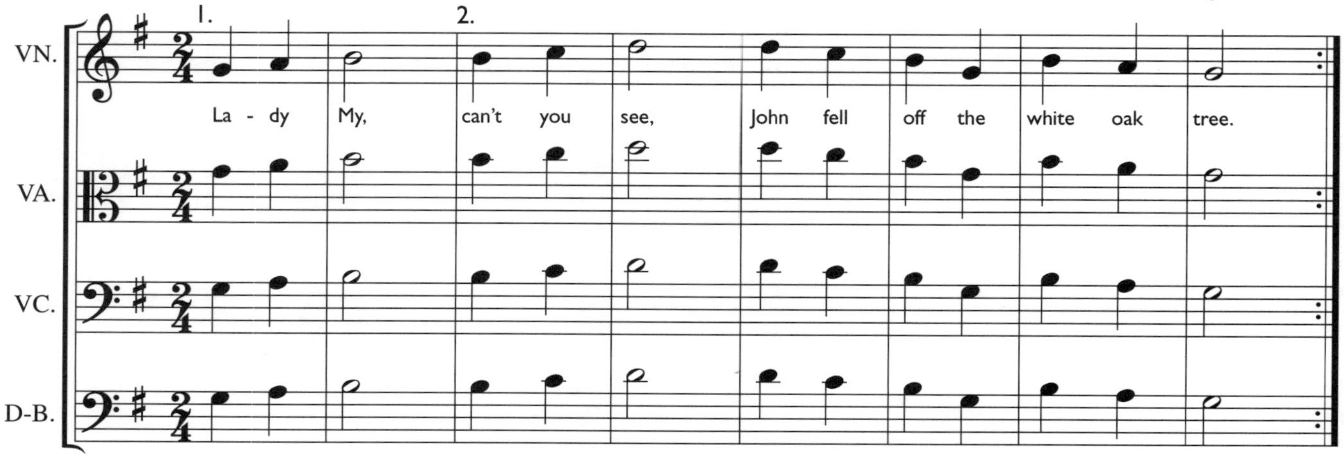

VN.

La - dy My, can't you see, John fell off the white oak tree.

VA.

VC.

D-B.

BLANK PAGE

STUDENT CD

Viola
Cello
Solo Trk 79
Accom. Trk 79-2

1 **Baa, Baa, Black Sheep** (IN MINOR TONALITY) FULL SCORE ON P. 29-E

France

Moderato

Fine

Baa, baa, black sheep, have you an-y wool? No, sir, nay, not one bag full.

D.C. al Fine

None for my mas-ter, none for my dame, None for the lit-tle boy who lives in the lane.

CANON — *Literally, a "rule" for realizing a composition. The rule dictates that each voice imitates exactly the melody sung or played by the first voice.*

2 **Tallis Canon** (4 VOICE CANON) FULL SCORE ON P. 29-F

Thomas Tallis (1510-1585)

Legato

1. 2. 3. 4.

All praise to Thee, my Lord this night. For all the bles-sings of the

light; keep me, Oh, keep us, King of Kings, be-neath Thine own Al-might-y wings.

Violin
Cello
Solo Trk 80
Accom. Trk 80-2

3 **Bingo** FULL SCORE ON P. 29-F

Gaily

American Game Song

There was a farm-er, had a dog, and Bin-go was his name - o. B - I -

N - G - O, B - I - N - G - O, B - I - N - G - O, and Bin-go was his name - o.

NATURAL (♮) — *A sign that cancels a flat (♭) or sharp (♯) in the measure or in the key signature.*

4 **French Cathedrals** (3 PART ROUND) FULL SCORE ON P. 29-G

French Lullaby

Stately

1. 2. 3.

Or - lé - ans, Beau - gen - cy, No - tre Dame de Clé - ry, Ven - dô - me, Ven - dô - me.

Rhythmic Flashcard Reading Option for *Baa, Baa, Black Sheep (In Minor Tonality)*

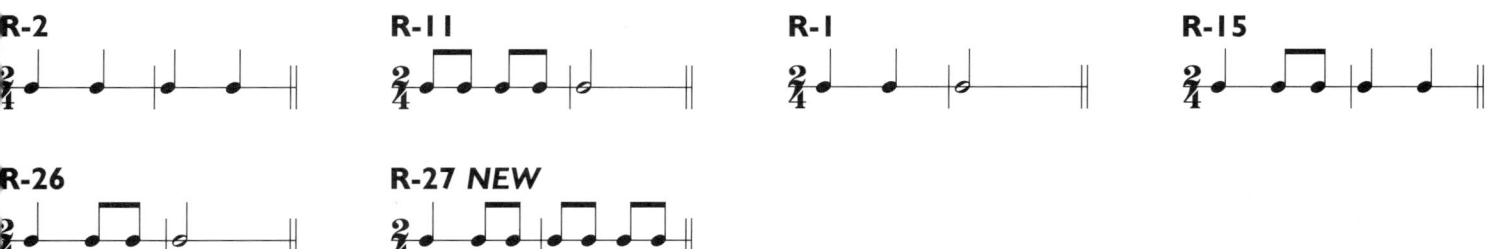

Rhythmic Flashcard Reading Option for *Bingo*

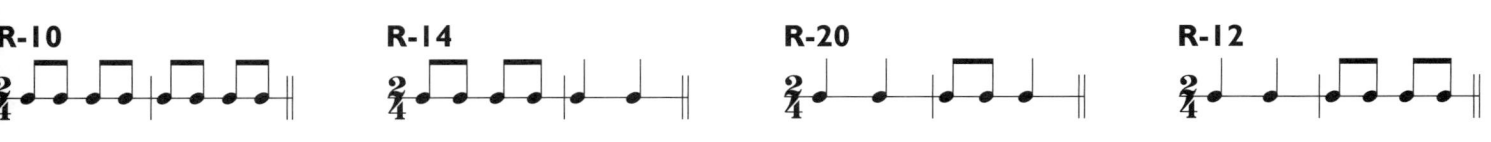

Rhythmic Reading Round

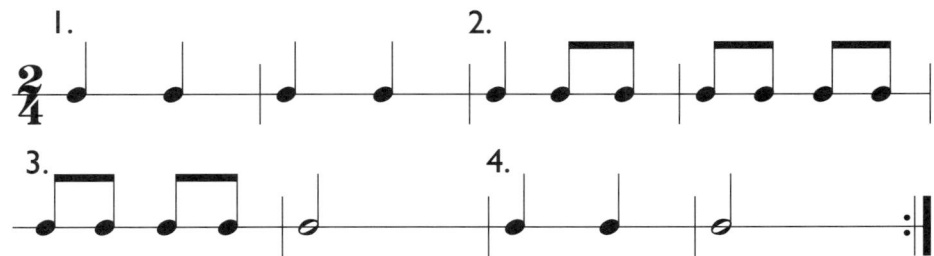

Rhythmic Reading Exercise (SEE PAGE 8-A FOR PROCEDURE)

A SPECIAL OPTION FOR SPONTANEOUS MUSIC MAKING

Blues in D (TEACHER CALL AND STUDENT RESPONSE)

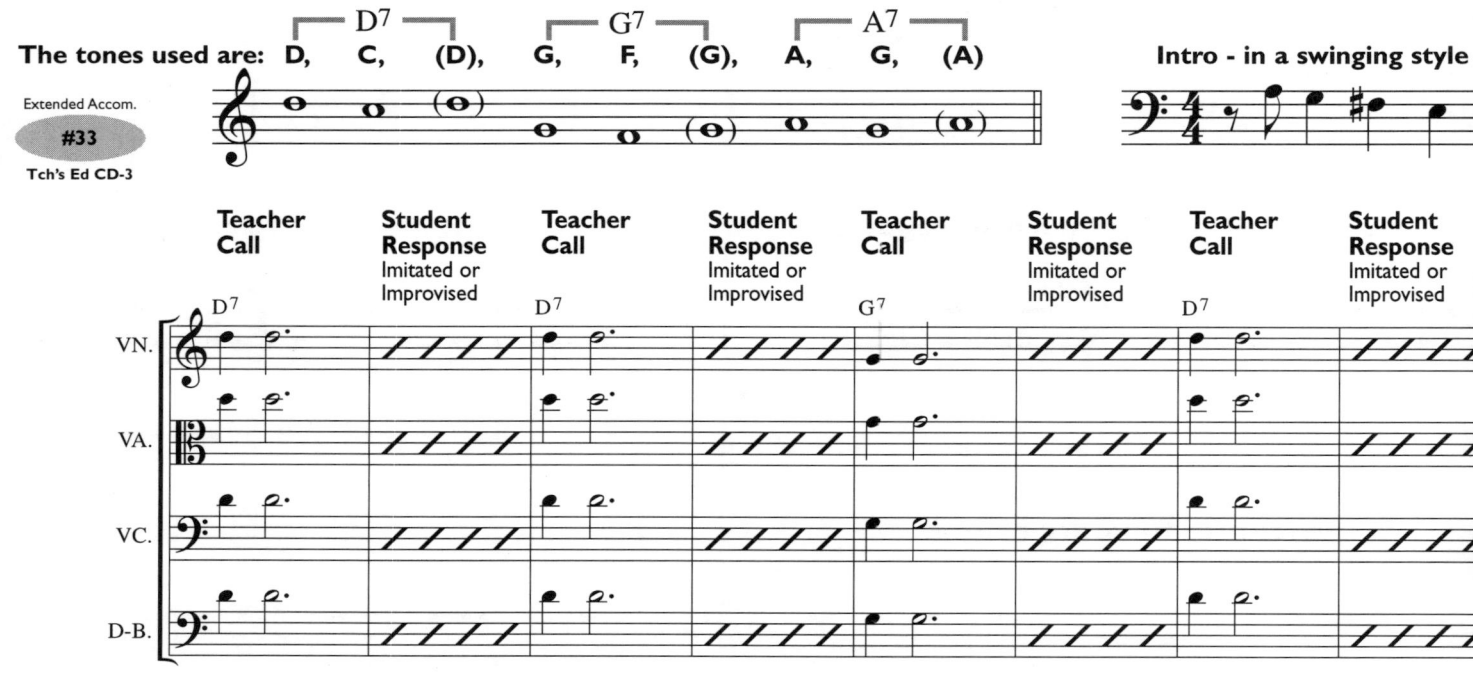

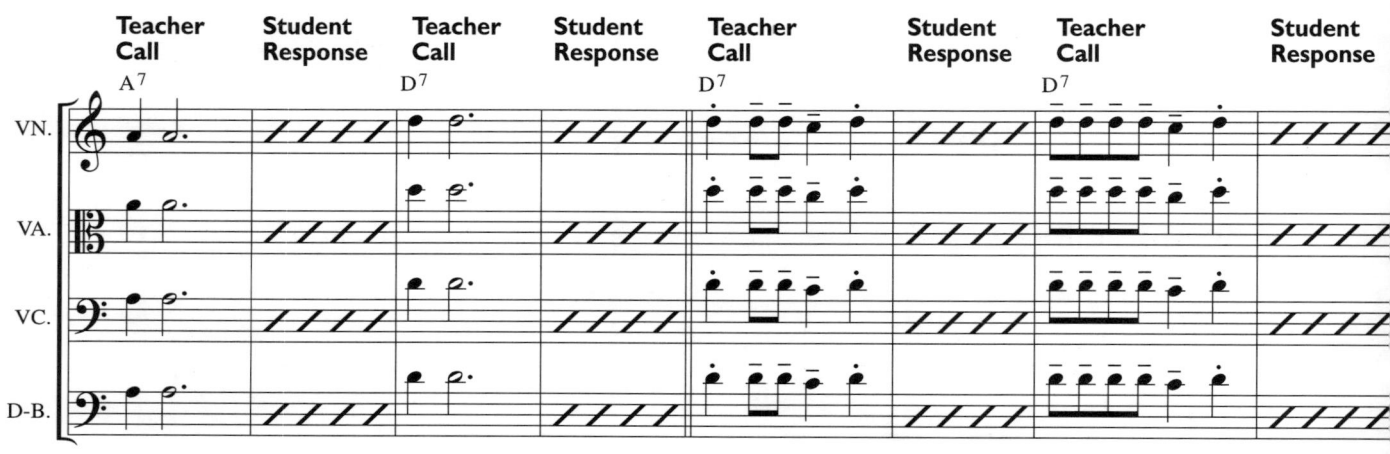

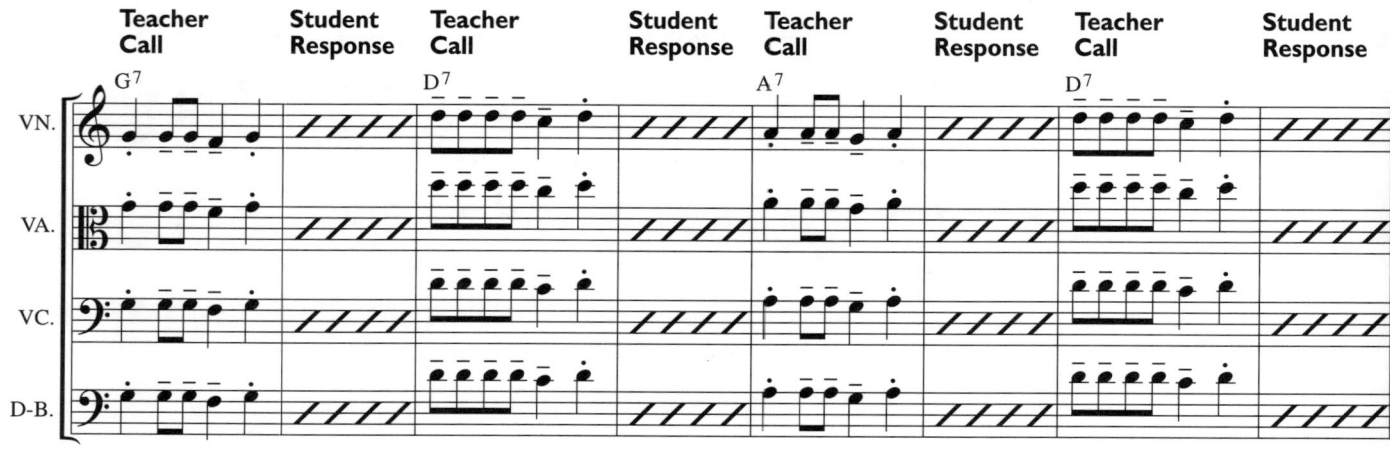

TRACKING THE BLUES IN D

Extended Accom.
#33
Tch's Ed CD-3

Blues in D "CALL AND RESPONSE" (AS PERFORMED BY THE TEACHER)

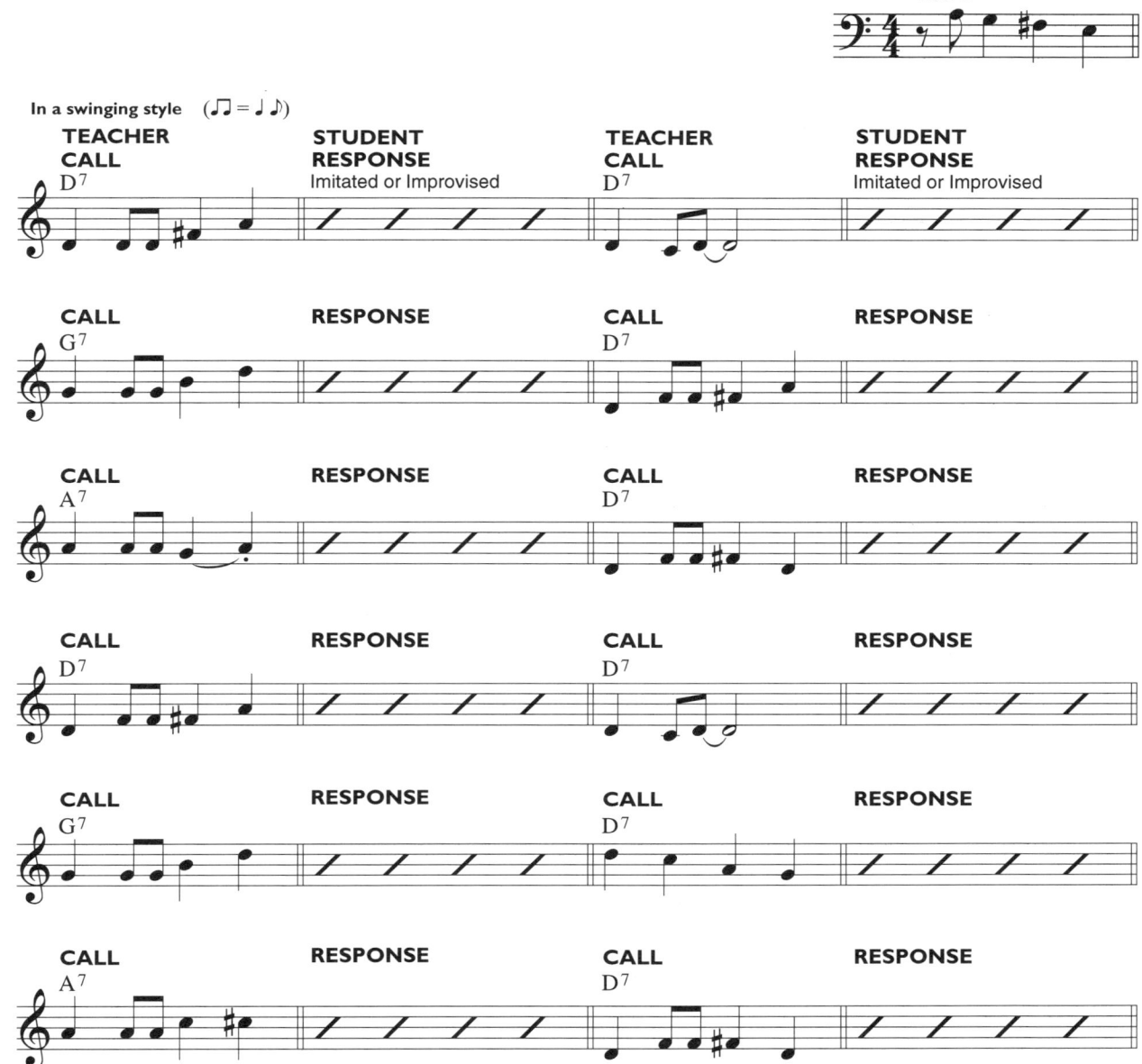

ANOTHER OPTION FOR SPONTANEOUS MUSIC MAKING
from the CD
DO IT! IMPROVISE *

"COOL JAZZ"

Procedure 1. Direct students to use the tones D, C, (D), F, and G.

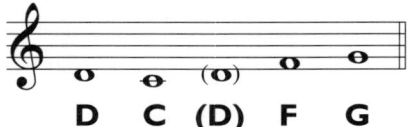

Procedure 2. Teach students to play a musical riff (ostinato).
(***Note:*** *Riffs may be improvised and taught to the class by the teacher or by the students.*)

Procedure 3. Direct students to "Continue the riff until the music ends."
(*For an interesting effect, perform Riff 1 and Riff 2 simultaneously.*)

Procedure 4. When individual students are chosen or volunteer, suggest that they:

A. "Play the riff,"

B. "Improvise a rhythmic variation on the riff, or"

C. "Improvise a rhythmic/melodic variation on the riff."

Procedure 5. Encourage students to notate their best improvised riffs. (See page 41-F for Cool Jazz Composition Worksheet)

* *Do It! Improvise* (CD Backgrounds and Scale Notations for Entry-Level Music Improvisation - MLR 422) Albert Blaser and James Froseth, © 1994 GIA Publications Inc., 7404 South Mason Avenue, Chicago, IL 60638

NEW NOTES

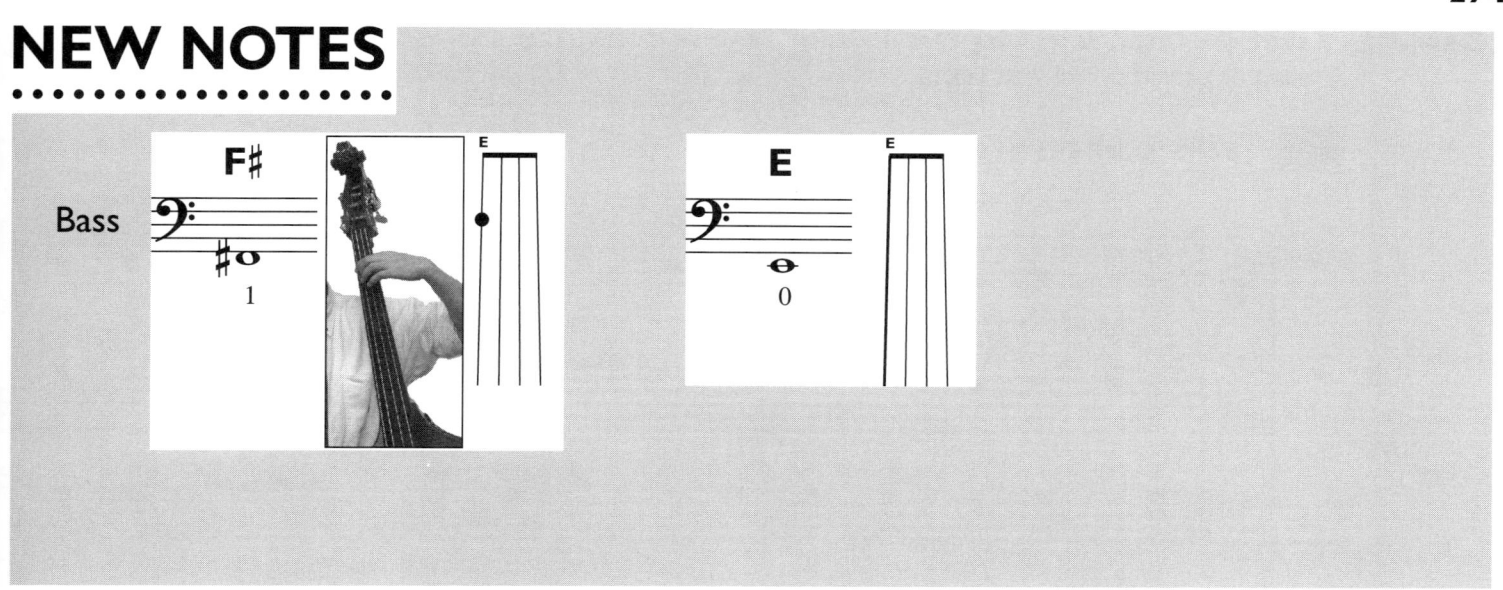

Bass

F# 1

E 0

1 **Baa, Baa, Black Sheep** (IN MINOR TONALITY)

Viola
#49
Tch's Ed CD-3

Cello
#50
Tch's Ed CD-3

Accom.
#51
Tch's Ed CD-3

Moderato

France
Fine

VN.

Baa, baa, black sheep, have you an - y wool? No, sir, nay, not one bag full.

VA.

VC.

D-B.

D.C. al Fine

VN.

None for my mas - ter, none for my dame, None for the lit - tle boy who lives in the lane.

VA.

VC.

D-B.

* Cued notes do not appear in the Student Text. See Special Project below.

SPECIAL PROJECT — ⭐ **(Bass only) Learn to Play** *Baa, Baa, Black Sheep* **8va**
Higher "By Ear" (See score above)

CANON — *Literally, a "rule" for realizing a composition. The rule dictates that each voice imitates exactly the melody sung or played by the first voice.*

2 **Tallis Canon** (4 VOICE CANON)

Thomas Tallis (1510-1585)

Legato

VN.

VA.

VC.

D-B.

All praise to Thee, my Lord this night. For all the bles - sings of the

light; keep me, Oh, keep us, King of Kings, be - neath Thine own Al - might - y wings.

Violin
#52
Tch's Ed CD-3

Cello
#53
Tch's Ed CD-3

Accom.
#54
Tch's Ed CD-3

3 **Bingo**

Gaily

American Game Song

VN.

VA.

VC.

D-B.

There was a farm - er, had a dog, and Bin - go was his name - o. B - I -

4 **French Cathedrals** (3 PART ROUND)

Stately

French Lullaby

STUDENT CD

1 Raindrops   FULL SCORE ON P. 30-F

Violin
Cello
Solo Trk 81
Accom. Trk 81-2

Lightly   Traditional

Hear the gen-tle rain-drops pit-ter pat-ter. See them danc-ing light-ly on the win-dow pane.

2 Raindrops Variation   FULL SCORE ON P. 30-F

Accom. Trk 81-2

Lightly   Traditional

3 Aura Lee   FULL SCORE ON P. 30-F

Viola
Cello
Solo Trk 82
Accom. Trk 82-2

Gently   American Ballad

As the black-bird in the spring, 'Neath the wil-low tree,___ Sat and piped, I

heard him sing, Sing-ing Au-ra Lee. Au-ra Lee, Au-ra Lee,

Maid of gold-en hair, Sun-shine came a-long with thee, And swal-lows in the air.

4 Sleep, Baby, Sleep (Schlaf, Kindlein, Schlaf)   FULL SCORE ON P. 30-G

Violin
Cello
Solo Trk 83
Accom. Trk 83-2

Lightly   German Lullaby

Schlaf,   *Kind - lein,*   *schlaf.*   *Der*   *Va - ter*   *hüt'*   *die*   *Schaf.*   *Die*   *Mut - ter*   *schüt - telt's*
Sleep,   ba - by,   sleep.   Thy   fa - ther   guards   the   sheep.   Thy   mo - ther   shakes   the

Bäum - e - lein,   *Da*   *fällt*   *her - ab*   *ein*   *Träum - e - lein,*   *Schlaf,*   *Kind - lein,*   *schlaf.*
dream - land   tree,   and   from   it   fall   sweet   dreams   for   thee.   Sleep,   ba - by,   sleep.

Rhythmic Flashcard Reading Option for *Raindrops* and *Raindrops Variation*

R-14

R-2

R-11

R-10

R-13

Rhythmic Flashcard Reading Option for *Aura Lee*

R-3

R-4

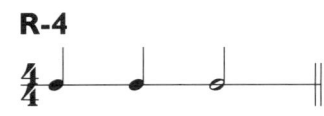

R-6

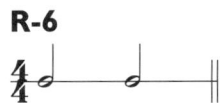

R-5

R-43 *NEW*

R-44 *NEW*

Rhythmic Reading Exercise

Rhythmic Reading Round

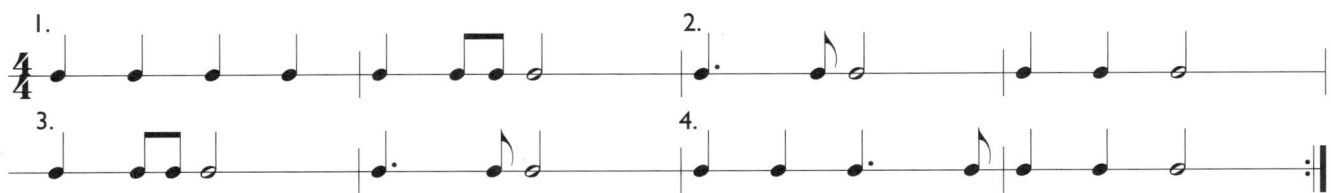

RHYTHMIC BOWING PATTERNS FOR TECHNICAL DEVELOPMENT

Procedure 1. Repeat a line. Direct students to "Repeat the chosen (or assigned) rhythm pattern line until you can play it with ease."

Procedure 2. Combine patterns. Direct students to "Play the rhythm pattern lines, with or without repeat, in order."

Procedure 2a. Combine patterns in ensemble. Assign sections or groups of students a line or lines. Direct students to "Play the assigned rhythm pattern line, and listen carefully to keep a steady beat."

Assign students:

- **an open string pitch or harmonic**
- **any fingered pitch (unison)**
- **their choice of chord tones (Ex. "Play any D, F♯, or A on your instrument.")**
- **the sequential pitches of a scale (Ex. "When you repeat or change lines, move to the next scale tone.")**

SPECIAL PROJECT – **Analysis of Music Compositions for the Use of the Motif**

MOTIF (MOTIVE) – *A short melodic pattern; a musical idea composed of two or more notes.*

Procedure: Notate the melodic motif that provides the basis for the following compositions. (Use the clef for your instrument.)

Shepherd's Hey (PAGE 16)

Shoheen Sho (PAGE 27)

Starlight (PAGE 37)

SPECIAL PROJECT — **Compose a Tune Based Upon an Original Motif**

Procedure 1.   Compose a one-measure (two-beat) motif.
Direct students to use the tones E, G, and A.

My Original Motif

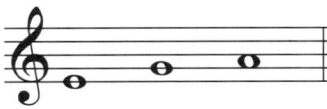

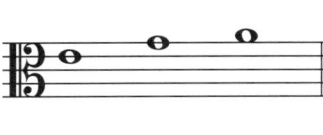

Procedure 2.   Compose three one-measure (two-beat) segments that employ the Structural Elements of Repetition and Variation.

MY COMPOSITION

My Motif   Segment One   Segment Two   Segment Three

A SPECIAL MUSIC COMPOSITION OPTION
CREATING COMPOSITIONS FROM A SINGLE MUSICAL IDEA

MOTIF (MOTIVE) – *A short melodic pattern; a musical idea composed of two or more notes.*

EXERCISE ONE - COMPOSE A FOUR-NOTE TUNE FROM A SINGLE MUSICAL IDEA (MOTIF)

Step 1: Compose a one measure (two beat) motif
Direct students to use the tones D, E, G, and A.

Step 2: Compose three one measure (two beat) segments that employ the Structural Elements of Repetition and Variation, and the Expressive Elements of Sound and Silence, Articulation, and Musical Dynamics.

Composition No. 1

The Motif	Segment One	Segment Two	Segment Three

Composition No. 2

The Motif	Segment One	Segment Two	Segment Three

EXERCISE TWO - COMPOSE A FIVE-NOTE TUNE FROM A SINGLE MUSICAL IDEA (MOTIF)

Step 1: Compose a one measure (two beat) motif
Direct students to use the tones D, E, F♯, G, and A.

Step 2: Compose three one measure (two beat) segments that employ the Structural Elements of Repetition and Variation, and the Expressive Elements of Sound and Silence, Articulation, and Musical Dynamics.

Composition No. 3

The Motif	Segment One	Segment Two	Segment Three

Composition No. 4

The Motif	Segment One	Segment Two	Segment Three

Extended Accom.
#57
Tch's Ed CD-1

Down By the Station - Return to the Musical Dialogue
(A TYPE OF IMPROVISED CALL AND RESPONSE BETWEEN TWO PERFORMERS)

MUSICAL DIALOGUE – *An improvised conversation between two performers. A performer initiates a "Dialogue" with a 4-beat improvised "Statement" or a 4-beat improvised "Question." A second performer responds with a 4-beat improvised "Answer," a 4-beat improvised "Statement," or a 4-beat improvised "Question."*

A musical "Statement" usually starts on the resting tone and always ends on the resting tone. (D is the resting tone for Down By the Station*)*

A musical "Answer" usually starts on a tone other than the resting tone and always ends on the resting tone.

A musical "Question" can begin on any tone but always ends on a tone other than the resting tone.

Direct students to employ one of the following options:

A. "Use the tones D, E, and F#" or   **B.** "Use the tones D, E, F#, and G" or   **C.** "Use the tones D, E, F#, G, and A"

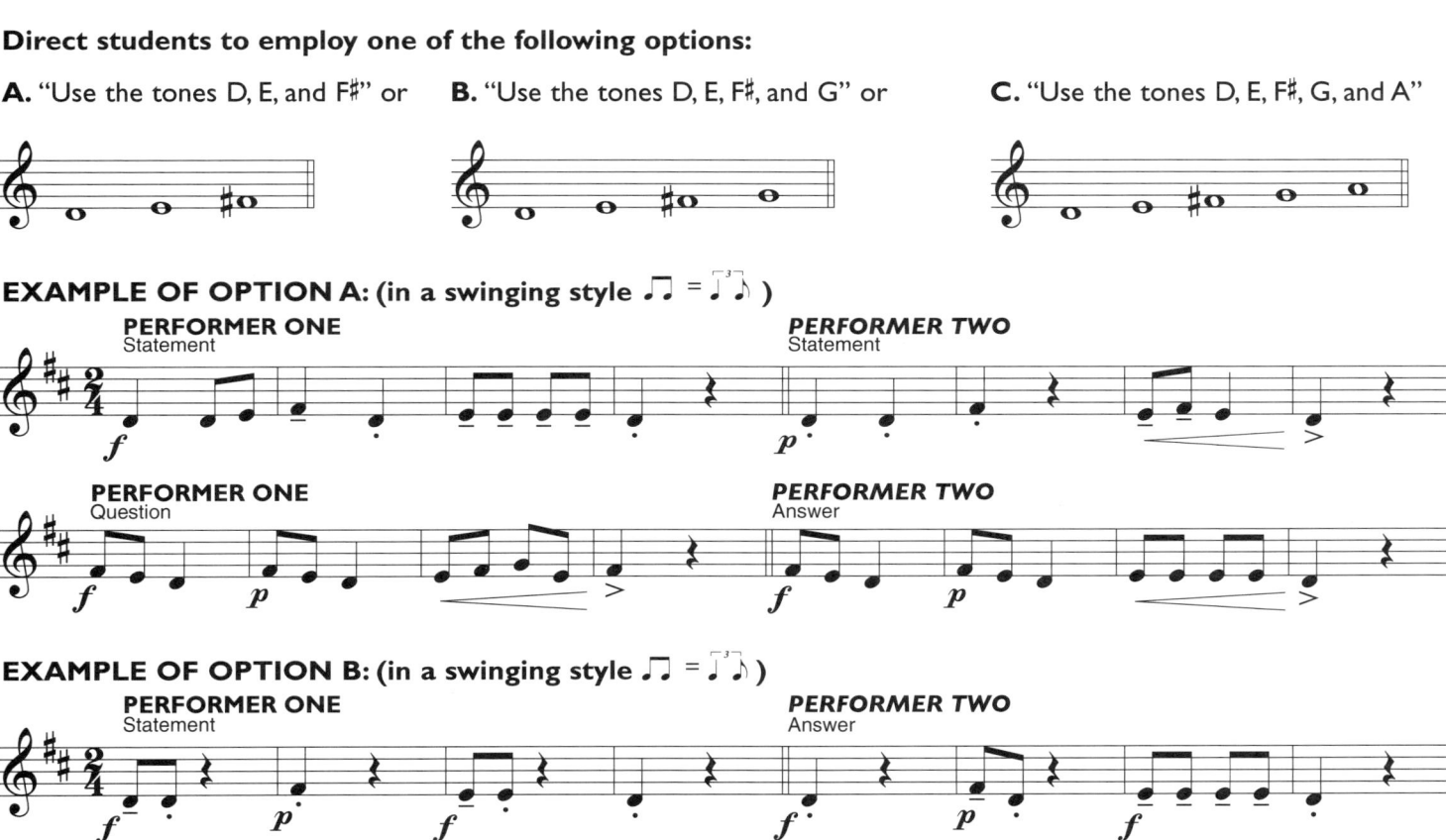

G.I.A. Publications, Inc. grants permission to the purchaser to duplicate this worksheet as an overhead transparency or student handout.

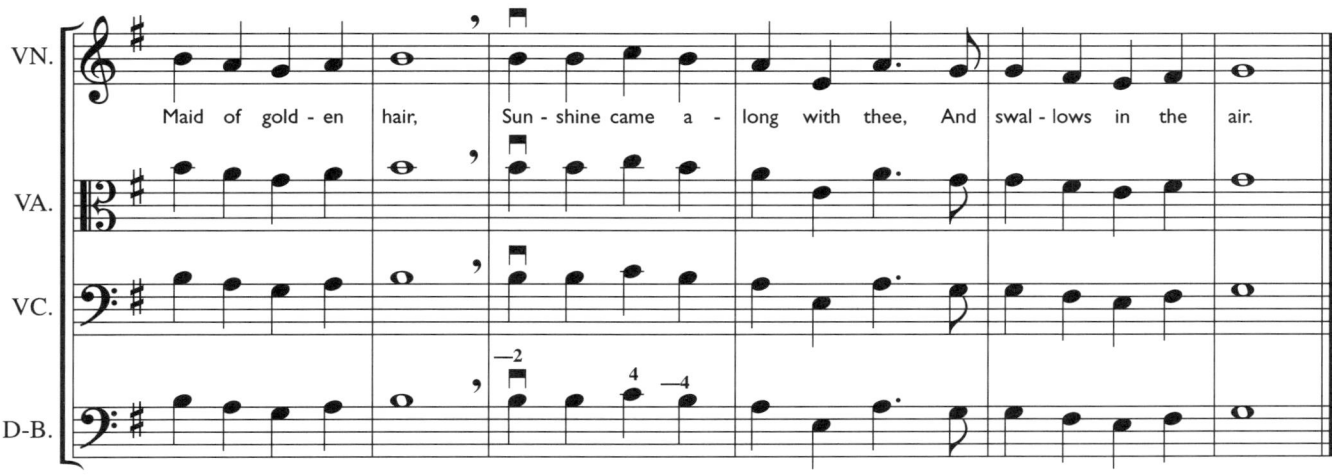

VN.
VA.
VC.
D-B.
Maid of gold - en hair, Sun - shine came a - long with thee, And swal - lows in the air.

Violin
#61
Tch's Ed CD-3

Cello
#62
Tch's Ed CD-3

Accom.
#63
Tch's Ed CD-3

4 Sleep, Baby, Sleep (Schlaf, Kindlein, Schlaf)

Lightly

German Lullaby

VN.
VA.
VC.
D-B.
Schlaf, Kind - lein, schlaf. Der Va - ter hüt' die Schaf. Die Mut - ter schüt - telt's
Sleep, ba - by, sleep. Thy fa - ther guards the sheep. Thy mo - ther shakes the

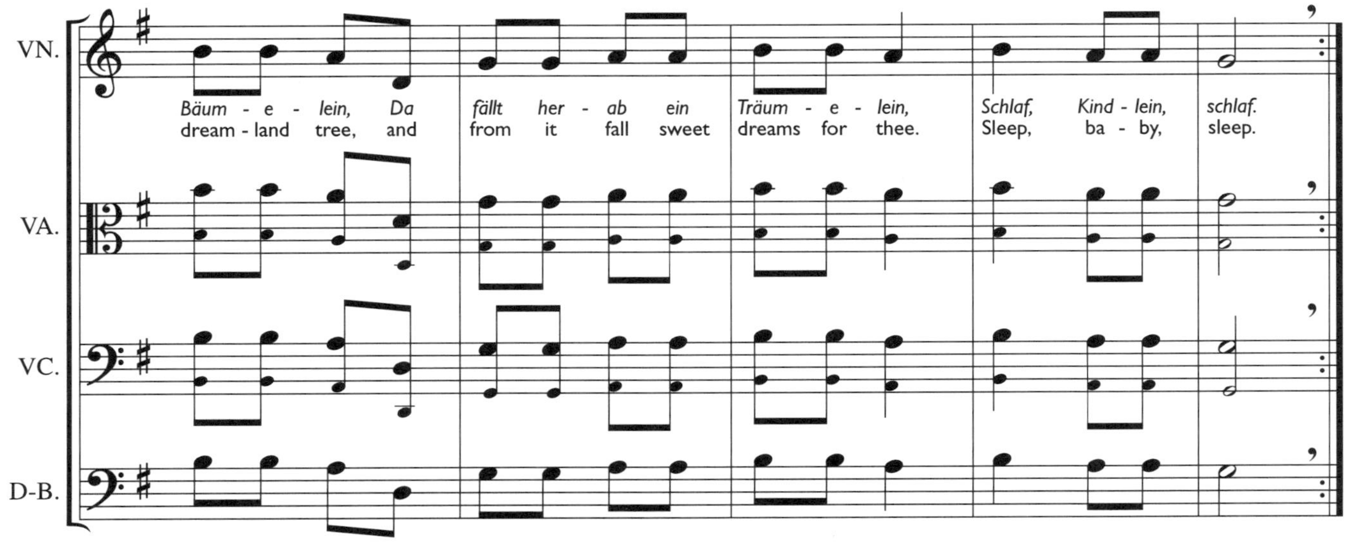

VN.
VA.
VC.
D-B.
Bäum - e - lein, Da fällt her - ab ein Träum - e - lein, Schlaf, Kind - lein, schlaf.
dream - land tree, and from it fall sweet dreams for thee. Sleep, ba - by, sleep.

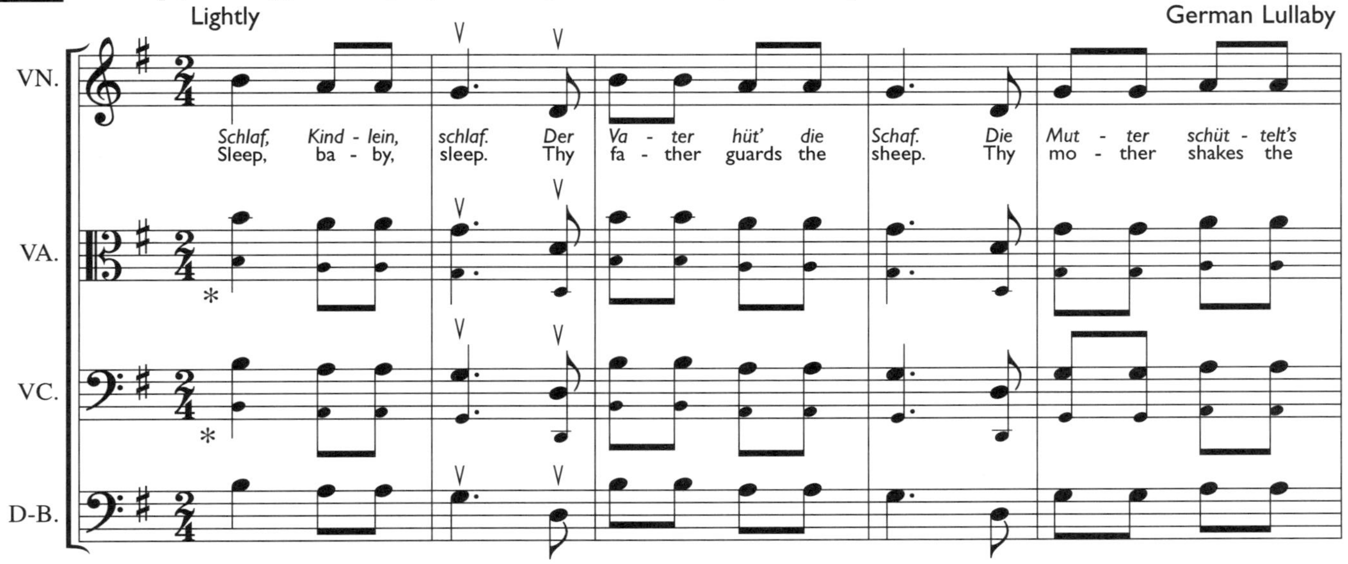

STUDENT CD

Violin
Cello
Solo Trk 84
Accom. Trk 84-2

Sur la Pont D'Avignon (On the Bridge of Avignon) (SOLO OR ENSEMBLE 2-6 PARTS)

Lightly   **FULL SCORES ON PP. 31-D and 31-E**   French Folk Song

OSTINATO — *A melodic pattern that is repeated over and over to accompany a principal melody.*

2 Melodic Ostinatos to *Sur la Pont D'Avignon*   **FULL SCORES ON P. 31-F**

FOLK HYMN — *A song of worship with a religious text that has been set to a folk melody.*

Violin
Cello
Solo Trk 85
Accom. Trk 86

3 Amazing Grace   **FULL SCORE ON P. 31-G**

John Newell (1779)
Early American Melody

GOSPEL — *African-American church music characterized by expression, improvisation, and a strong sense of celebration.*

Violin
Cello
Solo Trk 87
Accom. Trk 88

4 ★ SOLO — **Amazing Grace** (GOSPEL STYLE - "BY EAR" STARTING ON D)

Accom. Trk 88

5 ★★ SOLO — **Amazing Grace** (IMPROVISE IN GOSPEL STYLE - "BY EAR" STARTING ON D)

Rhythmic Flashcard Reading Option for *Sur la Pont d'Avignon* and Melodic Ostinatos

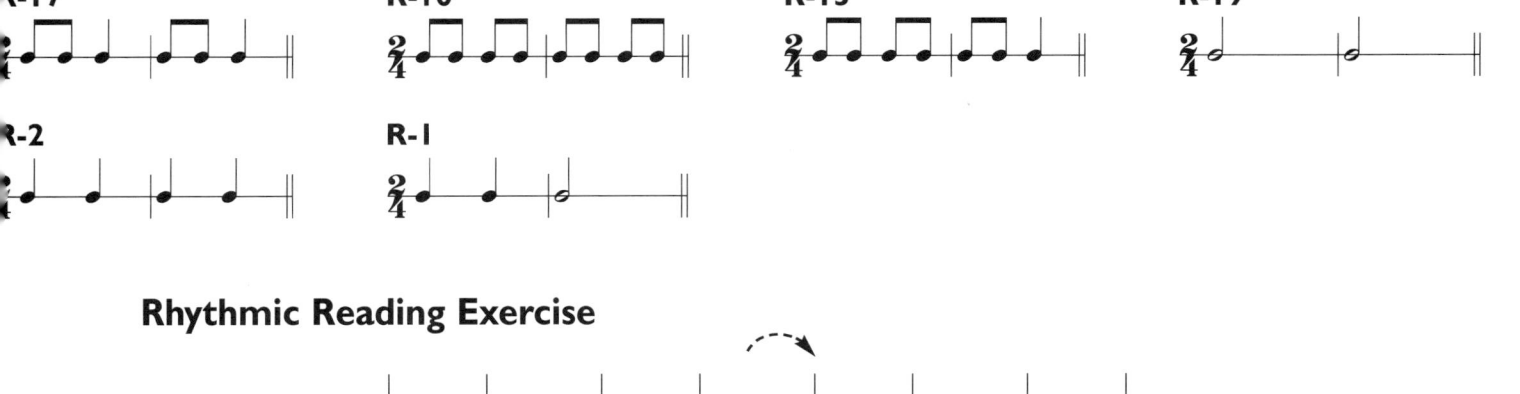

R-17   R-10   R-13   R-19

R-2   R-1

Rhythmic Reading Exercise

A
B
C
D

Rhythmic Reading Round

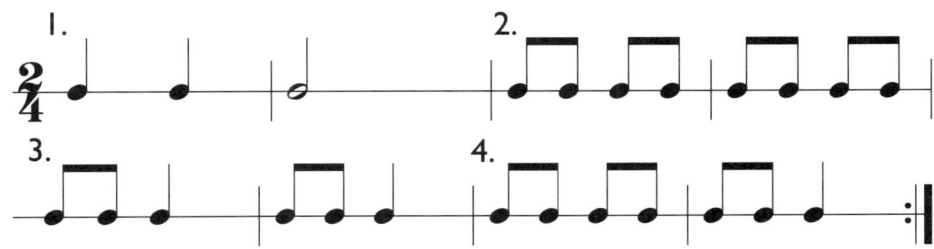

SPECIAL OPTION FOR GROUP MUSIC MAKING

CREATE A GROUP ARRANGEMENT OF *Sur la Pont D'Avignon*

- **Assign melody and ostinatos to various sections or individuals**
- **Decide on numbers of repetitions**
- **Experiment with musical elements like dynamics, articulations, pizzicato**

Accom.
#72
Tch's Ed CD-3

SPECIAL OPTION FOR SPONTANEOUS MUSIC MAKING

IMPROVISE RHYTHMIC VARIATIONS ON *Amazing Grace (Gospel Style)*

ANOTHER OPTION FOR SPONTANEOUS MUSIC MAKING
from the CD
DO IT! IMPROVISE *

Accom.
#98
Tch's Ed CD-2

"COOL JAZZ"

Procedure 1. Direct students to employ one of the following options:

A. "Use 4 tones of the D Minor Pentatonic Scale"

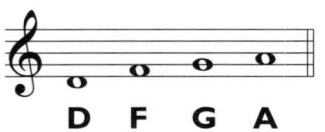

D F G A

B. "Use the tones of the D Minor Pentatonic Scale"

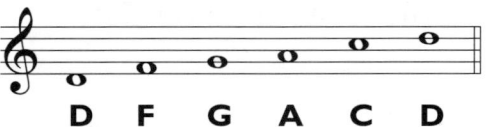

D F G A C D

Procedure 2. Teach everyone to play a musical riff (melodic ostinato) in a swinging style

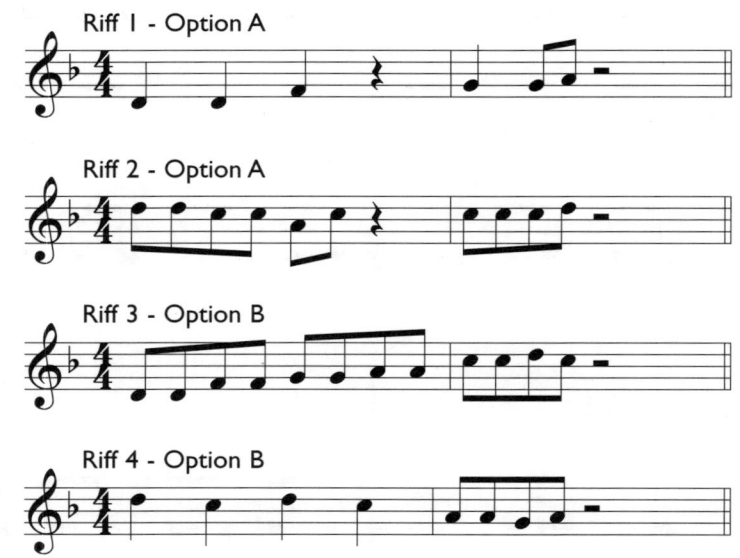

Riff 1 - Option A

Riff 2 - Option A

Riff 3 - Option B

Riff 4 - Option B

Procedure 3. Direct students to "Repeat the riff until the music ends."
(Two or more riffs may be played simultaneously.)

Procedure 4. When individual students are chosen or volunteer, suggest that they:

A. "Play the riff,"

B. "Improvise a rhythmic variation on the riff, or"

C. "Improvise a rhythmic/melodic variation on the riff."

Procedure 5. Encourage students to improvise and compose musical riffs. (See page 41-F for Cool Jazz Composition Worksheet.)

* *Do It! Improvise* (CD Backgrounds and Scale Notations for Entry-Level Music Improvisation - MLR 422) Albert Blaser and James Froseth, © 1994 GIA Publications Inc., 7404 South Mason Avenue, Chicago, IL 60638

DO IT! IMPROVISE *

Accom.
#98
Tch's Ed CD-2

COOL JAZZ – Teacher Call and Student Response (IN A SWINGING STYLE)

MORE OPTIONS FOR SPONTANEOUS AND CREATIVE MUSIC MAKING

OPTIONAL PROCEDURE #1. Ask for volunteers to lead the class with their own improvised calls

PROCEDURE #1-A. Direct the class to follow with imitated or improvised responses

OPTIONA PROCEDURE #2. Encourage students to notate riffs

PROCEDURE #2-A. Direct students to compose "Cool Jazz" melodies
(Refer to page 41-F for student worksheet)

* *Do It! Improvise* (CD Backgrounds and Scale Notations for Entry-Level Music Improvisation - MLR 422) Albert Blaser and James Froseth,
© 1994 GIA Publications Inc., 7404 South Mason Avenue, Chicago, IL 60638

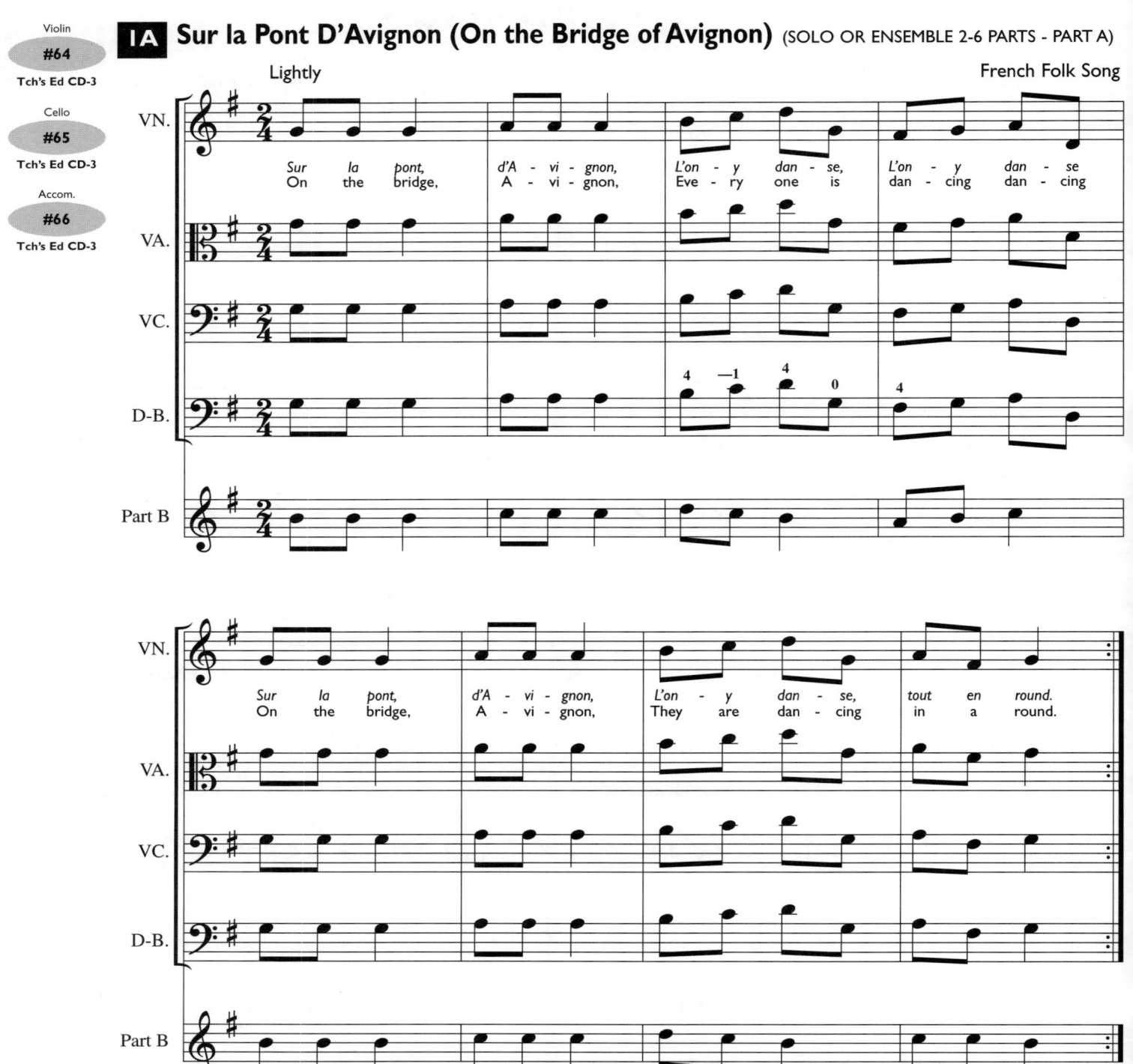

1A Sur la Pont D'Avignon (On the Bridge of Avignon) (SOLO OR ENSEMBLE 2-6 PARTS - PART A)

French Folk Song

1B **Sur la Pont D'Avignon (On the Bridge of Avignon)** (SOLO OR ENSEMBLE 2-6 PARTS - PART B)

Violin
#64
Tch's Ed CD-3

Cello
#65
Tch's Ed CD-3

Accom.
#66
Tch's Ed CD-3

Lightly

French Folk Song

Sur la pont, d'A - vi - gnon, L'on - y dan - se, L'on - y dan - se
On the bridge, A - vi - gnon, Eve - ry one is dan - cing dan - cing

Sur la pont, d'A - vi - gnon, L'on - y dan - se, tout en round.
On the bridge, A - vi - gnon, They are dan - cing in a round.

OSTINATO *— A melodic pattern that is repeated over and over to accompany a principal melody.*

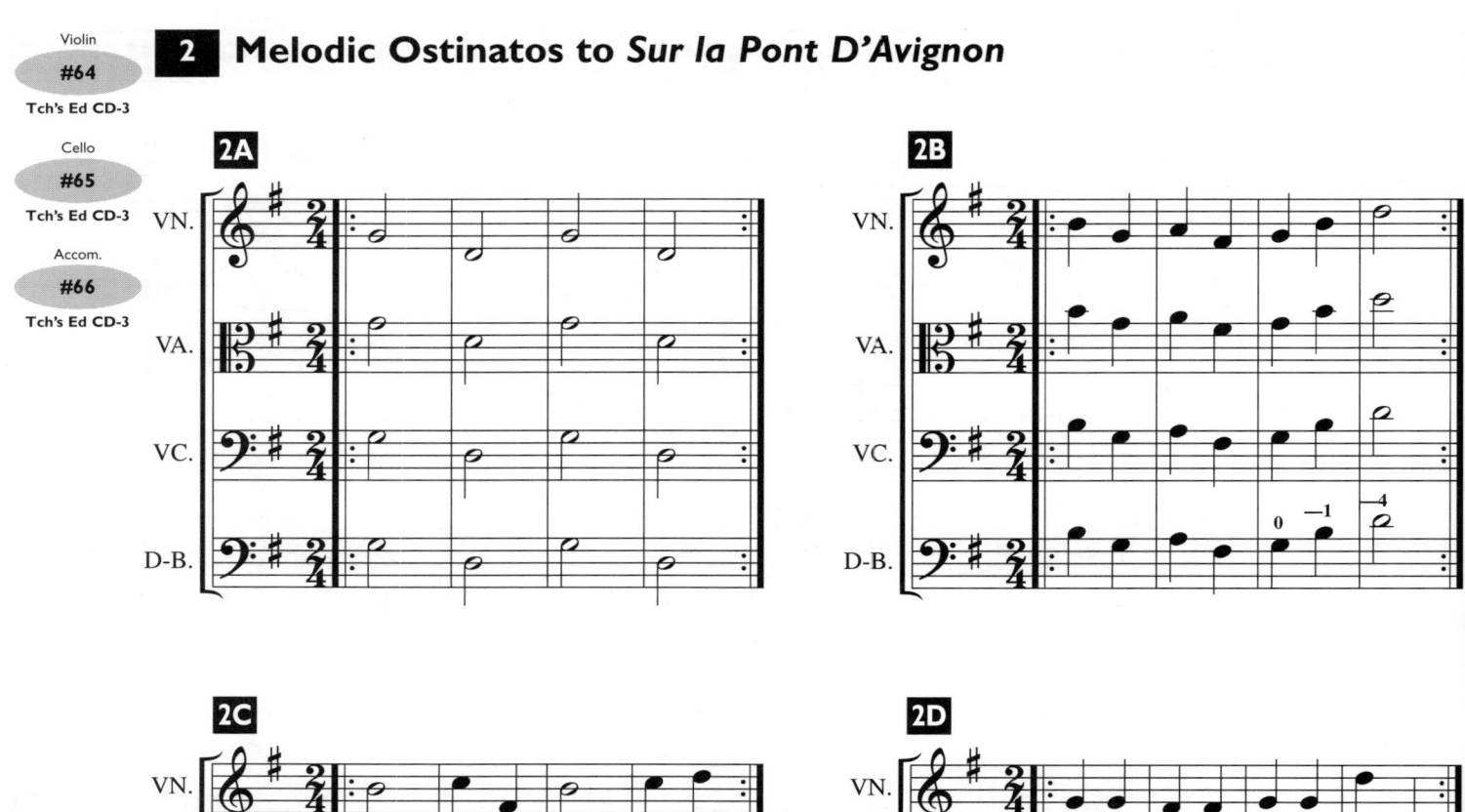

Violin
#64
Tch's Ed CD-3

Cello
#65
Tch's Ed CD-3

Accom.
#66
Tch's Ed CD-3

2 **Melodic Ostinatos to *Sur la Pont D'Avignon***

FOLK HYMN — *A song of worship with a religious text that has been set to a folk melody.*

3 **Amazing Grace**

John Newell (1779)
Early American Melody

Stately

* *Cued notes do not appear in the Student Text. See Special Project below.*

GOSPEL — *African-American church music characterized by expression, improvisation, and a strong sense of celebration.*

4 ☆ SOLO — **Amazing Grace** (GOSPEL STYLE - "BY EAR" STARTING ON D)

5 ☆☆ SOLO — **Amazing Grace** (IMPROVISE IN GOSPEL STYLE - "BY EAR" STARTING ON D)

SPECIAL PROJECT — ☆ **(Viola and Cello only) Learn to Play** *Amazing Grace* **8va Lower "By Ear"** (See score above)

Violin
#67
Tch's Ed CD-3

Cello
#68
Tch's Ed CD-3

Accom.
#69
Tch's Ed CD-3

Violin
#70
Tch's Ed CD-3

Cello
#71
Tch's Ed CD-3

Accom.
#72
Tch's Ed CD-3

1 Scotland's A-Burning (IN SIX-EIGHT TIME)   FULL SCORE ON P. 32-B   Traditional

2 Variation on *Scotland's A-Burning*   FULL SCORE ON P. 32-B

SPEAKER BALANCE
CONTROL
CD Trk 89
L   R
Violin   Accom.
Cello

3 Little Tom Tinker (4 PART ROUND)   FULL SCORE ON P. 32-C   Traditional Round

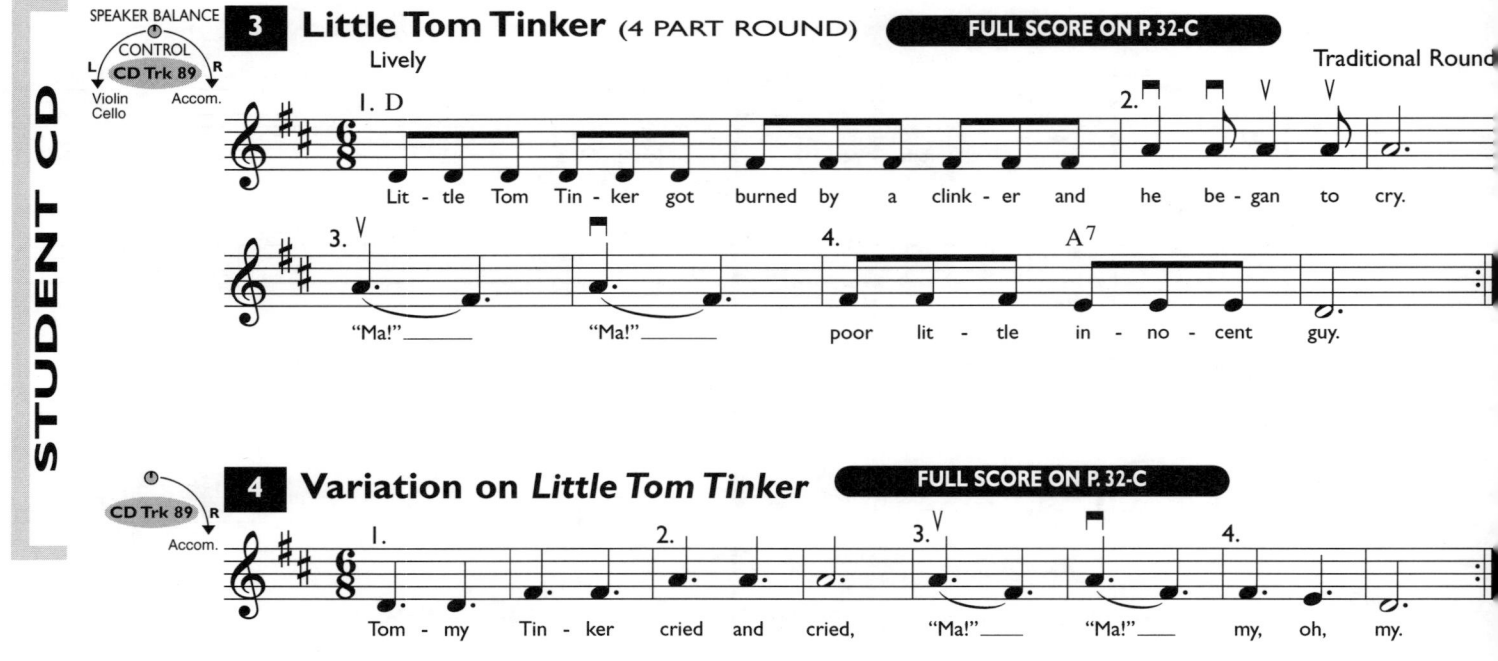

CD Trk 89   R
Accom.

4 Variation on *Little Tom Tinker*   FULL SCORE ON P. 32-C

5 Santy Maloney (4 PART ROUND)   FULL SCORE ON P. 32-D   England

Rhythmic Flashcard Reading Option for *Little Tom Tinker*

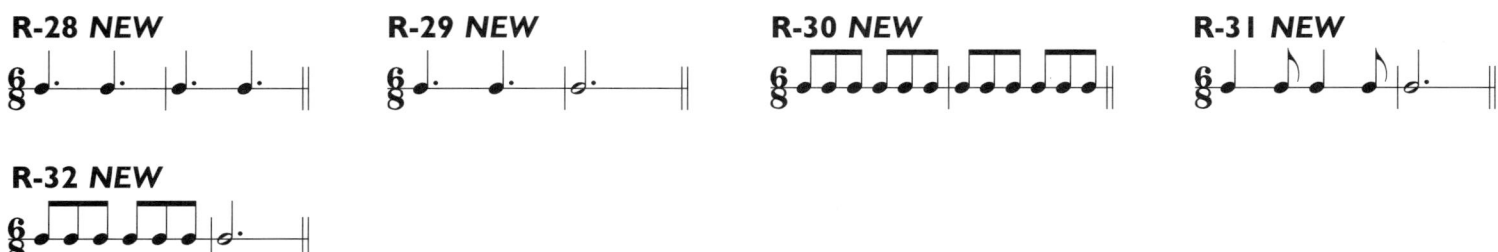

RHYTHMIC BOWING PATTERNS FOR TECHNICAL DEVELOPMENT

Accompaniment for Teacher Call - Student Response and Rhythmic Reading in 3s

#97

Tch's Ed CD-2

Procedure 1. Repeat a line. Direct students to "Repeat the chosen (or assigned) rhythm pattern line until you can play it with ease."

Procedure 2. Combine patterns. Direct students to "Play the rhythm pattern lines, with or without repeat, in order."

Procedure 2a. Combine patterns in ensemble. Assign sections or groups of students a line or lines. Direct students to "Play the assigned rhythm pattern line, and listen carefully to keep a steady beat."

Assign students:

- an open string pitch or harmonic
- any fingered pitch (unison)
- their choice of chord tones
  (e.g., "Play any D, F♯, or A on your instrument.")

- the sequential pitches of a scale
  (e.g., "When you repeat or change lines, move to the next scale tone.")

1 **Scotland's A-Burning** (IN SIX-EIGHT TIME)

* *Cued notes do not appear in the Student Text. See Special Project below.*

SPECIAL PROJECT — ★ **(Viola and Cello only) Learn to Play *Scotland's A-Burning* 8va Lower "By Ear"** (See score above)

2 **Variation on *Scotland's A-Burning***

3 **Little Tom Tinker** (4 PART ROUND)

Violin
#73
Tch's Ed CD-3

Cello
#74
Tch's Ed CD-3

Accom.
#75
Tch's Ed CD-3

Lively

Traditional Round

4 **Variation on *Little Tom Tinker***

Accom.
#75
Tch's Ed CD-3

5 **Santy Maloney** (4 PART ROUND)

England

Cued notes do not appear in the Student Text. See Special Project below.

SPECIAL PROJECT — ★ **(Viola and Cello only) Learn to Play** *Santy Maloney* **8va Lower "By Ear"** (See score above)

BLANK PAGE

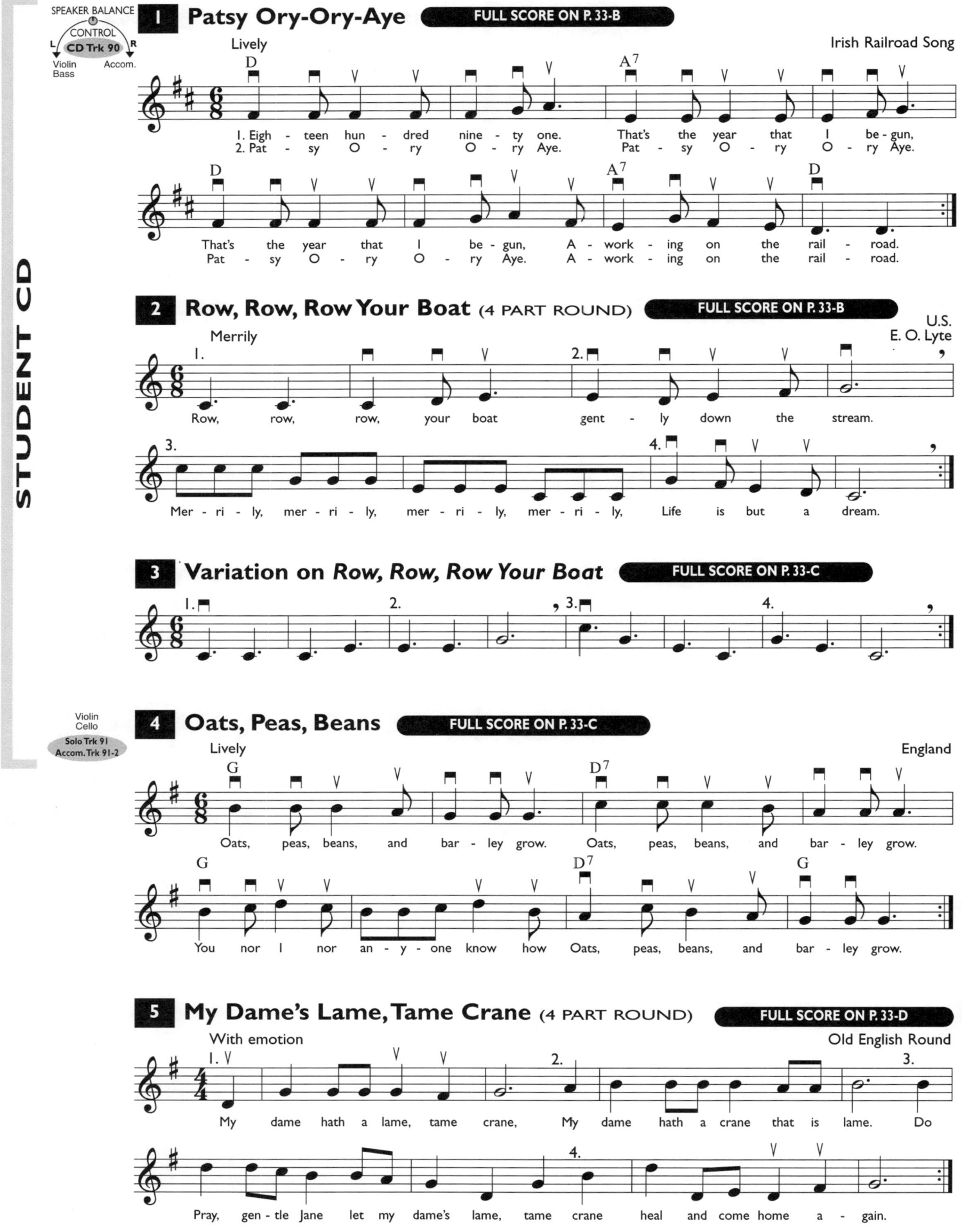

Rhythmic Flashcard Reading Option for *Patsy Ory-Ory-Aye*

R-33 *NEW*    **R-34** *NEW*

Rhythmic Flashcard Reading Option for *Row, Row, Row Your Boat* **and** *Variation*

R-37 *NEW*    **R-31**    **R-30**    **R-28**

Rhythmic Flashcard Reading Option for *Oats, Peas, Beans*

R-33    **R-35** *NEW*

Rhythmic Reading Exercise

Rhythmic Reading Round

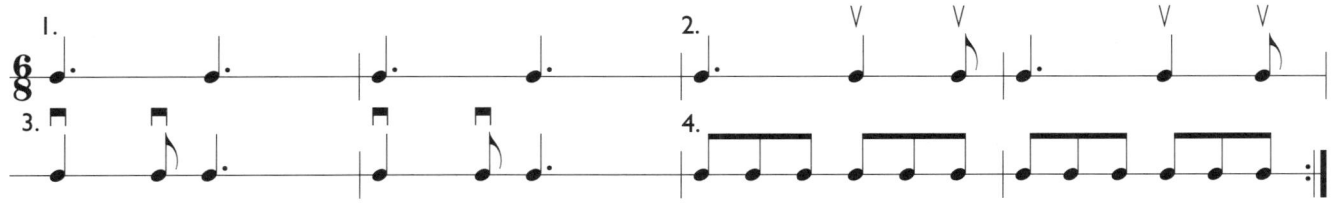

1 **Patsy Ory-Ory-Aye**

Lively

Irish Railroad Song

VN.
VA.
VC.
D-B.

1. Eigh - teen hun - dred nine - ty one. That's the year that I be - gun,
2. Pat - sy O - ry O - ry Aye. Pat - sy O - ry O - ry Aye.

VN.
VA.
VC.
D-B.

1. Eigh - teen hun - dred nine - ty one. That's the year that I be - gun,
2. Pat - sy O - ry O - ry Aye. Pat - sy O - ry O - ry Aye.

Violin
#76
Tch's Ed CD-3

Bass
#77
Tch's Ed CD-3

Accom.
#78
Tch's Ed CD-3

2 **Row, Row, Row Your Boat** (4 PART ROUND)

Merrily

U.S.
E. O. Lyte

VN.
VA.
VC.
D-B.

Row, row, row, your boat gent - ly down the stream.

Cued notes do not appear in the Student Text. See Special Project on page 33-C.

3 Variation on *Row, Row, Row Your Boat*

SPECIAL PROJECT — ★ (Viola and Cello only) Learn to Play *Row, Row, Row Your Boat* 8va Lower "By Ear" (See score on page 33-B)

4 Oats, Peas, Beans

Violin
#79
Tch's Ed CD-3

Cello
#80
Tch's Ed CD-3

Accom.
#81
Tch's Ed CD-3

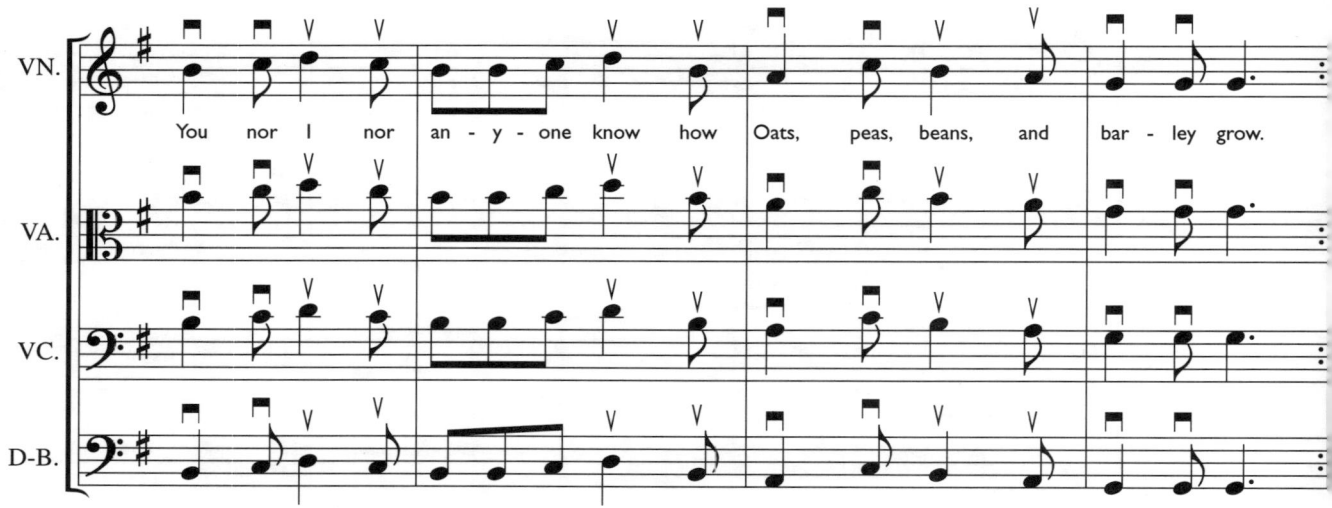

You nor I nor an - y - one know how Oats, peas, beans, and bar - ley grow.

5 My Dame's Lame, Tame Crane (4 PART ROUND)

With emotion

Old English Round

My dame hath a lame, tame crane, My dame hath a crane that is lame. Do

Pray, gen - tle Jane let my dame's lame, tame crane heal and come home a - gain.

BLANK PAGE

ACCELERANDO POCO A POCO — *Faster, little by little.*

Violin
Cello
Solo Trk 92
Accom. Trk 93

1 **The Shining Young Moon** FULL SCORE ON P. 34-B

Accelerando poco a poco

Russian Folk Melody

2 **Variation One on** *The Shining Young Moon* FULL SCORE ON P. 34-B

Accelerando poco a poco

Russian Folk Melody

SYNCOPATION — *A displacement of the natural pulse or accent of the music, usually to the second half of the beat, as in:*

3 **Variation Two on** *The Shining Young Moon* FULL SCORE ON P. 34-C

Accelerando poco a poco

Russian Folk Melody

4 **Variation Three on** *The Shining Young Moon* FULL SCORE ON P. 34-D

Accelerando poco a poco

Russian Folk Melody

RHYTHMIC BOWING PATTERNS FOR TECHNICAL DEVELOPMENT

Procedure 1. Repeat a line. Direct students to "Repeat the chosen (or assigned) rhythm pattern line until you can play it with ease."

Procedure 2. Combine patterns. Direct students to "Play the rhythm pattern lines, with or without repeat, in order."

Procedure 2a. Combine patterns in ensemble. Assign sections or groups of students a line or lines. Direct students to "Play the assigned rhythm pattern line, and listen carefully to keep a steady beat."

Assign students:

• an open string pitch or harmonic
• any fingered pitch (unison)
• their choice of chord tones (Ex. "Play any D, F♯, or A on your instrument.")
• the sequential pitches of a scale (Ex. "When you repeat or change lines, move to the next scale tone.")

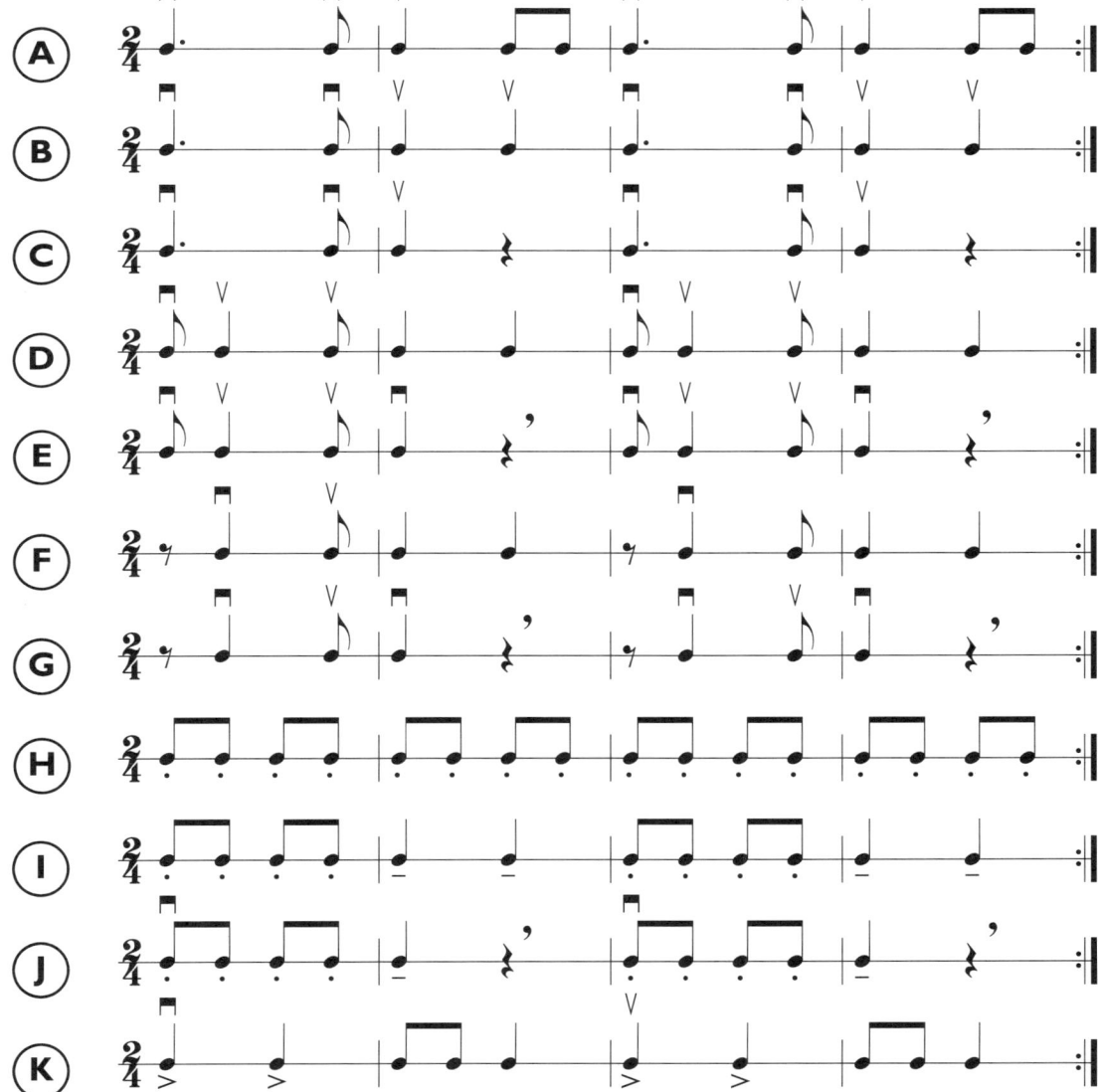

ACCELERANDO POCO A POCO — *Faster, little by little.*

Violin
#82
Tch's Ed CD-3

Cello
#83
Tch's Ed CD-3

Accom.
#84
Tch's Ed CD-3

1 ■ **The Shining Young Moon**

Accelerando poco a poco

Russian Folk Melody

Violin
#82
Tch's Ed CD-3

Cello
#83
Tch's Ed CD-3

Accom.
#84
Tch's Ed CD-3

2 ■ **Variation One on *The Shining Young Moon***

Accelerando poco a poco

Russian Folk Melody

SYNCOPATION — *A displacement of the natural pulse or accent of the music, usually to the second half of the beat, as in:* ♪ ♩ ♪

3 **Variation Two on *The Shining Young Moon***

Violin
#82
Tch's Ed CD-3

Cello
#83
Tch's Ed CD-3

Accom.
#84
Tch's Ed CD-3

Accelerando poco a poco

Russian Folk Melody

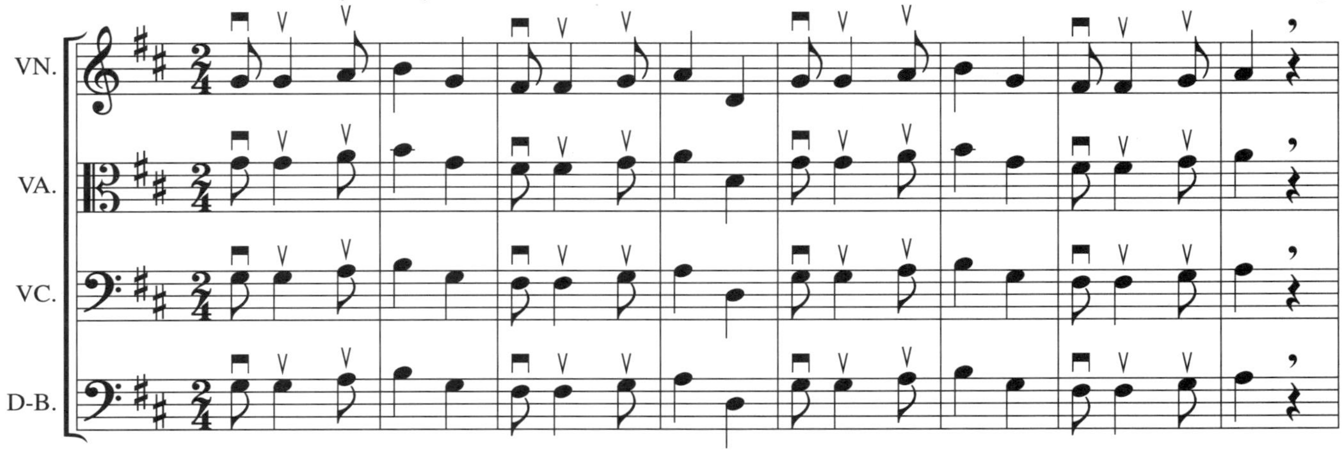

4 Variation Three on *The Shining Young Moon*

Russian Folk Melody

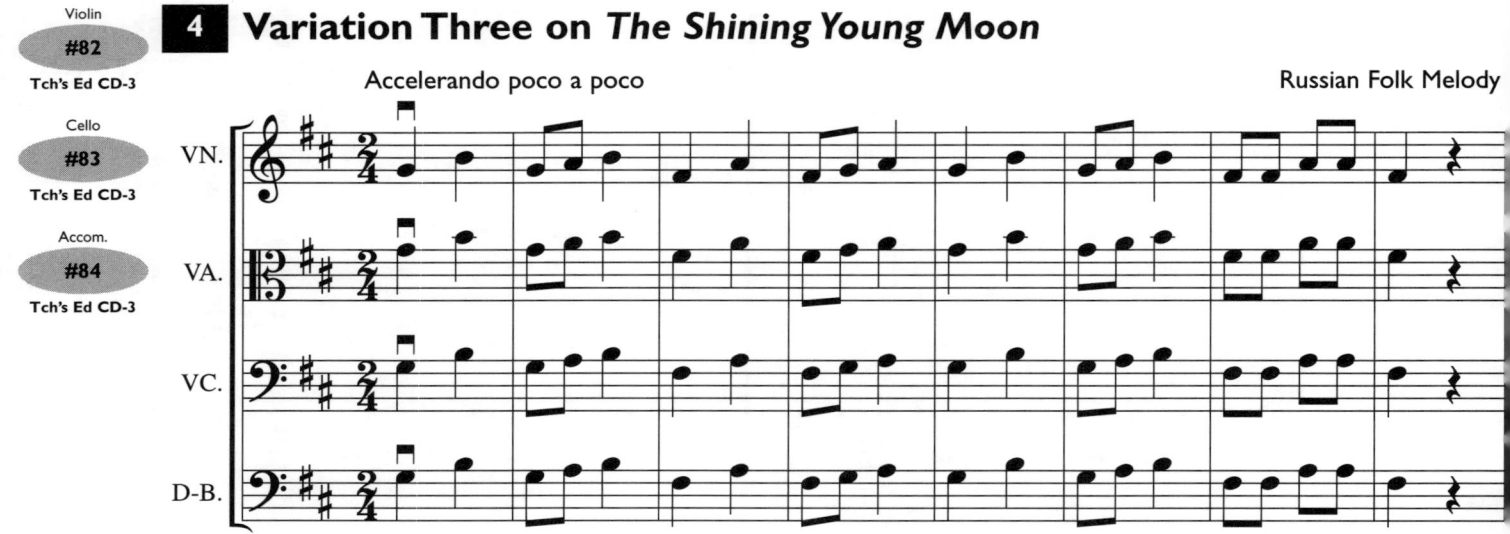

BLANK PAGE

5 **Variation Four on** *The Shining Young Moon*   FULL SCORE ON P. 35-A

Accelerando poco a poco   Russian Folk Melody

6 **Variation Five on** *The Shining Young Moon*   FULL SCORE ON P. 35-A

Accelerando poco a poco   Russian Folk Melody

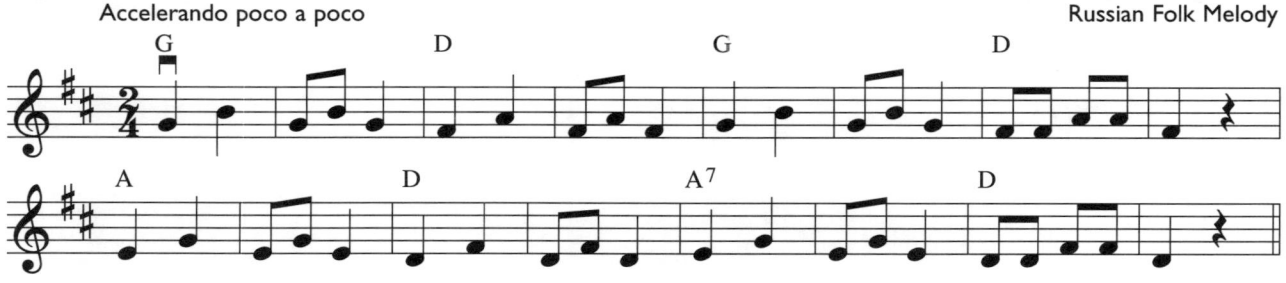

7 **Variation Six on** *The Shining Young Moon*   FULL SCORE ON P. 35-B

Accelerando poco a poco   Russian Folk Melody

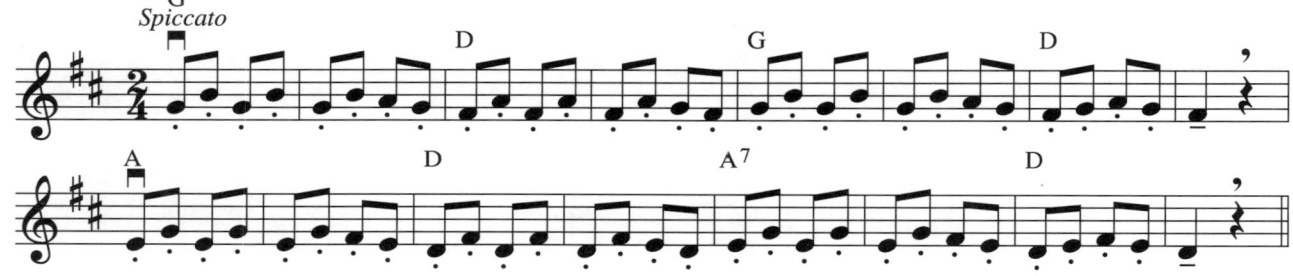

8 **Variation Seven on** *The Shining Young Moon*   FULL SCORE ON P. 35-C

Accelerando poco a poco   Russian Folk Melody

5 **Variation Four on *The Shining Young Moon***

Violin
#82
Tch's Ed CD-3

Cello
#83
Tch's Ed CD-3

Accom.
#84
Tch's Ed CD-3

Accelerando poco a poco

Russian Folk Melody

VN.

VA.

VC.

D-B.

6 **Variation Five on *The Shining Young Moon***

Violin
#82
Tch's Ed CD-3

Cello
#83
Tch's Ed CD-3

Accom.
#84
Tch's Ed CD-3

Accelerando poco a poco

Russian Folk Melody

VN.

VA.

VC.

D-B.

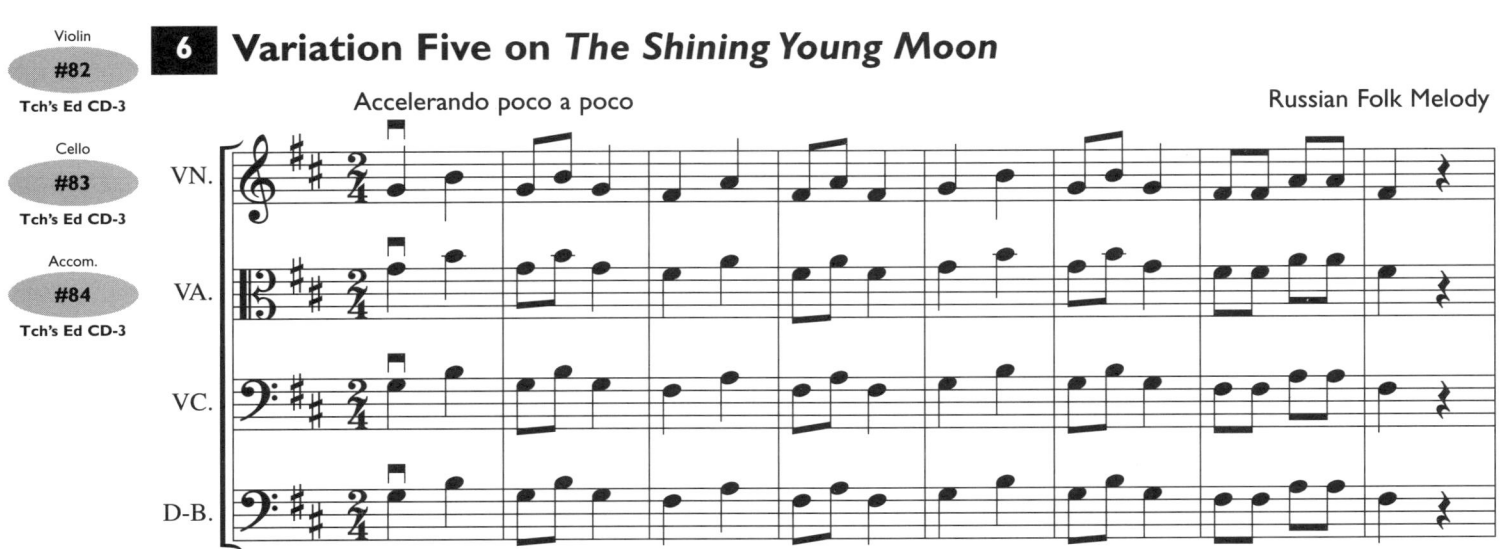

Violin
#82
Tch's Ed CD-3

Cello
#83
Tch's Ed CD-3

Accom.
#84
Tch's Ed CD-3

7 Variation Six on *The Shining Young Moon*

Accelerando poco a poco

Russian Folk Melody

8 **Variation Seven on *The Shining Young Moon***

Accelerando poco a poco

Russian Folk Melody

36

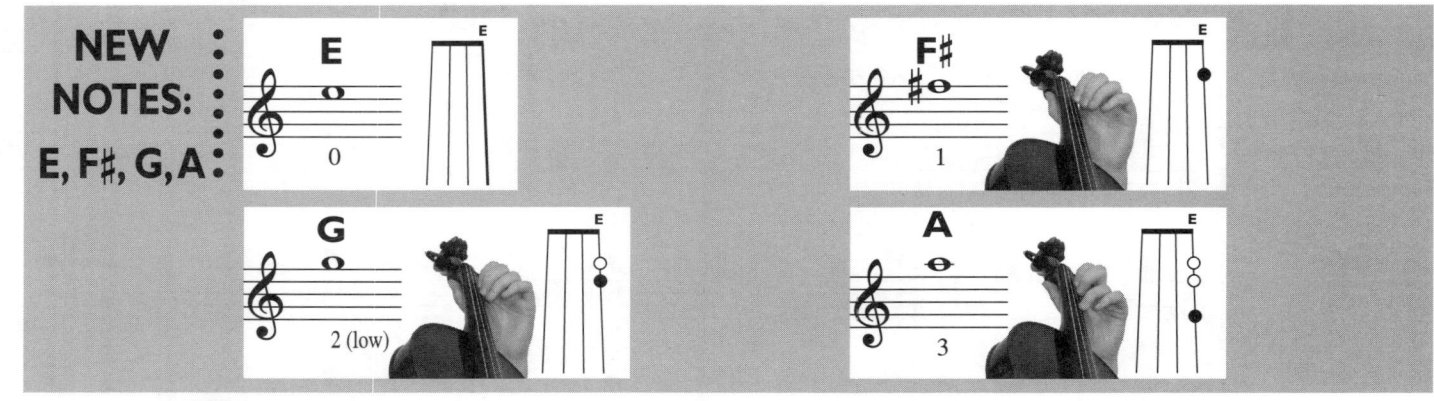

NEW NOTES: E, F♯, G, A

1 Singing Goose (4 PART ROUND)   FULL SCORE ON P. 36-D

With conviction

England

Why should-n't my goose, Sing as well as thy goose

When I paid for my goose, Twice as much as thou?

COL LEGNO — Tap the string with the bow stick.

Woodchuck (SOLO OR ENSEMBLE 2-4 PARTS)   FULL SCORES ON PP. 36-E and 36-F

Humorously

Dance Tune

Knock on instrument

STUDENT CD

3 Can Can Theme   FULL SCORE ON P. 36-G

Jacques Offenbach (1819-1880)

CD Trk 94

REVIEW OF STRATEGIES FOR CREATING MUSIC IMPROVISATIONS THAT ARE INTERESTING AND WELL-STRUCTURED

Extended Accom.

#57

Tch's Ed CD-1

For 𝄞 Instruments

The tune: *Down By the Station* (in a swinging style)

"I Don't Know What to Do"

1. **THINK**: *Rhythmic Subdivision* to create excitement and to energize your performance.

2. **THINK**: *Sound and Silence* to provide interest, variety, structure, and expression.

3. **THINK**: *Repetition (Rhythmic)* and *Variation (Melodic)* for interest and structure.

4. Another example of the use of *Repetition (Rhythmic)* and *Variation (Melodic)* as structural elements.

5. **THINK**: *Musical Articulation* to provide an expressive element to your performance.

6. **THINK**: *Musical Dynamics* as an expressive strategy.

7. **THINK**: *Blues Scale* to provide interest, variety, and expression.

Passing
tone

8. Another example of the use of selected tones of the *Blues Scale*.

9. Another example of the use of selected tones of the *Blues Scale*.

REVIEW OF STRATEGIES FOR CREATING MUSIC IMPROVISATIONS THAT ARE INTERESTING AND WELL-STRUCTURED

Extended Accom.

#57

Tch's Ed CD-1

For 𝄡 Instruments

The tune: *Down By the Station* (in a swinging style)

"I Don't Know What to Do"

1. **THINK**: *Rhythmic Subdivision* to create excitement and to energize your performance.

2. **THINK**: *Sound and Silence* to provide interest, variety, structure, and expression.

3. **THINK**: *Repetition (Rhythmic)* and *Variation (Melodic)* for interest and structure.

4. Another example of the use of *Repetition (Rhythmic)* and *Variation (Melodic)* as structural elements.

5. **THINK**: *Musical Articulation* to provide an expressive element to your performance.

6. **THINK**: *Musical Dynamics* as an expressive strategy.

7. **THINK**: *Blues Scale* to provide interest, variety, and expression.

Passing tone

8. Another example of the use of selected tones of the *Blues Scale*.

9. Another example of the use of selected tones of the *Blues Scale*.

BLANK PAGE

IA **Theme from "Spring"** (FOR STRING ORCHESTRA - VIOLIN I)

FULL SCORE ON P. 39-A

Antonio Vivaldi (1678-1741)
arr. Bret Smith

IB **Theme from "Spring"** (FOR STRING ORCHESTRA - VIOLIN II)

FULL SCORE ON P. 39-A

Antonio Vivaldi (1678-1741)
arr. Bret Smith

I Theme from "Spring" (FOR STRING ORCHESTRA)

Antonio Vivaldi (1678-1741)
arr. Bret Smith

Sakura FULL SCORE ON P. 41-A

arr. David Froseth

1 **Sakura**

arr. David Froseth

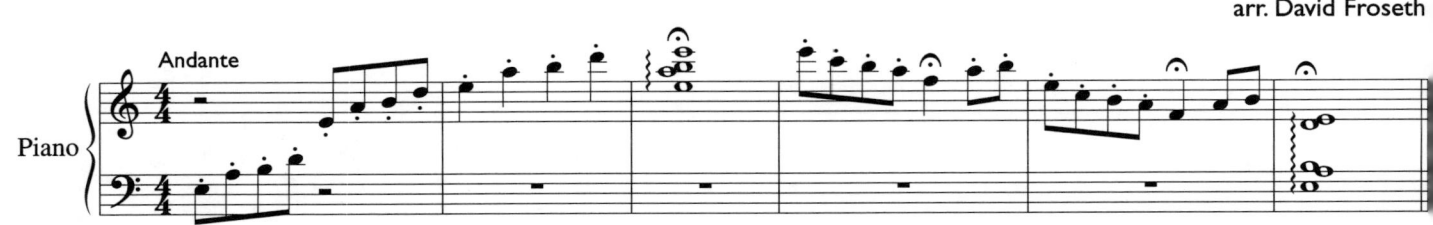

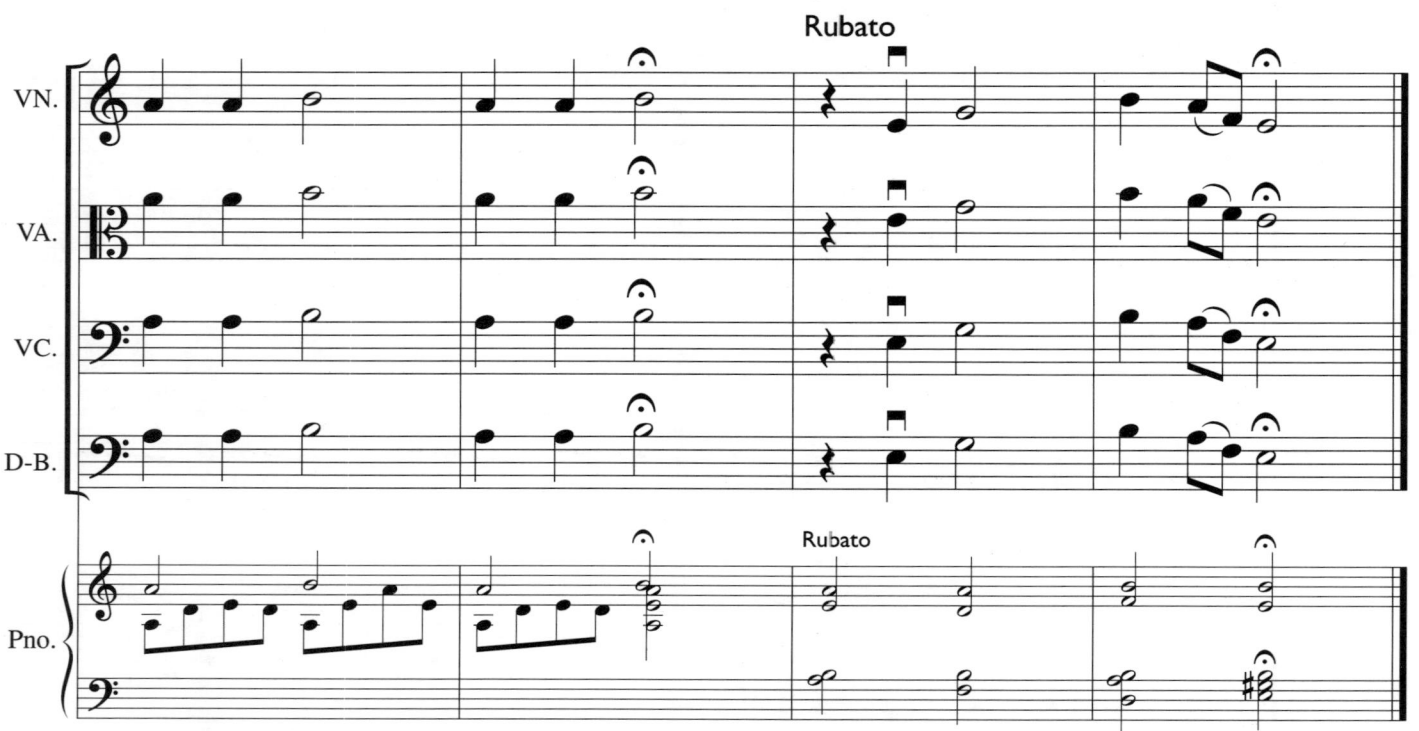

- STUDENT WORKSHEET -

Cobbler, Cobbler

CREATING COMPOSITIONS BY NOTATING AND COMBINING IMPROVISED RIFFS

PROCEDURES:

A. Improvise musical riffs over *Cobbler, Cobbler* background music.
(Riffs are usually four- or eight-beat melodic patterns.)

B. Notate your best improvised riffs.

C. Combine several riffs to compose a *Cobbler, Cobbler* melody.

D. Combine musically compatible riffs to compose two- and three-part pieces.

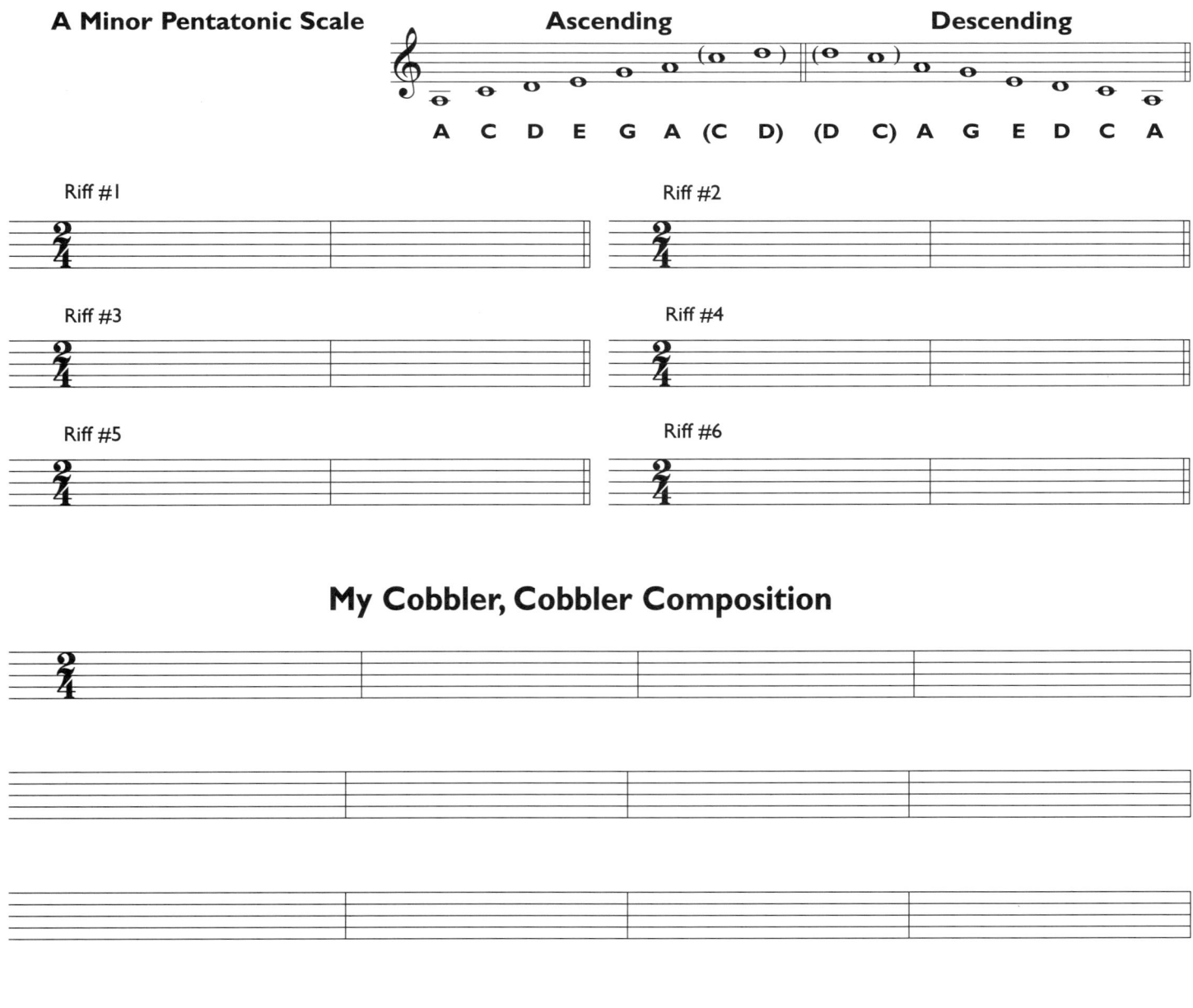

My Cobbler, Cobbler Composition

- STUDENT WORKSHEET -

Cobbler, Cobbler

CREATING COMPOSITIONS BY NOTATING AND COMBINING IMPROVISED RIFFS

PROCEDURES:

A. Improvise musical riffs over *Cobbler, Cobbler* background music.
(Riffs are usually four- or eight-beat melodic patterns.)

B. Notate your best improvised riffs.

C. Combine several riffs to compose a *Cobbler, Cobbler* melody.

D. Combine musically compatible riffs to compose two- and three-part pieces.

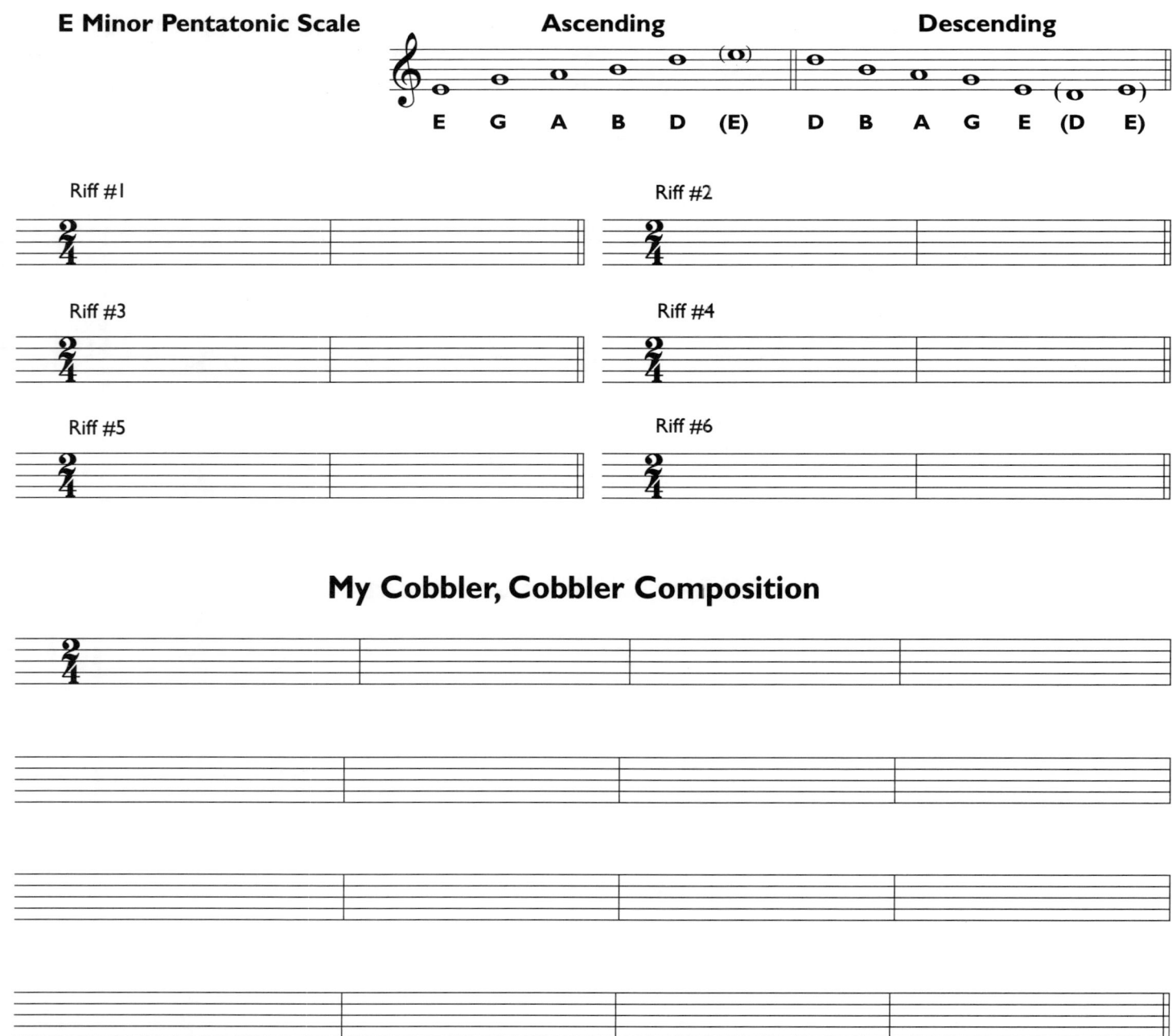

- STUDENT WORKSHEET -

Cool Jazz

CREATING COMPOSITIONS BY NOTATING AND COMBINING IMPROVISED RIFFS

PROCEDURES:

A. Improvise musical riffs over *Cool Jazz* background music.
(Riffs are usually four- or eight-beat melodic patterns.)

B. Notate your best improvised riffs.

C. Combine several riffs to compose a *Cool Jazz* melody.

D. Combine musically compatible riffs to compose two- and three-part pieces.

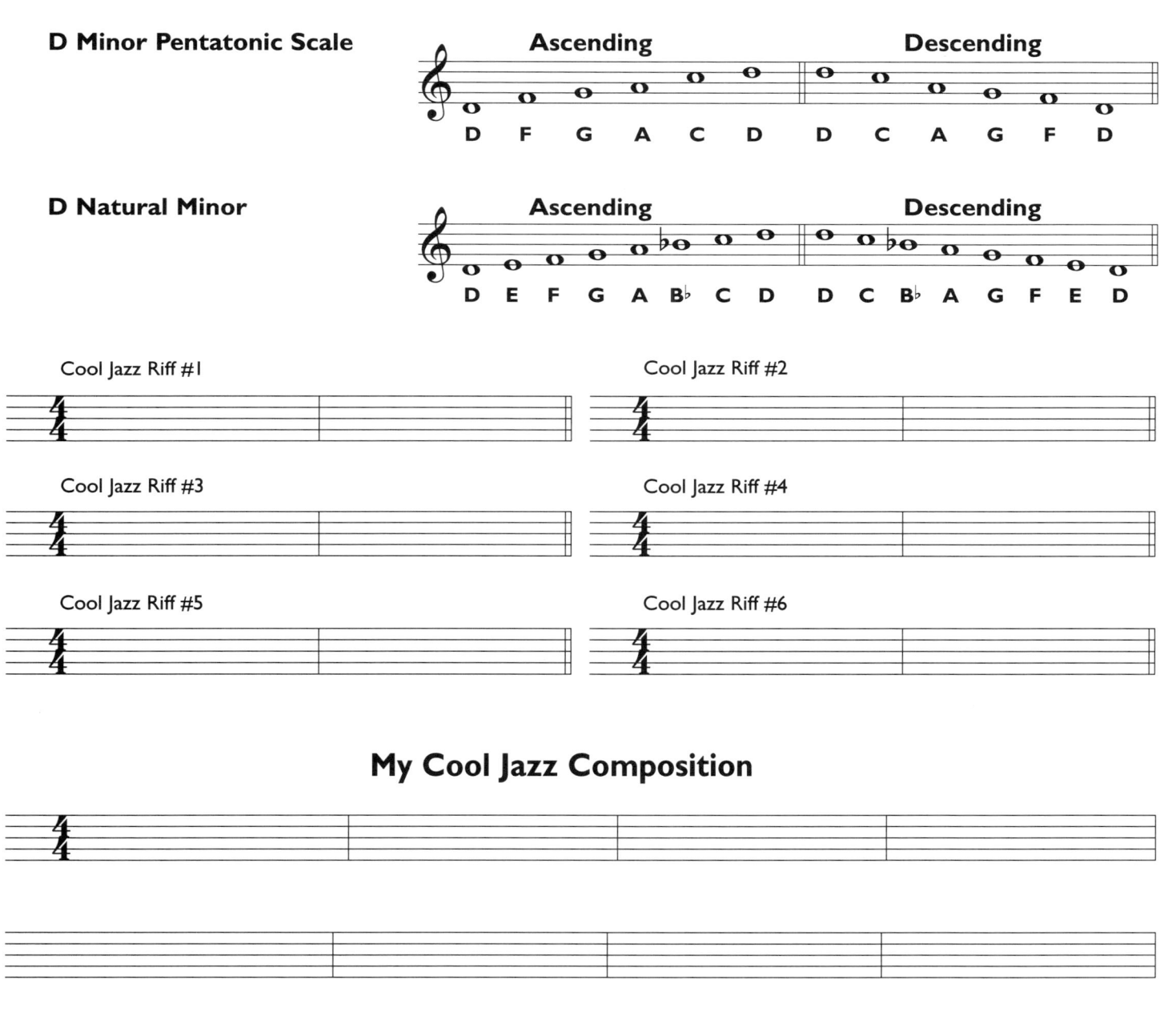

D Minor Pentatonic Scale

D Natural Minor

Cool Jazz Riff #1

Cool Jazz Riff #2

Cool Jazz Riff #3

Cool Jazz Riff #4

Cool Jazz Riff #5

Cool Jazz Riff #6

My Cool Jazz Composition

- STUDENT WORKSHEET -
Blues in D
CREATING COMPOSITIONS BY NOTATING AND COMBINING IMPROVISED RIFFS

PROCEDURES:

A. Improvise musical riffs over *Blues in D* background music.
(Riffs are usually four- or eight-beat melodic patterns.)

B. Notate your best improvised riffs.

C. Combine several riffs to compose a *Blues in D* melody.

D. Combine musically compatible riffs to compose two- and three-part pieces.

- STUDENT WORKSHEET -

Intry Mintry

CREATING COMPOSITIONS BY NOTATING AND COMBINING IMPROVISED RIFFS

PROCEDURES:

A. Improvise musical riffs over *Intry Mintry* background music.
(Riffs are usually four- or eight-beat melodic patterns.)

B. Notate your best improvised riffs.

C. Combine several riffs to compose an *Intry Mintry* melody.

D. Combine musically compatible riffs to compose two- and three-part pieces.

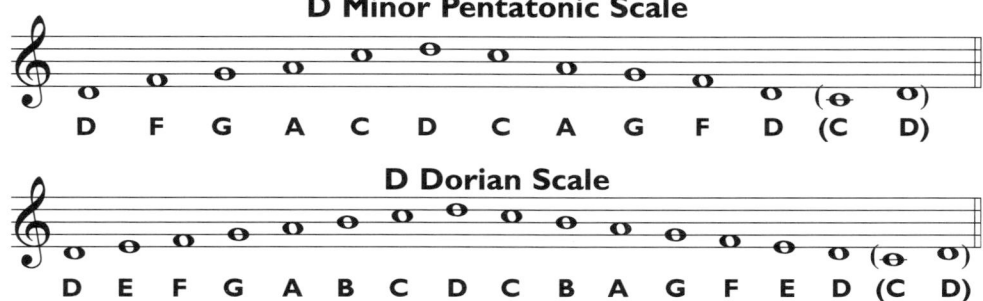

Riff #1

Riff #2

Riff #3

Riff #4

Riff #5

Riff #6

My Intry Mintry Composition

PRINCIPLES OF MUSIC NOTATION

Principle I.

The stem 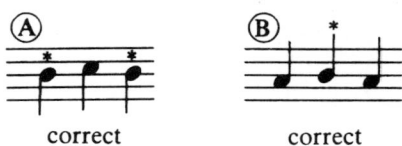 of a note on the middle line of the staff → can go up or down depending upon the notes before it and after it.

Examples of Principle I

correct   correct

Principle II.

Stems which go *up* are placed to the RIGHT of the note. Example:

correct   wrong

Principle III.

Stems which go *down* are placed to the LEFT of the note. Example:

correct   wrong

Principle IV.

All the notes *below* the middle line of the staff have stems that go *up*.

Example of Principle IV

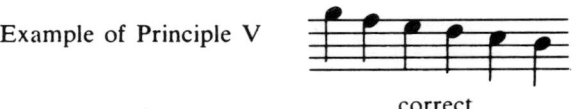

correct

Notice that the stem of the note on the middle line of the staff goes up. This is because all of the notes before it have stems that go up.

Principle V.

All the notes *above* the middle line of the staff have stems that go *down*.

Example of Principle V

correct

How to draw a TREBLE CLEF:

Practice drawing these three figures

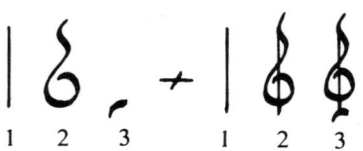

1   2   3   1   2   3

Notice that the treble clef circles the line G.

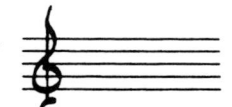

How to draw a BASS CLEF:

Practice drawing these two figures

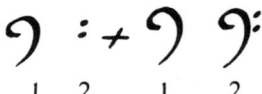

1   2   1   2

Notice that the two dots in the bass clef outline the line F.

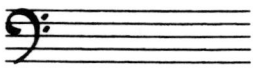

EXERCISES IN MUSICAL NOTATION

Instructions: Complete the exercises below by putting a stem on each note according to the principles outline above and by adding either a treble clef or a bass clef to each staff. Ask your teacher to check your work.

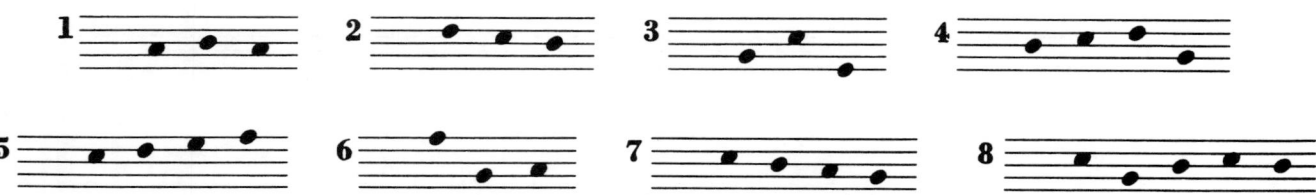

ONE-OCTAVE MAJOR AND MINOR SCALES AND ARPEGGIOS

VIOLIN

D major

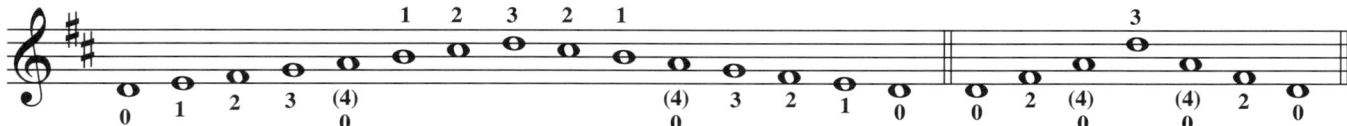

G major

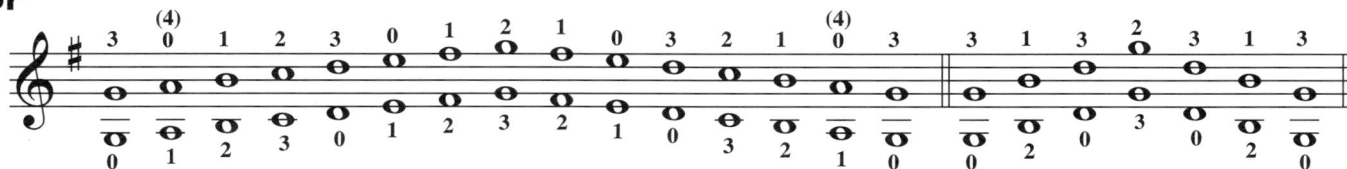

C major

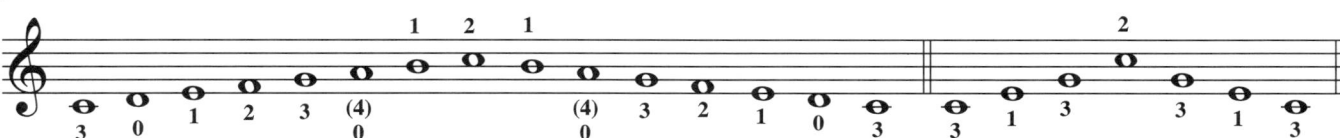

F major

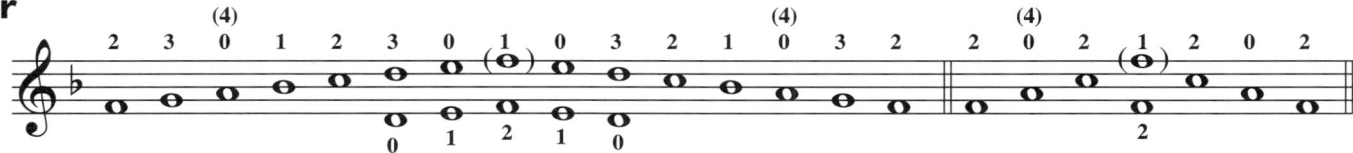

Bb major

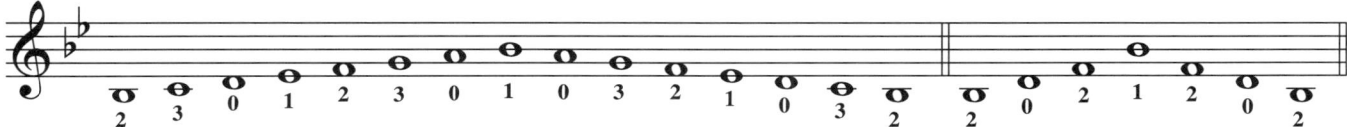

E natural minor

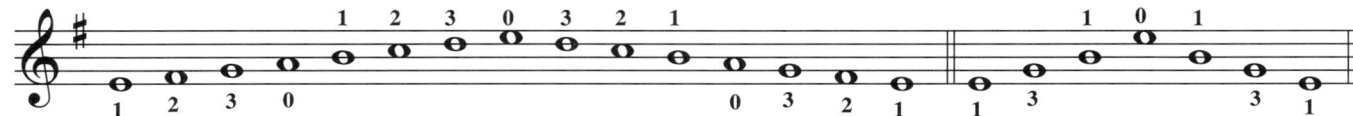

A natural minor

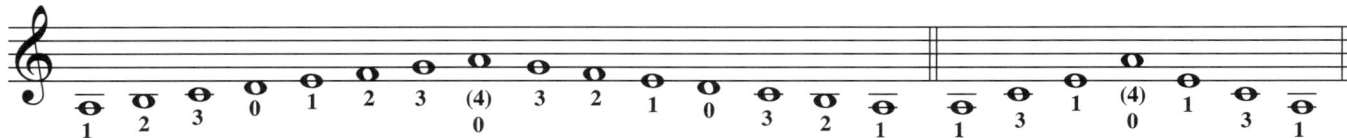

D natural minor

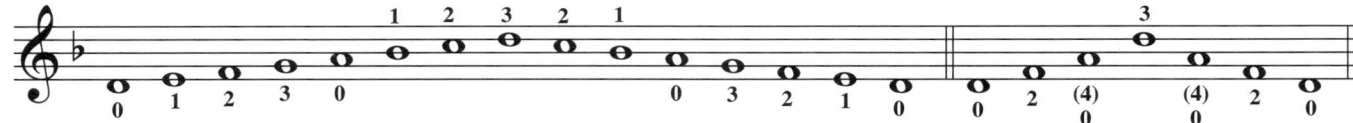

ONE-OCTAVE MAJOR AND MINOR SCALES AND ARPEGGIOS

VIOLA

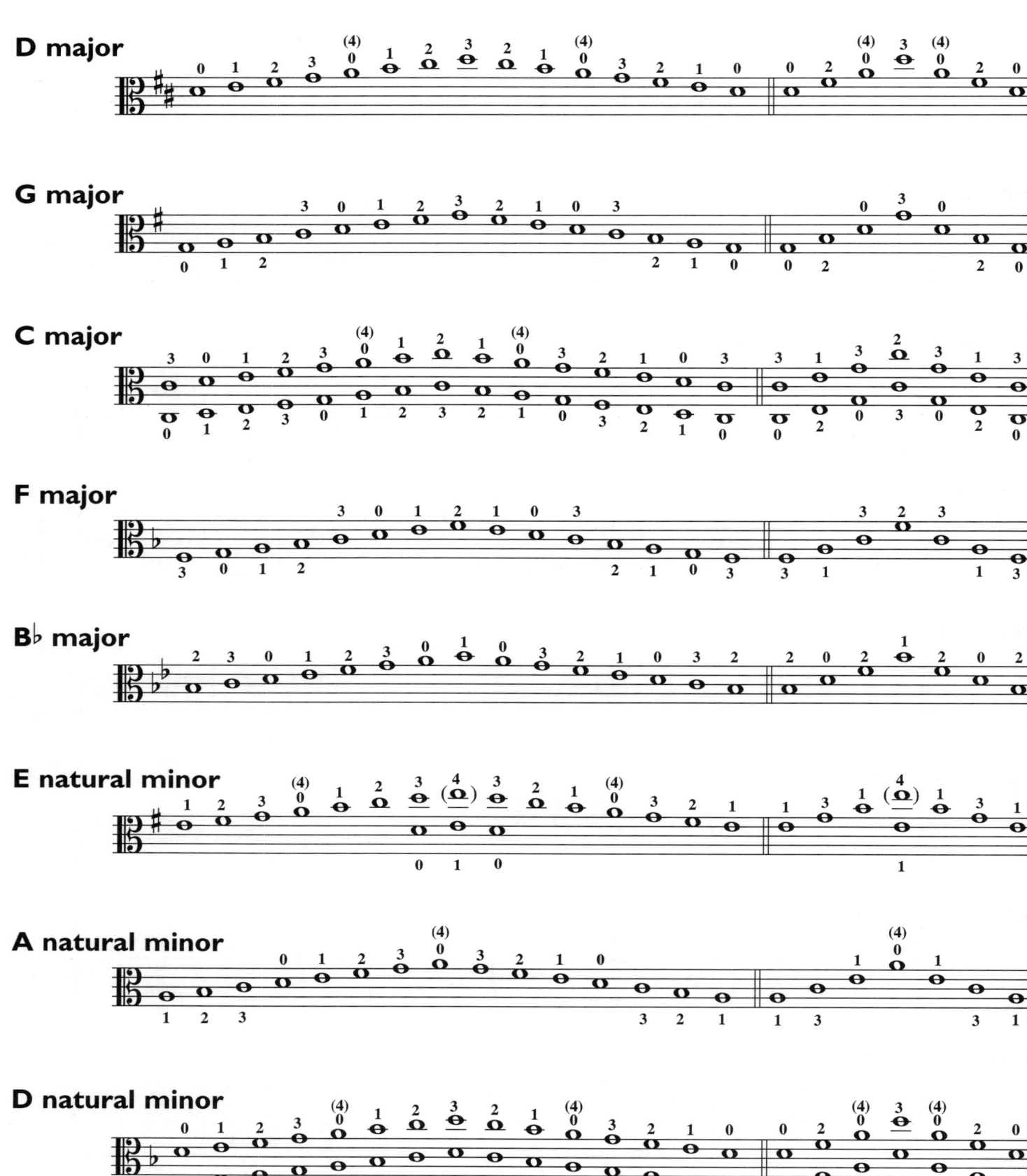

ONE-OCTAVE MAJOR AND MINOR SCALES AND ARPEGGIOS

CELLO

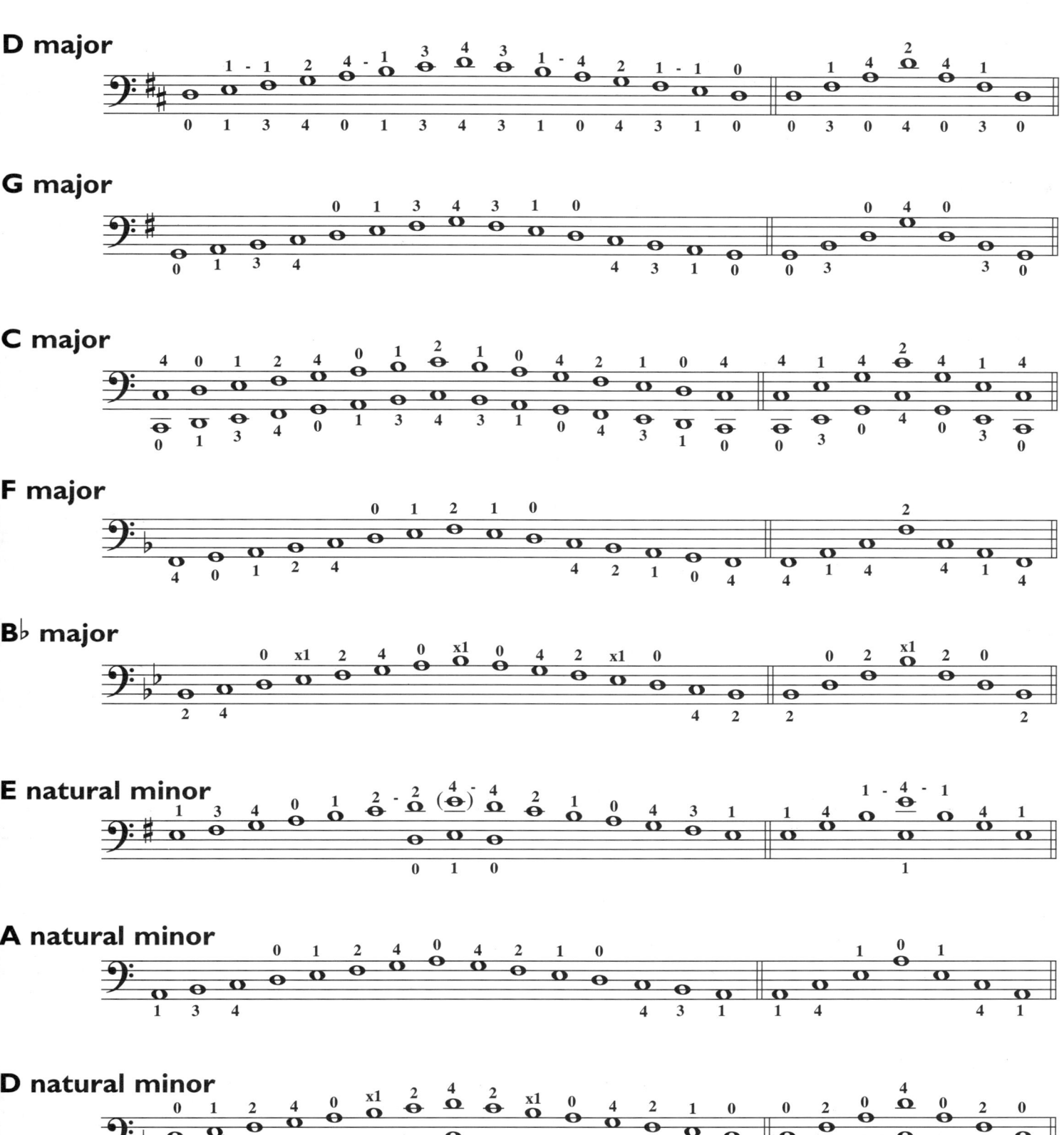

ONE-OCTAVE MAJOR AND MINOR SCALES AND ARPEGGIOS

BASS

D major

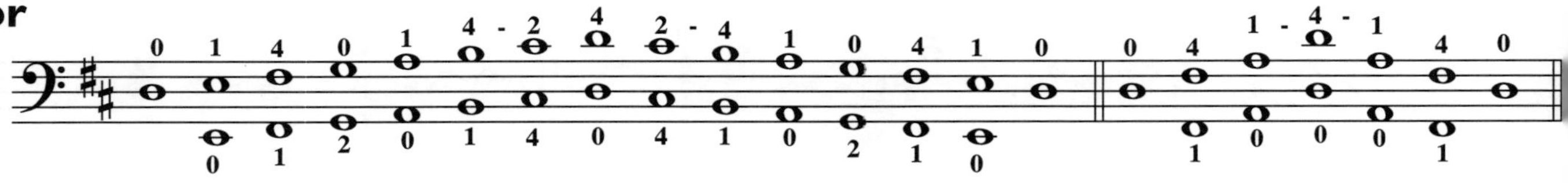

G major

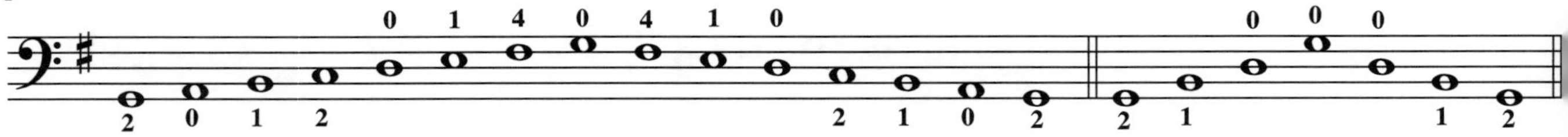

C major

F major

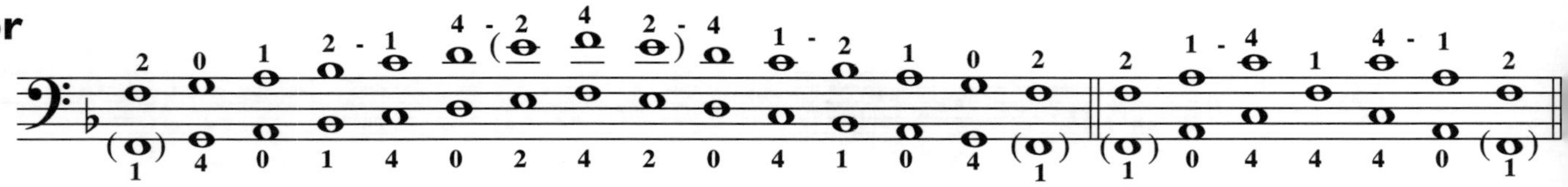

B♭ major

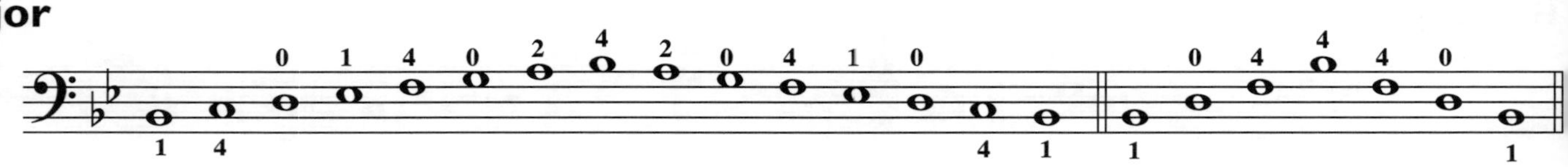

E natural minor

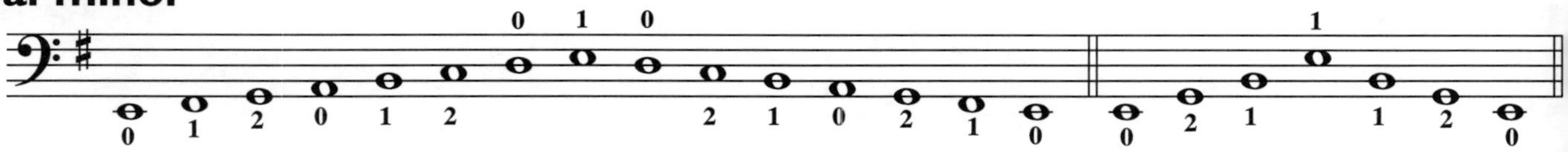

A natural minor

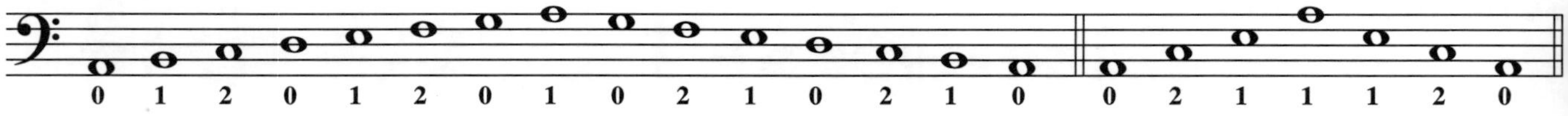

D natural minor

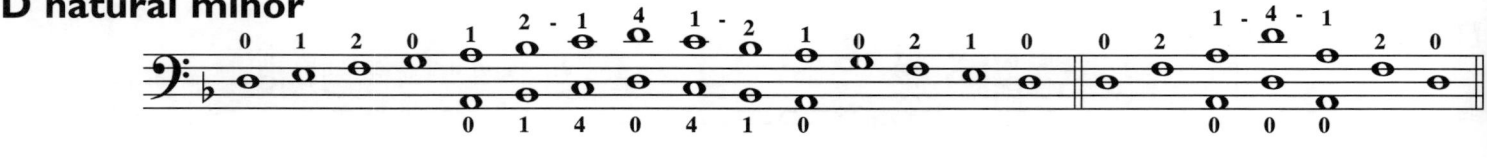

BLANK PAGE

8va	An abbreviation indicating that the melody should be played up or down an octave; in other words, the starting note is eight pitches higher or lower than notated. Pitch names remain the same.
Accelerando poco a poco	Faster, little by little.
Accent	"Look it Up" in the *Music Signs and Symbols Dictionary*-page 4.
Accidental	A flat, sharp, or natural sign that alters the pitch of a note.
Adagio	See **Tempo Markings** page 45.
Al Fine	To the end.
Allegro	See **Tempo Markings** page 45.
Andante	See **Tempo Markings** page 45.
Animato	In an excited, animated style
Arco	Performed with the bow.
Aural Transcription	Learning to play recorded music "by ear" without the aid of music notation. Also, the transfer of music heard to music notation.
Ballad	A short, simple song in a narrative or descriptive form, sometimes set to a romantic or historical poem.
Bar Line	"Look it Up" in the *Music Signs and Symbols Dictionary* page 4.
Bluegrass	A type of Anglo-American folk music originating around the mid 1940's in rural Appalachia.
Blues	An African-American folk music characterized by spontaneity and deep emotion.
Blues Scale	A six tone scale used to improvise over blues harmonies.
Bouffons	Costumed dancers of the 15th and 16th centuries.
Bow Lift	Lift the bow from the string and replace it nearer the frog.
Branle	A popular French dance of the 16th century in which all of the motions of the lead couple are imitated.
Call and Response	A musical alternation between two performers or a performer and a group of performers. The musical response to the call may be imitated or improvised.
Canon	Literally, a "rule" for realizing a composition. The rule dictates that each voice imitates exactly the melody sung or played by the first voice.
Clef	"Look it Up" in the *Music Signs and Symbols Dictionary* page 4.
Col legno	Tap the string with the bow stick.
Country Music	A popular style of American music originating in the South and West that usually expresses the feelingful elements of life.
Country Swing	A blend of Western, bluegrass, and swing styles originating in Texas during the 1940's.
D.C. al Fine	An abbreviation for "Da Capo al Fine" which means "go back to the beginning and end at the *Fine*."
Détaché	The bow stroke used to produce a legato style.
Dixieland Jazz	An early style of African-American jazz music originating in New Orleans.
Dolce	Sweetly.

Dorian	See Mode page 44.
Double Bar Line	"Look it Up" in the *Music Signs and Symbols Dictionary* page 4.
Down Bow	Draw the bow from the frog toward the tip.
Duet	A composition for two performers.
Dynamics	Degrees of softness to loudness.

ppp/pianississimo	very, very soft
pp/pianissimo	very soft
p/piano	soft
mp/mezzo piano	medium soft
mf/mezzo forte	medium loud
f/forte	loud
ff/fortissimo	very loud
fff/fortississimo	very, very loud

Flat	"Look it Up" in the *Music Signs and Symbols Dictionary* page 4.
Folk Hymn	A song of worship with a religious text that has been set to a folk melody.
Folk Song	A song reflecting the traditions of the people of a country or region and forming part of their characteristic culture.
Gospel	African-American church music characterized by expression, improvisation, and a strong sense of celebration.
Harmony	Two or more different tones played or sung at the same time.
Honky Tonk	A rowdy musical style characterized by a lively piano accompaniment.
Hooked Bow	Linking two down bows or two up bows together by stopping the bow and continuing in the same direction.
Hymn	A song of worship.
Improvisation	The art of creating music spontaneously, during performance; also a form of composition.
Jazz	Originally, a style of music characterized by strong rhythms and expressiveness, originating in the South by African-Americans.
Jazz Ballad	A slow, expressive vocal style characterized by extended jazz harmonies.
Jazz Waltz	An adaptation of jazz harmonies to 3/4 time characterized by a hard drving bass line and swinging drums, especially in the ride cymbal.
Key Signature	"Look it Up" in the *Music Signs and Symbols Dictionary* page 4.
Legato	With a smooth, connected style of articulation.
Lower Half (L.H.)	Play one or more notes from the frog to the middle of the bow.
Lullaby	A cradle song, usually sung by a mother to soothe or quiet an infant before bedtime.
Major Tonality	See Tonality page 45.
Marcato	Articulation with a marked emphasis on each tone.
March	Music for a procession or parade.
Martelé	A term describing an accented style of bowing. The arm and hand provide weight to the bow before the beginning of a tone, gripping the string, and releasing the weight as the bow is moved.
Measure	"Look it Up" in the *Music Signs and Symbols Dictionary* page 4.
Metronome Marking	A precise indication of the speed of the beat as expressed by Maelzel's Metronome. (The Metronome is a machine with a ticking pendulum patented by Johann Maelzel in 1816. M.M. ♩ = 96 means the tempo of the quarter note (crotchet) is 96 beats per minute.)
Minor Tonality	See Tonality page 45.

Mode
A term that embraces many ancient and contemporary concepts regarding the classification of scales and melodies. Today, the term usually refers to seven distinct scales derived from twelve ancient church modes. Below is an example of each mode starting on D.

D Ionian (Major) Mode

do re mi fa so la ti do

D Dorian Mode
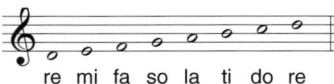
re mi fa so la ti do re

D Phrygian Mode
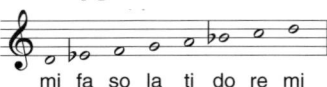
mi fa so la ti do re mi

D Lydian Mode
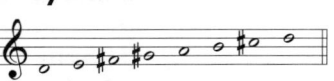
fa so la ti do re mi fa

D Mixolydian Mode
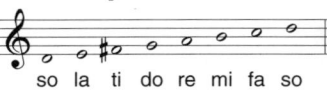
so la ti do re mi fa so

D Aeolian (Natural Minor) Mode
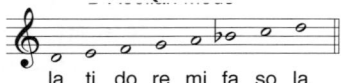
la ti do re mi fa so la

D Locrian Mode
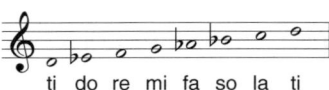
ti do re mi fa so la ti

Moderato	See Tempo Markings page 45.
Natural	"Look it Up" in the *Music Signs and Symbols Dictionary* page 4.
Obbligato	An accompanying part, usually ornamental in character.
Ostinato	A melodic pattern repeated over and over to accompany a principal melody.
Pentatonic Scale	A five tone scale. Examples are notated below.

Pick-up Note	One or more notes that come before the first full measure of a piece.
Pizzicato	Performed by plucking the string with a finger.
Plaintively	With sadness.
Poco a poco	Little by little.
Polka	A lively dance originated by Bohemian (Eastern European) peasants.
Quick Time	A doubling of the tempo that halves the performance time.
Reggae	A musical style mixing African and Carribean rhythms oftern attributed to Jamaican sources.
Rest	"Look it Up" in the *Music Signs and Symbols Dictionary* page 5.
Rhythm	An organizing principle of traditional music comprising three fundamental elements that are heard and felt. 1) A Primary Beat; the "basic" or "big" beat usually felt as the marching, walking or dancing beat. It is also the beat represented by the baton of a conductor. 2) Meter; the subdivision of the Primary Beat into twos and threes. Duple meter is the result when the Primary Beats are subdivided into two equal parts. Triple Meter is the result when the Primary Beats are subdivided into three equal parts. 3) Melodic Rhythm; the rhythm of the melody or the rhythm of the text. It is the result of virtually limitless combinations of beats, subdivisions, and elongations of the beat.
Rhythmic Improvisation	The act of expressing one's own rhythmic ideas while maintaining the basic melodic character of the piece.
Rock and Roll	A mid-1950's style of popular music featuring guitar and driving rhythms with accents of the off beats 1 2 1 2.
Round	A specially composed melody that allows two or more individuals to create interesting musical effects by starting the melody at different times.

Scale

Literally, a "ladder" or succession of eight tones ascending to or descending from a specific tonic (tonal center) to the tonic (tonal center) above or below. Examples:

C Major Scale

do re mi fa so la ti do

A Harmonic Minor Scale - Ascending

la ti do re mi fa si la

A Melodic Minor Scale - Ascending

la ti do re mi fi si la

A Melodic Minor Scale - Descending

la so fa mi re do ti la

Sea Chanty

A song sung by sailors to coordinate their movements while working.

Slur

"Look it Up" in the *Music Signs and Symbols Dictionary* page 5.

Solo

One player alone, with or without accompaniment.

Spiccato

A bowing style that allows the bow to spring or bounce away from the string between notes. The first of a series of spiccato strokes usually begins on the string. A dot (.) over or under a note can indicate a spiccato stroke.

Spiritual

A religious folk song of African-American origin.

Staccato

"Look it Up" in the *Music Signs and Symbols Dictionary* page 4.

Subdivision

The process of dividing a steady beat into even twos or threes.

Swing Style

A tyoe of Big Band jazz of the late 1930s and 1940s.

Syncopation

A displacement of the natural pulse of the music, usually to the second half of the beat as in:

Tempo

Rate of speed of the beat.

Tempo Markings

1. Symbols indicating rate of speed.

adagio	slow
andante	moderately slow
moderato	moderate
allegro	lively, brisk
vivace	fast
presto	very fast

2. Symbols indicating change of speed.

accelerando	increase speed
piu mosso	more motion
ritardando	decrease speed
meno mosso	less motion
a tempo	return to previous tempo
rubato	freely, with expression

Tenuto

"Look it Up" in the *Music Signs and Symbols Dictionary* page 4.

Theme and Variations

A musical form based upon a melody followed by a succession of composed rhythmic/melodic variations.

Tie

"Look it Up" in the *Music Signs and Symbols Dictionary* page 4.

Time Signature

"Look it Up" in the *Music Signs and Symbols Dictionary* page 5.

Tonality

A characteristic of Western music, referring to the relationship of pitches to a specific tonal center. If Do is the tonal center, the tonality is Major. If La is the tonal center, the tonality is Minor.

Treble Clef

"Look it Up" in the *Music Signs and Symbols Dictionary* page 4.

Up Bow

Draw the bow from the tip toward the frog.

Upper Half (U.H.)

Play one or more notes from the middle to the tip of the bow.

Waltz

A 19th century dance in triple meter.

Whole Bow (W.B.)

Play one or more notes from the frog to the tip of the bow.

RHYTHMIC PATTERN DICTIONARY

Hot Cross Buns (p 6 - CD # 1, 2, 3)
Twinkle, Twinkle, Little Star (p 15 - CD # 37, 38, 39)

Waltz (p 11 - CD # 20)

Mary Had a Little Lamb (p 6 - CD # 6, 7, 8)
Au Claire de la Lune (p 7 - CD # 10)
Vesper Hymn (p 13 - CD # 29)
Aura Lee (p 30 - CD # 82)

Lightly Row (p 14 - CD # 30, 31)
A Paris (p 22 - CD # 61)

Hot Cross Buns (p 6 - CD # 1, 2, 3)
Shepherd's Hey (p 16 - CD # 42)

Au Claire de la Lune (p 7 - CD # 10)

Au Claire de la Lune (p 7 - CD # 10)
Aura Lee (p 30 - CD # 82)

Variation on Cobbler Cobbler (p 10)
Variation One on The Shining Young Moon (p 34- CD # 92)

Variation Two on Stepping and Skipping (p. 7)

Shave and a Haircut (p 9)

Eighth Notes Duet (p 8)

Rocket Cruiser (p 8 - CD # 11)
Juba (p 10 - CD # 17)
Jolly Old St. Nicholas (p 16 - CD # 44)

Jolly Old St. Nicholas (p 16 - CD # 44)
Baa, Baa, Black Sheep in Minor Tonality (p 29- CD # 79)
Silent, Silent (p 28- CD # 78)

Lightly Row (Quicktime) (p 14 - CD # 33)

Down By the Station (p 8 - CD # 12)
Up On the Housetop (p 24 - CD # 66)
Sleep, Baby Sleep (p 30 - CD # 83)

Up On the Housetop (p 24 - CD # 66)

Aura Lee (p 30 meas 9 - CD # 82)
Sleep, Baby Sleep (p 30 - CD # 83)

Waltz (p 11 - CD # 20)

Die Abendglocke (p 24 - CD # 69)

On Top of Old Smokey (p 19 - CD # 53)

Fais Do Do (p 11 - CD # 19)
Scarborough Fair (p 38 - CD # 98)

Waltz Variation 1 (p 11)

Waltz Variation 3 (p 11)

Waltz Variation 2 (p 11)

Amazing Grace (p 31 - CD # 85)

Little Tom Tinker (p 32 meas 5-6 - CD # 89)
Row, Row, Row Your Boat (p 33)
Patsy Ory-Ory-Aye (p 33 - CD # 90)

Little Tom Tinker (p 32 - CD # 89)

Little Tom Tinker (p 32 - CD # 89)
Oats, Peas, Beans (p 33 - CD # 91)
Patsy Ory-Ory-Aye (p 33 - CD # 90)

Oats, Peas, Beans (p 33 - CD # 91)
Patsy Ory-Ory-Aye (p 33 - CD # 90)

Oats, Peas, Beans (p 33 - CD # 91)

Do It! Play Strings

Performing Artists

Violin and Viola

David Salness

Associate Professor of Violin and Chamber Music
University of Maryland, College Park

Cello

Bret P. Smith

Assistant Professor of Music Education
University of Maryland, College Park

Bass

George Vance

Soloist, Teacher, and Author
Silver Spring, Maryland

Ensembles, Studios, and Studio Musicians

James Dapogny and the **Chicago Jazz Band**

The Arco Iris String Quartet: Alejandra Urrutia, Violin; **Carolyn Lukancic,** Violin; **Judy Tay,** Viola; **Bret Smith,** Cello

Landmark Studio, Cleveland, Ohio: James Hillenbrand, Engineer; **Albert Blaser,** Leader/Musician; **Daniel Maier,** Piano; **Robert Fraser,** Guitar, Mandolin, Banjo, and Bass; **David Bird,** Bass; **Mark Gonder, David Bastian, Thomas Goldbach,** and **Robert McKee,** Drums. **Omega Studios, Rockville, Maryland: Shannon Follin,** Engineer. **Solid Sound Recording Studio, Ann Arbor, Michigan: Kenneth Abecing** and **Will Spencer,** Engineers. **Woodside Recording Studio, Evanston, Illinois: David Bjornson,** Engineer. **Audiomation,** Pittsburgh, Pennsylvania: **David Bastian,** Engineer. **Ann's Way Studio, Ann Arbor, Michigan: Kurt Wolak,** Engineer; **Aleksandr Chernyak,** Balalaika; **David Froseth,** Piano; **Bret Smith,** Guitar; **Kurt Wolak,** Accordion; **Cary Kocher,** Percussion.

Credits and Acknowledgments

Illustrations: Andrew Evansen. Photography: Bret Smith. Music Engraving and Layout: Paul G. Burrucker. Illustration and Photo Models: Sarah Pohl, Anna Psitos, and Amanda Walker. String Pedagogy Consultants: Michael Hopkins, Jerry Henry, and Martha Froseth. Editorial Assistance: Molly Weaver.
Special thanks to Kristie and Mathew Smith for patient support and to Ed and Alec Harris of G.I.A. Publications, Inc. for unqualified support.

BLANK PAGE

STUDENT CD MUSIC INDEX

A Paris p. 22: CD Tracks 61 & 61-2

Amazing Grace p. 31: CD Tracks 85 & 86

Amazing Grace *Gospel Style* p. 31: CD Tracks 87 & 88

Au Claire de la Lune *Major Tonality* p. 7: CD Track 10

Au Claire de la Lune *Minor Tonality* p. 12: CD Track 22 & 22-2

Aura Lee p. 30: CD Tracks 82 & 82-2

Baa, Baa, Black Sheep *Minor Tonality* p. 29:
CD Tracks 79 & 79-2

Bile'em Cabbage Down p. 10: CD Tracks 16 & 16-2

Bingo p. 29: CD Tracks 80 & 80-2

Birch Tree, The p. 17: CD Tracks 48 & 48-2

Blues in D *Melodic Patterns* p. 28: CD Track 72

Blues in D *Call and Response* p. 26: CD Track 73

Bouffons p. 25: CD Tracks 71 & 71-2

By the Fireside p. 17: CD Tracks 47 & 47-2

Can Can p. 36: CD Track 94

Champaigne Branie p. 11: CD Tracks 21 & 21-2

Cobbler, Cobbler *A Minor Tonality* p. 22: CD Track 62

Cobbler, Cobbler *E Minor Tonality* p. 10: CD Track 18 & 18-2

Cowboy Ballad p. 13: CD Track 27

Cuckoo Song p. 21: CD Tracks 56 & 56-2

Cuckoo Song *Jazz Waltz Style "By Ear"* p. 21:
CD Tracks 57 & 58

Dance in the Circle p. 19: CD Tracks 50 & 50-2

Die Abendglocke (Oh, How Lovely is the Evening) p. 24:
CD Tracks 69 & 69-2

Down by the Station p. 8: CD Track 12

Down by the Station *Jazz Style "By Ear"* p. 8: CD Track 13

Fais do do *Major Tonality* p. 11: CD Tracks 19 & 19-2

Fais do do *Minor Tonality* p. 12: CD Tracks 23 & 23-2

French Folk Song p. 19: CD Tracks 51 & 52

Gólya, Gólya Gilice (The Storks) p. 23: CD Tracks 65 & 65-2

Hot Cross Buns p. 6: CD Tracks 1 & 2

Hot Cross Buns *Honky Tonk Style "By Ear"* p. 6: CD Track 3

Hot Cross Buns *Rock and Roll Style "By Ear"* p. 6: CD Track 4

Hush My Baby p. 13: CD Track 26

Intry Mintry p. 27: CD Track 75 & 75-2

Jacob Drink *Bb Major Tonality* p. 37: CD Tracks 96 & 96-2

Jacob Drink *C Major Tonality* p. 23: CD Tracks 63 & 63-2

Jacob Drink *G Major Tonality* p. 9: CD Tracks 15 & 15-2

Jolly Old St. Nicholas p. 16: CD Tracks 44 & 44-2

Jolly Old St. Nicholas *Jazz Ballad Style "By Ear"* p. 16:
CD Tracks 45 & 46

Juba *D Major Tonality* p. 10: CD Tracks 17 & 17-2

Juba *G Major Tonality* p. 22: CD Tracks 60 & 60-2

Lightly Row p. 14: CD Tracks 30 & 31

Lightly Row *Country Swing Style* p. 14: CD Tracks 32 & 32-2

Lightly Row *Quick Time* p. 14: CD Tracks 33 & 33-2

Little Tom Tinker p. 32: CD Track 89

Mary Had a Little Lamb *Eb Major Tonality* p. 38: CD Track 97

Mary Had a Little Lamb *Bluegrass Style* p. 6: CD Tracks 6 & 7

Mary Had a Little Lamb *Reggae Style* p. 6: CD Track 8

Nonsense Song p. 21: CD Tracks 59 & 59-2

Norwegian Dance p. 25: CD Tracks 70 & 70-2

Notes *D Major Tonality* p. 6: CD Track 5

Notes *A Major Tonality with Slurs* p. 20: CD Track 54

Notes Leap p. 13: CD Track 25

Oats, Peas, Beans p. 33: CD Tracks 91 & 91-2

Oh, When the Saints Go Marching In *"By Ear"* p. 14:
CD Tracks 34 & 35

Old King Cole *D Major Tonality* p. 18: CD Track 49

Old King Cole *G Major Tonality* p. 9: CD Track 14

On Top of Old Smoky p. 19: CD Track 53

Patsy Ory-Ory-Aye p. 33: CD Track 90

Polka p. 12: CD Tracks 24 & 24-2

Practice Every Day March p. 13: CD Track 28

Rain, Rain *Call and Response* p. 14: CD Track 36, 36-2 & 36-3

Raindrops p. 30: CD Tracks 81 & 81-2

Rocket Cruiser p. 8: CD Track 11

Scarborough Fair p. 38: CD Tracks 98 & 99

Shepherd's Hey p. 16: CD Tracks 42 & 42-2

Shepherd's Hey *Quick Time* p. 16: CD Tracks 43 & 43-2

The Shining Young Moon p. 34-35: CD Tracks 92 & 93

Shoheen Sho p. 27: CD Tracks 74 & 74-2

Silent, Silent p. 28: CD Track 78 & 78-2

Sleep, Baby, Sleep p. 30: CD Tracks 83 & 83-2

Some Folks Do p. 28: CD Track 77 & 77-2

Starlight p. 37: CD Tracks 95 & 95-2

Stepping and Skipping *D Major Tonality* p. 7: CD Track 9

Stepping and Skipping *A Major Tonality with Slurs* p. 20:
CD Track 55

Sur la Pont d'Avignon p. 31: CD Tracks 84 & 84-2

Twinkle, Twinkle, Little Star p. 15: CD Tracks 37, 38, & 39

Twinkle, Twinkle, Little Star *Swing Style "by Ear"* p. 15:
CD Tracks 40 & 41

Up on the Housetop p. 24: CD Tracks 66 & 66-2

Up on the Housetop Swing Style *"by Ear"* p. 24:
CD Tracks 67 & 68

Vesper Hymn p. 13: CD Track 29

Waltz *C Major Tonality* p. 23: CD Tracks 64 & 64-2

Waltz *G Major Tonality* p. 11: CD Tracks 20 & 20-2

Yangtze Boatman Chanty p. 27: CD Tracks 76 & 76-2